Dedicated to the memory of my grandparents,
Sonia Bergmann, Felix Bergmann, and Israel Shekel

The Right to Religious Freedom in International Law

This book analyses the right to religious freedom in international law, drawing on an array of national and international cases. Taking a rigorous approach to the right to religious freedom, Anat Scolnicov argues that the interpretation and application of religious freedom must be understood as a conflict between individual and group claims of rights, and that although some states, based on their respective histories, religions, and cultures, protect the group over the individual, only an individualistic approach of international law is a coherent way of protecting religious freedom. Analysing legal structures in a variety of both Western and non-Western jurisdictions, the book sets out a topography of different constitutional structures of religions within states and evaluates their compliance with international human rights law. The book also considers the position of women's religious freedom *vis-à-vis* community claims of religious freedom, of children's right to religious freedom and of the rights of dissenters within religious groups.

Anat Scolnicov is lecturer and fellow in law of Lucy Cavendish College and deputy director of the Centre for Public Law, University of Cambridge.

Routledge Research in Human Rights Law

Human Rights Monitoring Mechanisms of the Council of Europe
Gauthier de Beco

International Human Rights Law and Domestic Violence
The effectiveness of international human rights law
Ronagh McQuigg

The EU as a 'Global Player' in Human Rights?
Jan Wetzel

Human Rights in the Asia-Pacific Region
Towards Institution Building
Hitoshi Nasu and Ben Saul

Vindicating Socio-Economic Rights
International Standards and Comparative Experiences
Paul O'Connell

The Right to Religious Freedom in International Law

Between group rights and individual rights

Anat Scolnicov

Routledge
Taylor & Francis Group

LONDON AND NEW YORK

First published 2011
by Routledge
2 Park Square, Milton Park, Abingdon, Oxon OX14 4RN

Simultaneously published in the USA and Canada
by Routledge
711 Third Avenue, New York, NY 10017

Routledge is an imprint of the Taylor & Francis Group, an informa business

First issued in paperback 2012

© 2011 Anat Scolnicov

The right of Anat Scolnicov to be identified as author of this work has
been asserted by her in accordance with the Copyright, Designs and
Patent Act 1988.

Typeset in Baskerville by Glyph International,

British Library Cataloguing in Publication Data
A catalogue record for this book is available from the British Library

Library of Congress Cataloging-in-Publication Data
Scolnicov, Anat.
The right to religious freedom in international law : between group rights and
individual rights / Anat Scolnicov.
    p. cm.
Includes bibliographical references.
ISBN 978-0-415-48114-4 (hardback) – ISBN 978-0-203-84263-8 (ebook)
1. Freedom of religion. 2. Freedom of religion (International law)
3. Human rights. 4. Women–Legal status, laws, etc. 5. Children–Legal
status, laws, etc. 6. Freedom of speech. I. Title.
K3258.S46 2011
342.08′52–dc22   2010012076

ISBN 13: 978-0415-48114-4 (hbk)
ISBN 13: 978-0415-81348-8 (pbk)
ISBN 13: 978-0203-84263-8 (ebk)

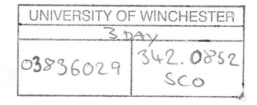

Contents

Table of abbreviations

Cases are cited in full in the text, except for decisions of the European Court of Human Rights and European Commission of Human Rights, which are cited in full in the Table of authorities.

Table of authorities

Treaties and international documents

International Treaties and Declarations

UN Resolutions

Bilateral Treaties

Regional Treaties and Instruments

Draft Conventions and Declarations

International Law Commission

Concluding Observations of the Committee on the Elimination of Discrimination Against Women

Reports by the Special Rapporteur on freedom of Religion and Belief

Concluding Observations of UN Human Rights Conventions Committees

Human Rights Committee

EU Directives

Restatement of Law

Table of Cases

**European Court of Human Rights and European
Commission for Human Rights**

(Decisions for which no published source was found are noted according to application number. All are available at http://www.echr.coe.int (accessed 14 December 2009).)

Privy Council

Inter-American Court of Human Rights

Communications to the African Human Rights Commission

Australia

Brazil

Canada

Germany

Hungary

India

Ireland

Israel

United States

Table of Statutes

Preface

This book is a revised version of my doctoral dissertation, undertaken at the London School of Economics. Its roots, however, are deeper than that. It is from my work as a barrister with the Association for Civil Rights in Israel and legal cases I represented on its behalf that I developed my quest to understand and shape the relationship between religion and state. I thank my colleagues there for inspiring this work.

Although through my experience I knew this to be a vital topic of practical legal implications, my main interest in writing this project was theoretical. It was to understand the roots of the conflict between two normative systems – religion and state – and offer a principled legal solution to this conflict, which must be applicable across a wide array of differing constitutional systems and religions.

However, through the years of writing my thesis this issue had gained urgent topicality, making the solution of this conflict vital for the peaceful existence of many states. I will only mention 9/11 and the questions this raised about the role of religion in world politics, which confounded academics and world leaders alike. Many issues of minorities in Europe came to the courts in the last years and the implications of these are also discussed here. New cases and legal issues in this topic arise constantly and, of course, those arising after submission of this book for publication are not included.

Portions of chapters 4 and 5 have previously appeared in the following articles: 'Religious law, religious Courts and human rights within Israeli constitutional structure', *International Journal of Constitutional Law* 4(4), 2006, 732–740; 'Multi-religious societies and state legal systems: religious marriages, the state and implications for human rights' in T. Wilhelmsson (ed.), *Private Law and the Many Cultures of Europe*, Kluwer Law International, 2007; 'Women and religious freedom: a legal solution to a human rights conflict?', *Netherlands Human Rights Quarterly* 4, 2007, 569–599; 'The child's right to religious freedom and formation of identity', *International Journal of Children's Rights* 15(2), 2007, 215–226. I am grateful to the various publishers for permission to use these materials in the current text.

It is the most pleasurable aspect of publishing this work as a book that I am finally able to thank properly all those who helped me in writing it. First and foremost, my thanks go to my inspiring doctoral supervisor, Christine Chinkin, and to Nicola Lacey, with whom I was privileged to work and who steered me through large parts of my work.

Friends and colleagues discussed, read, commented and encouraged – John Tasioulas, Shay Menuchin, Michal Levertov, Nomi Bar-Yaacov, and Rebecca Cox who offered words and whiskey. My mother, Hanna Scolnicov, cast her English literature scholar's eye over the draft manuscript. I thank them all.

I have many people to thank in Cambridge, my current academic home. James Crawford, formerly Chair of the Cambridge Law Faculty, encouraged me to publish this book. His successor, David Feldman, challenged my thinking on the topic of this book in many conversations. Without the help and patience of Leslie Dingle, librarian of the Squire Law Library, this book would never have been finalized. LLM students at the Cambridge law faculty heard and discussed my ideas. Lucy Cavendish College and its fellows provided me with an academic place for my work. Special thanks go to Michelle De Saram and Andrew Sanger for research assistance in the completion of the manuscript. My gratitude goes to all.

I gratefully acknowledge scholarships received from the Overseas Research Scholarships Fund and from the London School of Economics during my research period and funding from the Feinberg Fund for the completion of the manuscript.

Finally, no words could convey the gratitude I owe to my dear father, Samuel Scolnicov, who helped me through the period of writing the PhD and subsequently this book.

Cambridge, 2010

Introduction

'What is the area within which the subject ... is or should be left to do or be what he is able to do or be without interference from other persons?' ... 'What or who is the source of control or interference that can determine someone to do, or be, this rather than that?' The two questions are clearly different even though the answers to them may overlap.

(I. Berlin, *Four essays on liberty*, Oxford: Oxford University Press, 1969, 118)

Freedom of religion is a seeming contradiction in terms. Freedom is the absence of constraint; religion is a self-imposed constraint on freedom. Freedom of religion is thus a unique human right. Religion is an all-encompassing normative system, providing a complete value system for all aspects of life. Therefore, it poses an authority alternative to that of the state. In this, religious freedom is different from other human rights. Other human rights, such as free speech or privacy, are not associated with an alternative normative system. There is simply no such thing as a normative system of speech or of privacy. The construction of the right of freedom of religion must therefore deal with elements of constraint as well as freedom, and so the interpretation and protection of religious freedom as a human right is more complicated than that of other rights.

Because of this nature of religions as systems of rules, religions might claim group or institutional determinations to supersede individual autonomy. In fact, a vital constitutive part of many religions might be the ability of the group or its institutions to make binding determinations for its members. As will be seen, the group can stand in conflict not only with non-members but also with its members and its own dissenting subgroups.

Religions as communal normative systems, alternative to legal authorities, operate on different levels, from the smallest community – the family – to transnational communities. Religion can form an important part of state identity, particularly in the process of state building, as did, for instance, the rise of autocephalous churches in the states of the former Soviet Union (manifested in the legal regulation of registration of religions).[1] Religion can be a force behind regime change (the Islamic revolution in Iran), or aligned with it (Franco's Spain). Legitimation of religion can be associated both with democratization (post-Soviet Russia) and with a transition to totalitarianism. Religion is often entwined with other aspects of the state.

Indeed, the relationship between state and religion is not static. Religious changes can cause constitutional changes, and changes of regime can use religion to power the political and constitutional change. With the arrival of new religious groups, through immigration or mass conversion, states that before had only to determine their legal relationship with a predominant religion, now have to do so with several religions, which may serve for their members as competing sources of authority with the state.

Any determination in international law as to how states must accord the right to religious freedom restricts the state's ability to manifest its own ideology and restricts its sovereignty. This is true regarding all international protection of human rights, but especially so with religious freedom, as the religious, or alternatively secular, outlook is often an important part of the state's self-definition. Nevertheless, perhaps even more so because of this, it is a restriction that must be made in order truly to accord religious freedom.

This study argues that central to the interpretation of religious freedom is the understanding of the clash between individual claims and group claims. It argues that religious freedom is foremost an individual right; a right of groups can only be a right derivative of individual rights, and thus can never supersede them. Conceptually, group rights of religious freedom do not exist except as aggregates of individual right. Therefore, such rights should not be recognized (except as derivative rights). States do, in practice, recognize group rights. For this reason, I will refer to group rights, where such have been recognized, even though their existence and legitimacy is disputed in this work. (I refer to group rights and community rights interchangeably, as there is no meaningful difference between the terms for the purposes of this work.)

The argument in this book is both that the supremacy of individual rights to group rights *ought* to be the interpretation of international law, and that largely it *is* so. Those instances in which states or international law have not followed this approach are shown precisely as illustrations of the problems such deviation creates.

First, this work pursues a theoretical examination of what is meant by a group right and by an individual right, and by group and individual justifications for rights. It draws conclusions about the interpretation that should be preferred. This conclusion on different legal examples, looking at how they were decided, and how the analysis suggested here might lead to a different coherent analysis. The purpose of these examples is twofold: they both implement the thesis in specific cases, and thus show that indeed this is the best conclusion in each case, they strengthen the original thesis.

Cases from different jurisdictions, both international and domestic, are used as examples of such conflicts of rights. International case law is scarce, consisting of few decisions of the UN Human Rights Committee. General Comments and Concluding Observations on State Reports by the various committees under the UN human rights conventions were also helpful in analysing existing law and its required changes. More abundant is the regional case law of the bodies of the European human rights system. The few cases in this area of the African and American regional mechanisms are also utilized.

A conscious attempt was made to use examples from a variety of Western and non-Western jurisdictions, referring, if possible, to states with differing religious composition. The only criterion of choice was which cases best exemplified the problem discussed. Of particular importance to my work was the use of as wide as possible a spectrum of national and international jurisdictions. There is a predominance of cases from democratic states, as these are the most interesting for my discussion. While it is not surprising that states that are not democratic and do not respect human rights infringe religious freedom, it is more interesting to understand why states that *are* democratic and generally committed to human rights principles infringe this right. It is because the conflicts inherent within this right, exposed in this study, make it an impossible right to implement without following a conscious and coherent interpretation, which this work will try to suggest.

Domestic law can be evidence of state practice, and therefore of the existence of customary international law.[2] In order to prove that state practice exists, uniform and extensive state practice must be shown to exist, accompanied by a belief of states that they are acting according to international law. As will be seen, there is mostly no uniform state practice that can be said to apply in the situations raised in this work, much less indications of *opinio juris*. Indeed, this work is not intended as a survey of the practice of states regarding religious freedom. Such surveys have been carried out elsewhere.[3] The recourse to analysis of domestic law in this work serves another purpose: by seeing how states have dealt with problems involving the implementation of religious freedom, particularly those involving a conflict between individual and group rights, an insight into substantive arguments for group-rights approaches and for individual-rights approaches can be gleaned. The discussion of the conflicts in this work looks to reasonings of domestic courts, legislators and writers, which can further conclusions on desirable solutions in international law.

It may be noted, that there is an inherent problem in ascertaining general international law from the practice of states in the field of international human rights law, including religious freedom. Ascertaining the uniform practice of states would, in many cases, lead to the lowest common denominator of protection of rights, encouraging a 'race to the bottom', rather than setting a legal standard which reflects norms to which should aspire, and with which they must comply.

International law serves as the starting point of the discussion and as its end point. The aim of this work is to uncover the principles that should lead the implementation of this right in international law. It aims, through theoretical discussion and examination of practical examples, to show points of conflict of rights that international law has so far not addressed well, or at all. This discussion will lead to a conclusion about how it should address them in the future.

Chapter 1, a short introductory chapter, provides a point of reference for the substantive legal discussion to follow. It introduces the main legal documents of existing international legal protection of this right, showing the elements of individual and communal protection in the text of the documents themselves.

Chapter 2 sets out the main thesis of this work: that a key to understanding the right of religious freedom lies in the conflict between its interpretation as an individual right or as a group right. These interpretations will be learned from analysis of the classical liberal formulations of this right and their criticisms. The preferred interpretation is that of an individual right. A group (or community) right of religious freedom is only a derivative of individual rights and can never supersede them. This is correlated with, but not identical to, two perceptions of religious freedom: as a right of expression and as a right of identity.

The following chapters will show how the analysis introduced in Chapter 2 can further our understanding of human rights conflicts involving religious freedom and what problems it encounters. The subjects of these chapters reflect a choice of different types of conflict between group and individual in realization of the right to religious freedom. Each different type of conflict illuminates the main thesis from a different aspect.

Chapter 3 looks at the legal structures of religions within the state and how they impact on freedom of religion. Particularly, how the constitutional structure of the legal regulation relates to the interpretation of this right is examined. To an extent, the following chapters of the book extrapolate the theme of this chapter to specific areas in which the legal regulation of the state impacts on religious freedom.

Chapter 4 looks at the conflict between the individual rights of women and a group right of religious freedom, perhaps the most ubiquitous example of the clash of claims regarding religious freedom, one that and continues to be a major stumbling block to universal realization of human rights. It is also a clash rooted in principle, as the assignation of gender and family roles is a central tenet to the doctrine of many religions.

Chapter 5 looks at religious freedom of children. The case of children raises a conflict between the individual and a different type of group from those previously discussed: the family. Additionally, there are conflicts involving the wider religious community. The chapter centres on the process of formation of religious identity, primarily through education. Thus, this chapter examines not only the religious freedom of students, but also that of teachers, within the education system.

Chapter 6 revisits the distinction between religious freedom as a right of identity and religious freedom as a right of expression, introduced in Chapter 2, and asks how analysis that calls attention to these two perceptions can help in deciding what will be offences of religious speech acceptable in a democratic society that respects human rights.

Some issues run throughout this study. One such is the issue of discrimination in the workplace, addressed in Chapters 3, 4 and 5. The position of the worker in institutions of religious character emanates from the legal status accorded to religious organizations within the state. This status has particular implications for women workers and for workers in educational institutions. The problem of religious discrimination in the workplace is thus intertwined with the issues of education of children and of the rights of women within the public and private sphere.

Another important issue that runs throughout this work is the public/private distinction. The classification of bodies or activities as 'private' traditionally excludes them from the ambit of human rights law. This dichotomy will be questioned in the context of this work. Religion is a social institution that has a dual nature: it is private but it is also public. It must be protected from encroachment by the state, but individuals must also be protected from it.

Another of the classical liberal assumptions challenged is that of voluntary choice and its implications. The often implicit presumption, that individuals willingly enter groups and thus accept all their rules, will be seen in different instances to be a fallacious basis for various legal determinations regarding individuals within the religious group, whether as employees in institutions, students in schools or men and women within a family. Throughout this work, it will be seen that legal determinations have been made, based on assumptions of free will, which are at odds with the constraints imposed by the interacting forces of family, religion and community. The interpretation of religious freedom should take these into account.

Some issues will not be separately addressed, such as the claims of religious minorities themselves against the state (such as access to places of worship, right to communicate with co-religionists abroad). This work does not examine the claims of groups towards the state, but the conflict between individual and group claims of religious freedom. The issues of legal requirements to address religious needs of religious communities, particularly minority communities, have been comprehensively discussed elsewhere.[4]

The right included in most national and international documents is that of freedom of religion, conscience and belief or a right to freedom of religion and belief. I will not deal with the right to freedom of conscience, but only with freedom of religion and religious belief. Neither will I deal with freedom of belief that lies outside the ambit of religious belief. This study is thus restricted, as the conflict of individual and group rights is a key to the understanding of the right of freedom of religion and religious belief, because of the nature of religion as a social institution. Freedom of conscience has been studied elsewhere.[5]

This study enquires as to the nature of the right. It shows that recognition of group rights is not only opposed to the idea of human rights, but also results in inconsistent and unjustified determinations.

Major studies of the legal right to religious freedom include that of Tahzib,[6] who surveys the existing international legal instruments protecting religious freedom, and examines the possibility and desirability of a completion of a binding convention safeguarding this right. Taylor[7] offers a current discussion of religious freedom in UN and other international documents.

An important collection of essays edited by Witte and Van der Vyver[8] comprises two volumes: one of religious perspectives on religious freedom and one of legal perspectives. These include both articles from specific legal systems and articles relating to international law, covering a wide spectrum of countries and disciplines.

Carolyn Evans examines the principles that shape the jurisprudence of the European Court of Human Rights (and of the European Commission for Human Rights),[9] while Malcolm Evans[10] examines international law on religious liberty in Europe in the context of the historical development of the right to religious freedom. The collection of essays edited by Janis[11] deals with a separate but connected topic of the way in which religions influenced the development of international law.

Boyle and Sheen[12] provide an extensive survey of the compliance with international law of countries across the world. The aspects of English law dealing with minorities and freedom of religion and law are comprehensively described by Knights.[13] In a recent book, Ahdar and Leigh[14] argue for greater inclusion of religious, particularly Christian, perspectives, within the liberal state. Influential earlier work in the field includes studies commissioned by UN bodies engaged in the development of protection of religious freedom,[15] notably that of Krishnaswami.[16]

The recognized right under international law, including in the International Covenant on Civil and Political Rights and the 1981 UN Declaration on the Elimination of All Forms of Intolerance and Discrimination Based on Religion and Belief is a right to freedom of religion *or* belief. Since the term 'belief' is broader than 'religion', this work does not need to rely on a definition of religion. The definition of religion has been subject of much debate.[17] Substantive definitions are based on concepts of theism, or belief in a supernatural being.[18] Functional definitions more broadly encompass any belief system.[19] All of these would be included in the broader term 'belief', as would atheism and agnosticism. Indeed, 'belief' includes ideological or philosophical beliefs that do not take a stand on religious issues. This delineation does not concern this work and has been studied elsewhere.[20] The beliefs, practice and institutions of religions are protected under the right to freedom of religion in international law, to different extents. The extent of protection of religious institutions, especially, will be influenced by the approach taken to this right, whether as an individual or a group right.

The analysis presented in this work of the conflict between individual and group interpretations of religious freedom will shed light on the problematic nature of this right. Moreover, it will provide insight on the relationship between the constitutional structure of the state and the right of religious freedom.

Notes

1 See discussion in Chapter 3.
2 M. Shaw, *International law*, 6th edn, Cambridge: Cambridge University Press, 2006, 72–77.
3 See K. Boyle, J. Sheen (eds), *Freedom of religion and belief: a world report*, London: Routledge, 1997.
4 See, for example, P. Thornberry, *International law and the rights of minorities*, Oxford: Clarendon Press, 1990.
5 See, for example, L. M. Hammer, *The international human right to freedom of conscience*, Aldershot: Ashgate, 2001. Hammer examines solely the rights to freedom of conscience, offering discussion of issues deliberately not covered in this work such as conscientious objection to military service and to the payment of taxes.
6 B. Tahzib, *Freedom of religion or belief – ensuring effective international legal protection*, The Hague: Martinus Nijhoff Publishers, 1996.
7 P. M. Taylor, *Freedom of religion: UN and international human rights law and practice*, Cambridge: Cambridge University Press, 2005.
8 J. Witte and J. D. Van der Vyver, *Religious human rights in global perspective*, Vols. I and II, The Hague: Martinus Nijhoff Publishers, 1996.
9 C. Evans, *Freedom of religion under the European Convention on Human Rights*, Oxford: Oxford University Press, 2001.

10 M. Evans, *Religious liberty and international law in Europe*, Cambridge: Cambridge University Press, 1997.

11 M. W. Janis (ed.), *The influence of religion on the development of international law*, Dordrecht: Martinus Nijhoff Publishers, 1991.

12 K. Boyle and J. Sheen (eds), *Freedom of religion and belief: a world report*, London: Routledge, 1997.

13 S. Knights, *Freedom of religion, minorities and the law*, Oxford: Oxford University Press, 2007.

14 R. Ahdar and I. Leigh, *Religious freedom in the liberal state*, Oxford: Oxford University Press, 2005.

15 As will be discussed later.

16 A. Krishnaswami, *Study in the matter of religious rights and practices – Report of the Special Rapporteur of the Sub-Commission on Prevention of Discrimination and Protection of Minorities*, New York: United Nations, 1960.

17 For some discussions of the definition, see N. Smart, *The philosophy of religion*, New York: Oxford University Press, 1979, 4–34; K. Greenawalt, 'Religion as a constitutional concept', *California Law Review* 72, 1984, 753. For some of the legal implications of these definitions, see P. Edge, *Legal responses to religious difference*, The Hague: Kluwer Law International, 2002, 5–17.

18 Associated with German phenomenology and the work of Weber, Otto, Wach, and Berger. See J. D. Hunter, 'The challenge of modern pluralism', in J. D. Hunter and O. Guinness (eds), *Articles of faith, articles of peace: the religious liberty clause and American public philosophy*, Washington: Brookings Institution, 1990, 54, 58.

19 Associated with structuralism and the work of Durkheim, Malinowski and Talcott Parsons and with German sociological materialism and Marx, Engels and Harrington. See, Hunter, ibid.

20 C. Evans, *Freedom of religion under the European Convention on Human Rights*, Oxford: Oxford University Press, 2001.

1 Existing protection of religious freedom in international law

International law is both starting and end point for this study. However, this study is concerned not with the existing international law regarding religious freedom, but with how it should be developed. It seeks to uncover the problems regarding this right that are largely disregarded by existing international law. It will do so by drawing on a theoretical proposal and discussion of legal examples.

Before turning, in Chapter 2, to the thesis of this work, and to an analysis of the right to freedom of religion and belief, this chapter briefly examines the existing protection of religious freedom in international law.

The right to freedom of religion is recognized in international law and in all major human rights systems, recognition that is often given without much thought given to the problems it creates. Often, the most pervasive infringements of rights emanating from the state's actions towards religion are not viewed as issues of religious freedom. Only an analysis of the principles behind this right will allow a conclusion as to how it should be implemented in international law. However, to see how this analysis might fit into the existing legal framework and build on it, we must first examine, in brief, the relevant international legal documents. The analysis will bring us back, throughout this study and its conclusion, to an understanding of how this right should be perceived and developed in international law.

The historical development of the right to freedom of religion and its incorporation in international legal documents reflects a move from protection of groups to recognition of the rights of the individual. A start of a countermove is currently seen towards the incorporation of the protection of the rights of the group. While the current protection of religious freedom under international law is based on individual rights, a growing trend will be seen, reflected in proposed international documents and some regional documents towards recognition of group rights. However, this would be a problematic development for the protection of the right to religious freedom, as will be discussed in this chapter.

1.1 Historical underpinnings

A principle of tolerance of other religions was already recognized by several religions in antiquity.[1] But the emergence of a legal principle of religious freedom parallels the emergence of international law itself. Initially, this freedom was recognized only as a freedom of the ruler to choose the religion of his territory, *cuius regio eius religio*. The Peace of Augsburg (1555) gave Lutheran princes the same status as Catholic princes and let the lay princes decide which of the two religions to adopt within their territories (with limited concession to those people already Lutheran to continue observing their faith) and gave the Lutheran Church self-governance. The Peace of Westphalia Treaties in 1648 concluded the Thirty Years War by setting up a regime of states with different Protestant faiths, obliging them to respect the diverging religious beliefs of individuals subject to their jurisdiction.[2] The state borders no longer paralleled the religious border, and religious freedom in a true sense was recognized. The authority of the sovereign under this regime was no longer seen to emanate from divinity but from the will of people. Thus, legal positivism in international law was born. The Treaty of Westphalia guaranteed freedom of religion for three religions (Calvinist, Lutheran and Catholic Christian faiths). The Union of Utrecht (1579), which later became the Constitution of The Netherlands, had already guaranteed general freedom of religion. So, international law developed a right of religious freedom, but religious freedom, in turn, was pivotal to the development of international law.

Protection of religious minorities through bilateral treaties continued after the Peace of Westphalia, which modified the previous rule of *cuius regio eius religio*, the freedom of the ruler to choose the religion of his territory. Bilateral treaties since the 17th century incorporated religious protection clauses, usually on a basis of reciprocity between the signatories.[3] Religious rights were, in some cases, a condition for territorial arrangement or recognition of states.[4] This development in international law was the practical manifestation of the contemporary liberal philosophy, which wished to distinguish religion from state, in order to avoid conflict.[5] Since the Ottoman Empire, the Muslim powers too accepted these principles of European international law including full recognition of non-Muslim states, abandoning the *shari'a* principles of non-recognition of non-Muslim states and of a permanent state of war with such states.[6]

The era of modern protection of freedom of religion started after the First World War, with the League of Nations and the Minority Treaties. The Covenant of the League of Nations did not include a proposed Article (Draft Article 20) prohibiting the parties from interfering with religious exercise. A set of minority treaties was entered into.[7] Typical among these was the 1919 Minorities Treaty between the Principled Allied and Associated Forces and Poland,[8] which committed Poland to non-discrimination of (among others) religious minorities, equal funding for educational, religious and charitable causes of minorities, and specifically Jewish education (an arrangement which failed in practice),[9] as well as an undertaking not to disadvantage Jews because of Sabbath observance. The treaty was monitored by the Council of the League of Nations. The structure of the treaty was triangular: Poland's obligations towards the minorities were explicitly deemed international obligations between the signatories. The members of the Council of the League of Nations, and not the minorities themselves, were accorded the right to bring infractions to the attention of the Council or, ultimately, to the Permanent Court of International Justice.

1.2 Right to freedom of religion in the major UN documents

Following the Second World War, it became clear that the League of Nations method of upholding religious freedom through group protection had collapsed. This was due to its failure of enforcement, and, ultimately, to its use by Hitler as a pretext for the invasion of Poland, and start of the Second World War.[11] The approach to the protection of human rights in the international arena changed from a minorities protection approach to a conception of universal individual rights as manifested in the early documents of the United Nations.

The United Nations Charter, drafted in 1945, states in Article 1, among the purposes and principles of the United Nations[10]:

> (3) To achieve international co-operation in solving international problems of an economic, social, cultural, or humanitarian character, and in promoting and encouraging respect for human rights and for fundamental freedoms for all without distinction as to race, sex, language, or religion.

The phrase 'without distinction as to race, sex, language or religion', copied in subsequent human rights documents, was formulated in the San Francisco negotiations. The importance of this wording is the conceptual choice it reflects. A norm of anti-discrimination was chosen instead of any mention of minority protection, a preference furthered mostly by immigrant-absorbing countries such as the United States which feared the implications of minority-based wording.[12]

The Universal Declaration of Human Rights [UDHR][13] adopted on 10 December 1948, states, in Article 18, that:

> Everyone has the right to freedom of thought, conscience and religion; this right includes freedom to change his religion or belief, and freedom, either alone or in community with others and in public or private, to manifest his religion or belief in teaching, practice, worship and observance.

The main point of contention in drafting this Article was the right to change one's religion. The inclusion of this right, together with Article 16 (which mandates equality in marriage) caused Saudi Arabia's abstention on the vote on the Declaration[14] as irreconcilable with the teachings of Islam.

Article 2 of the Declaration, the non-discrimination Article, includes religion as an impermissible ground of discrimination in Declaration rights.

The Universal Declaration refers throughout to individual rights, except Article 26,[15] which does not establish a right but refers to a duty to promote tolerance between religious groups. This conception of rights as individual rights is due, in part, to the position of Eleanor Roosevelt, as head of the first Commission on Human Rights, who was opposed to the idea of minority rights, and saw the solution to the problems of minorities in respect for human rights.[16] This position was supported by immigrant-absorbing states such as Chile,[17] and by those, like the Belgian delegate, apprehensive of provisions relating to minorities, because of the use of the presence of German minorities in other countries by Hitler as a pretext for German intervention.[18] The historical failure of the Minority Treaties in group protection thus played an important role in the shift towards protection of individual rights.

1.3 The International Human Rights Covenants

The same individual approach is evident in the UN Human Rights Covenants adopted in 1966. The International Covenant on Civil and Political Rights [ICCPR][19] states, in Article 18, a clear individual rights provision, that:

1.   Everyone shall have the right to freedom of thought, conscience and religion. This right shall include freedom to have or to adopt a religion or belief of his choice, and freedom, either individually or in community with others and in public or private, to manifest his religion or belief in worship, observance, practice and teaching.
2.   No one shall be subject to coercion which would impair his freedom to have or to adopt a religion or belief of his choice.
3.   Freedom to manifest one's religion or beliefs may be subject only to such limitations as are prescribed by law and are necessary to protect public safety, order, health, or morals or the fundamental rights and freedoms of others.
4.   The States Parties to the present Covenant undertake to have respect for the liberty of parents and, when applicable, legal guardians to ensure the religious and moral education of their children in conformity with their own convictions.

All rights in the Convention are guaranteed without discrimination on enumerated grounds, which include religion.[20] (Similarly, the International Covenant on Economic, Social and Cultural Rights [ICESCR][21] mandates that all the rights which are included in that Covenant must be exercised without discrimination on certain grounds, including religion.)[22]

These provisions are complemented by Article 27 of the ICCPR, which accords specific rights to members of religious (and other) minorities.[23] It should be noticed that Article 27 is carefully worded, so that individuals are still the bearers of the rights it accords. The Sub-Commission on Prevention of Discrimination and Protection of Minorities discussed drafts of Article 27[24] submitted to it.[25] The Sub-Commission changed the wording of the Article from a collective wording: 'Ethnic, religious and linguistic minorities shall not be denied the right to enjoy their own culture, to profess and practice their own religion, or to use their own language' to the individual subject: 'persons belonging to minorities shall not be denied the right'. This was done because minorities were not seen as subjects of law. The Sub-Commission did acknowledge a communal character of the right by inserting the words 'in community with the other members of their group'.[26] The addition of the qualifying phrase '[i]n those states in which ethnic, religious or linguistic minorities exist' opened the door for states to argue that there are no minorities residing in their boundaries, thus allowing states an interpretation that the Article does not apply to them.[27]

Collective (or group) rights in UN human rights conventions appear regarding self-determination, in common Article 1 of the ICCPR and the ICESCR, which states the right of 'all peoples' to self-determination and to free use of their natural resources. (Collective rights also appear in Article 1 of the Declaration on the Rights to Development,[28] which declares that the right to development is a right of 'every human and all peoples'.) Some commentators have noted, that the right to development is meaningless except as a right to be exercised by groups,[29] although others have claimed that the right to development is not and cannot be a collective human right.[30]

Article 27 of the ICCPR, stating the right of persons belonging to ethnic, religious or linguistic minorities, to enjoy their culture, process and practice their religion and use their language, is clearly different. Although couched in terms of individual rights, it has been described as 'inherently collective'.[31] The Human Rights Committee[32] stated that this is an individual right, but may give rise to a state duty towards a minority to protect its identity. This is clearly different from a group right of religious freedom.

If there were to be recognized a group right of religious freedom, it would raise a set of problems not encountered with the recognition of group rights to self-determination and development, relating to potential conflict between the rights of the group, as they are exercised, and the rights and choices of individuals within it. Group decisions, which exercise existing collective rights (such as the right to self-determination and use of natural resources in common Article 1), may conflict with choices of individuals within the group. (Someone may object, for instance, to the way natural resources are used.) But the conflict between the exercise of religious rights of the religious group and freedom of belief of its members is inherent. This is because religions, by their very essence, seek to regulate every aspect of the lives of their members – public and private, moral and spiritual. In this respect, recognition of group rights of a religious group would be more problematic than recognition of group rights of linguistic or cultural groups. Language and culture typically encompass only some, mostly external, aspects of their members' lives. The potential for conflict between group and individual determinations is therefore greater in respect of religion.

1.4 The UN Declaration on the Elimination of All Forms of Intolerance and of Discrimination Based on Religion and Belief (1981)

A subtle shift towards protection of group aspects of religious freedom can be seen in the newer, more particularized documents on religious rights. Following the report commissioned by the Sub-Commission on Prevention of Discrimination and Protection of Minorities from Special Rapporteur Arcot Krishnaswami,[33] efforts to achieve a binding convention on freedom of religion or belief have been made. These have not, so far, been successful, culminating in the aborted 1967 Draft Convention on the Elimination of All Forms of Religious Intolerance.[34] What was achieved is the 1981 UN Declaration on the Elimination of All Forms of Intolerance and Discrimination based on Religion and Belief,[35] which is the most detailed international instrument on religious rights and freedoms to date.[36]

The Declaration is stated in terms of individual rights, but elaborates, in Article 6, on recognition of rights which are individual but exercised communally, such as the rights to worship or assemble in connection with religion, to teach religion or belief, to train and appoint leaders and to communicate with other communities in matters of religion.[37] The Article is phrased in terms of individual rights, as it is merely an explication of what the right to freedom of thought, conscience, religion or belief includes. These are individual rights exercised communally rather than group rights. Thus, they do not raise the problems, which will be examined in this study, inherent in recognition of group rights.

The idea of the group as a unit of protection of religious freedom is, however, reflected in Article 5. The group protected is the most intimate one, the family – a building block of the larger religious community. The parents are given the rights to organize life within the family in accordance with their religion and belief. This right is given in the context of the status of the child, but the right to organize the religious life of the family introduces a broader idea, of the family as an autonomous unit, a subject of rights, within the state. The implications and criticism of this approach will be seen in the discussion of the formation of religious identity and affiliation of children in Chapter 5.

The right to change one's religion or belief was omitted in the Declaration. This omission might be thought to detract from the individual aspect of religious freedom, as the right to change religion is important precisely to the dissenter, to the individual who wishes to distance himself from the group into which he was born. However, this omission is more a concession to expediency than principle, as, in practical terms, the right was preserved. The right to change belief was included in the UDHR. While the 1981 Declaration does not expressly mention the right, it declares in Article 8, that nothing in the Declaration shall be construed as restricting or derogating from any rights defined in the UDHR or the international human rights covenants. So, the shift is only illusory.[38]

Finally, discrimination on the basis of religion might also be prohibited by customary law.[39] However, it appears that only non-discrimination, which is an independent right as well as one aspect of religious freedom, is partially protected by customary law, while all other aspects of religious freedom are not.

1.5 International documents relating to national, religious and linguistic minorities and to indigenous peoples

The UN Declaration on Persons Belonging to National, Religious and Linguistic Minorities 1992[40] indicates a further step in the direction of according rights to minority groups. Although the rights in this Declaration are accorded individuals belonging to religious (and other) minorities,[41] it also declares that states must protect the religious identity (as well as other identities) of minorities.[42] The individual character of the rights is, however, retained and reinforced by the explicit right of minority members to choose to exercise their right either individually or in community with others.[43]

The Declaration provides that: 'No disadvantage shall result for any person belonging to a minority as the consequence of the exercise or non-exercise of the rights' in the Declaration.[44] However, it is not made clear if it is the state that may not cause such disadvantage to any person, or if also the minority group itself may not disadvantage the individual for his choice. (Indeed, if the state permits the group to cause such disadvantage, it is the state itself that is responsible for the infringement, as will be seen in Chapter 3.)

One further step in recognition of group rights over individual rights is evident in an evolving category of international human rights documents regarding rights of indigenous peoples (a category that includes some, but not all, religious minorities). The newly adopted UN Declaration on the Rights of Indigenous Peoples[45] differs markedly from existing UN instruments in that it is worded in the language of group rights.[46] The inherent problems of this approach are implicit in Article 34, which declares that '[i]ndigenous peoples have the right to promote, develop and maintain their institutional structures and their distinctive customs, spirituality, traditions, procedures, practices and, in the cases where they exist, juridical systems or customs, in accordance with international human rights standards.'

Thornberry, reflecting on the Draft Declaration,[47] suggested that, despite opposition from some representatives of indigenous peoples, both the collective right to indigenous juridical procedures, and its qualification, to adherence to human rights, should be retained in the Declaration. He suggested that a balance should be sought between individual and collective rights.[48] This is a problematic solution, as it is not clear who will decide on the balance of rights, and it gives no coherent reason as to why some individuals, but not others, must forsake their rights to the group. Indeed, the Declaration, which retained this right from the proposed declaration, was not uncontroversial, passing by an overwhelming majority, but against the votes of Canada, Australia, New Zealand and the United States.

Similarly, the Proposed American Declaration on the Rights of Indigenous Peoples[49, 50] declares that indigenous law shall be recognized as a part of the states' legal system,[51] that indigenous peoples have the right to maintain and reinforce their indigenous legal systems and apply them to matters within their communities,[52] and that procedures concerning indigenous peoples shall include observance of indigenous law and custom.[53]

However, indigenous juridical customs, many of them religious, may stand in conflict with human rights norms. A right to a legal system is a group right, and hence it is in potential conflict with rights of individuals within the group. While Article 43 of the UN Declaration on the Rights of Indigenous Peoples guarantees the rights recognized in the Declaration equally to male and female indigenous individuals, it ignores the possibility that the rights enumerated in the Declaration itself, such as an indigenous juridical system, may operate in a manner discriminatory to members of the group. The Proposed American Declaration too ignores altogether the possibility of gender discrimination within indigenous law and custom.

1.6 Regional instruments

The right to freedom of religion is also recognized in major regional human rights instruments. Differences between formulations of the right in these documents indicate different perceptions of this right as a right of individuals or of groups and of its place in the state.

1.6.1 The Americas

The regional American approach to human rights is consistently one of individual, rather than group, protection.[54] It is also the approach of various Latin-American constitutions.[55] It stems from a view that, as immigrant-absorbing countries, rights are granted to immigrants on the premise of their assimilation into society as a whole and not as separate groups.[56] However, as mentioned earlier, in stark contrast to this approach, the Proposed American Declaration on the Rights of Indigenous Peoples is one of the most group rights-oriented documents.

The American Convention on Human Rights protects religious freedom[57] as a right of the individual, offering particularly broad protection to the right of the individual to dissent from the group. This is done both by specific mention of the right to disseminate one's religion or belief,[58] and by adding to the right to change one's religious belief the prohibition of any restrictions on this right.[59] This would prohibit laws that place restrictions on proselytizing, which impair the right to change religion.[60]

1.6.2 Africa

The African Charter on Human Rights and Peoples' Rights[61] includes, in Article 8, the right to freedom of religion.[62] While other regional instruments allow the right to be qualified in certain conditions, the African Charter is the only such instrument to allow the right to be qualified under such a broad condition as 'subject to law and order'. The reason for this qualification in the African Charter was the insistence of the Islamic signatory states, to which this qualification was important.[63] This gives considerable scope to the state to restrict religious freedom. However, it does not mean that Article 8 cannot be effectual. For instance, the African Human Rights Commission found Zaire in violation of Article 8 in its harassment of Jehovah's Witnesses without proof that the practice of their religion 'threatens law and order'.[64]

1.6.3 Europe

In Europe, two main regional legal frameworks exist that protect human rights: that of the Council of Europe, through the European Convention for the Protection of Human Rights and Fundamental Freedoms,[65] and that of the European Union, within its competence, in relation to member states of the EU and the EU itself. As well, there exist the non-legal instruments of the Conference on Security and Cooperation in Europe.

The European Convention guarantees a right of religious freedom in Article 9.[66] A right to equality in protection of religious freedom is granted in Article 14.[67] It is not a general prohibition of discrimination on grounds of religion, but is limited to discrimination regarding Convention rights. A general prohibition on discrimination on any right in law is included only in Protocol 12 Article 1 to the Convention.[68]

Importantly, during the Cold War era,[69] the 1975 Final Act of the Conference on Security and Cooperation in Europe,[70] a non-legally binding instrument, provided that the participating states will recognize and respect the freedom of the individual to profess and practice, alone or in community with others, religion or belief. The later 1989 Concluding Document of the Vienna Follow-up Meeting of Representatives of the Participating States of the Conference on Security and Co-operation in Europe[71] referred specifically to the rights of religious communities in Principle 16.

The later Document of the Copenhagen Meeting of the Conference on the Human Dimension of the Conference on Security and Cooperation in Europe (1990) guarantees an individually formulated right to freedom of thought, conscience and belief.[72] However, Part IV recognizes rights of national minorities, including the rights to religious identity, maintenance of religious institutions, and the right to profess and practice their religion.[73] Here religious rights, even the right to profess and practice religion, are directly accorded to the group. Furthermore, participating states are required to create conditions for promotion of the religious (as well as ethnic, cultural and linguistic) identity.[74] The right to religious identity is accorded to the national minorities, while no separate mention is made of religious minorities. Religion is seen only as one of the defining characteristics of the national group. Identification as a member of the national minority is left to the individual's choice.[75] However, no mention is made of the rights of an individual who chooses to be part of the group, but would like to opt out of some of the group's actions. (The importance of such a possibility will become apparent in the substantive discussions which follow, for instance, of women within religious communities in Chapter 4.)

The Council of Europe Framework Convention for the Protection of National Minorities[76] similarly recognizes religion only as a component of national minority identity,[77] and not as a group identity on its own. It too protects the choice of the individual, whether or not to be part of the minority, without suffering disadvantage as a result of this choice.[78] This, again, is an 'all or nothing' choice. No protection is given for an individual's choice to be considered part of a minority for some purposes, but not for others.

The European Union has progressively adopted treaty provisions that protect religious freedom. The Treaty Establishing the European Union, as amended by the Nice Treaty[79] includes a provision concerning discrimination, whereby within its competence, the European Union may take appropriate action to combat discrimination based on religion or belief (among other grounds).[80]

The negotiations on the Draft Treaty Establishing a Constitution for Europe[81] exposed deep divisions regarding the inclusion of a mention of Christianity, mostly between Catholic states such as Poland, which demanded it, and secular states such as France, which opposed it. In the end no mention was made of Christianity, the Preamble referring only to the 'spiritual and moral heritage' of the European Union. The proposed constitutional treaty came to an abortive end, but the Lisbon Treaty[82] which replaced it similarly mentions the 'cultural, religious and humanist inheritance of Europe'.

Planned as a comprehensive human rights convention for the Union, the Charter of Fundamental Rights of the European Union has received the legal status of a treaty with the entry into force of the Lisbon Treaty. It includes the right to freedom of thought, conscience and religion,[83] a general non-discrimination provision on grounds which include religion[84], and a provision that 'the Union shall respect cultural, religious and linguistic diversity'.[85]

A right related to religion, the right to marry and found a family,[86] is made subordinate to national legislation. Although subordination to national legislation is not exclusive to rights concerning religion,[87] it is notable that such deference to national law is present regarding family life, seen as a deeply cultural choice, which religion underlies. Thus, even this new international document shows deference to member states, precisely in those areas that religion underlies. An investigation of the rights of religious freedom of the individual vis-à-vis the group is thus as important as ever.

Protection of religious freedom in international law has shifted from group protection to individual right. It now shows signs of shifting to incorporation of aspects of a group right, this study will show next why the conception of religious freedom should remain one of an individual right. The discussion in the chapters ahead will show why this move should cause concern, and why the conception of religious freedom should remain one of an individual right.

Notes

1 See Chapter 2, section 2.4, and discussion of the relation between religion and the sources of the law of nations in antiquity in D. J. Bederman, *International law in antiquity*, Cambridge: Cambridge University Press, 2001, 48–85.

2 M. Evans, *Religious liberty and international law in Europe*, Cambridge: Cambridge University Press, 1997, Chapter 2. But religion did not cease to influence statecraft after Westphalia (W. A. McDougall, 'Religion in world affairs: Introduction', *Orbis*, 42, 1998).

3 Such as the Treaty of Vienna (1606) and the Treaty of Carlovitz (1699) between Austria and Turkey (22 CTS 219). See A. W. B. Simpson, *Human rights and the end of empire*, Oxford: Oxford University Press, 2001,110–111.

4 N. Lerner, 'Religious human rights under the United Nations', in J. van der Vyver and J. Witte Jr. (eds), *Religious human rights in global perspective Vol. II – legal perspectives*, The Hague: Martinus Nijhoff Publishers, 1996, 94.

5 This will be discussed in greater detail in Chapter 2.

6 An-Naim, *Towards an Islamic reformation: civil liberties, human rights and international law*, Syracuse: Syracuse University Press, 1990, Chapter 6.

7 Seventeen states were involved in 14 treaties. F. Capotorti, *Study of the rights of persons belonging to ethnic, religious and linguistic minorities*, New York: United Nations, 1979, 18. See list in H. Lauterpacht (ed.), *Oppenheim's international law*, Vol. I, London: Longman, 1948, 713 fn. 1.

8 Treaty Series, No. 8 (1919). Reprinted in J. Robinson et al., *Were the minority treaties a failure?*, New York: Institute of Jewish Affairs, 1943, appendix I.

9 Ibid. 73.

10 For an up-to-date survey of UN documents relating to freedom of religion, P. M. Taylor, *Freedom of religion: UN and international human rights law and practice*, Cambridge: Cambridge University Press, 2005.

11 J. Morsink, *The Universal Declaration of Human Rights: origins, drafting and intent*, Philadelphia: University of Pennsylvania Press, 1999, 27. See details of the developments in Polish–German relations in 1930–1931 leading up to this, F. P. Walters, *A history of the League of Nations*, Vol. 1, Oxford: Oxford University Press, 1952, 446–468. Today, as will be seen in this and following chapters, different enforcement mechanisms of different international and regional instruments protecting religious freedom have varying degrees of effectiveness.

12 P. Thornberry, *International law and the rights of minorities*, Oxford: Clarendon Press, 1990, 122–123.

13 UNGA Res. 217 A(III) (1948).

14 J. S. Nielsen, 'Contemporary discussions on religious minorities in Islam', *Brigham Young University Law Review*, 2002, 356.

15 Article 26(2): 'Education shall ... promote understanding, tolerance and friendship among all nations, racial or religious groups.'

16 M. Evans, *Religious liberty and international law in Europe*, Cambridge: Cambridge University Press, 1997, 182.

17 J. Morsink, *The Universal Declaration of Human Rights: origins, drafting and intent*, Philadelphia: University of Pennsylvania Press, 1999, 251 (see also UN Doc. E/CN.4/SR.15/p.6 discussed, ibid, 271).

18 E/CN.4/SR.73/ at 6, quoted in Ibid. 274. (The Belgian delegation later reversed its stand on this issue.)

19 Adopted 16 December 1966, 999 UNTS 171.

20 Article 2.

21 Adopted 16 December 1966, 999 UNTS 3.

22 Article 2, para. 2.

23 Article 27: 'In those States in which ethnic, religious or linguistic minorities exist, persons belonging to such minorities shall not be denied the right, in community with the other members of their group, to enjoy their own culture, to profess and practise their own religion, or to use their own language.'

24 Report of Sub-Commission UN Doc E/CN.4/358, paras. 39–48.

25 Pursuant to UNGA Res. 217c(III) adopted 10 December 1948.

26 P. Thornberry, *International law and the rights of minorities*, Oxford: Clarendon Press, 1990, 149.

27 The Human Rights Committee has not yet examined a claim from a member of a religious minority under Article 27. A. M. De Zayas, 'International judicial protection of peoples and minorities', in C. Brolmann, R. Lefeber and M. Zieck (eds), *Peoples and minorities in international law*, Dordrecht: Martinus Nijhoff Publishers, 1992 points to HRC Comm. No. 208/1986 *Singh Bhinder v. Canada* UN Doc. A/45/40 Vol. II p. 50, in which the issue could have been raised but was not.

28 UNGA Res. 41/128 (1986).

29 Bedjaoui, M. Bedjaoui, 'The rights to development', in M. Bedjaoui, *International law: achievements and prospects*, UNESCO, Norwell: Martinus Nijhoff Publishers, 1991, 1182.

30 R. Higgins, 'Comments', in C. Brolmann, R. Lefeber and M. Zieck (eds), *Peoples and minorities in international law*, Dordrecht: Martinus Nijhoff Publishers, 1992, 30.

Higgins claims that the term 'rights of peoples' implies rights of the citizenry of the state as a whole, as distinct from minority groups within it (as in Article 27 of the ICCPR) and so it is misleading to refer to these rights as group rights.

31 H. J. Steiner, and P. Alston, *International human rights in context: law, politics, morals*, 2nd edn, Oxford: Oxford University Press, 2000, 993.

32 General Comment 23 (CCPR/C/21/Rev. 1/Add, 5) para. 6.2.

33 A. Krishnaswami, *Study in the matter of religious rights and practices – Report of the Special Rapporteur of the Sub-Commission on Prevention of Discrimination and Protection of Minorities*, New York: United Nations, 1960.

34 UN Doc A/8330 App. III (1971). See B. Tahzib, *Freedom of religion or belief – ensuring effective international legal protection*, The Hague: Martinus Nijhoff Publishers, 1996, 145–155 (a narration of the events leading to the Draft Convention), and ibid, 423–483 (appraisal of the current prospects for such a convention).

35 UNGA Res. 36/55 adopted 25 November 1981.

36 While UN General Assembly resolutions and declarations, such as the 1981 declaration, are not formal sources of law within the categories of Article 38 (1) of the Statute of the International Court of Justice, the resolutions are very influential in the development of customary international law. See O. Schachter, *International law in theory and practice*, Dordrecht; Boston: M. Nijhoff Publishers, 1991.

37 Article 6: 'In accordance with Article 1 of the present Declaration, and subject to the provisions of Article 1, paragraph 3, the right to freedom of thought, conscience, religion or belief shall include, inter alia, the following freedoms:

(a) To worship or assemble in connection with a religion or belief, and to establish and maintain places for these purposes;

(b) To establish and maintain appropriate charitable or humanitarian institutions;

(c) To make, acquire and use to an adequate extent the necessary Articles and materials related to the rites or customs of a religion or belief;

(d) To write, issue and disseminate relevant publications in these areas;

(e) To teach a religion or belief in places suitable for these purposes;

(f) To solicit and receive voluntary financial and other contributions from individuals and institutions;

(g) To train, appoint, elect or designate by succession appropriate leaders called for by the requirements and standards of any religion or belief;

(h) To observe days of rest and to celebrate holidays and ceremonies in accordance with the precepts of one's religion or belief;

(i) To establish and maintain communications with individuals and communities in matters of religion and belief at the national and international levels.

38 Elizabeth Odio Benito, the former Special Rapporteur Sub-commission on Prevention of Discrimination and Protection of Minorities, believes this right is included in the 1981 Declaration even without reference to Article 8 (E. Odio Benito, *Elimination of all forms of intolerance and discrimination based on religion or belief*, New York: United Nations, 1989, 50).

39 At least regarding systematic discrimination on grounds of religion. See: The Restatement [Third] of the Foreign Relations of the United States (1987) § 702 comment (j).

40 UNGA Res. 47/135 of 18 December 1992.

41 See Article 2.

42 Article 1.

43 Article 3(1).

44 Article 3(2).

45 UN Doc. A/61/L.67 (7 September 2007).

46 Indeed, France viewed this as an attempt to provide new rights in international law (UN Doc. E/CN.4/1997/102 para.108), and the Netherlands expressed concerns about this (UN Doc. E/CN.4/1997/102 para.109).

47 UN Doc. E/CN.4/Sub.2/1993/29/Annex I.
48 P. Thornberry, *Indigenous peoples and human rights*, Manchester: Manchester University Press, 2002.
49 Proposed American Declaration on the Rights of Indigenous Peoples (Approved by the Inter-American Commission on Human Rights, 26 February 1997) OEA/Ser/L/V/.II.95 Doc.6.
50 Although the proposed American Declaration does not define indigenous people, it refers to groups with their own customs and traditions and distinguishing culture, but does not refer to religion (in Article 1). However, Article 10 protects freedom of religion and spiritual practice, as well as associated rights to sacred sites.
51 Article 16(1).
52 Article 16(2).
53 Article 16(3).
54 P. Thornberry, *Minorities and human rights law*, Minorities Rights Group, 1991, 20.
55 Such as those of Brazil, Argentina, Chile and Mexico.
56 This approach was evident, as discussed above in the American delegates' positions in the drafting of the UDHR (J. Morsink, *The Universal Declaration of Human Rights: origins, drafting and intent*, Philadelphia: University of Pennsylvania Press, 1999, 251.
57 Article 12 of the American Convention on Human Rights, 22 November 1969, 1114 UNTS 123:

1. Everyone has a right to freedom of conscience and religion. This right includes freedom to maintain or to change one's religions or beliefs, and freedom to profess or disseminate one's religion or beliefs, either individually or together with others, in public or in private.
2. No one shall be subject to restrictions that might impair his freedom to maintain or to change his religion or beliefs.
3. Freedom to manifest one's religion and beliefs may be subject only to the limitations prescribed by law that are necessary to protect public safety, order, health or morals, or the rights or freedoms of others.
4. Parents or guardians, as the case may be, have the right to provide for the religious and moral education of their children or wards that is in accord with their own convictions.

58 Article 12(1).
59 Article 12(2).
60 Such restrictions in Israel, Germany, Greece and France are discussed in Chapter 6.
61 Adopted 26 June 1981, OAU Doc. CAB/LEG/67/3 Rev. 5. 21 ILM 58.
62 Article 8: 'Freedom of conscience, the profession and free practice of religion shall be guaranteed. No one may, subject to law and order, be submitted to measures restricting the exercise of these freedoms.'
63 D. Johnson, 'Cultural and regional pluralism in drafting the UN Convention on the Rights of the Child', in M. Freeman and P. Veerman (eds), *The ideologies of children's rights*, Dordrecht: M. Nijhoff, 1992, 95.
64 Comm. 25/89, 47/90, 56/91, 100/93 *Free Legal Assistance Group v. Zaire*.
65 Adopted 4 November 1950, 213 UNTS 221.
66 Article 9 states:

(1) Everyone has the rights to freedom of thought, conscience and religion; this right includes freedom to change his religion or belief and freedom either alone or in community with others and in public or private, to manifest his religion or belief, in worship, teaching, practice and observance.
(2) Freedom to manifest one's religion or beliefs shall be subject only to such limitations as are prescribed by law and are necessary in a democratic society in the interests of public safety, for the protection of public order, health or morals, or for the protection of the rights and freedoms of others.

67 Article 14 states that: '[t]he enjoyment of rights and freedoms set forth in this Convention shall be secured without discrimination on any grounds such as … religion.'

68 It states: '(1) The enjoyment of any right set forth by law shall be secured without discrimination on any ground such as sex, race … religion … (2) No one shall be discriminated against by any public authority on any ground such as those mentioned in paragraph 1.'

69 T. Buergenthal, J. R. Hall, *Human rights, international law and the Helsinki Accord*, Montclair: Allanheld Osmun, 1977, 134–140.

70 Final Act of the Conference on Security and Co-operation in Europe (adopted 1 August 1975) 14 ILM 1292.

71 28 ILM 527.

72 Article 9.4.

73 Article 32.

74 Article 33.

75 Article 32.

76 1 February 1995, 34 ILM, (1995) 351. See, generally, G. Oberleitner, 'Monitoring minority rights under the Council of Europe's Framework Convention' in P. Cumper and S. Wheatley (eds.), *Minority rights in the 'new' Europe*, The Hague: Martinus Nijhoff Publishers, 1999, 71.

77 Along with language, traditions and cultural heritage, in Articles 5 and 17. Articles 7 and 8 guarantee every person belonging to a national minority (among other rights) freedom of religion, conscience and belief, and the right to manifest religion and belief, and establish religious institutions, organizations and associations.

78 Article 3.

79 OJ C80, March 2001.

80 Article 13, The Consolidated Version of the Treaty Establishing the European Union, OJ C321, 29 December 2006.

81 OJ C169, 18 July 2003.

82 Article 10:

  (1) Everyone has the right to freedom of thought, conscience and religion. This right includes freedom to change religion or belief and freedom, either alone or in community with others and in public or in private, to manifest religion or belief, in worship, teaching, practice and observance.

  (2) The right to conscientious objection is recognized, in accordance with the national laws governing the exercise of this right.

83 Article 21(1): 'Any discrimination based on any ground such as sex, race, colour, ethnic or social origin, genetic features, language, religion or belief, political or any other opinion, membership of a national minority, property, birth, disability, age or sexual orientation shall be prohibited.'

84 In Article 22.

85 Article 9.

86 See for example Article 27 (workers' right to information and consultation).

87 Indeed, Protocol 7 to the Charter, which states that the Charter does not extend the powers of the European court of Justice to find the laws of Poland inconsistent with fundamental rights was framed at Poland's insistence to be able to maintain its national laws on issues such as abortion.

2 Why is there a right to freedom of religion?

2.1 Introduction

It is my purpose in this book to explain how international law should interpret the right to freedom of religion or belief, and how it should protect this right. The right to freedom of religion or belief should be understood and protected, first and foremost, as an individual right and only in furtherance of individual rights should it be protected as a group right. In this chapter this argument is based on a theoretical analysis of the right. The following chapters will argue for a coherent interpretation of international law based on the principles introduced in this chapter.

Other themes emerge throughout the discussion, in particular the meaning of religion and its role in society and in individual life is culture-specific. More than the subjects of other human rights, such as 'torture' (Universal Declaration of Human Rights [UDHR], Article 5) or 'slavery' (UDHR, Article 4), 'religion' is a concept defined by the culture to which it belongs. This concept loses much of its meaning outside its cultural context. Therefore, more than other human rights, freedom of religion can be interpreted differently by different cultures. Indeed, the different interpretations of this right were evident during the drafting of the article guaranteeing its protection in the Universal Declaration.[1]

According legitimacy to disparate policies regarding freedom of religion, as well as other rights, is at the centre of the debate between adopting a cultural approach to human rights or a universalist approach to human rights[2]. However, relativistic interpretations of the right to freedom of religion are intrinsically problematic,[3] as claims to such an interpretation of this right often clash with the rights of individuals, including those of women, children and dissenters, as will be illustrated in later chapters.

The law on freedom of religion must be interpreted in light of the unique role religion plays as a source of authority independent of and competing with state authority. Historically, of course, the process was the opposite one: it was the secular state that was set up as a rival source of power to religion through the mechanism of separation of state from church. Because of this, religion occupies a place in law distinct from other civic organizations, and guaranteeing its freedom is a more complex legal matter than ensuring other freedoms.

A state might deal with religion as a competing source of authority in one of two ways: on the one hand, it may view religion as a threat to itself, one that must be curtailed; on the other hand, it may co-opt religion for its own needs. History provides numerous examples of both these processes.[4] Religion may serve an important part in the formation of national identity and cohesiveness, and, indeed, may underwrite nationalism. This continuing struggle and engagement of religion and state is reflected, in different ways, in almost all modern constitutions.[5]

This chapter explores the justifications of religious freedom. Understanding the reasons for the recognition of freedom of religion as a human right is necessary for the resolution of legal conflicts surrounding the application of this right. First, the difference between a group right and an individual right is explained (section 2.2). I argue that the dual nature of the right to religious freedom creates a tension between liberty and equality, a tension that is manifested in the legal protection accorded to this right (section 2.3). I then examine the reasons given in liberal theory for protecting religious freedom in order to find which interpretation of the right to religious freedom they support. I examine the concept of liberal religious neutrality and the claim that this concept is not, in fact, neutral between religious and non-religious doctrines, and may conflict with how some religions view their own role and that of the state (section 2.4). The different reasons offered for promotion of religious freedom are reviewed, focusing on approaches which centre on the individual's relationship to community and culture (section 2.5). These are contrasted with views of religious freedom espoused by religions themselves (section 2.6). In view of the tensions inherent in the different conceptions of the right to religious freedom, I consider the problem of applying liberal theory to legal protection of religious freedom regarding two issues: the treatment of anti-democratic religious parties and the legitimacy of the use of religious reasons for legislation (section 2.7). This chapter concludes that religious freedom can only be an individual right, but exposes the difficulties that must be overcome in such an approach because of the group aspects of this right.

2.2 Can freedom of religion be a group right?

In this section, it is argued that religious freedom can only be an individual right, because rights, as such, cannot be attributed to groups. Rights are limits on a collective goal. Group power over individuals, like state power over individuals, may be justified in certain cases by other reasons, but not by assertion of rights. The exercise of rights depends on recognizable decisions by autonomous individuals. There is no one obvious way to recognize group members and identify legitimate processes of decision making. Saying that what will be recognized is whatever the group decides concerning its membership and procedures is not helpful, being nothing more than circular reasoning. Rights cannot be said to belong to groups because there is no undisputed way in which the bearer of the right (the group) may exercise the right. It is argued alternatively, and shown in the following chapters, that even if rights, including religious freedom, can be attributed to groups, rights of groups to religious freedom should not be allowed to override individual rights.

2.2.1 What would a group right be?

To understand how a group right to religious freedom could be conceived, we should first clarify what such a right is not: it is not an aggregate of individual rights, even individual rights that are exercised communally. Religion is a case in point. Religion is a social institution, and its practice implies the existence of more than one participant. A single person may hold a belief, but not a religion. Therefore, one may think that the right to freedom of religion is a group right (even if the right of freedom of belief is an individual right).

However, this conclusion is based on a faulty understanding of the distinction between an individual right and a group right. The mere fact that more than one person is needed for the exercise of a given right is not a sufficient condition for making that right a group right. Thus, freedom of association is an individual right, although it cannot be practised alone. Freedom of expression is an individual right, although it, too, cannot be meaningfully practiced alone. The speaker needs an audience, as the worshipper needs his co-religionists, but the respective rights to express and to worship are theirs as individuals.

The concept of a group right must mean something more: it must mean a right of the group as such. A group right would supervene on the rights of individuals but would not be reducible to an aggregate of individual rights (just as water is wet, but the molecules of which it is comprised are not). An obvious example of a group right is a right of the group that, by its nature, must override the rights of the group's individual members. For instance, a group could have a right to a legal system with jurisdiction over internal legal disputes.[6] A legal system, in order to operate, must override the freedoms of its litigants in that they must accept its verdict. The right to a legal system is properly a right of the group, not reducible to rights of individuals within it. So it is these types of right, rights that belong to the group as a whole and whose exercise may impact individuals within the group, that must be justified by those arguing for recognition of group rights.

However, while such putative rights might be accorded to groups by states or international law, there is no justification for considering them to be rights as such. As Waldron points out: '[i]f the whole point of rights for individuals is to place limits on the pursuit of some communal goal, it will hardly do to characterize that goal as a community right which may then conflict with, and possibly override, the rights of individuals.'[7] Rights are promoted as a way to counter the defects of utilitarianism,[8] but giving the group the power to exercise rights, necessarily overriding individual choices, is itself utilitarian. It would be absurd to set up rights as a response to a communal goal, and then define the communal goal as a right.

Indeed, as Sieghart warned,[9] rights given to 'a people' are given to an abstraction. Rights given to abstractions (like 'the state' or 'the true faith') encompass a danger that they will be used as a pretext for violation of human rights. Sieghart's pertinent concern was that individual rights should never become subservient to the rights of individual people.

2.2.2 *How to identify a group*

The concept of group rights also creates a problem of recognition. In order to recognize a group right we must have a rule for identifying group membership, and a rule for identifying the legitimate decision-making process for exercising this right.[10]

2.2.2.1 *Self-identification*

A seemingly straightforward solution is to make self-identification the criterion for membership of the group. The UN Committee on the Elimination of All Forms of Racial Discrimination[11] stated that identification of individuals as members of racial or ethnic groups shall be based on self-identification. This might seem to be an equally applicable criterion for defining membership of religious groups. There is however an important difference between race and religion. Religious groups often claim as part of their doctrine the defining criteria of membership.[12] Indeed, religious doctrine creates the group in the first place. Thus, this is a controversial solution to the question of defining membership of a religious group.[13] If a legal criterion of self-identification is accepted, then acceptance of religious freedom as an individual right over group rights is necessarily implied.

2.2.2.2 *Identification by the group*

A different possible principle is that of definition of the group by the group itself. Such an approach was taken by the US Supreme Court in *Santa Clara Pueblo v. Martinez*[14] (relating to a tribal rather than religious group). The Supreme Court decided that a Federal Court had no authority to intervene in the decision of the Pueblo, pursuant to its Membership Ordinance, which discriminated against women, granting membership to children of a Santa Claran father and a non-tribe mother, but not to children of a Santa Claran mother and a non-tribe father. The principled argument behind the case, as given by the first instance District Court, was that the membership rules were 'no more or less than a mechanism of social … self-definition … basic to the tribe's survival as a cultural and economic entity'.[15] The Court asserted that 'the equal protection guarantee … should not be construed in a manner which would require or authorize this Court to determine which traditional values will promote cultural survival… [S]uch a determination should be made by the people of Santa Clara; not only because they can best decide what values are important, … [but because] to abrogate tribal decisions, particularly in the delicate area of membership … is to destroy cultural identity under the guise of saving it.'[16]

The District Court, and eventually the Supreme Court, which affirmed its decision, upheld the discriminatory tribal decision. A comparable decision of state or federal authorities would have been viewed as discriminatory and would not have been upheld. Thus, a principle recognizing an unrestricted group right to definition of its membership has unacceptable consequences: by means of its self-definition, the group can infringe the recognized human rights of members. In this case a recognized right to equality between the sexes was infringed.

2.2.2.3 *Objective identification*

A third approach to the definition of group membership is one of external definition by means of objective criteria. This approach was used by the UN Human Rights Committee [HRC] in its *Lovelace*[17] decision. Sandra Lovelace was born and registered as 'Maliseet Indian' but had lost her rights and status as an Indian after having married a non-Indian, in accordance with section 12(1)(b) of Canada's Indian Act. She claimed her rights to membership of an ethnic and linguistic minority under Article 27 of the ICCPR were infringed.

The Committee decided that '[p]ersons who are born and brought up on a reserve who have kept ties with their community and wish to maintain these ties must normally be considered as belonging to that minority within the meaning of the Covenant. Since Sandra Lovelace is ethnically a Maliseet Indian and has only been absent from her home reserve for a few years during the existence of her marriage, she is, in the opinion of the Committee, entitled to be regarded as "belonging" to this minority and to claim the benefits of Article 27 of the Covenant.'[18]

Thus, the HRC chose to define membership of a group, for the purposes of Article 27, not according to the group's definition and not according to self-definition but according to what the Committee saw as objective criteria. Of course, such 'objective' criteria could also be subject to controversy. Such criteria are particularly controversial when defining a religious group. A religion, by its nature, is always defined from within. Any imposition of external criteria can itself be perceived as an infringement of religious freedom.

Thus, even the preliminary step of deciding who belongs to a group is highly controversial and open to manipulation, an unsure platform upon which rights can be distributed.

How to recognize legitimate decisions of the group for exercising its right to religious freedom is also problematic. McDonald suggests[19] a rule on decision making according to which group rights can only be exercised through group decision making. This suggestion is unhelpful: it is not clear how to define the members who may or may not consider themselves part of the group against the group's rules, or who disagree with its process of decision making.[20] If there is no recognized legitimate way for a group to exercise its rights, this casts doubt on the possibility of recognizing group rights at all.

But if we do not recognize group rights, including religious group rights, are we not being inconsistent? Can one deny the acceptability of group rights without rejecting the legitimacy of states?[21] The state itself, according to this argument, exercises collective rights, rights that may override individual liberties (such as through the powers of the criminal justice system). However, this argument for group rights must be rejected. Historically, rights were defined as rights of the citizens against the state. The liberal concept of rights was developed primarily as a defence of the individual against the exercise of state power.[22] State sovereignty and the justification of the state's legitimacy in wielding power against its citizens are not rights-based.[23] While the concept of rights has been broadened (for instance, to rights against private actors), using it to mean the exact opposite of its original meaning renders it void of any meaning at all.

2.2.3 Can group rights ever be recognized?

In view of such objections to the possibility of recognition of group rights, can group rights ever be recognized? It has been suggested by some writers that some concerns of groups are not addressed by the classic formulations of human rights and therefore merit recognition as group rights. Nettheim[24] identifies land ownership, cultural identity and socio-economic disadvantage as concerns of groups meriting group rights protection, with which international law has started to engage.[25] These could have relevance to religious freedom.

A number of bases advocated for advancing group rights merit closer examination. As will be seen, these arguments, in general, are not necessarily inconsistent with the argument advanced in this study, that a group right to religious freedom should not be recognized except as a right derivative of individual rights and never paramount to them. Crucially, these arguments and the examples given to support them support recognition of external group rights directed against the state. At the core of the demands for religious group rights, however, are internal group rights, directed against individuals within the group. In such cases, I argue and show that these arguments cannot justify recognition of group rights.

2.2.3.1 Historical considerations

Rectification of historical wrongs is one consideration that may be taken into account when interpreting and according rights such equality as religious freedom. In cases based on historical justifications, it can be argued that the right in question can only be accorded to the wronged group. An important manifestation of a group right is the communal right to land. This could be a right to ownership but could also be a right to spiritual use, particularly relevant to the discussion of religious freedom. Kingsbury[26] criticizes the US Supreme Court decision in *Lyng v. Northwest Indian Cemetery Protective Association*,[27] in which a claim by Native Americans that a road built on public land would breach their religious freedom to meditate in this traditional religious area was rejected. The group's religious freedom, just like the religious freedom of anyone else, was deemed by the Court not to extend to control of public lands. Kingsbury argues that the historical loss of control of Indian lands should have been seen as a relevant factor leading to recognition of the Native Americans' right. Such a right based on historical considerations can only be attributed to a community, not an individual. But this is a community right against a state, and thus presents no conflict with the rights of individuals within the community. Therefore, it can be accepted even alongside the thesis advanced in this work.

2.2.3.2 *Community survival*

A further justification for recognition of group rights in certain cases is that otherwise the community will assimilate and cease to exist. Indeed, this reason was mentioned by the US court in *Santa Clara Pueblo v. Martinez*,[28] discussed in section 2.2.2.2, for preferring the rights accorded by law to the group over gender equality. Kingsbury[29] argues that domestic courts should allow group rights that cause discrimination on the basis of gender when dealing with small indigenous groups departing from the universal arrangement (as Navajo in the USA), but not allow them for one of a number of major groups in a state based on a plurality of customary law systems (as in Tanzania). I find this distinction incoherent. Individuals' rights (in this case, women's rights) within the group should not be more or less important depending on the position of the group within the state. Women (or, indeed, other individuals whose rights require legal protection) should not have to pay the price, that is sacrifice their individual rights, for cultural survival of the group. The justification of community survival is relevant also to religious freedom. Religious law and the religious legal system are often claimed to be essential to the survival of the religion in question. Indeed, they are an inherent component of some religions. The counterargument that this justification should not override individual rights would also apply to religious groups. Religious legal systems, as will be seen throughout this study, especially in Chapters 4 and 6 (regarding, respectively, the rights of women and dissenting speech), often do not adhere to internationally accepted human rights norms.

2.2.3.3 *Cultural interpretation of rights*

Another deficiency of recognized rights in human rights instruments, it has been argued, is that they exclude different, especially non-Western, cultural interpretations of concepts used. A suggested solution has been to interpret existing rights within a cultural context, thus effectively recognizing group rights. In *Hopu and Bessert v. France*,[30] the Human Rights Committee accepted that the rights to family and privacy of Tahitians were violated when the French government allowed the building of a hotel over an ancient Polynesian grave. This was so even though the authors of the communication were not direct relatives of those buried. Thus, in effect, a communal right over the use of the land was recognized as part of the right to respect for family life.

This reading of Covenant rights as according communal rights creates a right against the state, not against individuals within the community. This type of recognition of group rights is not, in any way, incompatible with the thesis of this work, namely that there are no group rights to religious freedom which can trump individual rights. However, in other cases in which a cultural context interpretation would cause group rights to become paramount to individual rights, the criticism would be the same as that raised previously. Such a definition of rights would merely transfer power over individuals from the state to other groups, whose use of power is not checked by the human rights obligations which states are obligated to uphold. There is a danger that rights to family and to privacy, for example, would be interpreted as allowing the group to exclude state intervention which protects the rights of weaker members of the group. Under the thesis advanced in this work, such an interpretation must be avoided.

2.2.3.4   *Protection of the rights of individual members of minorities is not sufficient for the special protection needed for minorities*

Leuprecht[31] argues that particular rights beyond the rights of individuals, including administrative autonomy and special forms of participation in public decision making, are needed to protect minorities. These, indeed, would be paradigmatic group rights. Applied to religious groups, such rights would give the religious group an enhanced position in the law-making sphere, either over its own members or in the formation of law over all citizens. As will be demonstrated in this study, such rights unavoidably conflict with individual rights. Administrative autonomy (such as over marriage and divorce) will be seen in this study (Chapters 3 and 4) to affect adversely individual rights, particularly the rights of dissenting groups within the religions recognized by the state, and in the case of some major religions will affect adversely the rights of women. According special forms of participation in public decision making to religions, other than through the general democratic process, will also be seen to be problematic, potentially breaching the human rights of individuals (see the discussion of abortion legislation in Chapter 4).

Waldron suggests a solution, according to which group rights may be asserted externally (against claims from outside the group) but not internally (when there is a direct conflict between group and individual).[32] This solution must be faulted for pragmatic reasons. While Waldron's approach may have use regarding other rights, it is especially unsatisfactory in the context of religious freedom in which a large part of the group's demands is directed internally. Religions, by definition, mostly address themselves and their precepts to their members. Recognizing religious group rights except when directed internally takes out a large part of what having a group right means for religious groups. The position of religious groups can be contrasted with that of other groups, such as racial or ethnic groups. Precepts directing how members must behave are not an inherent part of racial or ethnic groups, but are part and parcel of religious groups.

The suggestion of limiting recognition of group rights to external rights would solve some of the problems associated with group rights. However, even if a compromise recognizing externally directed group rights is be a useful solution for recognizing the rights of other groups, it is certainly not so for religious groups. As will be seen in the cases examined in this study, individual and group rights were in sharp conflict, a conflict which must be coherently resolved by giving paramountcy to individual rights.

The uneasy basis for group rights in general, and for religious group rights in particular is evident also in international law, as will become apparent in this study. Although some mention of collective rights appears in international legal documents, this has been done without satisfactory theoretical debate as to the existence and meaning of the concept of collective rights prior to their inclusion.

The concept of a group right is difficult to justify. This is because the concept of a group right is antithetical to the idea of rights as a limit to collective power. The means of recognizing the group and its legitimate decisions are undecidable. Even if the concept of a group right has been recognized in international law, it application regarding religious freedom is incoherent and raises unique problems and conflicts which must be addressed and will be addressed in this work.

2.3 Freedom of religion: between liberty and equality

Religious freedom is a unique right, a double-sided right based on two aspects of religion: one conception of religion for the purposes of this right stresses the expressive activity of belief, criticism and inquiry. This derives from an individualist perception of religion, which relates to the liberal view, and entails *freedom* of religion. The second conception of religion, related to a communitarian view, stresses the identity aspect of religion. This entails *equality* between religions, and relates religion to groups, although equality is not necessarily thereby conceived of as a group right.[33] The conception, and protection, of religion as an attribute that marks membership of a group is becoming ever more prevalent in international human rights law and discourse.

Religion is both similar to, and different from, other characteristics that define groups. The similarities between religion and other group-defining characteristics, such as race, are highlighted by those who wish to accord them similar protection,[34] whether in national or international law. One difference between race and religion is obvious. While race is immutable, religion is not. In fact, one of the justifications given for upholding a right to religion freedom is to enable everyone who wishes to do so to change their religion. The right to do this is legally protected in international law.[35] But the mutability of religion does not mean religious affiliation is less deserving of legal protection than immutable characteristics. A person's right to change religion is protected, but so is his right to keep his religion. Religion is as much a part of identity, of personhood, as race or nationality.

Freedom of religion is unique. There is no correlative right regarding race or nationality. It is not possible to choose race, and there generally is no right to choose nationality, but there is a right to choose religion or belief. Religion is both a subject of liberty (like freedom of speech), and a subject of equality, a characteristic of the individual which merits the protection of the law (like gender, race or nationality). One can be of a certain race and be entitled to protection from discrimination based on race, just as one can be of a certain religion and be entitled to protection from discrimination based on religion. But it is meaningless to speak of 'freedom of race', while it is meaningful to protect freedom of religion. This is because religion is not only an identity. It is also an activity of thought, criticism and speech, an activity that merits protection in its robust and open manifestations.

Because religious freedom has two equally important aspects, religion as key to critical thought and religion as identity, both liberal and communitarian theories may offer important insights in their perceptions of religion. On this duality, the right to religious freedom should be constructed. This dual conception has important implications in current legal debate. These can be seen clearly in two examples of importance in international law: the prohibition of incitement to religious hatred and the prohibition of discrimination.

2.3.1 Liberty or equality: prohibition of incitement

The unique treatment accorded to religion, stemming from the tension between religious equality and religious liberty, can be seen in the framing of international law provisions prohibiting hatred and incitement. The argument in support of prohibition of incitement to religious hatred highlights the group-identity aspect of religion and frames the right in terms of equality of religions. A member of a religion cannot effectively exercise his right to be treated as a citizen equal to members of other religions in the public place if his religion is constantly denigrated and vilified. The only way to guarantee such equality is by prohibition of, at least, the most injurious religious hate speech.

The argument against such prohibition highlights the individual-inquisitive-expressive aspect of religion: since freedom of religion is about questioning and defending beliefs, doctrines and ideas, a robust exchange of ideas, even one which some people may find insulting or injurious, is important for society. The right to call non-believers infidels who will burn in hell, for example, is as integral to religious freedom as any other part of this right. Curtailing such religious debate would arguably infringe the right to free religious expression, an important component of religious freedom.

International law (like domestic legal systems) exemplifies both conceptions: that which treats religion like all other group characteristics on which incitement can be based, and that which sees religion as different from all other group characteristics. The International Covenant on Civil and Political Rights makes no distinction in its provision on incitement between religious hatred and racial hatred. Article 20(2) mandates that: '[a]ny advocacy of national, racial or religious hatred that constitutes incitement to discrimination, hostility or violence shall be prohibited by law.' Likewise, the Proposal for a European Union Framework Decision on Combating Racism and Xenophobia[36] does not deal differently with race and religion. It defines 'racism and xenophobia', which its provisions prohibit, as 'the belief in race, colour, descent, religion or belief, national or ethnic origin as a factor in determining aversion to individuals or groups'.[37]

However, the International Convention on the Elimination of All Forms of Racial Discrimination [CERD],[38] which deals with discrimination on the grounds of race, colour, descent, or national or ethnic origin, but *not* religion, has a much broader provision mandating that states prohibit acts and organizations promoting incitement and theories of superiority (Article 4).[39] While a ban on organizations advocating theories of racial superiority is deemed acceptable under CERD, such a ban on religious organizations and theories is not. Indeed, a ban on *religious* theories that claim superiority over other religions or beliefs may contravene the right to religious freedom. Many religions claim to be the one true religion, claiming superiority over other religions which are false (as indeed atheism claims that all religions are false). Such claims may be of core doctrinal importance to their believers. Why is there such a distinction between religion and race? The distinction seems to relate again to the analysis of religion as idea rather than identity. Religion is seen as a collection of ideas while a race is seen as a collection of people. It is acceptable to vilify ideas, not to vilify people, as vilifying people infringes upon their right to equality. But of course religions are both collections of ideas and of people. There is nothing wrong with claiming superiority of one doctrine over another, but much wrong with holding people who belong to one religious group to be better than others. International law might attempt to separate those two aspects, but, in practice, the difference between the two will not be so clear.

This is a problem not only of international law, but of domestic law as well, especially as state parties to the conventions mentioned above are obliged to implement their provisions. The debate over the dual character of religion was reflected in the controversy in the United Kingdom regarding a legal amendment to broaden the existing prohibition on incitement to racial hatred to cover religious hatred as well. Initially the amendment proposed by the government was not approved by Parliament, and the law passed by Parliament, the Anti-Terrorism, Crime and Security Act 2001, did not include this proposed controversial measure.[40] The government re-introduced the measure in Section 119 of the Serious Organised Crime and Police Bill, and by the Racial and Religious Hatred Act 2006 broadened the offence of incitement to racial hatred under the Race Relations Act 1965 and Part III of the Public Order Act 1986 to cover religious hatred (Section 29B).[41] Thus, it is the duality of the right to religious freedom, although it has not been so perceived, which causes difficulty in addressing religious incitement. The issue of incitement will be revisited in Chapter 6, where an approach to this offence will be suggested, based on this analysis.

2.3.2 Group or individual: implementation of religious equality

A dual perception of religion, as giving rise to a group right or to an individual right, can be seen in another example, namely the way international human rights law interprets the right to non-discrimination on the basis of religion. The right to equality, or non-discrimination, on the grounds of religion is complementary to the right to freedom of religion. Without it the right to freedom of religion is worth little. Currently non-discrimination on the grounds of religion is becoming the focus of religious rights in international law.[42] The right to non-discrimination based on religion in international law is drafted similarly to those based on race, nationality or gender.[43] Religion is seen as a subject of the universal prescription of equal treatment, like other characteristics whose bearers merit the same protection. The right not to be discriminated against on religious grounds is generally framed as an individual right in international law.[44] Every person has the right to be treated equally to others regardless of their religion. The claim of each individual to equality is to be assessed independently of the claims of other individuals who belong to the same or other groups. This is the approach that arises from the liberal interpretation of the right to religious freedom.

From a point of view that examines the effect of equality on society, especially a society in religious conflict, other considerations may be raised. A unique provision[45] in the EU Directive on Equal Treatment pertaining to Northern Ireland (the only state-specific provision of this Directive) allows differential treatment in recruitment to police and teaching positions to redress religious imbalance, as specified by national legislation.[46] In this case, the parties agreed to sacrifice equality of religion as an individual right in order to achieve equality between religious groups (Catholics and Protestants). Under this provision a qualified individual may be treated unjustly and less favourably based solely on his religion. Of course, this measure is intended to achieve a worthwhile cause – an end to historic conflict and a just peace between religious communities, in which policing and education are key issues. In one sense, this furthers equality. Members of both religious communities must feel equal to each other, and feel that they are treated equally, especially in their ability to influence their co-religious society through education and access to implementation of government policy (in this case through policing). In its individual sense, equality is sacrificed in order to achieve group equality.

Such an exception in a human rights document raises complicated questions. Conflict between religious groups is not unique to Northern Ireland. When, if at all, is it legitimate for international law to substitute a group-equality approach for an individual-equality one? It was precisely prevention of religious conflict that set in motion the movement to recognition of a principle of religious freedom in Enlightenment liberalism.[47] But a return to group-based equality can jeopardize our protection of individual rights. The important theoretical debate over the dual conception of religious freedom has, therefore, very practical legal implications. The tension between individual and group demands in the application of this right must be addressed by any legal system which accords this right. This is true for domestic legal systems and for international law.

As exemplified in this section, the right to religious freedom, more than other recognized human rights, is one that sees the individual and the group at odds. Theories which have tried to define and justify this right were confronted with the need to address the two competing aspects of this right. How they have fared is discussed in the following section.

2.4 Religious freedom in liberal political theory

An understanding of how the right to freedom of religion should be interpreted can be gained by analysing the different rationales for the right advanced by the political theories which were influential in developing our current understanding of this right. A principle of religious tolerance was not unrecognized in ancient cultures.[48] It is neither a modern nor a Western phenomenon. Thus, it has been suggested, that Ashoka's Rock Edicts, dating from the 3rd century BC, aimed at resolving the conflict between Brahmanism and Buddhism, were the first laws to recognize the principle of religious toleration.[49] The edicts embody the Buddhist spirit of toleration, which has its origins in Hinduism, a religion in which no one view is held as the one true view.[50] The Jewish tradition, too, has accorded an important role to tolerance of others. In the Bible, the Noachide Covenant sets basic moral rules for non-Jews,[51] thus accepting the morality of those who are not Jewish as long as they adhere to a basic moral code not related to a particular belief.

2.4.1 Justifications for religious freedom in liberal thought

While other and earlier philosophies embodied a principle of religious toleration, the idea of religious freedom as a right is most developed in liberal thought. It was first articulated under liberal philosophy as part of a set of rights. It is therefore especially relevant to understand the justifications for a right to religious freedom in liberal theory, and hence how this right should be coherently interpreted in law.

The idea of freedom of religion was an important force in the formation of liberal theory itself.[52] From the liberal literature of the Enlightenment and of the present-day debate, several important reasons for upholding freedom of religion emerge. While the basis for the right is individualistic, it is also related to a demand for the co-existence of religious groups. Out of liberal writings at least three different indi-vidualistic justifications for religious freedom are discernible as well as justifications that are based not on the rights of the individual but rather on the relations between religious groups. Each of these justifications has different implications for the legal right that religious freedom should protect. Each of them also has severe shortcomings in the protection of religious freedom as will be discussed later.

2.4.1.1 Individual religious freedom as critical capacity

The first reason for according a right to religious freedom is embedded in one of the central ideas of Enlightenment-era liberalism. Freedom of religious belief is key to the existence of men as rational free-thinking individual citizens in the state. It emanates directly from a normative premise of equality, the demand that every doctrine should be open to scrutiny, and a belief that no dogma can be held with certainty.[53] Thus, religious toleration is one of the hallmarks of the liberal state.

This highly individualistic reason for religious freedom emphasizes religious belief, personal decision and individual choice, rather than other aspects of reli-gion (such as worship, ritual or institutions). If this is the reason for upholding religious freedom, then the legal right to religious freedom must be interpreted accordingly. If religious freedom is protected because no religious dogma can be held with certainty, then those who challenge the existing dogma should be encouraged and not punished. It follows that activities such as blasphemy and proselytism, which do exactly that, must not be criminalized. Critique, discussion and a robust exchange of ideas are best promoted when individuals are free to convince others to convert to their belief, and to speak for and against religions, even in ways that may be deemed by some inappropriate, free from fear of prosecution. The implications of the conception of religious freedom as freedom of thought for the legal regulation of conversion, proselytism and blasphemy are explored in Chapter 6.

It further follows that if the ability to question dogma is the ultimate reason for religious freedom, then it should not be possible for the right holder himself or herself to waive, or to compromise, his or her capacity to continue to be able to think and make religious choices as an individual. A legal approach which attempts to preserve this critical ability can be seen in the implementation of religious freedom in France, in the concept of *laïcité active*. This concept was deployed to justify a recently enacted French anti-cult law.[54] The French government justified the law on the grounds of promotion of freedom of belief over freedom of religion.[55] It explained that the purpose of the law was to limit the religious liberty of the 'cult', in order to protect each individual's freedom to formulate belief free from constraint, such as that imposed by 'cults'.[56] This reasoning demonstrates a preference for the critical-individualistic aspect of religious liberty – a person must retain his ability to formulate and criticize any belief – over the aspect of religious liberty which promises freedom to identify with any religious persuasion and belong to a religious group. Even someone who wishes to exercise his religious freedom by relying on the decisions of the 'cult' is not permitted to waive his continuing individual capacity.

Such a strictly individualist conception of religious freedom leads to a regime that advances freedom of certain religions and beliefs but hinders the freedom of others.[57] As seen in the last example, religions which are deemed by the authorities to be 'brainwashing' or to reduce the critical capacity of individuals, that is, usually new and unknown religions, will be adversely affected. But such a limited view of religious freedom, which effectively excludes certain religions, has its base in early liberal thinking.

The conception of freedom of religion as an individualist charter of freedom of thought carried with it a severe limitation on religious freedom. Locke, the major proponent of this approach, who addressed the subject in his *Letter on Toleration* and other works, did not extend the right to atheists and Catholics.[58] According to Locke, atheists could not be trusted because they would not take an oath on the Bible; Catholics could not be trusted because they owed a double loyalty, a political theology at odd with liberal principles.[59] This reasoning reveals the very individualistic approach of Locke's liberal theory. This approach is actively opposed to a group approach to religious liberty,[60] excluding from the ambit of this right a religion whose doctrine contains a collective political element; a competing power to state authority is not to be recognized.[61] The same exception, which Locke uses against extending religious freedom to Catholics, could be used against extending religious freedom to Jews or Muslims. Judaism, although highly decentralized at Locke's time, and certainly not as institutionalized politically as Catholicism, is also not merely a religion but a social-normative regime for its members. Liberalism is very much a political approach best suited to one religion, Protestantism, and, indeed, historically was entwined with it.

But Locke's view of religious freedom, individualistic to the extent of exclusion of any group components, does not necessarily render freedom of religion an empty shell.[62] The extreme but logically possible conclusion would be that all religions based on institutions and not merely on individual belief should be excluded from the scope of protection. This, indeed, is Locke's conclusion. But such a conclusion is, of course, discriminatory and, as such, is unacceptable.

However, we can derive more moderate conclusions from Locke's exclusively individualistic view of religious freedom, for instance, that protection of a right to freedom of religion will be granted to adherents of all beliefs but not to religious institutions. This conclusion, too, is unsatisfactory. Protection of only the individual aspects of all religions does not necessarily translate to equal protection of all religions. Institutional aspects of religion are central to some religions, peripheral to others, and non-existent in yet others. For practical reasons, too, such a rule will be hard to implement, as the dividing line between the individual and institutional aspects of a religion is not always clear cut.

The highly individualistic view of religious freedom, grounded in the importance of guaranteeing the capacity for criticism, would thus entail extensive, non-waivable legal protection of the individual aspects of religious freedom, particularly those maintaining the ability to change religion and to influence others to do so. However, such a view may lead not only to a lack of protection of the collective and institutional aspects of religion, but also may prove highly discriminatory towards some religions.

2.4.1.2 *Individual religious freedom as equal liberty*

Other rationales for an individualistic interpretation of religious freedom can be discerned from the work of other liberal theorists with different implications for the legal interpretation of this right. The second individualistic justification for religious freedom is premised not on the importance of the individual faculty for criticism, but rather on a principle of equality. This justification emanates from the egalitarian strand of liberalism, which followed from the work of Rousseau,[63] who, among the early liberals, emphasized the need for equal political liberties. It is currently exemplified primarily in the work of John Rawls and Ronald Dworkin.[64] They emphasize the danger to liberty from a society that is unequal and unjust and the need for positive action for the realization of social freedom.[65] Dworkin[66] defines liberalism through a principle of 'rough equality': resources and opportunities should be distributed in roughly equal shares to accommodate different personal preferences. This is so not just for material goods, but also for political decisions. Political decisions must reflect some accommodation of the differing personal preferences everyone has for themselves, but may not reflect preferences people have about what others shall do or have. Rawls formulated liberal political theory so as to incorporate a principle of equality into liberal theory. The first principle of his theory of justice is that each person is to have an equal right to the most extensive liberty compatible with similar liberty for others.[67]

What are the implications of these approaches for religious freedom? Dworkin's approach, by virtue of its egalitarian principles, clearly entails an individualistic interpretation of all basic rights, including religious freedom. Because it disallows preferences people have about what others shall do or have, it will disallow exercises of group rights which override individual preferences. Rawls includes liberty of conscience in the basic liberties comprised in the first principle. By mentioning freedom of conscience rather than freedom of religion, it seems that Rawls emphasizes the internal, individual right over the institutional right. In his later writing on 'political liberalism', though, he refers to liberty of conscience as a liberty that both protects individual against Church and protects Church (= any religious association) against state.[68] As we shall see, these two types of liberty will often be antagonistic to each other. If the Church demands that the state respect its liberty even when its actions override individual rights, which liberty prevails?

Although Rawls leaves this question unanswered, his first principle is compatible with only one option. The demand that persons enjoy an *equal right* to religious liberty is important in solving this conflict of liberties. This is because it will be impossible to claim a right to religious liberty which is incompatible with equal liberties for each person. This principle, therefore, places limitations on group rights when they are incompatible with equal individual rights, and places religious liberty on a strong footing as an individual right.

Following the principle of liberty as equality should have implications for the legal interpretation of the right to religious liberty. If equality of opportunity or equality of treatment are seen as key to religious liberty, then international law should impose minimum standards ensuring equality of enjoyment of basic human rights, including religious freedom to everyone, especially to members of groups that are underprivileged in society such as women, children, homosexuals and religious dissenters, even where this entails intervention in group or state policy. In contrast with the reasoning of rights ownership, which will be discussed in the next section, the political-equality reasoning mandates at least a basic level of protection of individual religious freedom, even when the individual who chooses to become or remain a member of a religious group waives his/her right. Equality of opportunity can only be achieved in a society in which everyone has a basic level of political freedoms that cannot be relinquished to the group.

Rawls further individualizes religion by introducing to his political theory a principle of neutrality, which demands that states should be neutral between the various conceptions of 'the good'. This principle renders religion an individual, rather than a group, concern by displacing it from the legitimate realm of public affairs and maintaining it in the realm of personal affairs. One important legal implication of this demand regarding the use of religious reasons for legislation will be discussed in section 2.7.1.

The principle of neutrality was introduced not in order to deal particularly with religions, but rather as a principle relating to all doctrines of the good; however, it has particular importance with regard to religion. This is because religions, more than other civic institutions, prescribe complete moral and ethical programmes of the good in all areas of personal and public life, and these programmes often conflicts with liberal assumptions about the same issues.

The principle of neutrality has been attacked from within liberal debate. Crucially, Barry shows that the principle of neutrality may not be a sound basis for guaranteeing religious freedom. He argues that in order to accept the principle of neutrality, one must have accepted already many tenets of liberalism. Neutrality is not a position that can easily be reconciled with a religious position. Many religions will view the principle that every view of the good must be treated equally in the public sphere as morally reprehensible. Doctrines that call on the state to take a position on the public good[69] are central to their tenets. The Catholic Church, for instance, does not see its teachings as something for individual belief only, not to be used in the public sphere.[70] So, in fact, many non-liberals will not be able to accept the principle of neutrality.

In an attempt to respond to his critics, Rawls introduced the distinction between comprehensive liberalism and political liberalism.[71] Comprehensive liberalism includes, besides a political component, a prescription for the culture of civil society. Political liberalism is more minimalistic, and assumes that society may contain a plurality of reasonable yet incompatible comprehensive doctrines, religious as well as non-religious. This further attempt to reconcile liberalism with the plurality of non-liberal opinion has been countered by the criticism that a political theory that has no claim to any view of the good is an impossibility.[72]

A more fundamental criticism of the idea of liberal neutrality has been waged inside the liberal camp by perfectionists, such as Haksar, who claims[73] that liberal political theory must take a stand as to whether humans fare better under liberal institutions or under non-liberal ones. He argues that liberalism cannot and must not treat all value choices as equal, because some value choices *are* intrinsically better than others.[74]

Political liberalism not only may be unworkable but also undesirable. Elshtain[75] rejects Rawls' political liberalism, which demands that religious reasons not be brought into the public policy debate. She wants to acknowledge religious plurality and opposes the monist liberal stand. She rejects the view that this is neutrality. In her view, the separation of Church from state does not require the separation of Church from politics. The neutrality that disallows religious reasoning from the public political debate silences free religious expression rather than enhances it.

The place of religion in the public sphere and its uneasy relationship with individual liberty have remained a contentious point of the liberal programme. Many liberal states have refrained from adopting a principle of neutrality. As discussion of US Supreme Court cases in Chapter 3 will show, it is not clear if, and to what extent, such a principle can be implemented. Unsurprisingly, the discussion of neutrality by Rawls, Dworkin and Ackerman[76] is concurrent with important developments in US Supreme Court jurisprudence[77] concerning non-establishment of religion.[78]

As seen, basing religious freedom on a principle that demands equality will entail legal protection of equality of opportunity in utilization of this right for everyone. This will mean rights of individuals should be protected even within groups, such as those of members, employees or students of religious organizations. Equal liberties in society can be maintained only if individuals are never deemed to have waived fundamental liberties, even by joining an organization voluntarily. The introduction of a principle of neutrality, which is intended to further a society of equal liberties, will be seen by some as, in fact, curtailing liberties of freedom and belief in a discriminatory manner. Introducing a demand for neutrality in the state will limit lawmakers, public officials, judges and even citizens, in the legal decisions which they make if they rely on religious grounds as the basis for those decisions. This is a limitation whose implications and difficulties will be discussed in a later section of this chapter.

2.4.1.3 Individual right as property of the right holder

A third individualistic justification for religious freedom in liberal theory is offered by libertarian-liberal theory. It is based neither on the importance of individual critical capacity nor on a principle of equal religious liberties, but rather is rooted in the principle of minimal intervention by the state, as the perceived danger to liberty emanates from the state.[79] This strand of liberal thinking is notably expressed by Nozick[80] in his development of Lockean liberalism.

Although Nozick's[81] theory is based on individualistic principles that put individual choice above all other aspects of religious freedom, his theory ends up protecting the group over the individual. In his view, although the framework of the state is libertarian and laissez faire, individual communities within it need not be. Many communities may choose internal restrictions that the libertarian would condemn if they were enforced by a central state apparatus. In a free society, people may contract into various restrictions that the government may not legitimately impose on them.

Nozick's theory emanates from a perception of rights ownership[82] that implies that rights can be waived at will. Locke (whose ideas form the foundation of Nozick's theory) saw rights as non-alienable, so that no one can contract away his rights. Nozick's reading of Locke as an ultra-libertarian may be wrong on the issue of ownership and waivability of rights. Nozick believes personal religious freedom is owned by the individual, and can be used by him in any way he wishes, including by giving this right away. However, from our previous reading of Locke, it can be seen that according to Locke's view personal religious freedom is not absolutely waivable. At the least, it appears that under a Lockean analysis an individual cannot waive unto the group his right to make his own choices in matters of religion, especially not to a group whose governing principles compete with the liberal state, such as the Catholic Church. Rights cannot be sold or bargained away like property, as an individual cannot sell his freedom away to become a slave. Even in a proprietary model of rights, a different relation between the right holder and the right is possible. For example, Waldron[83] supports the understanding, based on the philosophy of Locke and Thomas Jefferson, that rights are not owned but held in trust by the right bearer.

Nozick argues that if one contracts into the community one buys the whole 'package'. But the reality, especially in the case of religious communities, is more complex. An individual's affiliation with a religious community may be a product of circumstance, of deep-rooted belief, or of choice. In some cases, an individual may not effectively be able to leave – his or her home, family, and social connections belong to the religious community. In other cases, an individual may not want to leave. It is precisely because of the importance of religion to the person that one should not be made to choose, on an all or nothing basis, between belonging to a religion and enjoying basic rights.

Nozick's approach results in harming individual freedoms. This radical liberal approach, which is generally perceived as ultra-individualistic, achieves a similar outcome to the communitarian approach, in contrast to other liberal approaches. Allowing people to contract away their freedoms unrestrained gives more power to the underlying forces operating in the community at the expense of individual liberties. Even the contractual argument – that members choose voluntarily to belong to a community and so have waived their right – is misleading. Often people are born into a community and face costly (not just economic) barriers of exit. This analysis of Nozick's argument shows that ultra-liberalism in fact diminishes the aggregate freedom of individuals rather than enhancing it.

If freedom of action and freedom of contract are the fundamental principles underlying religious freedom, and the state should not intervene in the exercise of this right, as the libertarian approach claims, then people are to be respected in their choice of living in communities that do not uphold principles of religious freedom. If we accept that it is illegitimate for the state to intervene in the functioning of religious communities, then we must also accept that it will also be illegitimate for international law to intervene. But, as I have argued, these assertions, based on a fiction of contractual freedom, must be criticized. This approach will have practical legal implications regarding restrictions imposed by religious communities on their members, in particular restrictions on women's rights, analysed in Chapter 4.

Thus, liberal thought propounded important justifications for religious freedom: that of rational criticism, that of equality in according liberties, and that based on a principle of non-intervention of the state. This last basis will be criticized in subsequent chapters.

2.4.2 *Justifications based on relations between religious groups*

An important reason given by Enlightenment liberalism for religious freedom was an individualistic reason, the encouragement of critical debate. No less important in the development of the liberal project was the Enlightenment liberals' group-based reasoning for religious freedom: the prevention of conflict between religious groups and the advancement of toleration. These are utilitarian justifications, but they are not to be separated from the rights debate. Not only were these arguments historically intertwined, but also, to this day, the separation of Church from state which follows from this reasoning both complements the principle of religious freedom in liberal ideology and sits uneasily with it.

The group-based justification that emerges from Enlightenment liberalism for religious freedom is that disentangling the people's choice of faith from the coercive power of the state will prevent violent conflict.[84] Rousseau saw this as key to solving the conflicts which plagued the ancient world in which:

> [S]ince each religion was thus attached exclusively to the laws of the state which prescribed it, and since there was no means of converting people except by subduing them, the only missionaries were conquerors; and since the obligation to change faith was part of the law of conquest, it was necessary to conquer before preaching conversion.[85]

The important aspect of religious freedom, under this reasoning, is separation of religion from state as a required constitutional principle. This demand was not accepted by many liberal states or by current international law, as discussed in Chapter 3. The controversial proposal of separation of Church from state *as pre-requisite to religious freedom* is a direct consequence of the particular nature of religion as a competitor to state authority. Such a structural constitutional imposition forming an essential aspect of a human right is unique to the right of religious freedom. There is no correlative demand regarding any other right; for instance, freedom of speech does not imply, under any political theory, that groups which engage in organized expressive activity will take no part in the governance of the state.

If religion as a source of law is incompatible with religious freedom, there are even more far-reaching implications than separation of religion from state. Not only is the attachment of religion to the state problematic, but so is the attachment of religion to political debate. The demand for the separation of religion and political debate was linked to the reasoning that resolution of conflict could only rely on accessible rational means, and not on external divine authority. As Stout explains:

> Any point of view in which religious considerations or conceptions of the good remained dominant was, in the early modern context, incapable of providing a basis for the reasonable and peaceful resolution of social conflict. Incompatible appeals to authority seemed equally reasonable, and therefore equally suspect, as well as thoroughly useless as vehicles of rational persuasion.[86]

This controversy over the involvement of religious argumentation in politics remains as pertinent today as it was then, as will be discussed in a later section of this chapter on religious reasoning in politics.

The justification for religious freedom which is based on the attempt to prevent conflict and the futility of coercion is closely related to the idea of toleration. The concept of religious toleration in Enlightenment liberalism had two distinct meanings: toleration as the best way to discover the one true course (Locke's meaning) and toleration as a way to accept different ways as valid and to co-exist with them (Hobbes' approach).[87] These two approaches may well be precursors of two different goals for the current liberal project, in Rawls' terminology comprehensive liberalism and political liberalism. They re-appear in a new guise in the debate over liberalism's claim to neutrality.

But the problem with defining religious freedom in terms of toleration is that toleration is extended to something which is to some degree undesirable but where there is a reason to tolerate.[88] Toleration is considered a virtue precisely because the tolerant person refrains from curtailing some thing he believes is unworthy.[89] In the case of religious toleration, the reason is the collective good: harmonious relations between religious groups and the prevention of social strife.

This is an instrumental, pragmatic reason for recognizing religious freedom and therefore is problematic. States will respect it as long as it fulfils their social goals, but will infringe this freedom when they find it socially expedient to do so, for instance when the religious dissenters are a small and socially insignificant minority.[90] The weakness of the toleration argument is that it does not establish an independent value of a human right to freedom of religion. In the words of Thomas Paine: '[t]oleration is not the opposite of intolerance, but it is the counterfeit of it. Both are despotisms. The one assumes to itself the right of withholding liberty of conscience, and the other of granting it.'[91] A social justification for religious freedom in lieu of an individual-rights justification cannot be the basis for effective protection of religious freedom.

But the justification of religious freedom as a way to prevent conflict and harmonize relations between groups has important legal implications. As we have seen, this view justifies interpreting equality on the basis of religion as equality between groups, rather than equality between individuals. If the object is to promote harmonious relations between groups, then each group must be treated equally, even if individuals are treated less favourably than they would be without regard to their religion. Conversely, if utilitarian reasons are unacceptable as a basis for human rights, group equality must be rejected in favour of a universal standard of individual equality.

2.5 Community and identity

2.5.1 Communitarian approaches

The liberal view of religious freedom has come under attack from writers, broadly classed as communitarians, who challenge liberalism's view of man as autonomous and place religion within its social context. All such approaches explore the concept of religion as identity and emanate from communitarian criticism of liberal theory.[92] While communitarian analysis may be thought to lead to an interpretation of religious freedom founded on the group rather than the individual, I argue that analysis of communitarian writers leads to a more complex conclusion.

While we have seen that group justifications were present in liberal conceptions of religious freedom, these were utilitarian justifications, which justified religious freedom based on advancement of the general public good rather than based on rights. Communitarians, however, offer a more direct *rights* basis for religious freedom that is derived from group affiliation. In the discussion that follows, I draw a distinction between a communitarian approach of self-identity, which forms a basis for individual rather than group rights, and a different communitarian approach of group identity, which forms a basis for group rights.

One explanation of the shift from viewing religion as choice to viewing religion as social affiliation is an historic one. The liberal theorists of 17th-century England saw religion as the product of individual decision. Glaser[93] claims that such an approach was applicable for a community that *was* homogeneous except for differences of religion. He questions why, however, this approach should still guide contemporary liberals such as Rawls, since nowadays religion is determined more by the community in which a person is born than by individual decision. Protecting the communal rather than the individual aspects of religion is therefore more conducive to safeguarding religious liberty today.

Religion also plays another important role, according to the communitarian account, as a social bond which provides a goal for society. Taylor[94] views civic freedom, complementary to the 'liberal' freedom of lack of government intervention in private life, as the freedom of a society to govern itself free from despotism. He argues that for such civic freedom to exist, a sense of cohesion or shared morality is required, something that can be given by religion. Liberal freedom in itself is a 'hollow' freedom. The conception of a positive freedom, a freedom beyond merely a lack of government interference in life, shares something with the postliberal critique of liberalism, which also demands a substantive, positive freedom. But here these two critiques of liberalism diverge. While feminists, other postliberals, and even egalitarian liberals demand a positive freedom that provides opportunity for *self*-realization of the individual, Taylor's approach demands a substantive freedom that is exercised by society as a *group*.

However, while having common goals may be of worth to society, the individuals and the groups that make up society often do not have a common goal, as Taylor himself concedes. The whole point of freedom is that we are allowed to pursue our own goals. Furthermore, it is not clear, both historically and conceptually, that religion leads to the sort of civic freedom that fosters a society capable of staving off despotism. Quite the contrary: shared goals (such as religion or nationalism) are just as capable of promoting tyrannies in society. Taylor's emphasis is on finding a common goal in society, besides the complementary freedom from government imposition of religion, which is part of the 'liberal' freedom. Such a position neither promotes the religious freedom of individuals nor of groups within society.

Religion may also be seen as an issue of identity in a different sense, not of communal identity but of personal identity. Although this conception of religion has been offered as part of communitarian philosophy, I wish to distinguish this reasoning from the reasoning that views religion as forming communal identity and constituting a person's identity through membership in the community. The role religion plays in constituting personal identity is an individualistic justification for respecting freedom of religion. In protecting freedom of religion we are protecting and assisting people in holding on to and cultivating their spiritual identity.

Such a view of religion can be discerned from Sandel's criticism of the liberal approach. Religion (and sometimes the lack of it) comprises part of a person. Demanding neutrality concerning religion on any level may require the denial of one's innermost convictions. This relates to Sandel's general criticism of liberalism as a deontological view of the person, whose purpose, ties and morals are deemed to be a product of choice. According to his view, the problem with liberalism is that it claims we must view ourselves as independent, in the sense that our identity is never tied to our aims and attachments; however, living by these aims and attachments is inseparable from understanding who we are as persons.[95] Applied to the issue of religious freedom, this might mean that religion should be accorded some kind of 'trump' value when it is in conflict with other considerations, because it is not just a rational or deliberative choice of a person, like political affiliation, but part of the person's constitution.

The idea of religion as self-identity rather than community identity that defines the individual is inherent in Sandel's strand of communitarianism. Although the community (family, religion, school) shapes and even constitutes the person, there is a personal, subjective conception of personhood, which includes contemplation of self-identity and personal commitments as well as relationship to society. Under this view, the person is not identical with his communal or social connections.[96] This version of communitarianism can be distinguished from a 'stronger' conception of communitarianism (such as that of MacIntyre, who views individuals as inheriting a specified social space)[97] in which the self is almost entirely a product of circumstances (including religion).[98]

Sandel claims[99] that belief is not a product of choice, like lifestyle, but is constitutive, a deeply rooted component of the individual. That is why freedom of conscience is unalienable. However, he refers to the source of belief as conscience, not social position but individual conscience, something that is influenced by, but also distinct from, social context. This view does not stand in contradiction to the claim that religious freedom is an individual right, although it may have ramifications on how that right is to be implemented.

Thus, there are two principal views of religion as identity in communitarian writing: that of religion as group identity and that of religion as individual identity. It appears that some communitarian writing obscures the difference between religion as community dentity and religion as self-identity. The relationship between a person and his/her community is crucial precisely because he/she forges his/her self-identity through confrontation with his/her surrounding community and attempts to differentiate himself/herself from it. As object relations theory of psychoanalysis suggests, individual identity is based on the separation of self from others. Although initially this concept refers to separation from the mother (real or symbolic),[100] it also refers, more importantly for our purpose, to separation from family and community.[101]

The interpretation of religion as constitutive of individual identity will be important in the discussion of legal issues in later chapters, such as that of children's religious freedom and the rights of the parents over the religious choice and education of their children, and in the discussion of proselytism.

2.5.2 *Freedom of religion as protection of minorities in a multicultural society*

An important reason to protect freedom of religion as a human right is the protection of minority religions in society. By guaranteeing all aspects of freedom of religion, we guarantee the preservations of these religious cultures and communities, and prevent their disappearance by assimilation into mainstream society. Two separate reasons justify this approach: One is that preservation of a variety of cultures, social systems and religions, and maintenance of the social dialogue between them will reap benefit to society as a whole (a public good argument). The other is based on the intrinsic right of each cultural (or religious) group to exist with equal respect. This last reason can also be couched in terms of individual rights. If minority cultures no longer existed, minority members' choices of culture would become restricted, and their freedoms would be curtailed.[102]

While these reasons apply equally to minority and majority religions, the emphasis is placed on minority religions as they are the ones likely to be adversely affected without this protection. Furthermore, historically, adherents of minority religions bore the brunt of persecution and discrimination. Thus it is justified that the protection of the rights of adherents of minority religions may be different from that accorded to the majority religion. (In the international context, of course, 'minority' is a relative term. A majority religion in one state may be a minority religion in another.) The different treatment may not only be a function of majority/minority status, but of the inherent differences between the religions themselves. If we accept these arguments, we must tailor the interpretation of religious freedom to fit disparate religions residing together. Parekh[103] argues that '[e]quality between cultures is logically different from and cannot be understood along the lines of equality between individuals ... It is not enough to appeal to the general right to equality. One also needs to show that there is equality in the relevant feature of the context and that it entails identical treatment.'[104]

The case of *Ahmed v. UK*[105] illustrates what equality between cultures entails.[106] A Muslim employee of a UK school asked to be given time off a regular workday to attend religious services and was denied. Following his failed domestic litigation, his application to the European Court of Human Rights, in which the applicant argued that his Article 9 (religious freedom) rights were breached, was also denied.[107] If the cultural context is ignored, Ahmed indeed is seen as asking not for equal treatment but for preferential treatment. He is asking to work four and a half days a week, while his colleagues work five days. However, the context in which this case took place creates inequality between cultures. The days of rest, Saturday and Sunday, conform to a Judeo-Christian tradition. To redress this inequality, an exception to the rule must be made for those whose religions require other rest days and the right under the Convention should be interpreted accordingly.

Parekh believes religious equality is an individually exercised collective right.[108] I disagree: although a correct analysis of equality should assess equality in the relevant cultural context, it is an individual right to equality of religious freedom that is protected. Ahmed's right and his choice to exercise it, and incur the risks associated with doing so, are his own. The fact that other devout employees of the same faith did not make the same demands, or even did not think this exemption was warranted by their faith, does not detract from the legitimacy of his claim. Religious freedom and religious equality should be understood and assessed in their cultural context, but this does not make them rights of the group rather than the individual.

My first disagreement is conceptual. Parekh argues collective rights do and should exist, and may sometimes trump individual rights. These include rights, such as the right of the Catholic Church, recognized by states, to grant or refuse divorce to its members. This is properly a group right (in his terms, a collectively exercised collective right), because it overrides the rights of individuals. But such a right is problematic precisely for this reason, even if individuals submit freely to the Church's power over them. Parekh dismisses the argument that groups should not be granted rights because such rights will threaten individual rights. He argues that individuals can misuse their rights against others as well, yet we recognize individual rights; why then should we not recognize group rights?

This argument seems to miss the point. Of course individual rights can be misused, but granting rights to groups essentially entails granting the group power over individuals.[109] States have power over individuals; indeed states are defined as having a monopoly of such power. A state may have legitimate reasons to divest power to other institutions, but it is not clear why transfer of such power over individuals from state to group, including religious groups, constitutes a right of the group.

My second disagreement is policy based. Parekh relies on the shared doctrine the group wishes to maintain as a justification for community rights, particularly pertinent to religious group rights. This, he maintains, is why most states respect the Catholic Church's right to excommunicate its members or deny them divorce, and grant it exemption from sexual discrimination laws, even though this severely restricts individual liberties. These examples illustrate the problems created by recognition of religious group rights. The powers of the Catholic Church, which are recognized in liberal states, raise the question of how such erosion of individual rights can be justified within a liberal framework. One answer is that in any state that recognizes the right to freedom of religion, every member is free to leave the Church. But this is not a sound justification: it is precisely because men and women are part of the society in which they live that the Church should not be able to override indiscriminately members' rights, even if the membership of the individual in the Church is voluntary. Voluntariness is a question of degree. Just because someone lives in a Catholic community does not mean that they agree that a refusal to grant divorce should be outside the realm of the law. While refusing to grant divorce may or may not contravene the Church member's rights, the fact that membership is voluntary should not automatically exempt the Church from scrutiny of the law.

Religious institutions, although they are private institutions, operate in the public realm. For instance, by allowing religious institutions the power to create legally recognized marriage and grant legally recognized divorce, the state is transferring to them regulatory power in a crucial area of public life.[110] The distinction between organs of the state belonging to the public realm and religious institutions belonging to the private realm does not represent reality. When a church hires or fires employees or excommunicates its members, it is not just a private institution that is enforcing its doctrine; it is a public organization implementing a system of morality that must stand up to generally accepted principles of human rights.

While accepting the premise of the communitarian approach, namely that the individual is part of a social context, my conclusion is not that religious communities should be left alone to formulate their own rules, but rather that basic human rights provisions should apply to them albeit adapted to their dual character.

2.5.3 Groups that violate the human rights of their own members

A lingering dilemma with no satisfactory resolution from any approach that advocates acceptance of a plurality of cultural doctrines while upholding basic principles of human rights is that of a group that discriminates against some of its own members or against non-members who are reliant on the group. The latter case concerns, for instance, employees who do not belong to the religious group but work in its schools, hospitals or other institutions.

The issue of groups that violate the human rights of their own members (especially socially weak members and dissenters) is nowhere more evident than in the context of religious communities and religious ethical codes. Kymlicka, who attempts to reconcile liberal theory with communitarian challenges, deals directly with the dilemma of how liberalism should treat groups that violate liberal principles. He argues that the fact that some group systems are deficient from a liberal point of view does not mean that liberals can impose their principles on them.[111] This is obvious to him in the transnational context: liberal states will not intervene in how an illiberal state is run. Kymlicka argues that national minorities (we may add, religious minorities) deserve to be treated similarly to foreign states, namely that liberal principles should not be imposed on them.

However, this reasoning can be argued the other way around. If some principles are justified as human rights minimums within the state, which the state may impose on private groups and institutions within it, then there also should be human rights principles which the international community is justified in demanding that states observe. This is not a new view. Tesón[112] traces the concept of human rights in international law to Kant, and explains that under Kantian theory, respect for human rights is a fundamental prerequisite of the state. However, this remains a controversial question in international law. How it directly impacts religious freedom will be revisited in Chapter 3.

2.5.4 Group rights: the utilitarian argument

An argument that promotes group rights above individual rights, for a completely different reason than communitarian arguments, can be termed the group-rights-utilitarian argument: individual rights can be protected only by giving power to the group. While the ultimate goal is to protect the individual's rights, this must, paradoxically, sometimes be achieved by favouring the group over the individual. Gedicks claims[113] that religious groups protect individual liberty precisely because they challenge the power of the state, something which individuals are incapable of doing alone in the modern world. To allow groups the freedom they require to fulfil this role, they should be allowed to trump individual liberty in cases where group rights and individual rights conflict.

This may be likened to the powers accorded by some laws to labour unions over workers. Organized labour is seen as the only power strong enough to challenge employers and authorities, and to protect individual workers' rights, something the individual worker is unable to do. To ensure unions have these powers, for instance to deploy strikes, the decisions of individual workers must give way to union decisions. Similarly, the rights of individuals against the state can only be protected if power is given to popular social institutions, like religions, to override individual preferences.

The group-utilitarian justification provides no answer for those individuals whose rights are infringed by religions. By transferring authority from the state to religions, authority which may be paramount to individual right, we are merely transferring the power to infringe individual rights, not protecting them.

2.6 Religious views and liberal prescription of religious freedom

Religions that view themselves as all-encompassing social prescriptions for the community of their adherents stand completely at odds with the liberal view of the role of religion. A key idea of liberalism is the autonomous individual – an individual who is not ruled by others and rules himself[114] – a view which is inherently incompatible with many religious world views.

As part of the liberal ideology, religious toleration is perceived to be compatible with Protestantism, the religion historically associated with the rise of liberal thought. However, even this is not entirely the case and historically has not necessarily been so. Liberalism has been an important tradition in Protestantism, owing to the Protestant emphasis on private judgment.[115] But Protestant Christianity developed an affinity not just with the individualistic aspect of liberalism, but also with the other defining characteristic of the liberal movement, the rise of the nation-state.[116] The Protestant Reformation, although ultimately conducive to religious freedom, also encompasses a history of religious intolerance. While Protestantism empowered the individual in exercising personal religious freedom, it utilized the power of the state to establish religion, aligning the state-religion with the newly emerging nation-state. While some aspects of the Reformation worked in favour of religious liberty and separation of Church from state (especially among minority groups such as the Baptists and Anabaptists which were not aligned with the state), the main Reformers such as Luther and Calvin actually helped reinforce the principle of one religion in one state, and put the power of religion directly behind the secular authority.[117] While today there is no such relation between Church and state in those states which are traditionally linked with Protestantism, as will be seen in Chapter 3 their history shows a complex relationship to the liberal principle of freedom of religion.

The conflict may be even more pronounced in the case of religions that are not aligned with the philosophical tradition of liberalism. The Muslim political theorist Mernissi argues that lack of public–private demarcation is inherent in the Islamic state. She claims[118] that being Muslim is not a matter of personal choice, but of belonging to a theocratic state. Being a Marxist or an atheist does not contradict obeying national law, but being a Muslim is inherently a matter that is not disjointed from the public code. This would be impossible to reconcile with a liberal state's conception of freedom of religion. Mernissi's conception has direct implications in the international sphere. A view of the right to religious freedom in international law exclusively as a right of the sovereign state was expressed by the Saudi Arabian government.[119] It argued that this right comprises the freedom of any country to adhere to, preserve and protect its religion, and show respect and tolerance towards religious minorities of the country's citizens as long as the former respect the constitutional tenets of their country.

Non-monotheistic religions and the political traditions they inform have other views on the respective roles of the individual, the state and religion. Those Asian states in which Buddhism and Hinduism are predominant tend to espouse non-separation of state and religion, integration of the individual and the public, and a grant of formal power to the state without clear theories of accountability.[120] These are at odds with Western ideas of constitutionalism and individual freedom, as well as with the possibility of separation of state from religion. In Japan, for instance, it has been asserted that the post-war 1947 constitution, which was drafted by US occupation forces, instituted foreign Christian values.[121] Separation of religion from state in that constitution, imposed by the allied forces, certainly introduced foreign, American, ideals, as will be discussed in Chapter 3.

However, other aspects of the liberal concept of religious toleration may be particularly suited to non-monotheistic religions: Monotheistic religion, suggests the Buddhist philosopher Abe, is apt to be intolerant due to its emphasis on one absolute god. Religions based on exclusive faith generate intolerance. In contrast, Buddhism does not compel its adherents to 'have no other god'. It has no dogma, as Buddha's teachings are just one of the many ways to enlightenment.[122] Hinduism encompasses two aspects: the ever present moral order of the universe (*dharma*) but also individual devotion (*bhakti*).[123] The second, more individualistic and less authoritarian aspect, is more easily reconciled with the liberal concept of religious freedom, but Hinduism is, is fact, a mixture of both.

As we can see even from this small sample, religious views and religiously informed state views on different aspects of religious freedom have varied enormously. If such are the divergences in the political philosophies of the states and the religious philosophies that inform them, both historically and currently, it is obvious that grave obstacles stand in the way of achieving a consensus on an international right to freedom of religion. This difficulty will be explored in later chapters.

2.7 Religious political participation

There are problems inherent in the concept of religious freedom that make religious freedom impossible to realize within the state. If religious freedom includes the freedom to use religion to oppose the state and its political underpinnings (in a liberal state, democracy, human rights, and, possibly, neutrality), the state cannot maintain both itself and complete, unabridged religious freedom. The state will necessarily provide incomplete protection of religious freedom, especially under the view that claims religious freedom is a group right. While an individual may wish to use religion against principles of the state, organized political activity is much more central to the exercise of religious freedom by a group. Therefore, any limitation on religious participation in the political sphere is injurious to the exercise of group religious freedom. Conversely, any justification of limitations of religious political activity may contribute to a political argument in favour of recognizing religious freedom as an individual, rather than group, right. Examples of such limitations will be discussed in this and in the following sections.

In the context of religious freedom, competition between the authority of religion and the authority of the state makes the conflict between group and individual rights much sharper compared to other human rights. It raises some profound problems in all states, and particularly in liberal democracies. These problems, both in quality and in quantity, are distinct from any that arise with other civil institutions. This is because religions are coherent, all-encompassing, externally derived, alternative normative systems to the state. Both problems analysed show that religious freedom might be harder to define and more difficult to achieve than other human rights.

The first problem, discussed in section 2.7.1, is that of the legitimacy of using religious reasons for legislation. Law in a democracy is made by majority vote, regardless of the subjective motivations people have for casting such vote. Each vote is equal. But there are limitations on the power of majority vote. Respect for human rights, including religious freedoms, is one of these limitations. But is prohibition of legislation based on religious doctrine one of these limitations? If democracy is based on collective decision making by rational autonomous agents, when these agents are deciding according to predetermined external doctrine, they are bypassing substantive, if not procedural, democracy. These two opposing arguments mean that democracy and liberalism stand in irreconcilable tension regarding the status of religion in the state.

The second problem, discussed in section 2.7.2, is that of the right of religious political parties that are opposed to democracy to participate in the democratic process. If religious freedom is recognized as a collective right, one of its most important manifestations is the ability to participate in democratic elections. This presents a conflict between democracy as a free and equal election process, and the limitations on it necessary to make democracy both meaningful and sustainable. This conflict is fundamentally unsolvable.

2.7.1 Are religious reasons for legislation a breach of religious freedom?

One of the difficult problems regarding the permissible bounds of religion in the state, in states which *are* liberal democracies, is that of religious motivation for legislation. This question, of the legitimacy of use of religious reasons in the democratic political process, is pivotal both to theory and practice of the liberal state. The resolution of this question is necessary to resolve the fundamental question: Can a liberal state and religion co-exist in the same society? The answer to this question has direct bearing on the interpretation of freedom of religion as a group or individual right, and is ultimately at the core of understanding religious freedom. This problem will be revisited, with some its practical manifestations regarding women and religion, in Chapter 4.

On the one hand, if the legislative process is the culmination of the free marketplace of ideas, then religious ideas must be as eligible to compete in it as any other idea. On the other hand, if the resulting law is equivalent to the religious norm, and the reason for its adoption is religious dictate on which the legislators acted, is that not tantamount to imposition of religious norms in contravention of the religious freedom of all citizens?

In the discussion that follows, it is clearer to focus on primary religious reasons, that is, religious reasons given as the direct justification for the legislation. There are many cases of hidden or secondary religious reasons, that is, reasons that are based on social or cultural norms, which are ultimately derived from religious teachings even if religion is no longer seen as their justification.

When asking whether religious reasons are legitimate, different answers must be given for different actors in the political system. I will analyse them in order, from the actor for which it is most permissible to use religious reason to the one for which it is least permissible.

First, *individual citizens*. Principles of individual freedom and individual choice mean that individual citizens may generally make decisions as they please, for any reasons they feel are apt, or for no reason at all. But is this true also when they act as voters? Of course, there is no possibility of placing legal restrictions on citizens' reasons for voting as they do, but should there be any such moral constraints? I think not, as citizens should enjoy absolute personal freedom in forming their decisions. Others see a social reason for reaching the same conclusion. Not only are religious reasons perfectly legitimate reasons for voting, but their inclusion may even serve a social function, argues Weithman.[124] He argues that to achieve liberal democratic citizenship, as many citizens as possible must participate in political life. This entails, he claims, allowing moral and religious argument from citizens and even some moralizing by government. Many people become involved in public life through participation in churches, and their participation in political life would be curtailed if this could not be the platform for their own political agenda.

However, it may be argued that when exercising their right to vote individual citizens cannot legitimately act as they please. Rawls argues that not only should legislators and officials be limited to public reason in political decisions, but citizens should likewise be limited when they are acting politically, as voters, rather than in their personal lives. Their limitation to reliance on public reason means that they should be able to explain their actions in terms others could accept as consistent with their freedom and equality.[125]

Some attempt has been made to reconcile these opposing views. Liberal democracy and religious public reasoning are not contradictory. Greenawalt argues that it does not follow from a secular and separationist form of a liberal democracy that people should eschew their religious convictions when making political choices.[126] At least in choosing between several reasonable possibilities given by public choice, he suggests that one may use a non-public (or religious) reason.[127]

Second, there are *individuals who hold institutional religious positions* and the *organizations they represent*. These may, of course, use religious reasons in conducting the affairs of their religions, but the question is whether they may rely on their religious authority in the political discussion, use the power of religious institutions to advance political goals, and involve themselves in the political process. Among opponents of the legitimacy of such involvement, Audi[128] demands that those bearing institutional religious positions refrain from pressing for specific public policies. Greenawalt[129] likewise argues that religious leaders should steer clear of endorsing political parties, because such action will make religion political and alienate those with opposing religious views. However, he fails to explain why making religion political is an undesirable thing. It could be argued that making religion political means being part of robust discussion in society and is therefore a beneficial result.

Weithman[130] argues that religious institutions may legitimately be involved in politics, citing two examples: the first is of US Catholic Bishops writing a letter in support of economic justice, the second is Church support for the US civil rights movement in the 1960s. However, the content of the involvement – the fact that religious institutions supported worthwhile causes[131] (from a liberal viewpoint) – demonstrates little about the principled political legitimacy of such institutional involvement. If such involvement is legitimate when it furthers causes compatible with liberalism, it must also be legitimate when it furthers causes which liberals would oppose.[132] An argument for institutional religious involvement in political life based on the content of the involvement in particular cases is lacking in principle.

A middle way between prohibition of institutional religious involvement in politics and grant of equal participation in the political process is taken by US law. The limitation on the involvement of religion in politics is indirect. In the USA, churches are prohibited from endorsing or opposing political candidates if they wish to enjoy tax-exempt status.[133] Although enforcement was not rigorous, and perhaps because of this very fact, claims were made that the prohibition was discriminately applied. Discrimination in application is one of the dangers of rules that allow religion into politics, but it is one of the dangers of legislation that excludes religion from politics as well. The other danger of any regulation that decides how much religious speech may legitimately be included in the political process is that the state becomes a 'speech police'.

The third party is the *legislators*. A legislator does not enjoy the unencumbered freedom of the voter. They are elected to act in promotion of the public good not their idiosyncratic preferences. But legislators could claim that they were elected to promote a platform chosen by those who voted for them. If this platform relies on religious reasons, it is not only the legislator's right but also his or her duty to use them to enact conforming legislation. Some attempt has been made to reconcile these demands on the legislator. Greenawalt[134] argues that legislators may use religious reasons for themselves, but should publicly develop non-religious arguments. Similarly, Perry argues that it is constitutionally permissible for legislators to make a political choice based on religious argument but only where a plausible secular argument supports the same conclusion.[135] He argues that only citizens may articulate religious grounds for their political decisions and use them in public argument.

The legitimacy of reliance by legislators on a religious source should be differentiated according to the type of religious source used: legislation based on the idea that there is a God-created order fundamental to moral truth; legislation based on the idea of a God-inspired text; and legislation based on the directives of a God-anointed figure, like the Pope, believed to teach moral truth.[136] The political legitimacy of these as a basis for legislation is not equal. The difference between them is in the degree to which the legislator divests himself/herself of the exercise of personal judgment. Reliance on a general belief in a God-ordered universe may be permissible; disallowing it transgresses on the individual realm of freedom of belief. However, deference of the legislator to a non-state religious figure (such as the Pope) may well be considered an illegitimate use of institutional religion in the state.

It finally should be noted that any limitations on lawmakers relying on any aspect of religion, whether confessional or institutional, as a basis for their legislation conflicts with one aspect of religious expression of the group that some religions see as vital to their message – a religious political party.[137]

Unelected public officials must exercise their judgment in making decisions of public policy on which they may hold a religious opinion. Unlike legislators, unelected public officials cannot claim to have been elected to their position by their voters to promote a particular religious viewpoint. They have an equal duty towards all citizens. Even if it may be legitimate for legislators to use religious reasons, public officials must rely only public reasons.

Judges[138] are the final category to be examined. Even if it is legitimate for citizens and legislators to draw on their religious affiliation in choosing how to exercise their public decision making, it is different for decisions made by judges. Judges who bear religious allegiance may face a conflict between their belief and what is laid down by the law that they must interpret. In a liberal democracy, the case seems clear – rule of law must prevail and the judge must lay his or her personal beliefs aside. Judges must rule according to law, and not according to religious dictate.

Anything else would be a breach of the rule of law principle as well as an illegal imposition of the judge's religious beliefs on the litigants. However, from the judge's point of view, the case may not be so simple. A religious judge may feel that it is difficult to separate the personal from the professional. He or she may feel that their religious freedom is breached when they are *not* allowed to bring their religious beliefs into consideration.[139] In many legal cases, moral determinations necessarily must be made. Indeed, according to natural law theories, a judge is bound to do so in every case. Ethical considerations can serve as protection against automatic application of unjust laws by judges. So why should only religious considerations be excluded?

This dilemma is not just a theoretical one. Recently, US Supreme Court Justice Antonin Scalia (himself a Catholic) opined in a public lecture that any Catholic judges who follow the Church's teaching (promoted by Pope John Paul II) that capital punishment is wrong should resign.[140] But would judges who follow such religious teaching be doing something wrong? One factor to consider is that religions constitute a comprehensive normative system, and in that they are different from other moral beliefs. As in the case of legislation, we should differentiate between institutionalized and personal religious reasoning. A judge's reliance on institutional religious dictates (such as a direct command from a religious leader) in adjudication is very obviously wrong. It may be somewhat easier to argue in favour of a judge who relies on personal religious belief and not on religious dictates. However, in the case of judges the arguments against using religious reasons are the strongest of all the cases of use of religious reasons by political actors. These arguments must outweigh the injury to the religious beliefs of a judge and mandate against use of religious arguments by a judge.

How should international law treat domestic religiously motivated legislation (or other legal decision making) of the different types just analysed?

The different ways in which religion motivates legislation is evident in the legislation in various states. For instance, the debate regarding legislation on abortion in many states, such as Ireland,[141] has seen the use of religious reasons in the political forum, whether by the discussants resorting to religious moral codes or by direct involvement of the clergy.[142] Likewise, religious reasons were present in different states in the debates on the legal rights of homosexuals (regarding criminalization of homosexual acts, same-sex marriage, and adoption by same-sex parents). Another recent use of religious reasons was the mobilization by the Greek Orthodox church against the elimination of registration of religion on identity cards in Greece.[143]

Viewing religion as a group attribute makes for a stronger claim that religion cannot be dissociated from political life than if religion is viewed as merely an individual concern. The group is emasculated if it is not allowed to operate in the prime public sphere of the state. But it is precisely the *group* characteristics of religion – its ordered hierarchy, lack of individual moral reasoning, and acceptance of pre-written decisions – which make the use of religious public reasons anathema to the proponents of liberal democracy.

Of course, if the positions advocated lead to contravention of the state's international human rights obligations, the objection to them is clear, but human rights discourse has not yet analysed whether intervention by clergy or by those relying on religious arguments is legitimate in cases that do not involve a breach of specific human rights obligations of the state.[144] Equal freedom of belief for all is breached, especially of those who do not share the religious belief, when religious reasons are used for decisions of the state regardless of the resulting decision. However, if the legislators' reasoning is taken into account when deciding on the legislation's legality, then the same law could be deemed legal in one state (in which its enactment was motivated by religion) but not in another (in which it had a different basis).[145] International law must assess here very different legal and moral cultures and cannot provide one satisfactory answer.

2.7.2 *Democratic participation of non-democratic religious parties*

Democratic participation and the continued observance of human rights may not always go hand in hand, as many commentators assume, but may pose conflicting demands on a state. This conflict occurs in democracies that face the rise of intolerant political parties through the democratic system. Numerous examples of this phenomenon exist in recent years: in 1996 Mahatir bin Mohamad, Prime Minister of the Federation of Malaysia, threatened to suspend the government of the state of Kelantan, thus pressuring the state government to abandon Islamic penal legislation that contravened personal freedoms. In Algeria in 1991 the second-round election was cancelled;[146] the state justified the cancellation by claiming the Islamic FIS Party a threat to the secular Algerian state.

When a political party opposes democratic elections or threatens the continuing respect of basic human rights, it has been claimed by Fox and Nolte, the state may be justified, under international law, in curtailing this institution's participation in the democratic process.[147] The dilemma is addressed by the ICCPR. While Article 25 of the ICCPR mandates that:

> Every citizen shall have the right and opportunity ... without unreasonable restrictions ... to vote and to be elected ... guaranteeing the free expression and will of the electors.

Article 5(1) of the ICCPR declares that:

> Nothing in the present Covenant may be interpreted as implying for any State, group or person any right to engage in any activity or perform any act aimed at the destruction of any of the rights and freedoms recognized therein or at their limitation to a greater extent than is provided in the present Covenant.

Fox and Nolte argue that Article 5(1) manifests the principles of substantive, rather than formal, democracy. They point to its application by the HRC in removing an Italian fascist party from the protection afforded by the Covenant,[148] and to similar jurisprudence by the European Commission for Human Rights, permitting such restrictions to apply to 'persons who threaten the democratic system'.[149] Fox and Nolte suggest that international law views democratic procedure not as an end but as a means to creating a society in which citizens enjoy certain basic rights.[150] If so, democratic elections may be curtailed or restricted in order to protect the continuing enjoyment of such rights.

However, when restriction on the activities of a party is triggered by its religious ideology, it is freedom of religion, as well as rights of association and political participation, which is being curtailed. If the religious group defines itself through its participation in public life, it is meaningless to talk of a group right of religious freedom and bar its participation in elections. In this sense the concept of freedom of religion as a group right is inimical to liberal democracy.

Religious group rights are not contradictory to a democratic regime that respects human rights, insofar as what is included in the religious group right is defined from a liberal perspective. For those religious groups that view their political aspect as part and parcel of their religious self-identity, such a definition of what the group may or may not do or say will not be acceptable.

Dombrowski[151] argues that where a particular religion has a comprehensive conception of good such that it will survive only if it controls the machinery of the state and practices intolerance, it would effectively cease to exist in a politically liberal society. If this is a descriptive claim, it is simply not true. It is precisely in those cases in which a religion with a comprehensive conception challenges the authority of the existing state that the politically liberal society is strained to its limits.

Rawls, while presenting a rather optimistic picture of the way intolerant religious sects will be whittled down naturally in a politically liberal society, ultimately concedes that he has no solution for the problem of intolerant religions in the liberal state:

> Even if an intolerant sect should arise, provided that it is not so strong initially that it can impose its will straight away ... it will tend to lose its intolerance and accept liberty of conscience ... Of course, the intolerant sect may be so strong initially or growing so fast that the forces making for stability cannot convert it to liberty. This situation presents a practical dilemma which philosophy alone cannot resolve.[152]

2.8 Conclusion

Religious freedom is unique, a double-sided right, encompassing the freedom to criticize and change ideas, and the right to preserve identity, a freedom of doing and of being. The term 'religious freedom' holds an internal contradiction. While freedom of religion, like all rights, is intended to ensure liberty, religion itself is also defined by the constraints it imposes. Freedom of religion protects both self-imposed and group-imposed constraints. For this reason, it is a liberty that sees the individual often at odds with the demands of the group. As we have seen, various theories which have tried to define and justify this right confronted the need to address two competing aspects of this right: liberty or equality, individual or group. This important theoretical debate has, crucially, very practical legal applications. The tensions between individual and group demands on the application of the right to religious freedom must be taken into account by any legal system that accords this right. This chapter has argued and demonstrated that the right to religious freedom is an individual right, but has also highlighted the difficult problems associated with denial of group-related aspects of this right. These concerns exist for domestic legal systems and for international law, and will be exemplified and analysed in the various legal issues discussed in the following chapters.

Notes

1 See M. A. Glendon, 'Religious freedom and the original understanding of the Universal Declaration of Human Rights', Conference: Religious liberty and the ideology of the state, Prague, 2000, available at http://www.becketfund.org/other/Prague2000/GlendonPaper.html (accessed 8 December 2009). Glendon highlights the fact that the main controversy surrounding the drafting of the UDHR related to Article 18, specifically to the inclusion in it of the right to change religion. While all delegates agreed as to the importance of the inclusion of the right to freedom of religion in the Declaration, the Saudi Arabian delegation objected to the inclusion in it of a right to change one's religion based on the tenets of the Islamic faith. The Pakistani delegate was influential in bringing about the final inclusion of this right, based on the interpretation he gave to relevant passages of the Koran. This incident supports a wider claim: that in fact much more representative inter-cultural and inter-faith dialogue had taken place in the drafting of the Declaration than many commentators assume and that the final consensus was reached as much by non-Western as by Western contributions.

2 For the debate on universalism versus cultural relativism in the specific context of the UDHR, see K. Mickelson, 'How universal is the Universal Declaration?', *University of New Brunswick Law Journal*, 47, 1998, 19. For cultural-relativist criticism of the UDHR, see A. Pollis and P. Schwab, 'Human rights: a western construct with limited applicability', in A. Pollis and P. Schwab (eds), *Human rights: cultural and ideological perspectives*, New York: Praeger, 1980, 1. The authors claim that human rights is a Western concept that cannot be transplanted outside its cultural context, that it philosophically stems from Western Enlightenment-era philosophy of the autonomy of the individual, and that the UDHR was historically adopted when Western states were dominant in the international community, and so cannot be said to reflect universal values. For the view that the UDHR, although based on a human rights concept of Western origin, has universal applicability in the modern word, see R. E. Howard and J. Donnelly, 'Human dignity, human rights and political regimes', in J. Donnelly, *Universal human rights in theory and practice*, Ithaca: Cornell University Press, 1989, 66. On the wider debate on the universality of human rights, for a philosophical basis for the claim of universality of human rights, see R. Panikkar, 'Is the notion of human rights a Western concept?', *Diogenes* 120, 1982, 75. For a perspective that challenges the dichotomy of both pervasive views and argues that universalism/relativism is not an east/west distinction, see Y. Ghai, 'Human rights and interethnic claims', *Cardozo Law Review* 21, 2000, 1093, 1137. For further articles dealing with cultural implications of human rights, see A. An-Na'im (ed.), *Human Rights in Cross-Cultural Perspective*, Philadelphia: University of Pennsylvania Press, 1992. For a relativist criticism waged against the UDHR in a statement by the American Anthropological Association, see A. D. Rentelin, *International human rights: universalism vs. relativism*, Newbury Park: Sage, 1990, 83.

For a recent comment on the universality of human rights, see Hoffmann, 'The Universality of Human Rights', *Law Quarterly Review* 125, 2009, 416–432. For an evaluation of the current standing of the UDHR, see J. Von Bernstorff, 'The changing fortunes of the Universal Declaration of Human Rights: genesis and symbolic dimensions of the turn to rights in international law', *European Journal of International Law* 19(5), 2008, 903–924.

3 For the universalist/cultural debate on the UDHR as applicable to religious freedom, see M. A. Glendon, 'Religious freedom and the original understanding of the Universal Declaration of Human Rights', Conference: Religious liberty and the ideology of the state, Prague, 2000, available at http://www.becketfund.org/other/Prague2000/GlendonPaper.html (accessed 8 December 2009); A. An-Na'im, *Towards an Islamic reformation: civil liberties, human rights and international law*, Syracuse: Syracuse University Press, 1990; A. E. Mayer, 'Universal versus Islamic human rights: a clash of cultures or a clash with a construct?', *Michigan Journal of International Law*, 15, 1994, 307.

4 The first occurred, for example, when Turkey limited by law the power of Islam (C. Evans, *Freedom of religion under the European Convention on Human Rights*, Oxford: Oxford University Press, 2001, 19), and the second occurred when the rulers of pre-revolution Mozambique used Catholicism to enhance their legitimacy in the eyes of the country's citizens (D. D. Nsereko, 'Religion, the state and law in Africa', *Journal of State and Church* 28, 1986, 285).

5 See J. F. Maclear, *Church and state in the modern age: A documentary history*, New York: Oxford University Press, 1995 for a collection of documents chronicling the development of constitutional relations between Church and state in Western states from the 17th century onwards. For discussions of some constitutions by state, see A. An-Na'im, 'Human rights in the Muslim world', *Harvard Human Rights Journal* 3, 1990, 13; K. Boyle and J. Sheen (eds), *Freedom of religion and belief: a world report*, London: Routledge, 1997 (world survey).

6 See, e.g., the UN Declaration on the Rights of Indigenous Peoples, UN Doc. A/61/67 (Adopted 7 September 2007), which guarantees the right to an internal legal system to indigenous groups.

7 J. Waldron, *Liberal rights: collected papers, 1981–1991*, Cambridge: Cambridge University Press, 1993, 364.

8 See R. Dworkin, *Taking rights seriously*, London: Duckworth, 1994, especially 94–105.

9 P. Sieghart, *The international law of human rights*, New York: Oxford University Press, 1983, 368.

10 A definition of 'religious group' is required not just for the interpretation of human rights, but also, for instance, for the purposes of the Genocide Convention. (See discussion of how the ICTY and ICTR defined this term: R. Wilson, 'Defining genocide at international criminal tribunals: towards a political understanding of genocide', abstract available at http://www.allacademic.com/meta/p_mla_apa_research_citation/1/7/7/0/4/p177046_index.html (accessed 8 December 2009).

11 General Comment 8, UN Doc. A/45/18.

12 For example, Jewish law considers Jews only those who are born to a Jewish mother or convert to Judaism under supervision of a Rabbinical Court. (Israeli Supreme Court: HCJ 72/62 *Rufeisen v. Minister of the Interior*, 16 PD 2428.)

13 This will be seen in the discussion in Chapter 3 of schismatic groups and state recognition of leadership of religious communities and in the discussion in Chapter 6 of religious dissenters.

14 *Santa Clara Pueblo v. Martinez* 436 US 49 (1978).

15 402 F. Supp 5, 15 (1975).

16 Ibid, 18.

17 Comm. No. 24/1977 *Lovelace v. Canada* CCPR/C/13/D/24/1977.

18 Ibid.

19 M. McDonald, 'Should communities have rights – a reflection on liberal individualism', in A. An-Na'im (ed.), *Human rights in cross-cultural perspective*, Philadelphia: University of Pennsylvania Press, 1992, 134–135.

20 The practical problems in defining membership of the group can be seen when advancing the concept of a group right one step further to include a collective right to compensation for past grievances to the group. See J. Edwards, 'Collective rights in the liberal state', *Netherlands Quarterly of Human Rights* 17, 1999, 259.

21 C. H. Wellman, 'Liberalism, communitarianism and group rights', *Law and Philosophy* 18, 1999, 37.

22 The idea influentially developed by J. Locke, *Two treatises of government*, ed. M. Goldie, London: Everyman, 1993. See also D. Miller (ed.), *The Blackwell encyclopedia of political thought*, Oxford: Blackwell, 1991, 222.

23 But relies on other reasoning, such as social contract and collective benefit.

24 See G. Nettheim, ' "Peoples" and "populations" – indigenous peoples and the rights of peoples', in J. Crawford (ed.), *The rights of peoples*, Oxford: Clarendon, 1988, 107.

For more recent commentary, see G. Pentassuglia, 'Evolving protection of minority groups: global challenges and the role of international jurisprudence', *International Criminal Law Review* 11(2), 2009, 185–218; R. Kuppe, 'The three dimensions of the rights of indigenous peoples', *International Criminal Law Review* 11(1), 2009, 103–118; and W. Kymlicka, 'The internationalization of minority rights', *International Journal of Constitutional Law* 6(1), 2008, 1–32.

25 See the ILO Convention No. 107 of 1957 Concerning the Protection and Integration of Indigenous and Other Tribal and Semi-Tribal Populations in Independent Countries and other instruments discussed in Chapter 1.

26 B. Kingsbury, 'Competing structures of indigenous people's claims', in P. Alston (ed.), *People's rights*, Oxford: Oxford University Press, 2001, 69, 73–74.

27 485 US 439 (1988).

28 436 US 49 (1978).

29 B. Kingsbury, 'Competing structures of indigenous people's claims', in P. Alston (ed.), *People's rights*, Oxford: Oxford University Press, 2001, 69, 83.

30 UN Doc. CCPR/C/60/D/549/1993.

31 P. Leuprecht, 'Minority rights revisited', in P. Alston (ed.), *People's rights*, Oxford: Oxford University Press, 2001, 111–123.

For recent theoretical commentary on minority rights in international law, see P. Macklem, 'Minority rights in international law', *International Journal of Constitutional Law* 6(3/4), 2008, 531–552.

32 J. Waldron, *Liberal rights: Collected papers, 1981–1991*, Cambridge: Cambridge University Press, 1993, 366.

33 See section 2.3.2.

34 For example T. Yang, 'Race, religion and cultural identity', *Indiana Law Journal* 73, 1997, 120 argues that race and religion in US law should be treated alike as a constitutional matter.

35 Article 18 UDHR but not explicitly in Article 18 ICCPR or in the 1981 UN Declaration. See further Chapters 1 and 6.

36 OJ 2002 C75E/269.

37 Article 3.

38 (Adopted 1966) 660 UNTS 195.

39 N. Lerner, *Religion, beliefs and international human rights*, Markinoll: Orbis Books, 2000, 53 assumes Article 4 implicitly applies to religion as well, but I believe the wording clearly omits religion from the ambit of this Article.

40 See also the House of Lords Select Committee Report on Religious Offences in England and Wales, 10 April 2003, Volume I, HL Paper 95–I.

41 See further discussion in Chapter 6.

42 This is even indicated in the name of the 1981 UN Declaration, which mentions 'intolerance and discrimination' but not 'religious freedom'. See further international legal documents indicating this trend in Chapter 1.

43 ICCPR Article 2(1): 'Each State Party to the present Covenant undertakes to respect and to ensure ... the rights recognized in the present Covenant, without distinction of any kind, such as race, colour, sex, language, religion'; ICESCR, Article 2(2): 'Each State Party to the present Covenant undertakes to respect and to ensure ... the rights recognized in the present Covenant, without distinction of any kind, such as race, colour, sex, language, religion'.

The UNESCO Convention Against Discrimination in Education, Article 1: 'Each State Party to the present Covenant undertakes to respect ... the rights recognized in the present Covenant, without distinction of any kind, such as race, colour, sex, language, religion'.

ILO Discrimination (Employment and Occupation) Convention (No. 111) concerning Discrimination in respect of Employment and Occupation, Article 1: 'For the purpose of this Convention the term "discrimination" includes: (a) Any distinction, exclusion or preference made on the basis of race, colour, sex, religion, political opinion, national extraction or social origin, which has the effect of nullifying or impairing equality of opportunity or treatment in employment or occupation.' There are also, at least in 'soft law' instruments derivative duties of states to prevent behaviour which infringes these rights: UN Declaration on the Elimination of All Forms of Intolerance and Discrimination based on Religion or Belief (1981) Articles 4, 7. See also the draft Convention on the Elimination of All Forms of Religious Intolerance (1965) Articles VI–VIII.

44 See provisions in previous note.

Also Declaration on the Elimination of All Forms of Intolerance and of Discrimination Based on Religion or Belief, Article 2:

'(1) No one shall be subject to discrimination by any State, institution, group of persons, or person on the grounds of religion or other belief.

(2) For the purposes of the present Declaration, the expression "intolerance and discrimination based on religion or belief" means any distinction, exclusion, restriction or preference based on religion or belief and having as its purpose or as its effect nullification or impairment of the recognition, enjoyment or exercise of human rights and fundamental freedoms on an equal basis.'

45 Council Directive 2000/78/EC of 27 November 2000 establishing a general framework for equal treatment in employment and occupation OJL 303, 02/12/2000, 16–22.

46 See Section 46 of the UK Police (Northern Ireland) Act 2000.

47 See section 2.4.2.

48 For pre-modern historical development see J. Newman, *On religious freedom*, Ottawa: University of Ottawa Press, 1991, 101–113.

49 See for example: 'All religions should reside everywhere, for all of them desire self-control and purity of heart.' Rock Edict No. 7 'Contact (between religions) is good. One should listen to and respect the doctrines professed by others. ... [A]ll should be well-learned in the good doctrines of other religions.' Rock Edict No.12

The Edicts of King Ashoka, English: V. S. Dhammika, Buddhist Publication Society, Kandy, Sri Lanka 1993, available at http://www.cs.colostate.edu/~malaiya/ashoka. html (accessed 8 December 2009).

50 Ibid.

51 Genesis: 9.

52 J. Raz, *The morality of freedom*, Oxford: Clarendon, 1988, 252. For a general introduction to early liberal theory see J. Rawls and J. B. Herman, *Lectures on the history of moral philosophy*, Cambridge, MA: Harvard University Press, 2000; J. Gray, *Liberalism*, 2nd edn, Bristol: Open University Press, 1995.

53 B. Barry, *Liberty and justice*, Oxford: Clarendon, 1990, 23. See, for instance, the reasoning of Anthony Collins, the 18th-century outspoken critic of religion in *A discourse of free thinking*, reprinted in I. Kramnick (ed.), *The portable Enlightenment*, New York: Penguin, 1995, 101, who argues that arriving at the truth can only be achieved through free thinking.

54 Law n° 2001–504 of June 12, 2001.

55 Intervention of the French delegation to the OSCE Supplementary Meeting on Freedom of Religion, Vienna 1999, quoted in: M. Introvigne, 'Freedom of religion and belief in the Christian/western world', Introductory lecture at the conference organized by the International Humanist and Ethical Union, 4 May 2001, available at http://www.cesnur.org/2001/mi_osli_en.htm (accessed 8 December 2009), fn. 7.

56 I will disregard, for the purposes of this discussion, the veracity of the claim that certain religions, which were classified as cults, constrain individual thought more than others, as my interest is only in analysis of the justification offered.

57 Asma Jahangir, the UN Special Rapporteur on Freedom of Religion or Belief, also thought that this government policy, specifically the inclusion of certain groups in a list, negatively affected the right to freedom of religion or belief of members of these groups (Report submitted by, the Special Rapporteur on her Mission to France (18 to 29 September 2005), Addendum 2. Available at http://www.cesnur.org/2006/UNCHR_report_on_France.pdf (accessed 9 December 2009).

58 He refers to Catholics indirectly: '[t]hat Church can have no right to be tolerated by the magistrate which is constituted upon such a bottom that all those who enter into it do thereby ipso facto deliver themselves up to the protection and service of another prince.' J. Locke, *A letter on toleration*, trans. J. W. Gough, Oxford: Clarendon Press, 1968, 133.

59 B. Elshtain, 'State imposed secularism as a potential pitfall of liberal democracy', Conference on religious liberty and the ideology of the state, Prague, 2000, available at http://www.becketfund.org/other/Prague2000/Elshtainpaper.html (accessed 8 December 2009); M. Cranston, 'John Locke and the case for toleration', in S. Mendus and D. Edwards (eds), *On toleration*, Oxford: Clarendon Press, 1987, 101, 106.

60 Although see the opposite view of Richard Ashcraft, quoted by J. P. Martin, 'Religion, human rights and civil society: lessons from the seventeenth century for the twenty first century', *Brigham Young University Law Review*, 2000, 933, 938, that under the guise of appeal to individual reason, Locke was, in fact, attempting to rely on community prejudices (against Catholics) to further his cause.

61 Of course, it is also blind to religions that are not Bible adherents, but that is another matter.

62 B. Elshtain, 'State imposed secularism as a potential pitfall of liberal democracy', Conference on religious liberty and the ideology of the state, Prague, 2000, available at http://www.becketfund.org/other/Prague2000/Elshtainpaper.html (accessed 8 December 2009) citing McConnell. See also: M. W. McConnell, 'The origins and historical understanding of free exercise of religion', *Harvard Law Review* 103, 1990, 1409, 1430–1436. McConnell shows that Locke's writing was the intellectual basis for the constitutional framing of religious freedom in the USA, but the Americans importantly departed from his views. Locke did not object to religious patronage, while the Americans finally prohibited establishment of religion, and Locke gave the magistrate (the secular power) the supremacy in conflict with individual religious conscience, making the limits of religious freedom subject to the government's perception, while American jurisprudence adopted constitutional judicial review over legislation, thereby denying government the last word over permissible limitation of this freedom.

63 J. J. Rousseau, *The social contract*, Harmondsworth: Penguin Books, 1968, Book II, Chapter XI.

64 For a Kantian analysis of equal political liberties compare: J. Habermas, *[Between facts and norms]: contributions to a discourse theory of law and democracy*, Oxford: Polity, 1996, 120–122.

65 See discussion in: J. Hampton, *Political philosophy*, Boulder, CO: Westview Press, 1997, 153–159.

66 R. Dworkin, 'Liberalism', in S. Hampshire (ed.), *Public and private morality*, Cambridge: Cambridge University Press, 1978, 113, 128–141.

67 J. Rawls, *A theory of justice*, 2nd edn, Belknap, Cambridge, MA: Harvard University Press, 1999, 53.

68 J. Rawls, *Political liberalism*, New York: Columbia University Press, 1993, 221, fn. 8.

69 An 'external preference' in Dworkin's terms. R. Dworkin, 'Liberalism', in S. Hampshire (ed.), *Public and private morality*, Cambridge: Cambridge University Press, 1978, 113, 133–134, limits legitimate political decisions to those that reflect some accommodation of the personal preferences of everyone for themselves, but not what he terms 'external preferences' – preferences people have about what others shall do or have.

70 B. Barry, *Liberty and justice*, Oxford: Clarendon, 1990, 34.

71 J. Rawls, *Political liberalism*, New York: Columbia University Press, 1993, especially 195–200.

72 J. Gray, *The two faces of liberalism*, Cambridge: Polity, 2000, Chapter 1.

73 V. Haksar, *Equality, liberty and perfectionism*, Oxford: Oxford University Press, 1979, 7.

74 For anti-perfectionist analysis, see also J. Raz, *The morality of freedom*, Oxford: Clarendon, 1988, 107–165.

75 B. Elshtain, 'State imposed secularism as a potential pitfall of liberal democracy', Conference on religious liberty and the ideology of the state, Prague, 2000, available at http://www.becketfund.org/other/Prague2000/Elshtainpaper.html (accessed 8 December 2009).

76 B. A. Ackerman, *Social justice in the liberal state*, London: Yale University Press, 1980, 12–15.

77 Such as: *Lemon v. Kurtzman*, 403 US 602 (1971) and its progeny; *Wisconsin v. Yoder*, 406 US 205 (1972); *Lynch v. Donnely*, 465 US 668 (1984).

78 B. Barry, *Liberty and justice*, Oxford: Clarendon, 1990, 29.

79 For the other major exponent of libertarian theory and critic of welfare liberalism, see F. A. Hayek, *The constitution of liberty*, London: Routledge & Kegan Paul, 1960.

80 R. Nozick, *Anarchy, state, and utopia*, Oxford: Blackwell, 1974, 320.

81 Ibid.

82 J. Gray, *The two faces of liberalism*, Cambridge: Polity, 2000, Chapter 1.

83 J. Waldron, 'Inalienable rights', *Boston Review*, 24, 1999, available at http:// bostonreview.net/BR24.2/Waldron.html (last accessed 8 December 2009).

84 Of course, often the individual reason and the social reason were both argued, as by 17th-century writer Pierre Bayle, in his *Philosophical commentary on the words of Jesus Christ, 'Compel them to come in'*, reprinted in I. Kramnick (ed.), *The portable Enlightenment*, New York: Penguin, 1995, 75, 79.

85 J. J. Rousseau, *The social contract*, Harmondsworth: Penguin Books, 1968, Book IV, Chapter 8, 178.

86 J. Stout, *The flight from authority: religion, morality, and the quest for autonomy*, Notre Dame: University of Notre Dame Press, 1981, 235.

87 J. Gray, *The two faces of liberalism*, Cambridge: Polity, 2000, 2–3.

88 C. Evans, *Freedom of religion under the European Convention on Human Rights*, Oxford: Oxford University Press, 2001, 22. P. King, *Toleration*, London: Allen & Unwin, 1976, 13 ff., suggested a distinction between tolerance and toleration. Tolerance is practised when one objects to something but voluntarily endures it, while toleration is defined as the negation of intolerance, which can include both mere endurance and positive support. While other writers have used these terms interchangeably, it is useful to note the two separate meanings of these terms.

89 J. Raz, *The morality of freedom*, Oxford: Clarendon, 1988, 401–407.

90 C. Evans, *Freedom of religion under the European Convention on Human Rights*, Oxford: Oxford University Press, 2001, 23.

91 T. Paine, *The rights of man, Part I*, in *Thomas Paine – political writings*, B. Kuklick (ed.), Cambridge: Cambridge University Press, 1989, 102.

92 For a communitarian theory overview, see A. Gutmann, 'Communitarian critics of liberalism', *Philosophy and Public Affairs*, 14, 1985, 308.

93 N. Glaser, 'Individual rights against group rights', in W. Kymlicka (ed.), *The rights of minority cultures*, Oxford: Oxford University Press, 1995, 123, 126.

94 C. Taylor, 'Religion in a free society', in J. D. Hunter and O. Guinness (eds), *Articles of faith, articles of peace*, Washington: The Brookings Institution, 1990, 93.

95 M. Sandel, *Liberalism and the limits of justice*, Cambridge: Cambridge University Press, 1998, especially 7–14, 62, 133–135.

96 For the development of the concept of identity, see C. Taylor, *The sources of the self: the making of modern identity*, Cambridge: Cambridge University Press, 1989; for development of the politics of identity, see C. Taylor, 'Multiculturalism: examining the politics of recognition', in A. Gutmann (ed.), *Multiculturalism*, Princeton: Princeton University Press, 1994, 25.

97 A. MacIntyre, *After virtue*, 2nd edn, Notre Dame: University of Notre Dame Press, 1984, 33–35.

98 E. Frazer and N. Lacey, *The politics of community: a feminist critique of the liberal-communitarian debate*, Hemel Hempstead: Harvester-Wheatsheaf, 1993, 158.

99 M. Sandel, 'Freedom of conscience or freedom of choice', in J. Hunter and O. Guinness (eds), *Articles of faith, articles of peace*, Washington: Brookings Institute, 1990, 74.

100 See J. S. Grotstein and D. B. Rinsley (eds), *Fairbairn and the origins of object relations*, New York: Guilford Press, 1994.

101 L. Gomez, *An introduction to object relations*, London: Free Association Books, 1997; and see E. Frazer and N. Lacey, *The politics of community: a feminist critique of the liberal-communitarian debate*, Hemel Hempstead: Harvester-Wheatsheaf, 1993, 174–175. Psychologists note that in non-Western cultures the self is viewed not as self-sufficient and autonomous. A. Roland, *In search of self in India and Japan: towards a cross-cultural psychology*, Princeton: Princeton University Press, 1988, refers to 'we-self', a concept of personal identity that includes the encircling group.

102 W. Kymlicka, *Liberalism, community and culture*, Oxford: Oxford University Press, 1989, Chapters 8, 9, p. 162 ff.

103 I use Parekh as a representative of multicultural thinkers. For other writers on multiculturalism, see A. Gutmann (ed.), *Multiculturalism*, Princeton: Princeton University Press, 1994 and C. Willet, *Theorising multiculturalism: a guide to the current debate*, Oxford: Blackwell, 1998.

104 B. Parekh, 'Equality in a multicultural society', in J. Franklin (ed.), *Equality*, London: Institute for Public Policy Research, 1997, 120, 142–143.

105 UK Court of Appeals decision: *Ahmed v. ILEA* [1978] QB 36, 1 All ER 574, CA; European Court decision: *Ahmed v. UK* (1982) 4 EHRR 126 ECtHR. See case analysis also in A. Clapham, *Human rights in the private sphere*, Oxford: Clarendon Press, 1993, 14–15, 316.

106 Compare: B. Parekh, 'Equality in a multicultural society', in J. Franklin (ed.), *Equality*, London: Institute for Public Policy Research, 1997, 120, 123.

107 For a similar case regarding a Sabbatarian Christian employee, see the European Commission's decision in *Stedman v. UK* [1997] 23 EHRR CD 168 EComHR. See now *Copsey v. WWB Devon Clays Ltd* [2005] EWCA Civ 932; [2005] IRLR 811. Mummery LJ took the extreme position that 'as far as working hours are concerned, an employer is entitled to keep the workplace secular'. In such cases, an employee is not in general entitled to complain that there has been a material interference with his Article 9 rights. Rix LJ, however, noted that the Commission in *Ahmed* emphasized the lengths to which the school had gone before declining to accommodate Ahmed's request, leading him to a more nuanced position on employers' obligations towards religious workers.

108 B. Parekh, *Rethinking multiculturalism: cultural diversity and political theory*, Basingstoke: Palgrave, 2000, 216.

109 In the previous examples, the Church is even given powers in the Hohfeldian sense (a right conferred by law to alter the legal relations of others). See P. J. Fitzgerald, *Salmond on jurisprudence*, 7th edn, London: Sweet & Maxwell, 1966, 228–229.

110 See, further, Chapters 3 and 4.

111 W. Kymlicka, *Multicultural citizenship: a liberal theory of minority rights*, Oxford: Clarendon Press, 1995, 165.

112 F. Tesón, 'The Kantian theory on international law', *Columbia Law Review*, 92, 1992, 53, 62–66.

113 F. M. Gedicks, 'Towards a constitutional jurisprudence of group rights', *Wisconsin Law Review* 99, 1998 159.

114 J. Gray, *Liberalism*, 2nd edn, Bristol: Open University Press, 1995, 59.

115 J. Newman, *On religious freedom*, Ottawa: University of Ottawa Press, 1991, 153.

116 T. G. Sanders, *Protestant concepts of Church and state – historical backgrounds and approaches for the future*, New York: Holt, Rinehart & Winston, 1964, 12.

117 J. Newman, *On religious freedom*, Ottawa: University of Ottawa Press, 1991, 107 ff.

118 F. Mernissi, *Women and Islam*, Oxford: Basil Blackwell, 1991, 20.

119 Report of the UN Special Rapporteur on Religious Intolerance, E/CN.4/1993/62, p. 85. See D. Shelton and A. Kiss, 'A draft model law on freedom of religion, with commentary', in J. D. van der Vyver and J. Witte Jr., *Religious human rights in global perspective Vol. II – Legal perspectives*, The Hague: Martinus Nijhoff Publishers, 1996, 559.

120 L. W. Beer (ed.), *Constitutional systems in late twentieth century Asia*, Seattle: Washington University Press, 1992, 17–18.

121 D. Forfar, 'Individuals against the state? The politics of opposition to the re-emergence of State Shinto', in I. Neary et al. (eds), *Case studies on human rights in Japan*, Surrey: Japan Library, 1996, 245.

122 M. Abe, 'The Buddhist view of human rights', in A. An-Na'im (ed.), *Human rights and religious values: an uneasy relationship?*, Amsterdam: Rodopi, 1995, 143.

123 C. van der Burg, 'Traditional Hindu values and human rights', in A. An-Na'im (ed.), *Human rights and religious values: an uneasy relationship?*, Amsterdam: Rodopi, 1995, 109, 110.

124 P. J. Weithman, 'Religious reasons and the duties of membership', *Wake Forest Law Review*, 36, 2001, 511.

125 J. Rawls, *Political liberalism*, New York: Columbia University Press, 1993, Chapter VI, changing his stand in J. Rawls, *A theory of justice*, 2nd edn, Belknap, Cambridge, MA: Harvard University Press, 1999.

126 K. Greenawalt, *Religious convictions and political choice*, New York: Oxford University Press, 1988.

127 But see also K. Greenawalt, *Private consciences and public reasons*, New York: Oxford University Press, 1995.

128 R. Audi, 'The separation of Church and state and the obligations of citizenship', *Philosophy and Public Affairs*, 1989, 259.

129 K. Greenawalt, 'Religion and American political judgement', *Wake Forest Law Review*, 36, 2001, 401.

130 P. J. Weithman, 'The separation of Church and state: Some questions for Prof. Audi', *Philosophy and Public Affairs*, 1991, 52.

131 Examples certainly abound, such as a recent call by bishops of the Church of England on the UK government for stricter regulation of arms exports to the third world. See G. H. Baldwin, 'Clergy lead attack on weapons export bill', *The Times*, 4 February 2002.

132 Such as the successful campaign by the Catholic Church in Portugal against liberalization of the law criminalizing abortion, in a 1998 referendum (G. Tremlett, 'Poverty, ignorance and why 17 women face jail for abortion', *The Guardian*, 18 January 2000).

133 The Internal Revenue Code 1986, Section 501(c)(3).

134 K. Greenawalt, 'Religion and American political judgement', *Wake Forest Law Review*, 36, 2001.

135 M. J. Perry, *Religion in politics: constitutional and moral perspectives*, Oxford: Oxford University Press, 1997, 3.

136 Ibid., at 664, fn. 2.

137 Such as Soka Gahkai in Japan (P. Arvin, *Buddhist politics: Japan's clean government party*, The Hague: Martinus Nijhoff Publishers, 1971).

138 See also J. Waldron, 'Judges as moral reasoners', *International Journal of Constitutional Law*, 7(1), 2009, 2–24; W. Sadurski, 'Rights and moral reasoning: an unstated assumption – a comment on Jeremy Waldron's "Judges as moral reasoners"', *International Journal of Constitutional Law*, 7(1), 2009, 25–45; and G. Beck, 'Human rights adjudication under the ECHR between value pluralism and essential contestability', *European Human Rights Law Review*, 2008 (2), 214–244.

139 Such an issue was raised in the UK case *McClintock v Department of Constitutional Affairs* [2008] IRLR 29. A magistrate's claim that his Article 9 right to freedom of religion was breached by the change in law, which meant that he would have to consider cases placing children with same-sex parents, was dismissed.

140 CNN, 'Scalia questions Catholic anti-death penalty stance', 5 February 2002.

141 This will be discussed in Chapter 4. See also G. Whyte, 'Some reflections on the role of religion in the constitutional order', in T. Murphy and P. Twomey (eds), *Ireland's evolving constitution: 1927–1997*, Oxford: Hart, 1998, 51. For a historical summary of events leading to Ireland's constitutional change allowing the Divorce Bill, see T. Barnes, 'Ireland's Divorce Bill: Traditional Irish and international norms of equality and bodily integrity at issue in a domestic abuse context', *Vanderbilt Journal of Transnational Law*, 31, 1998, 617.

142 Indeed, in the US Supreme Court Justice Stevens argued that religiously based premises about the value of life are illegitimate basis for such legislation (*Webster v. Reproductive Health Services* 492 US 490 (1989)).

143 See Y. Stavrakakis, 'Religion and populism: reflection on the "politicised" discourse of the Greek Church', Discussion Paper No. 7, May 2002, The Hellenic Observatory, The European Institute, The London School of Economics, available at http://www.lse.ac.uk/collections/hellenicObservatory/pdf/StavrakakisDiscussionPaper.pdf (accessed 8 December 2009).

144 The tacit assumptions concerning such religious involvement are rarely questioned in international law literature. Exceptionally see J. A. Coons, 'Book review: *Freedom of religion: a world report Ed. K. Boyle and J. Sheen*', *The American Journal of Comparative Law* 49, 2001, 161.

145 Compare M. J. Perry, 'Why political reliance on religiously grounded morality does not violate the Establishment Clause', *William and Mary Law Review*, 42, 2001, 663, 672.

146 G. H. Fox and G. Nolte, 'Intolerant democracies', in R. B. Roth and G. H. Fox (eds), *Democratic governance and international law*, Cambridge: Cambridge University Press, 2000, 393, 445.

147 Fox and Nolte, 'Intolerant democracies', in R. B. Roth and G. H. Fox (eds), *Democratic governance and international law*, Cambridge: Cambridge University Press, 2000, 393, 389–435, especially 396.

148 Comm. No. 117/1981, *M. A. v. Italy*, CCPR/C/OP/31,33 /1984.

149 Concerning the similar Article 17 of the European Convention on Human Rights, *De Becker v. Belgium* (1979–80) 1 EHRR 43 ECtHR. See also *Lawless Case v. Ireland (Merits)* 1 EHRR 15 ECtHR. See discussion in G. H. Fox and G. Nolte, 'Intolerant democracies', *Harvard International Law Journal*, 36, 1995, 41.

150 G.H. Fox and G. Nolte, 'Intolerant democracies', *Harvard International Law Journal*, 36, 1995, 41.

151 D. A. Dombrowski, *Rawls and religion: the case for political liberalism*, Albany: State University of New York Press, 2001, 103.

152 J. Rawls, *A theory of justice*, 2nd edn, Belknap, Cambridge, MA: Harvard University Press, 1999, 219.

3 Legal status of religion in the state

This chapter examines the implications of the legal status of religions in the state for the determination of how religious freedom should be interpreted. First, the different legal arrangements of the status of religion in the state will be distinguished, and then I argue that, regardless of the position adopted, religious freedom must be accorded as an individual right. This analysis should guide the interpretation of this right in international law.

The status of religion in the state, the degree of state involvement with religion and regulation of religion, are relevant not only to the degree of religious freedom, but also to its interpretation, whether as a group right or an individual right. Whatever legal status the state accords to religion, including according it no formal legal status (which is also a type of legal status), it must make choices between according this right to individuals, to groups or to subgroups. The state cannot escape from being entangled in deciding whether religious freedom is an individual right or a group right, whether religious groups themselves must respect religious freedoms and how groups, their members and their leadership are defined for state legal purposes. Thus, while freedom of religion is generally defined as a negative right – the state must not inhibit free religious belief and practice – we will see that what this right entails for the state is far more complex. In many cases positive involvement of the state is required to provide rights that are an integral part of religious freedom. While it can do so in different ways, the only principled way to do so is by interpreting them as individual rights.

PART A: LEGAL STATUS OF RELIGION IN THE STATE

There is an important relation between the stance of the state towards religion and the degree of religious freedom in the state. However, this is not a simple relation. States that are most closely identified with one religion may inhibit religious freedom, as may states that, at the other extreme, are hostile to religion.[1]

At one extreme, that of identification between state and religion, are states with an established religion.[2] Even these differ considerably. States in which religious doctrine, as such, is the law of the state, *because* it is religious doctrine,[3] or in which the law is subject to religious confirmation, such as Iran,[4] breach the right to religious freedom of those citizens who do not believe in the state religion or do not accept its doctrine.

Other states with a state religion, but with secular system of law, breach human rights obligations when religious dictates permeate state legislation. For instance, in Nepal, where Hinduism is the established religion,[5] the law discriminates against women by utilizing Hindu concepts about women's property rights in marriage.[6] It is not the establishment of religion as such, but the *influence of the established religion on positive law* that is in breach of international human rights obligations, specifically, in this case, that of non-discrimination on the grounds of sex.[7]

Establishment of religion exists in many liberal democracies, such as the UK,[8] which, while following the premise of religious freedom, have not accepted the correlative premise of Enlightenment liberalism of separation of church and state.[9] Unquestionably, the historical position of the Church of England as a state-church has given an advantage to the Anglican faith over other creeds.[10] Strictly speaking, an advantage given to one faith, the state-church, constitutes discrimination against other faiths. Undoubtedly, a state-race would not be permissible under international law. However, the religious and historical underpinnings of national identity[11] may permit a certain divergence from institutional equality between religions, even though, inevitably, the national religion will not be that of all the state's citizens.

The UN Human Rights Conventions and the 1981 Declaration are silent on the subject of what is a permissible status of religion in the state.[12] The 1967 Draft Convention on the Elimination of All Forms of Religious Intolerance[13] included in Article 1(d) the statement that 'neither the establishment of a religion nor the recognition of a religion or belief by a state nor the separation of Church from State shall by itself be considered religious intolerance or discrimination.' The Convention was never adopted, and the 1981 Declaration does not refer to this matter. The UN Human Rights Committee (in its General Comment to Article 18 of the ICCPR)[14] has not seen establishment of religion of itself as an infringement of religious freedom.[15] Likewise, the Special Rapporteur on Freedom of Religion or Belief has not seen establishment of religion in itself as breach religious freedoms.[16] The European Court has also not seen a state-church system in itself as breaching the state's duty to observe religious freedom.[17] Morsink,[18] however, argues that the Universal Declaration does not allow for state-sponsored religion. He bases his assertion on the freedom of religion and non-discrimination provisions of the UDHR, together with the purposeful omission of any reference to God in the Declaration, at the insistence of the French delegate René Cassin. This last opinion seems, however, to be against what little legal opinion of UN bodies exists on this matter, and contrary to state practice.

However, a danger in the acceptance in international law of the state-church status, is that the favoured status it confers on one religion will be seen as the starting point of the examination of religious freedom, rather than as an arrangement whose implications must themselves be scrutinized as to their compatibility with the principles of religious freedom and non-discrimination. This danger can be seen in a decision of the Human Rights Committee [HRC] on a communication by a teacher of religions and ethics at a public secondary school in Colombia.[19] He was removed from teaching religion because he followed 'liberation theology', which advocates views different from those of the institutional Catholic Church. The Committee decided that the teacher's right to profess or to manifest his religion had not been violated, and that Colombia may, without violating Article 18 of the ICPPR, allow the Church authorities to decide who may teach religion and in what manner it may be taught. Neither did the Committee think this violated Article 19. It said that Article 19 will usually cover the freedom of teachers to teach their subjects in accordance with their own views, without interference. But, in this case, it reasoned, because of the special relationship between Church and state in Colombia, exemplified by the applicable Concordat, the requirement by the Church that religion be taught in a certain way did not violate Article 19.

This seems an ominous precedent for the legal appraisal of the relationship between individual religious freedom and the state's established Church. An established Church is always at tension with individual religious freedoms. If an established religion is to be legitimate, it can only be so as long as it does not infringe individual rights, including individual religious freedom. In this case, the implication of the establishment of church is that only one religion is taught in public secondary schools and only teachers subscribing to that religion, and to its official interpretation by the state-church, may teach it. This breaches the religious freedom of both students and teachers. Had this been a private school of a religious community, there would be no difficulty with a policy requiring teachers of religion to conform to Church doctrine. However, the privileged position of one Church, giving it access to state secondary education, must not be used to infringe the rights of individual students and teachers.

The HRC itself revealed a different and preferable approach in its Concluding Observations on the Costa Rica state report.[20] It expressed concern that Costa Rican law (the Ley de Carrera Docente) confers on the National Episcopal Conference the power to impede the teaching of religions other than Catholicism in public schools and the power to bar non-Catholics from teaching religion in public schools. It concluded that the selection of religious instructors subject to the authorization of the National Episcopal Conference was not in conformity with the Covenant.

Indeed, the Human Rights Committee followed this reasoning in *Waldman v. Canada*,[21] a decision in which it rejected the state's argument that the privileged treatment of a religion (a Catholic school) was not discriminatory because it was a constitutional obligation.

One way in which states discriminate in favour of the established religion, is by supporting it, but not other religions, with state funding obtained through compulsory taxation. The conformity of this practice with individual religious freedom under the European Convention on Human Rights was challenged in *Darby*,[22] but was left undecided, as the Court found a breach of the Convention on other grounds. The existence of a privileged status of a state-church in itself has not yet been challenged under the European Convention. However, the European Court has decided there was unlawful discrimination, where a religious association was not accorded legal personality in public law, which would enable it to pursue legal action in courts, whereas other religions had such status.[23] In this case, the discrimination of the applicant Catholic Church was in relation both to the state religion (Greek Orthodox) and another religion (Judaism). There appears to be an incongruity between this determination and the implicit acceptance of the legitimacy of a state established religion by the European Court and Commission so far.[24] One religion may be given a privileged status, but more than one religion may not. It remains to be seen if the Court would entertain such a claim of discrimination, where the only privileged religion was the state religion, or if it would decide that some degree of discrimination between religious organizations was justified in states that have a state-church because of the historical significance of the Church to the state.

Between establishment and non-establishment of religion there is a continuum of legal arrangements.[25] A process of disestablishment of religion in the state, which nonetheless left an important constitutional role for the Catholic Church was instituted in formerly Catholic states by Concordats.[26] Concordats between states and the Holy See defined the status of the Catholic Church in the state, without preserving it as the state religion. It was often a pre-requisite for a transition to a civil constitution, disentangling the state from the church, fully or partially, as in Spain,[27] Italy[28] and South American states such as Peru.[29] Italy and Spain have also domestic agreements with other religious communities.[30] However, under this system, the legal status of all religions is not equal. In Spain, the Constitution was framed concomitantly with the conclusion of the Concordat. The Concordat will have great influence on constitutional interpretation, while the other agreements will not. Likewise the Lateran Pacts have a superior constitutional status to that of other agreements with religious communities in Italy.[31] The Concordats, as international agreements between two equal partners, put the Catholic Church in a privileged extra-constitutional position. Indeed, the Italian Constitutional Court upheld the disparity in treatment between Catholicism and other religions, because Catholicism is the religion of nearly the entire Italian population.[32]

Not only in these cases, but generally, states that grant religious rights by agreements with religious communities leave members of other, usually smaller, religions, having no such agreements, in an unequal position.[33]

Such processes of lessening of identification between church and state have occurred in other, non-Catholic states as well. The 1975 Greek Constitution[34] recognizes the Orthodox Church of Greece as the national religion of Greece. State structure, however, has become more secular, with recognition accorded to civil marriages in 1982 despite church opposition.[35]

At the other end of the spectrum of identification between state and religion from that of states with an established religion are states which espouse a principle of secularity.[36] Like establishment of religion, secularity translates into a variety of different stances of states towards religion, resulting in different degrees of respect for religious freedom. In its extreme, a principle of secularity seeks to privatize religion and remove it from the public sphere. As will be seen, by doing so it infringes religious freedom. This type of secularity in its extreme is a very individualistic conception of religious freedom, which delegitimizes any involvement of religion in public life. As such, it is hard to reconcile with any comprehensive notion of religious freedom. Even an individualistic notion of religious freedom must accept some involvement of religion in public life. The right of religious freedom includes the possibility of using religious conviction to influence the policy of the state.[37] Secularity means different things in different states spreading over a range of positions towards religion in the state, both formal and informal.

i Hostility

A hostile legal stance towards religion was evident in state constitutions in regimes that were trying to emerge from Catholic political hold. This hostile attitude has been now eradicated from the constitution and laws in these states. For instance, the 1931 Spanish Republican Constitution attempted to neutralize the competing power of religion, by dissolving religious orders (specifically, the Jesuits) that require a 'special vow of obedience to any power other than the state'.[38] It attempted to privatize religion, guaranteeing freedom of conscience to profess and practice any religion,[39] but allowing only private worship, and limiting public worship to that authorized by the state. Any form of state aid to religious bodies was disallowed. The reinstatement of Catholicism as state religion by Franco after the 1936 Civil War helped the regime take hold, as much as it helped the Church itself, attesting to the power of religion when used by the state.[40] It was finally the Vatican, and not the state that pushed for recognition of religious freedom in Spain,[41] commensurate with recognition of Church autonomy.[42] Today, Spain has struck a balance between secularity and establishment of the Catholic religion.[43]

Comparable developments in which states used their constitutions to neutralize the influence of the Catholic Church on the state occurred in Latin America. The Mexican Revolutions of 1910 and 1917 sought to oust religion from public life completely by a series of constitutional measures severely restricting all public manifestations of religion.[44] What is remarkable is not so much the restriction on religious freedom for an ostensibly liberal regime, but that a principle of individual religious freedom[45] was coupled with extreme displacement of religion from the public realm. The Mexican Constitutional amendment of 1992 rescinded many of the restrictions on the public aspects of religious life.[46] Some restrictions remain: Religious ministers are not allowed to hold public office within several years of leaving the ministry[47] and religious groups are not permitted to form political parties or associations with political goals. This is still an extreme privatization of religion, and exclusion of religion from political life.[48, 49]

ii Exclusion

Turkey, one of only few predominantly Muslim states described as secularist in their Constitution,[50] faces an ongoing struggle in which religion challenges the authority of the secular state.[51] In Turkey, the constitutional principle of secularism forbids the legal order of the state to be based on religious precepts,[52] effectively excluding religion from political public life, but generally not forbidding private or public manifestations of religion.

However, Turkey's constitutional principle of secularism entails a demand of loyalty from public servants, such as the military,[53] to this principle. The European Court accepted a state principle of secularism, in itself, as a sufficient reason for restricting religious freedom.[54] It would seem, rather, that because this principle restricts religious freedom, it should be subjected to scrutiny under Article 9(2) of the European Convention. A law that demands loyalty of public servants to one attitude towards religion should be presumed to breach religious freedom, unless it can be shown why such a demand would be justified in a particular case.

The principle of secularity itself did come under scrutiny in the European Court decisions in the case of *Refah Partisi*.[55] The European Court was called upon to examine the order of the Turkish Constitutional Court, which, in 1998, dissolved the Refah political party,[56] on the ground that it had become a 'centre of activities contrary to the principle of secularism'. On application to the European Court, both the Chamber of the 3rd section and the Grand Chamber, to which the judgment was referred, did not find a breach of Article 11 of the Convention (freedom of association), and saw no further issues arising under Article 9. The underlying issue in the case was that of the legitimate place of religion in the public life of the state. The Turkish government argued that the party in question, and political Islam, did not confine itself to the private sphere of relations between the individual and God but also asserted its right to organize the state and the community, posing a potential danger for Turkish democracy. The European Court rejected the application, finding that the measures imposed by the state met a 'pressing social need'. The Grand Chamber affirmed the decision, based on Refah's intention of setting up a plurality of legal systems and introducing Islamic law (*shari'a*), and its ambiguous stance with regard to the use of force to gain power and retain it. The Grand Chamber found that the state may forestall such a policy, which is incompatible with the Convention's provisions, before concrete steps are taken to implement it that might prejudice civil peace and the country's democratic regime.[57]

While not going so far as to legitimize banning a party, which, if it implemented its goals, would breach human rights guaranteed in the Convention, the Grand Chamber nevertheless mentions Refah's plans, which would breach religious freedoms, as legitimate reasons for curtailment of its rights.[58] This reasoning puts religious political parties in peril, insofar as a certain severity of breaches of human rights would be tantamount to undermining the democratic regime.

iii Neutrality

Neutral states are those espousing secularity which are neutral, rather than hostile, towards religion. As has been seen, even states that have an established religion may be neutral between religions and beliefs in other respects. But a secular state may, of course, claim to espouse a more consistent principle of neutrality. However, neutrality towards religion is manifested differently in different legal systems, for example in the attitude to state funding of religion, as will be seen in four examples from the range of different state interpretations of the principle of separation of religion and state.

France is defined in its constitution as a secular republic.[59] However, because of the historical position of religion (Catholicism) in the state, its principle of *laïcité*, which is ostensibly neutral, can work to the detriment of minority or newly introduced religions. French law prohibits government funding of religious bodies, but still allows public funds to maintain Roman Catholic churches built before 1905 (which were transferred to the ownership of the state).[60] This law prejudicially harms worshippers of religions mostly newer to France, such as Muslims,[61] as mosques are not provided for. The choice of a state to become completely neutral is not necessarily egalitarian. A "hands-off" approach to religion, coming after a historical association with one religion, gives an advantage to well-established religions, which have benefited from state endorsement in the past.

A second interpretation of neutrality and constitutional separation of religion from the state, with no such historical burden, is enshrined in the Constitution of the United States,[62] in two clauses of the First Amendment to the Constitution, the free exercise clause, which guarantees free exercise of religion,[63] and the establishment clause, which forbids establishment religion.[64] The tension between the two clauses has formed the backbone of religious freedom jurisprudence in the USA.[65] This tension is manifested in the long and tortuous line of Supreme Court cases regarding funding of religious bodies.[66] Under the US principle of separation of state and church, no funding of religious bodies is permitted. But under the free exercise clause, religious belief cannot be burdened more than non-religious belief. Thus, while it is clear that purely religious activities cannot be funded, much legal wrangling has defined the permissible line regarding funding of activities in parochial schools,[67] student newsletters,[68] and other activities that have a secular parallel.

As will be seen in this chapter, the principle of separation of religion from the state has resulted not in an absence of a constitutional status of religion, but rather in a legal determination that both preserves group autonomy at the expense of individual rights and does not take enough account of the different positions of members of majority and minority religions.

In Japan, the constitutional text requiring separation of state and religion is derived from, and similar to, that of the United States. However, since the cultural setting is different, the involvement of religion in public life is also very different. The principle of separation of religion and state and the abolition of the established status of Shinto shrines were incorporated into the 1947 Japanese Constitution at the behest of the American Occupying force, who wished to end the identification of the emperor as a god and the role of the Shinto religion as an ideology that underscores strong nationalism and statism.[69]

The Constitution prohibits any religious organization from receiving any privileges from the state,[70] prohibits the state from participating in any religious activity,[71] and mandates that the state budget remain strictly secular.[72] However, Japanese tradition has meant that the Shinto religion continues to play a role in the state.[73] The Supreme Court saw the separation of religion from state provision of Article 20 as an indirect guarantee of religious freedom, rather than an independent principle. Therefore it was interpreted as unlawful, at least in petitions of individual persons, only if the activity directly infringes on their religious freedom by imposing restriction on their exercise of religious freedom or by compelling them to attend religious activities.[74] Thus, deification of a veteran by the veteran's association, despite his widow's objection, was not considered a breach of religious freedom.[75] The majority of the Japanese Supreme Court considered the absolute separation principle of Article 20 an ideal which is impossible to achieve in a real social context, leaving a margin of permitted state funding for socio-cultural activities conducted by religious bodies[76] including certain religious ceremonies deemed to have a social rather than religious role.[77]

In recent decisions *Kohno v. Hiramatsu* and *Higo v. Tsuchiya*,[78] in which the Japanese Supreme Court ruled in favour of governmental involvement with Shinto and rejected the constitutional attack on attendance by municipal governors at *Daijosai*, a Shinto ceremony traditionally held when a new emperor succeeds to the throne.

In Germany, in yet a further interpretation of neutrality, the Basic Law bars the establishment of a state-church.[79] But a principle of coordination, rather than separation, is upheld.[80] Religions can be aided by state funding, as long as this funding is equitable. However, only religions that are recognized in public law can benefit from tax funding.[81] While avoiding the pitfalls associated with the US principle of separation, this system itself jeopardizes state neutrality. It involves the state in deciding upon the definition of religions; it is discriminatory toward those religions, especially new religions, which have not yet been able to achieve recognition in public law; and it may involve the state in deciding which groups claiming to represent the same religion should be acknowledged, as will be seen in the discussion later.[82]

The European Court had previously avoided ruling on the question whether Article 9 mandates neutrality of the state in all religious matters. In fact, as seen, many of the member states of the European Convention are identified with a religion in varying degrees. However, recently, in *Lautsi v. Italy*[83] the Court squarely based its decision that display of crucifixes in public schools is in violation of Article 9 on the principle of neutrality. The Court determined that the state must be religiously neutral in public spaces. The decision stressed that freedom not to hold a religious belief means not just freedom not to be compelled to participate in religious practice, but also be free from religious symbols and practices in public places that they could not reasonably avoid.

This acceptance of the Court that the principle of religious neutrality of the state is inherent in Article 9 could have far-reaching ramifications. The same principle could apply to displays of religion in courtrooms, voting stations and government buildings.

A forerunner of this decision is *Buscarini v. San Marino*[84], in which the Court referred to a principle of neutrality, as a basis for its decision that a demand that members of parliament take an oath on the Bible is a breach of Article 9. The *Lautsi* decision, however, is potentially much more far reaching. *Buscarini* demands that the state be neutral within its governing institutions. *Lautsi* demands that the state be neutral in its public *fora* (at least those dedicated to education of children, but the rationale of the decision could apply to all *fora* dedicated to public activities).

While it may be initially thought that the secular state, which is not involved with religion or which relegates religion to the private sphere, could guarantee freedom of religion while evading the need to decide to whom these rights belong, whether individuals or communities, this is clearly not the case. Secular states, just as states in which one or more religions are given a constitutional or legal status, need to make decisions about allocation of religious rights (religious freedom and religious equality). Against this background, I argue that the interpretation of religious freedom must be as an individual right. Community rights may be derived from the individual right, but they may not override it.

PART B: RELIGIOUS FREEDOM SHOULD BE AN INDIVIDUAL RIGHT IN PREFERENCE TO A GROUP RIGHT

Within the context of the various existing legal arrangements of religion in the state, four main arguments will be advanced in this chapter as to why religious freedom should be interpreted as an individual right, in preference to a group right:

1   Religions have a public or semi-public character and so must accord individual rights. This is so especially regarding state established religions, but also, in a lesser measure, regarding all religions.
2   The right of members and workers of religious organizations to belong to the religious community and participate in its activities does not mean they must shed their rights at the door.
3   According rights to groups inevitably involves the state in defining religious groups, thus breaching state neutrality in matters of religion.
4   Jurisdiction cannot be accorded to a religious community that does not respect individual rights, as some members may not have a real choice whether to belong to it. Even where there is a choice, the state should not allow individuals to waive rights of religious freedom to their communities.

I then proceed to argue that:

5   An individual conception of religious freedom should take into account the different positions of members of minorities and of majorities.
6   If religious freedom were to be recognized as a group right this would raise the further need to define group equality and to choose between individual equality and group equality.
7   States should not make value judgments of the social worthiness of religions, as this breaches state neutrality.

I pursue these arguments in the context of the different forms that state involvement (or non-involvement) with religion may take. Each argument is relevant to a different legal position of religion in different states. Several cases from different jurisdictions, which exemplify these problems, are examined. Often, these problems did not arise in discussions of international human rights law. Some issues are best illustrated by jurisprudence of the European Court of Human Rights, some arose in domestic cases in various jurisdictions, and some through examination of state constitutions, laws and agreements.

3.1 Religious institutions have a public or semi-public character and so cannot be granted rights that override individual rights

The public character of religious institutions provides a strong reason for demanding that they themselves respect individual rights, and do not benefit from a communal right to religious freedom that overrides individual rights. Where institutions belong to an established state religion, the status of the established religion and its affinity with the state make a particularly strong case for subjecting it to limitations based on individual rights of members and non-members. To a lesser extent, the argument of public character is true also for non-established religions.

As will be seen, under the European Convention, churches have rights, but actions of state-churches may also give rise to state obligations under the Convention. Some bodies of a state-church may be victims of violations under the Convention, but this does not rule out state obligations concerning other bodies or actions of state-churches. Public aspects of religious disciplinary proceedings of a state-church bear enough similarities to judicial proceedings to demand that they be subject to human rights guarantees. Internal judicial proceedings of other religions also share some of these characteristics in their implications for the individual subjected to them, but are left outside the scope of current human rights law.

Institutions of established religions, or at least some of them, can be subject to the international human rights obligations of the state, based on the claim that they are bodies of the state. Indeed, the obligation of states to ensure observance of the Convention by certain institutions of state-churches has been recognized to some extent in judicial interpretation of the European Convention, based on the role such institutions play in the administration of the state, as will be discussed later. It is possible to suggest an evaluation of the applicability of the Convention to religious institutions according to two criteria: The first is the constitutional position of the Church and its institutions, whether the Church is on a par with state authorities, giving its actions towards members and non-members the imprimatur of the state. (For example, the legislation of Measures of the General Synod of the Church of England is primary state legislation in the UK.) The second is the performance of functions of the state, or functions usually associated with the state, such as registration of marriages, undertaking burials, education and welfare functions. There is also a third consideration in attaching state responsibility to acts of state-churches, namely, that even when not directly fulfilling state functions, churches offer a comprehensive guide for peoples' lives, within an inclusive social and moral framework. This strengthens the case for including them within the state's human rights responsibilities, more than for comparable non-religious bodies that have a constitutional position or perform a state function. This third consideration, while not related to the status of the religious organization as a body of the state, is a further reason why the state should have to assure that Convention rights are respected, even within a religious organization.

In international law, there has not been recognition of a state obligation to ensure that religious organizations of non-established religions respect individual rights. However, there are reasons to favour such recognition. While the constitutional position of these religions is different from that of an established religion, non-established religions do perform both formal and informal governmental functions, such as marriage registration, burial, education and welfare care. Religious bodies to which legal state powers, such as marriage registration, are devolved, are exercising a government function and so the state should be held responsible for its compliance with the state's international human rights obligations.[85]

When to attribute responsibility to the state in international law is a difficult problem. The Articles on Responsibility of States for Internationally Wrongful Acts[86] support the above interpretation. Conduct of any organ of legislative, judicial or executive branch is considered an act of state (Article 4). So, clearly, decisions of a religious tribunal operating under law are state acts. More ambiguous is the inclusion as acts of state, in Article 5, of acts of an entity that is not a state organ but is empowered by state law to exercise governmental authority. So, for example, it would seem that registration of marriages by non-governmental religious registrars is a state act. Article 9 is even further reaching, including in the scope of act of state conduct exercised by persons in the absence of official authorities exercising governmental authority in circumstances that call for these. These could possibly include acts of religious charities, which provide basic needs that are not provided by government. When any of these breach the state's human rights obligations, the state could be responsible for contravening international law.

Other activities in which religious organizations perform functions primarily undertaken by the state, such as operating hospitals, or even schools, should also give rise to state responsibility. This was not the approach taken by the European Commission in *Rommelfanger*,[87] which viewed the Catholic hospital as a non-governmental organization not liable to obligations of the European Convention. A modification of this approach is signalled in *Costello-Roberts*,[88] in which the European Court stated that even when the state privatizes state functions, such as education, the Convention obligations remain.[89]

However, it is possible to include non-state actors that perform such functions within the scope of human rights obligations, while allowing for an interpretation of the rights within a religious organization that is different from that of rights outside.[90]

Indeed, some states, including Germany, have recognized religious organizations as public bodies, which need to respect constitutional rights just as other state bodies. In Germany, where there is no state-church, the Roman Catholic and Lutheran Churches are nevertheless public authorities subject to Article 19(4) of the German Basic Law, under which recourse to the court is granted in case of violation of rights by these authorities.

The need to assure an observance of basic human rights at least within some institutions of religious organizations is bolstered by observing that regulation of members' lives by non-established religions may be as influential and comprehensive, if not more so, than that of established religions. They may provide, in varying degrees, a personal moral and social framework and define a comprehensive community structure, which can encompass aspects from nurseries to pastoral care to the regulation of food sold to the community. Some of the examples discussed later in the chapter illustrate this.

3.1.1 Churches as bearers of rights and as bearers of obligations under the European Convention

The characterization of religious bodies as public or private has important consequences not just for their substantive rights, but also for their procedural ability to enforce these rights. The European Convention treats Churches both as rights bearers and, sometimes, as bodies with obligations under the Convention. Religious organizations are themselves able to use the European Convention to protect *their* religious freedom. They may have rights under the Convention as well as the competence to apply to the European Court to rectify such infringements.

Churches and similar organizations have been recognized by the European Commission for Human Rights as being capable of lodging applications and claiming rights in their own name. Non-governmental organizations and other groups have *locus standi* under Article 34[91] of the Convention, if a party to the Convention has violated its substantive Convention rights. Because of the nature of this right, the question addressed by the Commission was whether organizations, rather than natural persons, could claim a right to freedom of religion, conscience or belief. The Commission decided that they could do so.[92] Among the rights included in organizations' religious freedom, the European Court has acknowledged a right of religious organizations to be recognized as legal entities.[93]

It seems from the Commission's language, that it recognized Article 9 rights of organizations as aggregates of members' rights, rather than as group rights,[94] although neither the Commission nor the Court has yet had to decide on this question. While recognizing a right of a Church to organize its worship, the Commission was careful to note that the church was protected 'through the rights granted to its members'.[95] Recently the Court has accepted applications from religious organizations without question, but nothing in the decisions or their reasoning would suggest that they are no longer seen as claiming rights on behalf of their members.[96]

Evans believes that this difference is of no importance, because a church cannot manifest its beliefs independently of the actions of its members.[97] However, as will be seen, the difference between according religious communities or institutions substantive group rights and recognizing their rights as just an aggregate of individual rights is of significant practical and theoretical importance.

The European Commission distinguished religious organizations that can be 'victims' under the Conventions from those for whose actions the state bears responsibility under it. In *Finska forsamlingen I Stockholm and Hautaniemi v. Sweden,*[98] the Church of Sweden and its parishes were deemed to have non-governmental organization status, since they were not exercising governmental powers. Therefore, they could have *locus standi* as 'victims' (under Article 25)[99] to lodge an application against the state.[100] The Commission then decided that it follows that the state cannot be held responsible for a violation of parishioners' freedom of religion as a result of the decision of the Church Assembly.

Possibly, this decision should be read as limited to doctrinal, non-governmental functions, such as, in this case, prescribing the liturgy. But there are governmental activities of some state-churches,[101] and these will be subject to Convention obligations. The Commission, following Article 25, differentiates between non-governmental organizations and those bodies for whose actions the state is liable under the Convention. It is a preferable interpretation, to differentiate according to function, and thus not to exclude bodies of the state-church, from the ambit of the Convention, but to examine the body performing the act and the nature of the act performed. State-churches conduct government functions as well as acts of merely internal significance.

Indeed, it should not be the conclusion from *Finska* that state-churches are never deemed state organizations for which the state is responsible. That would be an undesirable interpretation, which would result in lack of redress under the European Convention for individuals whose human rights were breached by a church that may possess state powers affecting individuals and whose actions may be perceived by the public as those of the state. The state-church would benefit from both the autonomy of a religious community and the power, status and resources of a state endorsed religion, with no effective guarantee of the rights of individuals and subgroups within it.

A position of the Commission that the central institutions of state-churches are subject to the obligations of the Convention is discernible elsewhere. By agreeing to examine the merit of applications of clergymen of state-churches against the church, such as in *Williamson,*[102] the Commission implicitly accepted that state-churches can be subject to the substantive Articles of the Convention.

A distinction can be made based on the role that the church is playing and the legal authority or capacity it is exercising, to decide whether or not it is exercising a governmental function of the state. A distinction based on the role of the body concerned within the church was made in the *Case of the Holy Monasteries.*[103] Greece claimed that the applicant monasteries could not be 'victims' under former Article 25 of the European Convention, by pointing to their strong connection with the state. The European Court did not accept the argument, even though the monasteries were public law entities, because their role is spiritual and they have no administrative role in the state. They thus qualify as non-governmental organizations. It is left open in the Court's decision what these governmental or administrative roles might be. In keeping with the Court's decision, these could still be interpreted broadly, to include not just central government roles but also government in its role of serving the community so as to include functions such as education and welfare.

A distinction between different church bodies as well as a distinction between different functions exercised by church bodies has been made by the UK House of Lords. Because the European Convention has been incorporated into the UK Human Rights Act, the UK courts needed to define the status of the state-church and its institutions for the purposes of the European Convention. The House of Lords decided on the applicability of the Convention's provisions to a parish council of the Church of England.[104] The Lords interpreted the UK Human Rights Act to match the interpretation of the European Court and Commission as to when the European Convention would apply to church bodies. The Church of England itself is not a legal entity, but parish councils are. According to the Human Rights Act, the Convention would apply if the parish were a 'core' public authority, which fell under Section 6(1) of the Act, or a 'hybrid' authority, exercising a public function, falling under Section 6(3) of the Act. Section 6(1) refers to 'public authority', but does not define it. The Lords, in several separate opinions,[105] characterized it by possession of powers, democratic accountability, public funding, and an obligation to act in the public interest. One of the tests used[106] was based on *Holy Monasteries* and *Finska* – whether the body was established to be part of the process of government. None of the Lords thought that the parish council is a 'core' public authority, therefore they had to decide whether the parish council was a hybrid authority exercising a public function. Parishes do exercise public functions, such as registration of marriages and burials, but, in the particular case, which dealt with repairs to the chancel, all but one of the Lords also did not think the parish council was exercising public functions of a 'hybrid' body, under section 6(3), and therefore, in this case, the Human Rights Act did not apply. Further to this analysis, it appears that the provisions of the Act, and therefore of the Convention, would apply to the exercise of other functions of a parish, and to all acts of the central bodies of the Church of England.

This is the analysis under UK law, according to which first the body concerned has to be analysed, and then, if it is a 'hybrid' case, its function in the particular case. The European Commission had only distinguished between bodies of the church for the purposes of application of Article 9. It is suggested that the UK approach be adopted under the European Convention regarding 'hybrid' church bodies, distinguishing between their governmental and non-governmental functions.

3.1.2 Church employees and internal proceedings

One of the state-like activities conducted by religious organizations is having an internal legal and judicial system. It is, of course, only state *like*: it applies only to members, and in this sense it is voluntary; generally, the 'judicial' determinations may only be recognized in law through private law arrangements. But, effectively, such 'judicial' decisions of religious bodies may determine privileges, rights and responsibilities as recognized by the community, affecting members' lives as much as state judicial decisions. Thus, there is strong reason to suggest that internal proceedings in religious organizations follow basic safeguards of fair procedure. However, it is more questionable whether international human rights law can hold states responsible for enforcing fair procedure requirements in such cases.

There are three types of internal proceeding by religious organizations: disciplinary proceedings against clergy in a state-church, disciplinary proceedings against clergy in a religious organization with no constitutional status, and other proceedings in a religious organization that determine religious rights within the religious community. States may be responsible under international human rights law for guaranteeing fair procedure in the first case. In the second and third cases, there is a strong argument for the demand of such guarantees, but there is currently no basis to claim that these exist in international law.

A case of the first type was discussed in *Tyler v. UK*.[107] An Anglican minister argued that he should be guaranteed rights of fair procedure, according to Article 6 of the European Convention, in disciplinary proceedings against him in the ecclesiastical courts.[108] The UK government argued that his function was in a nature of a public service, rather than a private professional service, and so the proceedings were not a determination of his 'civil rights' within the meaning of Article 6(1). The Commission in *Tyler* did not rule on this argument, as it decided the ecclesiastical court did constitute an independent and impartial tribunal.

The term 'civil rights and obligations' in Article 6(1) is ambiguous. Its interpretation, given in Strasbourg jurisprudence, purposely ignores state classification, examining instead the contents and effects of the right,[109] and includes some public law and administrative procedures, especially, but not exclusively, those in which the authority is not acting as sovereign.[110] Pertinent among these were the determinations that classified disciplinary proceedings resulting in suspension from medical practice[111] and legal practice[112] as a 'civil right' within the ambit of 6(1). Disciplinary procedures in a state-church could similarly be said to determine 'civil rights' under this test. However, more relevant to disciplinary procedures in state-churches, which concern state employees, is the test regarding employment disputes of civil servants given in *Pellegrin*.[113] It includes in Article 6(1) employment disputes regarding civil servants, excluding only disputes regarding activities of public servants who are acting as a depository of public authority. Under *Vilho Eskelinen v. Finland*[114] the exclusion was narrowed further. Only a dispute regarding an exercise of state power will be excluded, not every dispute regarding an employee who has the authority to exercise state power. Thus, it appears that disciplinary proceedings against clergy of state-churches could be subject to Article 6(1).

Indeed, it would be advisable if disciplinary procedures against clergy in state-churches were included in the ambit of international human rights guarantees of fair procedure in determination of legal rights, such as Article 6(1).[115] The constitutional status of the ecclesiastical courts in the United Kingdom[116] should mean that Convention obligations must apply. Disciplinary proceedings in such a case are quasi-judicial proceedings, in which a legal mechanism associated with the state determines rights and privileges of individuals.

It is an inbuilt weakness of European Convention protection, because it creates obligations on states not private parties, that it would apply to disciplinary proceedings of a state-church but not to proceedings of another religion. Proceedings in religious institutions of religions other than state religions would not be subject to Article 6(1). But this leaves an important facet of individual rights unprotected. These are procedures that de facto determine significant aspects of the lives of members of the community or organization, including benefits, privileges, social standing or employment, as crucial to the lives of members as any official determination of rights. While the legal basis, if any, for such proceedings is rooted in private law, the determination may be more than a private matter, because of its severe ramifications in a cohesive community, and, at least in case of disciplinary procedures, the moral opprobrium of the individual concerned.

Such a case was a decision by the Chief Rabbi of the UK on a Rabbi's fitness to hold rabbinical office, following an investigation of allegations against him, discussed in an application for judicial review in the Divisional Court.[117] The Court decided it would not exercise judicial review, because the decision to be reviewed was not a regulation of a field of public life, for which the government would have provided a statutory framework, if regulation did not exist. The test for judicial review in UK law is not the same as that for the application of the European Convention (by means of the Human Rights Act). The judicial review test is broader, as it does not apply only to acts of government but to acts that would have been undertaken by government. It could be suggested that this is a preferable test to determine which bodies should be subject to human rights obligations. UK courts had previously found that some acts of NGOs are to be treated like government acts because they regulate a field that government would have regulated.[118] Governments do not regulate religions, but for the purposes of application of human rights guarantees possibly the criterion should be broadened to include acts similar to those which government regulates, which could include proceedings which are a determination of a person's reputation in the community. A further difficulty pointed out by the Divisional Court is that of disentangling procedural considerations of natural justice from Jewish law, which the Court must respect. This is a substantial difficulty, which should caution care, but should not prove an absolute bar to application of procedural guarantees.

Religions use internal proceedings that have a judicial character not only regarding employees. Proceedings of the London *Beit Din*, a tribunal appointed by the Chief Rabbi to decide on certificates of *kashrut* for food vendors, were examined by a UK court, which decided that there was no recourse to judicial review of the decision.[119] The *Beth Din* is a religious Jewish court. It is not a court of law of the state. Food vendors voluntarily decide if they wish to apply for its *kashrut* certificates, and thus submit to its decisions to revoke such certificates.

It does not decide legal rights, but it decides, in fact, on the livelihood of a member of the community, with a de facto significance much like that of a business licence. It is arguable that the religious institution cannot act regardless of the procedural rights of its member in such proceedings. However, in this case the argument is weaker than that regarding disciplinary proceedings, because there is no moral blame implied by the proceedings.

The right to have internal judicial or quasi-judicial procedures is a group right *par excellence*. If such rights are to be recognized as part of religious freedom, they should be subject to the proviso that individual rights of basic fair procedure (such as the rules of natural justice) are respected. However, there is a danger not only of interference in institutional religious autonomy, but also in matters of religious doctrine. Thus, not full judicial procedures, but rather rudimentary elements of fair procedure must be observed.

3.1.3 Democratic governance

If religious institutions of a state religion have legal status as public bodies, there is an argument that they must be subjected to requirements of democratic governance (as well as possibly other attributes of good governance, such as transparency and accountability). As will be seen, this is a requirement that has been raised both from within, by members of religious organizations themselves, and from without, by states in which they operate.

The requirement for democratic governance of religious institutions has not yet been raised in international law, and seldom in domestic law. It is not presently clear that a democratic governance requirement exists in international law even regarding state governance, although there is a strong claim for such a requirement, an issue of much recent debate.[120] However, even if a requirement for democratic governance of states exists in international law, current international law does not offer a basis for a possible demand for democratic governance of religious institutions in the state.

Nevertheless, it would be commensurate with the trend for strengthening democratic governance and human rights observance in civil society, if this requirement were demanded of civic organizations, including religious institutions, particularly institutions of state religions, concurrent with the implementation of human rights provisions.

This is not an easy argument. So far, democratic governance in religious institutions has seldom been demanded even in democratic states. It has never been raised as an international demand of religious bodies in other states. Even in the processes of state building in which the international community has participated (such as Afghanistan and Iraq) and raised demands for state democracy, religious organizations were left outside these demands.

Nevertheless, there are reasons to develop legal bases for enforcing at least some aspects of democratic governance on religious institutions, such as voting for the administrative bodies that oversee religious institutions, but not appointment of religious authorities. A religious institution, although rooted in a private law contract, does have a public aspect. Its members do have a claim, regardless of the private law instrument setting it up, as to the way it is run, and can legitimately demand that principles of democracy and accountability be upheld. Religious organizations often influence members' lives often as much as the state. They encompass in their actions and teachings all aspects of life, and form an important social, cultural and religious framework for members. In religiously pluralistic societies in Europe and elsewhere, religious organizations of different religions organize important aspects of individual and social life. It is important for the state to foster a plurality of organizations in civil society, but participation in civic society through its organizations should also mean that participants be able to oversee the civic organizations, including religious ones, in which they take part.

The argument for a requirement of democratic governance may be extended to institutions of religions that are not state religions. Some states that extend a requirement of democratic governance to certain private associations, exempt religions not only from human rights requirements imposed on private civic organizations, but also from democratic requirements of other civic organizations. This is a way in which states favour religious group rights over those of individual members. The decisions of the institution, according to its own rules, will be recognized over the wishes of individual members, even if they are a majority. For example, in Hungary, civic associations are required to have a democratic structure, but religions are exempt from the need to have a democratic structure in order to be registered.[121] Clearly, this exemption was given so as not to interfere in doctrinal matters. But the same attributes that favour a democratic governance requirement in civic organizations, namely that they manage important aspects of peoples' lives, perform social functions in the state and often receive funds from the state (directly or through tax exemptions), apply to religious institutions. Future debate is needed on how to reconcile democratic governance and doctrinal imperatives, possibly distinguishing between doctrinal decisions and administrative organization of the religious institution.

A requirement of democratic governance for religious organizations was debated in a US case in an indirect way. Courts in the USA are loath to intervene in church decisions, based on a principle of non-intervention in church affairs grounded in the First Amendment.

However, in *Jones v. Wolf*,[122] a problem arose of deciding which faction in a church dispute should prevail. The court majority decided on a rebuttable presumption that the church body decides by majority decision. The dissent on the court said there should be no presumption of a particular decision method, and the court should look only to church doctrine as to who is the qualified decision maker, otherwise the boundaries set by the First Amendment will be overstepped. While in practical terms, the difference is only one of evidentiary burden, there may be a more fundamental difference. The majority did not explicitly mention democratic ideals behind its presumption of majority vote. Nevertheless, in fact, the decision promotes principles of democratic governance, even if only in a weak (i.e. rebuttable) sense. This decision is an example, albeit a rare one, of imposition of principles of democratic governance on a religious organization by the state, the USA, even if this was done only implicitly.

Why religious community members would favour a democratic governance requirement can be exemplified by a decision of the UK Court of Appeal. It ruled that the decisions of an imam in compiling a list of members entitled to vote for mosque committee elections was not subject to judicial review, as his functions and decisions were not of a public nature.[123] The imam's actions were deemed binding on members by force of a private law contract. However, a mosque, as any religious institution, is not merely a product of a private law contract. It governs all aspects of adherents' lives as much as state organs do, even when not taking over directly functions of the state, such as education. Requiring democratic participation in decision making is part of assuring respect for human rights in carrying out these functions.

While currently there is no applicable legal requirement of democratic governance either in UK law or in international law, it could be an important development to participation in civil society if civic organization had a requirement of democratic governance that included at least the administrative functions of religious organizations. Of course, it may not be easy to delineate administrative functions from core religious functions. It is difficult presently to suggest how such a requirement could be introduced in future international legal instruments, but this should merit further consideration.

Thus, religious organizations bear characteristics of public bodies having human rights obligations, as employers, as civic bodies, or as regulators of social life. As such, they are not purely private bodies, and should not be exempt from the obligation to observe human rights, including religious freedom of individuals.

3.2 Religious freedom includes the right to participate in religious communities without waiving one's basic rights

Individuals who participate in religious communities, whether as members or employees, do not let go of their rights at the door of the community. Religious freedom encompasses the right to participate in religious community activities with basic rights such as freedom of expression, equality, and freedom of religious belief and practice. The normative claim regarding members is that the state must accord religious freedom equally and so their right to religious freedom is infringed if they cannot benefit from equal protection of the law in institutions of their religion. Because religion is part of one's identity, the individual should not be made to choose between participation in religious institutions and basic rights. It is the meaningful participation in religious life sought by members and workers as a manifestation of their religious freedom that calls for guarantees of rights by the state.

This is not just a normative claim. There are some indications of an existing basis in law for these claims, in European human rights law. The exclusion of this consideration, for instance in the developed case law of US courts, is unjustified.

The argument is strongest where a state religion is involved, because individuals have a strong claim that a religion that has the imprimatur of the state must respect their rights. Nevertheless, the argument that religious freedom must not mean having to waive basic rights by joining religious activities is valid for other religions as well.

3.2.1 European human rights law

The problem of squaring the autonomy of religious institutions with individual human rights is evident in the international as well as domestic legal context. The European Commission stated, that Article 9 does not oblige the High Contracting Parties to ensure that churches within their jurisdiction grant religious freedom to their members and servants. In a state-church, it reasoned, servants are employed for the application of a particular religious doctrine, and their religious freedom consists of their ability to leave the church.[124] It saw the church as protected in its autonomy in these matters. This broad qualification of Article 9 can be criticized. Individuals always have a right to religious freedom, even when they undertake a position within a church. People enter employment or otherwise associate themselves with religious organizations for a variety of reasons and exigencies. They do not, thereby, forfeit any right to freedom of religion and belief. This right should, however, be interpreted differently according to the context of the position they undertake within the church. The variable scope of individual religious freedom should depend on the position of the employee, his profession and the institution in which he serves. The applicants in *Karlsson* and *Knudsen* were clergymen, regarding whom it is most justified to view a church demand of religious conformity as not infringing their religious freedom.

The European Commission, however, followed its earlier reasoning also in the case of a non-established church, and viewed as legitimate a dismissal of a doctor in a Catholic hospital who expressed, in a private capacity, pro-abortion views,[125] because it reasoned that by entering employment with the church the doctor accepted a certain limitation of his freedom to criticize the church.

But, contrary to the reasoning of the Commission, when assessing the protection of employees' human rights in religious institutions, not all employees should be treated alike. Differentiation should be made between 'core' religious employees such as clergy, for whom an imposition of doctrinal conformity would be easier to justify, and other employees who may have valid claims to a broader interpretation of religious freedom. This argument regarding the Commission's qualification of Article 9 is especially strong when applied to state-churches or dominant religions in the state.

However, as will be discussed later, even this qualification of Article 9 does not mean that, under the European Convention, states do not need to assure that churches grant members and employees human rights. The permissible limitation of religious freedom remains the exception.

One of the main issues to cause concern for churches, in any state, were they to be subjected to international human rights requirements, is the ordination of women clergy. The claim of women who wish to be ordained exemplifies well the argument of this section. It is precisely because of their wish to play a meaningful role within the religious community, that the law must intervene within the realm of church autonomy to guarantee their right to equality.

This issue has not been raised directly in international fora. Neither the European Court, nor, previously, the European Commission, has confronted the question of whether state-churches must ordain women as part of their human rights obligations. But a correlative issue was presented to the European Commission.[126] The Commission decided that state-churches that ordain women clergy have not breached the right to religious freedom of clergymen who objected to such ordination on theological grounds. In *Williamson*,[127] the applicant, a clergyman, tried unsuccessfully to challenge the legality of the Ordination of Women Measure[128] as breaching his religious freedom. The Commission reiterated its established position that freedom of religion does not include the right of a clergyman, within the framework of a church in which he is working or to which he applies for a post, to practice a special religious conception.[129] However, the Commission, in dismissing his application, also noted that Article 14 of the European Convention prohibits discrimination in connection with Convention rights, discrimination that the Measure sought to eliminate. But the Commission did not go (and did not need to go) so far as to say that the Church of England, whose Measures are parliamentary legislation, *needed* to allow for ordination of women in order to abolish discrimination between men and women, so that the UK would be in compliance with the Convention. However, if Article 14 applies to state-churches, as applied by the Commission in this case, then not only is the church allowed to appoint women, but it *must* do so. Indeed, under the Commission's reasoning the UK itself is in breach of Article 14 by the Anglican church's failure to permit the ordination of women Bishops.[130]

A similar question is likely to arise as to the ordination of homosexual clergy. The question of ordination of gay clergy has arisen in internal religious debate, for instance in the Anglican Church.[131] It has yet to be framed as a human rights requirement to which the Church of England, or any state-church, must adhere. If such a claim would arise under the European Convention, the Court would have to examine whether refusal to appoint gay clergy breaches their right to equal enjoyment of religious freedom under Article 14 (in conjunction with Article 9) of the Convention. Sexual orientation is not one of the enumerated prohibited grounds of discrimination in Article 14, but it has been recognized by the European Court as one of the grounds of prohibited discrimination covered by the words 'such as' in Article 14.[132]

3.2.2 *Rights of employees of religious organizations – UK and Germany*

The unresolved conflict between church autonomy and individual freedom has been resolved differently in different states. The examples we turn to next, those of the UK and Germany, and then the USA, have each struck a different balance between church autonomy and individual freedom. The US case law leaves narrow the scope for protection of individual rights. German constitutional decisions have attempted a more balanced approach, but still give considerable protection to church autonomy over individual rights. In the UK, the balance between institution and employees is yet to be determined in the interpretation of new legislation.

One of the important areas in which individuals are pitted against private institutions is that of employment. A conflict between individuals' religious beliefs and the demands made by these institutions can arise where religious individuals are employees or apply for work in non-religious places of employment or in places of employment of a religion other than their own.

The place of work has become one of the important areas in which people spend much of their lives and so it exerts a strong influence on their lives, as much, if not more than the state. There, more than almost anywhere else protection of individual rights is needed.

The ILO Discrimination (Employment and Occupation) Convention (No. 111) prohibits discrimination in the workplace on various grounds, including religion. The EU has an given detailed protection to this act through the Council Directive Establishing a General Framework for Equal Treatment in Employment and Occupation.[133]

The Directive mandates the prohibition of direct and indirect discrimination on the grounds of religion or belief in employment and related areas.[134] The Directive qualifies this stricture in various ways, stating among them, in Article 4, that 'Member States may provide that a difference of treatment which is based on a characteristic related to any of the grounds referred to in Article 1 shall not constitute discrimination where, by reason of the nature of the particular occupational activities concerned or of the context in which they are carried out, such a characteristic constitutes a genuine and determining occupational requirement, provided that the objective is legitimate and the requirement is proportionate.'

In the UK, the Employment Equality (Religion or Belief) Regulations 2003 implemented the EU Equality Framework Directive[135] in regard to discrimination on the grounds of religion or belief. (The Equality Act 2006 outlaws discrimination on grounds of religion and belief in other contexts – including goods, facilities and services, education and public authorities.)

The UK Human Rights Act, which adopts the European Convention, does not state explicitly whether it upholds individual religious rights or religious group rights. However, Section 13 of the Act[136] instructs the courts to have particular regard to the importance of the right to religious freedom, when its exercise by a religious organization will be affected. The wording of the section is vague. It does not say the court must prefer the right of the religious organization to a conflicting right of religious freedom, for instance, that of a member. As the importance of the right to freedom of thought, conscience and religion which Section 13 stresses is also the right of individuals within religious organizations, it would be possible to interpret Section 13 so as not to prefer a right of the religious organization over that of its members or employees.

In Germany, a constitutional guarantee of a right of self-government to religious organizations[137] was interpreted by the Constitutional Court so that it may override constitutional rights of employees, including religious freedom. The workers to which such decisions referred ranged from a minister (who was suspended by his church upon being elected to the Bundestag, contrary to constitutional protection[138] of elected members)[139] to workers in non-religious roles that have a bearing on church ethics (doctor in Catholic hospital who expressed pro-abortion views),[140] to workers in purely non-religious roles (a bookkeeper of a Catholic youth home who had left the church).[141]

The range of workers whose rights were subject to the church autonomy guarantee was overbroad. However, differently from the US doctrine of 'ministerial exception', which will be discussed below, the German Constitutional Court, held that there *were* limits to the right of the church to impose its views on its employees. Churches could not put unreasonable demands of loyalty on employees. Thus, the German Court does not see church autonomy as a blanket exemption of the church from compliance with protection of individual rights. However, the results reached by the Court show that it did not differentiate between workers according to their roles.

3.2.3 United States

A well-established doctrine regarding rights of workers within religious organizations exists in US case law. However, under US religious freedom analysis, the rights of individuals in religious organizations are not adequately addressed. To see why this is so, the principles of the law of religious freedom in the US should be recalled.

The US religious freedom jurisprudence is based on the two religion clauses of the 1st Amendment to the US Constitution. It contains two clauses regarding religion: the free exercise clause, which guarantees freedom of religion, and the establishment clause, which forbids Congress from establishing religion.

Free exercise of religion can be restricted by law, according to the Supreme Court test in *Sherbert v. Verner*,[142] if such a law furthers a compelling state interest, and employs the least restrictive means in order to do so. The Court substantially modified this test in *Employment Division v. Smith*,[143] so that government can prohibit religious conduct without showing a compelling interest, as long as the law is neutral and generally applicable.[144] The Religious Freedom Restoration Act[145] [RFRA], which the US Congress enacted in 1993 to counter *Smith* and restore the *Sherbert* test, was struck down[146] by the Supreme Court decision *City of Boerne v. Flores*.[147] However, even under the *Smith* doctrine, when a law is not neutral and generally applicable, government must still show a compelling reason for restricting exercise of religion.[148] In *Gonzales v. Centro Espirita*[149] the Supreme Court, interpreted RFRA (which it implicitly accepted as in force in relation to the Federal government) as mandating a strict scrutiny test, meaning the government needed to show a 'compelling interest' to interfere with the free exercise of religion of the *particular* person affected, and it was not enough for the government to show that the measure was neutral and generally applicable.

However, outside the line of free exercise cases, the establishment clause gave rise to a broad doctrine of church autonomy. One of the important aspects in which church autonomy is elevated above individual human rights is the 'ministerial exception', defined thus: 'When a church makes a personnel decision based on religious doctrine … the courts will not intervene.'[150] However, there need not be reliance on church doctrine underlying each decision for the ministerial exception to apply. This means that churches and other religious organizations are exempt from a variety of employment laws,[151] including Title VII of the Civil Rights Act that forbids discrimination in employment on grounds of race, colour, religion, sex, or national origin.

The lower courts have asked whether the ministerial exception survives after the *Smith* decision. If government may burden individual religious practice by general neutral law even without a compelling state interest, may it also burden religious organizations by general neutral law, for instance, by employment equality legislation? All courts in which this question arose decided that the ministerial exception remains intact.[152] The reason given was that the ministerial exception addresses the rights of the church, while *Smith* refers only to the rights of individuals.[153] Some courts have, however, tailored the exception more narrowly, requiring the religious organization to show that may involve matters of church government, faith or doctrine.[154] The ministerial exception is rooted in Supreme Court cases affirming the church autonomy doctrine, which protects the fundamental right of churches to decide for themselves matters of church government, faith, and doctrine. The result is that concurrently *Smith* and its progeny allow the state to burden individual manifestations of religious freedom by neutral law while the doctrine of church autonomy does not allow burdening of religious organizations by similarly neutral laws.

But church autonomy is in fact one type of manifestation of religious freedom. Thus, one manifestation of religious freedom, a group manifestation, is given more constitutional protection than other, individual manifestations of religious freedom.

The ministerial exception is far reaching as it applies not only to clergy. The general rule is that 'if the employee's primary duties consist of teaching, spreading the faith, church governance, supervision of a religious order, or supervision or participation in religious ritual and worship, he or she should be considered clergy'.[155] This resulted in a range of cases in which individual workers were denied the opportunity to pursue discrimination claims against churches. For example, the Equal Employment Opportunities Commission could not bring suit under title VII of the Civil Rights Act alleging sex discrimination against a Catholic church for dismissing a female music director, even though a non-Catholic replaced her, as this was considered a doctrinal matter falling under the ministerial exception. Likewise a communications director for a church could not bring a claim under Article VII for discrimination on grounds of ethnic origin,[156] because her role was to advance the message of the church, and so fell under the 'ministerial exception', rather than any claim that the dispute itself had anything to do with religious doctrine.

The US Supreme Court decided on the constitutionality of an exemption from the Civil Rights Act Title VII prohibition on discrimination based on religion for religious corporations 'with respect to the employment of individuals of a particular religion to perform work connected with ... its activities'.[157] The Court rebuked the claim that the exemption 'offends equal protection principles by giving less protection to religious employers' employees than to secular employers' employees', because the statute 'does not discriminate among religions and, instead, is neutral on its face and motivated by a permissible purpose of limiting governmental interference with the exercise of religion'. The exemption is rationally related to the legitimate purpose of 'alleviating governmental interference with the ability of religious organizations to define and carry out their religious missions'.[158]

The Court decided that the exemption applies even to employees of non-profit organizations operated by churches who have no religious functions, such as workers of a church-owned gymnasium.[159] So, the freedom of churches to employ only members of their religion is even broader than the ministerial exception, as it applies to all workers.

Thus, in assessing whether the state breached principles of religious freedom, the Court looked only at whether there was discrimination between religions. But here there is a different religious freedom concern. The autonomy of the religious organizations is furthered but the religious freedom of workers is left unprotected. As was seen, the European Court has decided that member states do not have to guarantee religious freedom of workers in churches. The US Court does not even address this as a problem of protection of individual religious freedom inside a church.

The preference of institutional religious freedom to individual religious freedom in the USA can also be seen regarding another exemption of churches from laws that protect the rights of employees, an exemption from paying state unemployment contributions to religious bodies. A social worker of the Salvation Army who became unemployed was not eligible for state unemployment benefit, because the Salvation Army, like other religious organizations, was exempt by law from paying unemployment contributions. The 1st Circuit decided that this law did not breach 1st amendment principles of religious freedom. The Court[160] surmised:

> Establishment Clause concern is that of avoiding the effective promotion or advancement of particular religions or of religion in general by the government. Although favoritism toward any particular sect is not an issue raised by this appeal, it is not disputed that religious institutions as a whole benefit from the [...] tax exemptions. An incidental benefit to religion does not, however, render invalid a statutory scheme with a valid secular purpose ... [w]hile religious employers may be benefited, the employees of exempted religious institutions, as the appellant has discovered, may be ineligible to enjoy the attendant benefits of the unemployment compensation scheme. Thus, the primary effect of the exemptions is not to force the general public to subsidize religion.

The constitutional concern of the Court was whether the state advances or inhibits religion. The Court concluded that the law doesn't advance religion because the exemption is not at the expense of the public, but rather at the expense of the employees. In every religion whose employers benefit from the exemption, the employees lose their unemployment benefits. This means that institutions of the religion benefit at the expense of individuals of that religion. A worker who works for a religious institution because of a belief that furthers his participation in religious work is penalized for that religious choice. The purpose of the law is to protect religious freedom, by freeing religious institutions from government regulation. But it is protection of religious freedom of institutions at the expense of the religious freedom of their workers. Working at a religious institution is sometimes, though not always, a manifestation of a worker's religious belief. The religious freedom of such employees in making employment choices according to their religious beliefs is harmed by a law that disqualifies them from receiving unemployment benefits because they chose to work at a religious rather than a secular institution.

The US Supreme Court developed individual religious freedom and group religious freedom as two different strands of free exercise law. The D.C. Circuit Court in *EEOC* explained the distinction between them:[161] '[G]overnment action may burden the free exercise of religion, in violation of the First Amendment, in two quite different ways: by interfering with a believer's ability to observe the commands or practices of his faith … and by encroaching on the ability of a church to manage its internal affairs.' Out of the two, the Court saw a reluctance of the Supreme Court to interfere with the second.

Ironically, considering the highly individualistic notion of human rights in the context of the United States Constitution, in the USA the legal balance between church rights and individual rights is currently weighted quite heavily towards the church (or other religious organization). This is so in two ways: the first, in a conflict between the rights of a church and the rights of its employee, the church has the upper hand; the second, as far as state, rather than federal law is concerned, while individual religious freedom can be impinged upon by a general neutral law even absent a compelling state interest, internal church autonomy cannot be so impinged on.

The meaningful religious freedom for many members of religious communities is thus the protection of their ability to be members of religious communities without having to sacrifice their basic rights. This is the religious freedom which international and domestic law should protect.

3.3 Recognizing religious group rights inevitably involves the state in defining religious groups, thus compromising state neutrality in matters of religion

According legal status to groups is necessary for many of the functions and activities of communally exercised religious rights. Legal personality, for example, is needed, to acquire property and exercise functions of private law. Such rights, which individuals can only exercise communally with each other, are part of the right to religious freedom. Indeed, the European Court has increasingly come to recognize this. However, those instances in which the exercise of religious freedom is necessarily communal, such as choice of leadership, are also those in which it is important to uphold the rights of individuals and subgroups within the larger community. This is why it is important, especially in this context, to adhere to the principled view that a group's rights are derivative and cannot override the rights of the individuals who compose it.

Although necessary for implementation of certain rights, laws that accord legal status to religious groups are nevertheless troubling, because for their implementation the state must accept a certain determination of the group and its representative leadership. This is often unacceptable to subgroups, dissenting leaders or individuals within the group. Any determination between competing claims by the state means it will not remain neutral. While it is recognized in international law that states may have an established religion, with which they are historically associated and thus not remain neutral in this respect, nevertheless they do have an obligation of non-discrimination in their current actions towards all religions. As examples in this section will show, group determination is not only misguided in principle, but is also problematic in application.

An inherent problem with according groups rights of religious freedom is that of defining the group. This was shown in Chapter 2 to be a strong reason for according religious rights to individuals, rather than groups. The inevitability of the state being involved in such definition, as will be seen, reinforces this point.

One of the concerns over establishment of religion is the states' exclusion or, conversely, legal regulation, of minority religions. Specifically, any official state determination of the legal status, rights and obligations of minority religions raises a concern that the object of granting them an official status is to keep them under government control. Moreover, the legal status of minority religions poses crucial conflicts between group rights and individual rights.

In certain cases the state cannot escape from legally defining religious groups and maintaining their rights according to these definitions. This is true even in states that maintain separation of religion from state, as even they cannot escape entanglement of the state with religion.

I analyse instances in which states accord religious status to communities in order to further their ability to practice their religion. This is done by according them legal powers or by exempting them from general laws and by allocating them funds. I then look at the regulation of legal status of religions by means of registration and state power to appoint clergy. In all these cases, the inherent problems in defining religious groups will be evident.

3.3.1 Legal powers

When the state delegates to religious communities the legal power to perform state functions, the state must necessarily decide who constitute the religious group and who is its representative leadership. Thus, the empowerment of religious groups may mean an infringement of rights of sub-groups or alternative leaderships within the group. A particularly difficult situation facing the state is when a schism occurs within a recognized religion. Any position taken by the state, whether recognizing or refusing to recognize the splinter group, necessarily entails a judgment of the state on religious matters.

A refusal by the state to recognize a splinter group was sanctioned by the European Commission[162] as not incompatible with religious freedom. The Marriage Board of the Pentecostal Movement, which was authorized by the state to grant its pastors license to register marriages, had revoked the licenses of the applicant pastors who were deemed by the Pentecostal Movement to belong to breakaway factions. The Commission affirmed the actions of Sweden, which did not intervene in the decision of the Pentecostal board. The Commission decided that the state had no obligation to ensure that the Movement accepts those pastors, and the congregation they lead, as its members. Thus, it dismissed the application.

The Commission clearly favoured the religious autonomy of the Pentecostal congregation over the independent rights of its dissenting members. The Commission seems right in concluding that sometimes it is inevitable that the state decide which is the recognized leadership and what are the decision-making procedures of the group. Celebration of marriage is a group function, so the legal right to celebrate marriages must be accorded to religious communities, rather than to individuals. These religions are entitled to decide who may act in their name. However, the right ultimately derives from that of individuals. If individuals leave a known religion and want equal legal recognition for their schismatic group, they are entitled to it, whatever the objections of the main group. Had the dissenting pastors asked for separate certification from the state, equal respect for the right of religious freedom would have meant that they have a right to receive it.

A recent ECHR decision that appears to favour this approach is the *Holy Synod of the Bulgarian Orthodox Church v. Bulgaria*.[163] In this case, the Court determined that the authorities cannot take sides in an intra-religious dispute and use state power to suppress one of the sides to the dispute. Furthermore, the state cannot use the justification of 'unity' to impede a schismatic group from establishing a new church.[164]

But does this mean that any breakaway group, no matter how small or novel, must be given recognition? It seems so. If the state recognizes religious groups for legal purposes, then it cannot make any decisions as to their religious or social worth. Any religious group must be given equal recognition. This can be qualified by technical difficulties, such as a group that is too small too maintain a marriage registration board, or unreasonable financial burdens involved.[165]

Indeed, an approach that does not let the state-recognized religious community override the choices of other religious groups of the same religion, and does not accept as permissible a state decision on competing demands within a minority religious group, was taken by the US 2nd Circuit Court of Appeals. The case involved ritual Jewish dietary requirements.[166] The Court struck down as unconstitutional a New York state law which allowed food to be marked as 'kosher' only if approved according to standards maintained by an Orthodox Jewish board.

The decision was based on First Amendment constitutional principles of separation of church and state. But the resulting decision also affects the position of religious minorities in that jurisdiction. As a result of the decision, government will no longer be able to give legal status to one leadership of a religious group, when part of the religious group claims an alternative leadership and religious interpretation.

Certification of marriage registrars involves a function that the state must perform, while certification of religious dietary requirements is a function that the state chose to perform, but the conclusion in both cases is the same. As in the case of state certification of religious marriage registrars, so too in state certification of religious dietary boards, if the state legally empowers any religious group, it must likewise legally empower all interested religious groups including dissenting groups.

A state decision on the definition of a religious group is needed not only in order to give groups legal power, but also in order to exempt them from general legal requirements. Such involvement of the state in deciding those bodies of the religious group to which it grants the exemption from general law is, likewise, problematic, as can be seen in the following example.

The European Court of Human Rights was confronted with the question of the legality of a state decision on leadership of religious communities in *Cha'arei Shalom Ve'zedek*.[167] The case illustrates the problem discussed in Chapter 2 of recognition of group rights, that is, the determination of who has the power to define a religious group.

The applicant association wanted separate governmental certification as a religious organization, so that it could legally perform Jewish ritual slaughter (which was exempt from general animal slaughter regulations). The French government had already certified an association of the majority of the Jewish congregations, and refused to certify the *Cha'arei Shalom* organization, which had a stricter interpretation of the religious slaughter rules.

The majority of the Court decided that as long as the members of the community could obtain the stricter *glatt-kosher* slaughtered meat from another source, there was no breach of their religious freedom in not allowing them to obtain their own slaughter permit.

The Court seems to suggest that the individual's right is only to *receive* kosher food, and there is no separate right to *supply* kosher food. The state decided that one religious organization stands for an entire religion. But performing ritual slaughter is part of the communal manifestation of religion. A minority group of the religion should have an equal right to state exemption.[168] The right to receive the religious slaughter exemption is given to community slaughterhouses, but the substantive right is that of individuals. They do not have to belong to the community that represents the majority of believers, and do not have to adhere to its religious interpretations.

Rights are given to religious groups as a practical matter. It would be impractical to give every Jewish person a slaughter certification, but these are still in principle individual rights. When the state accords such rights to a religious community, individuals do not lose their claim to manifest this right in a different community of their choice.

3.3.2 *Budget allocation*

Allocation of state budget to religious organizations gives rise to a similar problem, even if it follows a principle of equality. The state must make a decision about who constitutes the religious groups. The budget is necessarily allocated to groups rather than individuals, even if the substantive right to the money belongs to individuals. However, if the right to state funding of religious activity is viewed as an individual, rather than a group right, then dissenting individuals within the religious groups have a right to demand allocation of funds to their subgroup. This should not be at the discretion of the state.

Germany allocates tax funding to religious organizations. The Central Council of German Jews, a Jewish umbrella organization, receives the proportion of state taxes ear-marked for the Jewish religious institutions. The Reform Jewish movement asked to receive a share of the funding from the state of Sachsen-Anhalt proportional to its membership in order to establish its own community centre.[169] As the Central Council decided that the Reform congregation did not follow Jewish tradition, it did not agree that a proportion of the funding for the Jewish community would be allocated to them. The Reform community petitioned the Federal Administrative Court (Bundesverwaltungsgericht) against the state, regarding its religious funding.[170] The officially recognized Jewish group saw the Jewish religious community as one, while the Reform sub-group saw itself as a religious community in its own right.

The Court ruled that there is not necessarily one single Jewish community. The Reform community may ask to be officially recognized as a separate Jewish community for funding purposes, if it can show that it has recognition by an international body of the movement of Reform Judaism. If so, in principle, any subgroup of a funded religion may claim similar recognition and funding. Thus, the state is faced with the prospect of having to decide on the identity of religious groups, namely, which separate religious group is group entitled to funding.

Thus, even in the distribution of state funds, which can only be allocated to groups, the ultimate bearers of the right to funding are individuals. Only individuals can define their religious group for funding purposes, and no religious group has a right to include individuals in its membership overriding individual or subgroup choice.

3.3.3 *Registration and freedom of religious association*

Granting legal status to religious minorities involves the state in the role of deciding what constitutes a recognizable religious minority group. Some states have set registration requirements quite obviously in order to avoid recognizing new and small religions, by setting a minimum number of members and a minimum period of operation in order to qualify for registration as a religion. This practice discriminates between religions and between members of different religions for no legitimate purpose. The registration requirement has become a focus of discussion in regard to post-Communist states in Eastern Europe, although they are not the only ones who have such requirements.[171]

In some states, registration of minority religions[172] (and in some, of all religions)[173] is either compulsory or a prerequisite for exercising certain manifestations of religious freedom, particularly the communal manifestations.[174]

The right to congregate in order to pray, preach, or educate are rights exercised communally. According to the classification introduced in Chapter 2 these are 'communally exercised individual rights'. So, their recognition and protection is consistent with a theory of individual rights, indeed required under it.

The requirement of registration can be seen, in itself, as a curtailment of freedom of religion and freedom of association. It can do so in several ways: the state might make rights which are part of religious freedom, such as congregating at a place of worship, contingent on registration, and withhold them from those religions which haven't registered. However, it cannot be a valid justification for a prohibition on prayer or communal study that a religion is not registered. (There might be *other* legitimate reasons for such prohibitions on communal activities, such as genuine health and safety considerations.)

Registration might be required by the state in order to recognize the legal personality of a religious organization. There is nothing in that requirement per se that breaches the religious freedom of the members of the religion. But, if the requirements are substantially more stringent for religious organizations than for other corporations, this may be a breach of the religious freedom of their members. Also, the requirements, although neutral on their face, might be such as to discriminate against minority religions.

The danger is that the registration requirement will serve as a means to monitor or curtail the activities of minority or dissident religions. Even when not used for discriminatory purposes, this requirement may cause the state to have to decide between competing religious groups, an unwanted scenario for maintenance of religious freedom.

This was the case in many former Soviet bloc states,[175] such as in Russia, with the introduction of the 1997 Russian Law on Freedom of Conscience and Religious Associations, which requires, among other requirements, that the religion has operated in Russia for a minimum of 15 years.

Not only former Soviet bloc states have used registration laws to impede new religions. Austria's 1997 Confessional Communities Law[176] was clearly adopted with the intent of discriminating between existing and new religions. The law requires for registration of a religion, that it has been in operation for a minimal, rather large, number of years[177] and has minimal, rather substantial, membership.[178] It must also show its distinction from other existing religions and have a 'positive attitude towards the society and state', and must not create 'an illegal disturbance of the relations of Churches and other religious communities'.[179] These requirements serve no legitimate state interest and discriminate against new religions.

The demands for registration have increasingly been the subject of litigation in the ECHR in recent years. In dealing with these applications, again and again the European Court has determined that the specific decisions denying registration of minority religions were arbitrary or ill founded. It has not, for the most part, pronounced on the legitimacy of the requirements for registration as such, even where the registration requirements discriminate against new religions. However, the more recent *Jehova's Witnesses* decision, analysed later, suggests a different, and preferable, view in the Court.

The line of cases pronouncing on specific registration denials centred on the requirements of Russia, Moldova and Bulgaria. In *Moscow branch of the Salvation Army v. Russia*,[180] the Court decided that freedom of association of the Salvation Army had been breached where its registration had been denied despite lack of evidence that it had any intention of breaching the law, as claimed by Russia. However, the Court did not pronounce on the legitimacy of such registration requirements for minority religions but not for the majority religion (as it might have done had it examined the alternative argument of the applicants under Article 14, the non-discrimination Article of the Convention).[181]

In Moldova, the Religious Denominations Act mandates that in order to be able to organize and operate, denominations must be recognized by means of a government decision. In *Metropolitan Church of Bessarabia v. Moldova*,[182] the Metropolitan Church of Bessarabia was denied registration by the government of Moldova, under the Moldovan Religious Denominations Act. Registration was needed to establish legal personality of a religion and was a prerequisite for marketing religious objects, and founding and distributing religious periodicals, among other things. The government denied registration because it considered the Church of Bessarabia as a schismatic group of the officially recognized Metropolitan Church of Moldova.[183] The Court ruled on the illegal application of the registration requirement in the particular case. The Court accepted that refusal to recognize a religion that acts in a harmful way was a limitation in pursuit of a legitimate aim, under Article 9(2) of the European Convention, but the claim of harm was not proven in this case.

The Court could have, but did not, rule on the legality of a registration requirement in itself. The Court did not use this opportunity to examine whether the demand for registration, in and of itself, as a prerequisite to conducting certain religious activities, is a breach of religious freedom. By refraining from doing so, the Court implied such a requirement is not. This seems an unadvisable conclusion. A registration requirement which makes vital religious activities, such as printing and distributing religious literature, producing liturgical objects, and engaging clergy,[184] *a priori* dependent on registration of the religion by the government should be considered a breach of religious freedom. As the Court itself said, the state's duty of neutrality and impartiality is incompatible with any state power to assess the legitimacy of religious beliefs. From this assertion, it should follow that any power of the state to require registration as a prerequisite to conducting certain group religious activities should be considered illegal.

The recent European Court decision *Religionsgemeinschaft der Zeugen Jehovas v. Austria*[185] differed in important ways from the previous cases dealing with registration. In Austria, Jehovah's Witnesses were, for a prolonged period, denied status of a religious community, and only had the status of a religious association (less advantageous in several ways, including tax exemptions).

In its decision on the denial of registration the Court progressed in several important ways from earlier case law on similar matters: It considered the requirements as set in law, not just as applied in this case. The law, which required the prolonged period (10 years) before recognition as a religious community in every case, was criticized by the Court. Differently than in similar cases discussed above, the applicants were not interfered with in any way by the government, but the Court stressed that being placed in an inferior status was in itself a violation of their religious freedom. The fact that they could achieve most of the advantages of being a 'religious community' through other means did not change that.

The Court considered not just Article 9, but also Article 9 in conjunction with Article 14 (non-discrimination). It decided that refusal to give the applicant religious organization the same status as other religions without justifiable reasons was discrimination in protection of religious freedom.[186] The Court moved towards further recognition of the communal and collective aspects of manifestation of religion as included in this right. It mentions both Article 11 and Article 6 as important for ensuring judicial protection of the rights enshrined in Article 9.

The Court's decision achieves the right outcome and should be preferred to that of the dissenting judge, who thought there was no infringement of the right as all the applicant's practical objectives of manifestation of religion could be achieved through other means.

The collective aspects of manifestation of religion should be protected. This is no way contradicts the individual understanding of this right. There is no contradiction in this case between protecting the individual and protecting the group. While the reading in conjunction of Articles 9 and 11 would seem to strengthen the claim to view Article 9 as a group right, in fact this is not so. This would be an example of a 'communally exercised individual right' according to the classification explicated in Chapter 2. There is no conflict between the claims of the individual members of Jehovah's Witnesses and the Church as an organization. The Church, on their behalf, is claiming the aggregate of their Article 9 and Article 11 rights, to manifest their religious belief in association with each other.

The conflict in these cases arose between state and group. There is no real conflict between the group and subgroups. So it is consistent with the view that group rights should not override individual rights. A conflict would arise where a religious group objected to registration of a schismatic group. In this context as well, a religious community should not have an overriding right to decide against separate recognition of a subgroup, because the right to register, although it can only be utilized by religious groups, is ultimately the right of the individuals who compose the group.

Indeed, in *Supreme Holy Council of the Muslim Community v. Bulgaria*,[187] the Court decided that a state may not force factions of a minority religion to have one unified organization, and must remain neutral on religious matters.

It had elsewhere decided that even regarding the state-church, a state could not compel a splinter faction to remain within the state-church, despite the social cohesion which the state may claim to be dependent on maintaining a unified church.[188]

3.3.3.1 State involvement in private disputes

Even when registration is not a prerequisite for engaging in vital religious activities, it gives power to the state in allocating rights to groups. When a schism occurs, the state may be forced to decide between religious subgroups. Even a non-biased government may find itself in an impossible position. Allocating group rights to one subgroup of a religion may be seen by the main institutions of the religion as impinging on its religious community's autonomy. This, again, points to the problem inherent in recognition of groups as subjects of religious rights. Recognition of groups and maintenance of group autonomy to conduct their internal affairs may entail non-recognition of schismatic subgroups. However, from a perception of religious freedom as an individual right it would follow that no group can object to the recognition of another which it views as its subgroup. Registration requirements can serve to hinder this interpretation, and should be revoked.

A breakaway subgroup is no less problematic in a state that eschews any kind of registration. Conflicts may involve private law rights such as use of churches, as happened in the US case of *Kedroff*.[189] The Convention of the North American Churches of the Russian Orthodox Church broke away from the hierarchy of the Supreme Church Authority in Moscow. In a dispute concerning use of a New York church, the Court invalidated a New York state law[190] that declared the autonomy of the American Church. The Court decided that it may only recognize decisions of the Church according to its hierarchy headed by the Moscow Church Authority, and not US government decisions which interfere with it. The Court recognized church autonomy as a constitutional principle. Courts have held that churches have autonomy in making decisions regarding their own internal affairs. The church autonomy doctrine prohibits civil court review of internal church disputes involving matters of faith, doctrine, church governance, and polity.

The Court preferred the (foreign) church even to the choices made by its (US) members. The recognition of church autonomy in a group rights interpretation of religious freedom has led to the unfortunate result that the religious freedom of members of the (American) subgroup was made subject to that of the group. This case shows why a group-rights approach leads to unwarranted results. Individuals of a faith who wish to determine their own decisions have no choice but to have this determined by the larger organization even one that is overseas.

Even a state that has no registration requirements is thus faced with a need to determine whether it should recognize, for legal purposes, religious subgroups despite opposition of the main religious group.

3.3.4 Claims of leadership

Legal powers of a state to appoint or change religious leadership may also involve the state in conflicting claims to leadership within the groups, highlighting, once again, the inherent problem of according rights of religious freedom to groups. Such powers can, of course, be misused by the state to breach religious freedom. Even if they are not deliberately misused, a decision about religious leadership by the state may involve it in making unwarranted decisions about claims concerning legitimacy of religious groups.

The European Court in *Hasan and Chaush v. Bulgaria*[191] decided that the rights of contenders to the leadership of the Muslim community to participation in the life of the community, protected by Article 9 of the Convention, as interpreted in the light of Article 11, had been breached when the state authorities were biased in exercising their power by law to decree the leadership of the Muslim community, rather than acting according to the election by-laws of the community. The Court made clear that state interference in the organization of the religious community was a breach of Article 9 rights of every member of that community. However, the Court refrained from deciding whether state legal powers to change leadership of religious communities infringe Article 9, because, even if legal *in principle,* discretion was obviously misused by the state in this case.

This was a missed opportunity to examine whether legal powers of the state to change the leadership of religious communities are a breach of religious freedom. The decision leaves states considerable power over religious communities. As a result, misuse of this power will be remedied by the Court in each case, but the state powers to appoint religious leaders remain intact. Better protection of religious freedom would have been given to religious communities, had the court set a priori limitations on state powers to register religions and change their leadership. A power of the state to decide who are the clergy and leaders of a religious community is unwarranted even where the state is acting neutrally. The state must decide who constitute the leadership, and so must accept one determination of the group, necessarily ignoring other factions of the group that do not agree with the majority view. Freedom of religion for all is guaranteed if everyone can choose their own leaders. However, as will be seen next this may not be possible when community clergy also discharge state functions.

The status of religions, including the rights of communities and the appointment of their leaders, has in the past sometimes been determined in bilateral agreements between state and representatives of religions in the state or by international agreement of the state with a co-religionist state of the minority. This would suggest a way for religious communities to take part in defining their own rights, but this method is not free of the problems inherent in according legal rights to religious communities.

Unusually, the Muslim minority in Greece remains protected by provisions of an international treaty between states regarding co-nationals,[192] as was prevalent before the Second World War.[193] The Treaty of Athens,[194] which obliged Greece to allow the Muslim community of Thrace to elect its own religious leaders, who also have jurisdiction over matters of personal law, was examined by the European Court in *Serif*.[195] Greece appointed by legislative decree a different mufti from that elected by the community. Serif, the community-elected leader, was convicted for usurping the function of a clergyman,[196] and he ultimately applied to the European Court.

The Court concluded that Greece acted in violation of Article 9 of the European Convention, by punishing a person for acting as a religious leader and by using the criminal law to prevent there being more than one leadership of a religious community. The Court did not examine the legality of the state powers to choose muftis or any other religious officials bestowed with state legal powers, as such a determination was not necessary in this case. The Court did not ask whether Article 9 includes a right for members of a community to choose their own leadership, both for religious functions and for judicial functions.

In this case, Serif was not exercising any judicial functions accorded to muftis by the state, but was only performing expressive religious acts. While regarding purely religious leadership the state has no legitimate interest to interfere with community choice, regarding judicial-religious appointments, this is not a simple question. If community autonomy is recognized by the state, as it was in this case, state powers to appoint its officials undermine it. Nevertheless, the state has a legitimate interest in the appointment of judges in jurisdictions that are devolved to religious communities, as they exercise legal powers of the state.

However, if the state undertakes to appoint religious leaders to state functions, such as granting them legal jurisdiction, it is effectively involved in choosing community leadership. This leaves hollow the religious rights of individuals and subgroups to choose their own religious leadership.

3.3.5 Conclusions

It is inevitable that states accord a legal status to religious groups. Religious groups exist, and the state, by recognizing or ignoring them, treating them favourably or unfavourably, gives them a certain legal status in the state. In some cases, the legal status given is a means of restricting and controlling religions, such as registration requirements and involvement in appointment of clergy. Such state regulation, which has the capacity for misuse, is unwarranted, whether in fact it is misused or not. In other cases legal status is given for benign considerations, and may even be necessary in order to provide complete religious freedoms. Such is the case when recognizing groups in order to bestow them with powers to perform public legal functions, exempt them from general laws that contradict their religious doctrine, and allocate state budget. However, the need to decide who constitutes religious groups involves the state in an exercise which itself possibly breaches both state neutrality and rights of claimant individuals, groups or subgroups which are not recognized. International human rights law has so far largely avoided these questions.

The implications for the thesis advanced in this work are complex: the problems of conflicting group claims support the argument for an individual right, but they also show that without recognition of groups as claimants, important aspects of religious freedom will be meaningless.

3.4 Jurisdiction cannot be accorded to a religious community to which individuals may not have chosen to belong. Even where such choice exists, the state should not allow individuals to waive rights of religious freedom to their communities

Some states have granted legal jurisdiction to religious communities, typically in matters of personal law.[197] This arrangement persists in those states for historical and political reasons related to internal conflicts about the role of religion in the state.[198] Such a grant of group rights comes at the expense of individual rights, which cannot be squared with international human rights standards.

The right to have religious tribunals and be able to administer religious law has not been explicitly recognized in international human rights documents. It has been claimed that it should be seen as included within Article 1 of the 1981 Declaration.[199] Even on this approach, because religious law can conflict with other human rights obligations, the extent of its application in such cases must be limited accordingly.[200] However, a prior question is whether there is such a right to a religious legal system, or whether there is no such right because religious legal jurisdiction as such breaches individual rights. By a right to religious law and jurisdiction, in this discussion, I refer to a right to exercise legal powers over the members of the community (as distinct from internal tribunals exercising jurisdiction over clergy or purely doctrinal matters).

A right to a religious legal system (comprising both substantive religious law and jurisdiction of religious courts) cannot be claimed to be part of the right to religious freedom for two reasons: first, a legal system necessarily has an element of coercion. Not every member of the religious community wants to be subject to religious law. Not every individual has consented to the imposition of religious law, but rather consent to the system of religious jurisdictions has been given by the representatives of the community. Even if a member of the community originally consented to its jurisdiction, for instance by entering a religious marriage, he or she may have entered a religious marriage for lack of choice, or may not have knowingly consented to different aspects of personal law that may be subject to such jurisdiction throughout his or her life.

Second, by relinquishing state power to the religious law, the state acknowledges an independent and equal source of law. State recognition cannot legitimize a source of law that does not emanate from the state. Religious law, even when recognized by the state, has a source external to the state. The demand for a right to a legal system is such a demand for state power. A right to religious freedom is a right against the state, but not a right to supersede the state.[201]

If a right to a religious legal system is recognized as part of the right of religious freedom, it applies not only to minority religions, but also to a majority religion. In the case of a sole dominant religion, the problem of the creation of an alternative source of law to that of the state, and its potential implications for human rights are underscored. This is so, as long as religious law remains unanswerable to international human rights standards. This danger exists, even where individuals have a choice not to a subject of this system.

The devolvement of legal power to the religious community cannot be predicated on members' consent either. While individuals can make contractual arrangements in matters of private law, personal law is not just a private matter but also a matter of state interest. It should not be permitted to be left entirely to private arrangement. Even provisions in personal law which are *jus dispositivus* are still subject to the state legal system. But the state cannot accept recognition of an entire system of religious personal law on the basis of mere agreement between community members.

A state that has only religious legal systems without a secular alternative breaches the religious freedom of agnostics/atheists and of those who do not belong to a recognized religious system but are forced into one of the existing systems.[202] Moreover, it also breaches the religious freedom of those members of existing religious communities who do not want to be subject to religious laws.

A state that offers concurrent religious and secular jurisdiction still encounters the problems discussed earlier, both of legitimacy of the source of religious law in the state and of the consent to being subject to what is often a lifelong jurisdiction under one religious system. Individual members of the community may not have accepted, merely by belonging to the community, to be under religious jurisdiction, and cannot opt out of it without forsaking their religious, social and cultural connections, which compose their identity, and in some cases cannot opt out at all.

In India, the claim that different personal laws for Hindus and Muslims discriminate on the ground of religion, contrary to Article 15(2) of the Indian Constitution, and therefore are null,[203] was discussed and rejected by the Bombay High Court in *State of Bombay v. Narasu Appa Mali*.[204] The claim in the particular case related to a law making bigamy an offence for Hindus but not for Muslims.[205] The Indian Court reasoned that the communities were governed by different religious texts providing for totally different concepts of marriage acknowledged by the Indian Constitution.

Today, such discrimination contravenes Article 26 (as well as Article 18) of the ICCPR. The argument that different personal laws constitute discrimination on the grounds of religion could apply to any aspect of personal law, not only regarding criminal sanctions, that treats individuals of different religions differently because they belong to different religions. The only way for the individual not to be discriminated against is to convert to another religion, clearly not always a viable choice. Thus, recognizing a right of communities to administer religious law both contravenes religious freedom of individuals and discriminates between individuals on the grounds of religion.

Other human rights besides religious freedom are infringed in community systems, including the right to equality on the basis of sex. These will be discussed in Chapters 4 and 5.

Such jurisdictions of religious communities are typically instituted to protect the autonomy of illiberal religious communities within a secular state structure. The question of compatibility of such regimes with Article 9 is apparent in cases before the European Court. So, in *Serif*,[206] discussed earlier, the European Court stated that Article 9 does not *require* states to give legal effect to religious marriages and religious judicial decisions. This had already been decided by the Commission in a previous case.[207] Religious freedom does not include a right to recognition of religious law as binding on the state. Indeed, as long as there is no prohibition on performing religious marriages, the religious freedom of those marrying is not infringed by the legal requirement of civil marriage. But it has to be acknowledged that this is a liberal view of religion, a view that displaces religion from the public sphere. From a religious point of view, especially that of a religious community, the constitutive power of religious acts is no less important than the ceremonial aspect.

Implicitly, the Court in *Serif* assumed that state parties *may* give legal effect to religious marriages and religious judicial decisions. However, the legality of this is far from clear. This may impinge on individual religious freedoms of people who might be under such jurisdiction involuntarily, including, for instance, minors.

The conflict of a religious legal system with the European Convention is evident in this same case. The muftis of the Muslim community in Greece are public servants. They are judges with concurrent jurisdiction over marriage, divorce, alimony, execution of wills, custody and emancipation of minors of this minority community.[208] Their judgments are given civil effect by civil courts, which only examine whether the muftis' judgment conforms to the Greek Constitution and is within its jurisdiction.[209] However, conformity to Greek law includes conformity to international law, which is paramount to domestic law in Greece.[210] So, judgments of muftis must conform to the European Convention, and thus must not be discriminatory, for example, on grounds of gender.[211] Such a conflict has not yet occurred in a case before either the European Court or domestic Greek courts. In the European Court, clearly the rights of the community would have to yield to individual rights protected by the European Convention. A Greek court would be faced with a decision whether to uphold the Muslim community rights protected by Greece's international obligations under the Treaty of Athens, or the individual rights to which Greece is committed under the European Convention.

The potential conflict between legal jurisdiction of religious communities and the European Convention came to a head in the European Court discussion of *Refah*.[212] The European Court dealt specifically with the Refah Party's manifesto to set up in Turkey a plurality of legal systems of the different religious communities. Refah claimed that, under the existing (secular) system, religious freedom is curtailed, and the solution would be to let everyone choose the religious community and respective legal system to which they would belong. The Chamber (3rd section) of the European Court rejected this sort of community-based argument, a decision affirmed by the Grand Chamber to which the case was referred.

The Chamber stressed 'the State's role as the guarantor of individual rights and freedoms', and rejected, as incompatible with the Convention, the plan which 'would oblige individuals to obey, not rules laid down by the State in the exercise of its above-mentioned functions, but static rules of law imposed by the religion concerned'.[213] It concluded that 'the State has a positive obligation to ensure that everyone within its jurisdiction enjoys in full, and without being able to waive them, the rights and freedoms guaranteed by the Convention.'[214]

The Grand Chamber was somewhat more reserved in its criticism of the idea of a plurality of legal systems. It expressly declined to form an opinion in the abstract on the advantages and disadvantages of a plurality of legal systems. In the case at hand it decided, that as Refah's policy was to apply some of *shari'a*'s private law rules to a large part of the population in Turkey (namely Muslims), within the framework of a plurality of legal systems, it was not compatible with the Convention. The Grand Chamber surmised that such a policy went beyond permissible state policy which accepted religious wedding ceremonies before or after a civil marriage (a common practice in Turkey) and accorded religious marriage the effect of a civil marriage.[215]

The Court gave a strong individualistic interpretation to religious freedom. Specifically, it rejected the possibility of a political system in which individuals waive their religious freedom to their chosen religious community. It viewed the individual right as inalienable. It saw the state's role as guaranteeing the continuous religious freedom of the individual, a role it does not fulfil if it allows individuals to choose religious systems that do not respect their Convention rights. The Grand Chamber implied that the system that Refah was proposing was not truly one of choice, it is only a system of choice in the sense that everyone can choose their religion, but once they choose a religion they are subject to its legal system. For most Turkish citizens, who are Muslims, conversion to another religion would not be a relevant choice, and they would be subject to Muslim law.

Other states outside Europe have pluralist legal systems in personal law. If a similar determination to that of the European Court were to be accepted in interpretation of international, not just European, human rights law, it would mean that pluralist religious legal systems of personal status law, such as exist in India[216] or Israel,[217] will be seen to infringe it. (In fact, personal law in Israel is still governed by remnants of the Ottoman *millet* system, which the Grand Chamber criticized.)

3.5 An individual conception of religious freedom should take into account the different positions of members of minorities and of majorities

An argument against the interpretation of religious freedom as an individual right is that individual protection does not differentiate between religions of minorities and the religion of the majority. Because members of minority religions are a priori less well placed to protect their rights, a seemingly equal protection of individual religious freedom will have unequal results for members of majorities and minorities. Indeed, individual rights analysis often does not take this difference into account, but it is possible to offer an individual rights analysis of religious freedom, which takes into account the unequal starting positions of members of minorities and members of majorities.

3.5.1 Employment

One problem that raises such considerations is that of the official days of rest. The state must make one determination on its day of rest, which cannot suit all religious groups. This issue reached the European Commission in the case of *Stedman*.[218] Stedman, a Christian, refused to work on Sundays, resulting in termination of her work contract. On her application, the Commission decided that her right to religious freedom had not been breached, because she was free to resign from the post. *Konttinen*[219], in which the applicant was a worker who was a Seventh Day Adventist, was similarly decided. Because of his religion, he refused to work on Saturday, and was dismissed from state employment. The Commission had applied in *Konttinen* the same reasoning that it later applied in the *Stedman* case. In both cases, the Commission found that Article 9 had not been breached, as the worker could leave his or her job, and maintain his or her religious holy day. Article 14 (equality in enjoyment of rights) had not been breached either, according to the Commission, because no individual is guaranteed that their holy day will be regarded as a state day of rest.[220]

In a similar case in the UK, *Copsey v. WWB Devon Clays Ltd*,[221] a worker was dismissed because he refused to work on Sunday, and claimed this was unfair dismissal. The Court of Appeal dismissed his claim. Mummery LJ, relying on the rulings of the ECHR in *Ahmad, Konttinen* and *Stedman*, decided that Article 9 was not engaged as the applicant could have chosen different employment in which he would not have to work on his day of rest. Rix LJ, however, found that the employer *does* have to provide reasonable accommodation to the employee, but that the employer had acted reasonably in this case. This seems the preferable approach in principle.

The argument of voluntary exit, used by the ECHR in *Stedman* and *Konttinen* and which has also been used on other occasions by the Commission,[222] is unsatisfactory, particularly in the case of employment. The worker may not have a choice. Economic and social considerations may preclude other employment. Allowing the worker a choice between losing his job and having to work on his holy day *does* restrict his religious freedom.

Such a restriction might be justified in some cases, but not in others. In Stedman's case it is justified, because she observes the day of rest of the majority. While some jobs necessarily must include Sunday work, her day of rest conforms to the general day of rest, and Sunday work is the exception required only in specific employments. In the case of Konttinen, the worker belongs to a minority religion, with a different holy day than the majority. Society does not accommodate his religious needs, as his holy day is not the general rest day. He has a stronger claim to infringement of religious freedom. Being a member of a minority religion, he is at an *a priori* disadvantage compared to the general population. There is a difference between the two cases. The social context, in this case the position of the religious majority and minority groups, must be taken into account in the analysis.

The argument that the membership in a majority or a minority group must be taken into account in assessing claims of religious freedom in employment was already raised in Chapter 2. There it was seen that the need to regard social context does not mean that the right is a group right. It is an individual right of the employee. The Commission did not err in assessing the right as an individual right, but rather in ignoring the social context in which it is set.

3.5.2 Exemptions from general rules

The need to take into account the majority or minority placement of those seeking equality of religious freedom arises also in view of the latest developments in US religious freedom jurisprudence. Discrimination between mainstream and minority religions was not often explored in US Supreme Court cases. However, in the pre-*Smith* case, *Larson*,[223] the Court struck down a state law that exempted, from registration for the purposes of charitable solicitation, religious organizations that solicited less than fifty percent of their contributions from non-members, but not those that solicited above this share from non-members: 'Free exercise thus can be guaranteed only when legislators – and voters – are required to accord to their own religions the very same treatment given to small, new, or unpopular denominations', noted the Court. However, this test was overlooked in later developments in US religious freedom jurisprudence.

Analysis of the ruling in *Employment Division v. Smith*[224] shows how the test formulated by the Court, whether the law is neutral and generally applicable, gives little attention to whether the law impacts differently on religious majorities and minorities. Laws that are generally applicable and neutral tend to consider the interests of majorities rather than minorities, not necessarily intentionally. The facts of *Smith* itself exemplify this assertion. The use of peyote was prohibited under the state drug laws, with no exemption for sacramental use. The prohibition on use of peyote, with no exemption for sacramental purposes, is general. But the lack of exemption is relevant only to a religious minority. But if the general category is framed as prohibition on use of intoxicating substances used for sacrament, inconsistently peyote is prohibited but wine is not. In the process of legislation, the majority is more likely to ban a substance used by a minority. The argument of minority protection was mentioned in passing in the concurring opinion and in the dissent in *Smith*.

In *Church of the Lukumi Babalu Aye v. City of Hialeh*,[225] the Supreme Court decided that when an ordinance is narrowly tailored and targeted to fit a specific religion it is not neutral and must pass the more stringent 'strict scrutiny' test. This decision provides important protection for minority religions, but it does not change from the *Smith* formula.

The problem is evident in a lower court's application of the *Smith* test, regarding the Jewish *eruv*.[226] A municipal ordinance prohibited placing any thing on public poles. Religious Jews had placed wires to mark an *eruv*, a boundary that, under Jewish law, permits carrying or pushing outside the home objects (including wheelchairs and prams) in the Sabbath. The Court found merit in the *eruv* supporters' free exercise claim because the law was only enforced against them and not others who contravened it. But had this not been the case, the analysis under the 'generally applicable and neutral' test would mean that the city could have taken down the *eruv*. Of course, the law is applicable to all religions, but it is only relevant to the practice of one religion. The only case in which a minority is given consideration under the post-*Smith* rationale is when it has been specifically targeted. In all other cases, in which some religious groups are placed at a relative disadvantage, the discriminatory result is disregarded.

It seems that an individualistic conception of religious freedom has led to unequal protection of religious freedom of members of minorities. But this need not and should not be the case. The majority or minority context should be taken into account when determining religious freedom, otherwise equality in according this right is impaired. This does not detract from the nature of the right as an individual right.

3.6 Apportioning equality between religious groups is inherently problematic

If religious freedom were to be recognized as a group right, it would entail two further problems. The first is concerned with equality between religious groups, and is raised next. The second, related problem is concerned with evaluation of the worthiness of groups and is discussed in section 3.7.

Recognition of religious freedom as a group right entails recognizing religious equality (one aspect of religious freedom) as a group right. This translates into two questions, namely, what does equality between religious groups entail (what are the criteria for equal allocation of religious freedom between groups) and whether religious equality of individuals takes precedence over religious equality between groups.

3.6.1 Equality in allocation of resources

Some of the rights included in religious freedom can only be utilized by a group and not by an individual. But these rights still constitute an aggregate of individual rights. Such is the right to funding of religious institutions, in those states in which the constitutional system interprets religious freedom to include this right. Funding for communal religious activities can only be given to groups, not to individuals.

The state must not only accord religious freedom, but it must do so in a non-discriminatory manner.[227] The provisions of international human rights law mandate non-discrimination between individuals.[228] However, if states recognize religious communities as entities that are subject holders of the religious freedom and religious equality, then it must be decided how equality should be assessed between religious groups. Relying on the principle that religious freedom is ultimately an individual right would seem to suggest that equal apportionment should be based on the number of members. Approaches that view groups, as well as individuals, as holding religious rights, could suggest other methods: A group that the state had persecuted in the past should be compensated in order to be treated equally.[229] Alternatively, on the assumption that religious plurality is inherently good for social discussion in society, each religious group deserves an equal share of public resource, or at least a critical minimal share of resources, which will allow it to function and propagate its ideas.

A clash between the different perceptions of equality in allocation of resources arose in Hungary. As in other post-Soviet states, the state set about restoring religious rights after decades of Communist rule. One of the tasks the state set itself was restoring to former owners confiscated church property. However, a legal challenge to the constitutionality of this arrangement claimed that rather than an equal treatment of religions, compensating churches according to the property they owned before confiscation, was an attempt to recreate a previous religious landscape. The Hungarian Constitutional Court rejected this claim, and viewed the arrangement as a correct implementation of the right of religious freedom.[230]

This is a restitutional perception of equal treatment of religious groups. Other, distributional perceptions of religious equality could have been suggested, such as starting with a 'clean slate' and providing all religions with public aid according to current membership. Whichever way the state decides to apportion this restitution, it would necessitate a decision on how to judge equality between religious groups.

In a different allocation of public resources in Hungary, public broadcast media allocates broadcast time to the eight major religious communities, taking into account the proportional membership of each out of the general population. Size of membership is indeed a relevant factor in allocating a public resource, such as broadcast time. But it must be recognized that this too is a value-judgments about what equality of religious freedom means. It could be argued that this helps maintain the supremacy of existing religions with large membership over new religions, which necessarily have a smaller membership to start with. According to this argument, equality of religious freedom means giving all religions an equal opportunity in the marketplace of ideas, i.e. all must receive an equal time slot to propagate their beliefs to the public.

This analysis shows the difficulties of applying equality of religious freedom to groups. State involvement in allocation of public goods to religious groups, whether funding, property, broadcast time or other public goods, necessarily requires the state to set criteria for equality, indirectly revealing a value-judgment of the state on the merits of the groups. The dilemma of equal allocation to groups is indicative of a more general problem, which is inherent in a conception of group rights. An individual rights approach would entail allocation according to membership. However, as shown above, this may not be an adequate solution to the dilemma of group allocation.

3.6.2 *Equality on the basis of religion between individuals or between groups*

Equality between religious groups, rather than individuals, has been attempted for the purpose of resolution of conflict between religious groups, through constitutional recognition of more than one religion on an equal basis. The result of laying down the rights and limitations of groups may involve infringing individual rights of group members. Equality on an individual basis is sacrificed for equality based on groups. For example, government positions are allocated according to group affiliation. A qualified member of one group may not have an opportunity to be a candidate for a government position, but overall equality between the groups will be maintained.

The 1990 amendment of the Constitution of Lebanon[231] exemplifies these principles. It divides parliamentary seats equally between Christians and Muslims, and proportionately between denominations within these.[232] Top-level (although not other) positions are to be divided equally between Christians and Muslims.[233, 234]

Similarly, in the 1960 Constitution of Cyprus, Muslims are deemed members of the Turkish community and they elect a Turkish Vice-President. Greek Orthodox Christians are deemed members of the Greek community and they elect a Greek President.[235] In the Cypriot case, the complexity of the arrangement is compounded by the fact that the dichotomy between the two groups is both ethnic and religious.

Both the Lebanese Constitution and the existing Constitution of Cyprus curtail individual religious equality. A Muslim Turk cannot become president of Cyprus, and a Christian-Greek cannot be vice-president. A qualified Christian or Muslim Lebanese cannot obtain a top-level public position if the denominational quota has been filled. This manifests a conception of religious equality (or approximate equality) between groups, even at the expense of individual equality.[236]

In Northern Ireland, while the general legal framework is one of equality on an individual basis,[237] as a temporary measure the police force is legally permitted to recruit new officers according to an equal sectarian quota.[238] This arrangement is different, as it is a measure of limited duration in a system that is based on individual equality.

The strong argument for the preference of equality of religious groups above equality of individuals is a pragmatic one, if arrangements based on equality between groups achieve the sought outcome of prevention of conflict, particularly in situations of conflict resolution. However, in practice this has not necessarily proved so.

3.7 States should not evaluate the social worth of religious groups as this breaches state neutrality

Sometimes, states have to make a value judgment about religious groups when they must perform distributive functions, as seen in the case of budget allocation. In cases in which no action of the state is required, it is unwarranted for the state to make such value judgments, as the state must remain neutral in matters of religion. But, if positive action of the state is required, it may have no choice but to make such value judgments.

One such case, in which the state is called on to make a judgment as to the social worth of institutions, is tax exemptions. In *Walz*,[239] the US Supreme Court decided that property tax exemptions awarded to organizations for properties used solely for religious worship do not infringe the First Amendment prohibition on establishment of religion. Justice Burger, who delivered the opinion of the

Court, stressed that any position that the government adopt on taxation of religious institutions – exemption from taxation, exemption only for social activities of religious institutions, or no exemption – would inevitably result in some government entanglement with religion. Therefore, the government choice to exempt all religious institutions was a legitimate option. There is no need to evaluate the social good that the religious institution contributes to society (in the form of schools, kindergartens etc.) in order to justify the exemption. The extent of social involvement may differ between religions, and it is best that state authorities are not involved in evaluating the social worth of religions.

The scheme approved by Justice Burger, in which all religious activity may be tax exempt, amounts to permissible indirect government subsidy for all religions. It is based on the alluring, if paradoxical idea that a state is truly separate from religions if it supports all their activities rather than only their social, not directly religious activities. In order to maintain state neutrality, the ultimate criterion for choosing the methods of allocation of resources (or, conversely, fiscal exemptions) must be such that the state refrain from evaluating the worthiness of activities of religions.

Other states in which religion is separate from the state, such as France,[240] do engage in making such evaluations and permit state funding of institutions of a social (rather than religious) function that are operated by religious bodies. This aid, it can be claimed, does not further religion, as it benefits society as whole.[241] But at the same time it works, of course, to enhance the influence in society of those religions receiving the funding and distributing aid.

The outcome of such evaluations as to whether the activity has a social purpose or is purely religious is, in any case, culture specific and religion specific, and so best avoided. So, for example, the Japanese Supreme Court, in trying to distinguish social functions from religious functions, regarded certain Shinto religious ceremonies, deeply embedded in the national culture, as serving a social, rather than religious function, and thus being legitimately state supported under Japan's principle of separation of religion from state.[242]

Evaluation of the worthiness of the religious principles themselves is certainly a breach of religious freedom, and its outcome will discriminate illegitimately between religions. The English law of charitable trusts admitted as charitable 'for the advancement of religion' those religious associations that 'confer a benefit' on society, such as the intangible benefits of edification,[243] which were deemed not to accrue, for example, if the worship is not conducted in public.[244] This assessment involves the state in a value judgment of religious principles, and today would have been illegal under the Human Rights Act, under Article 9 in conjunction with Article 14 of the European Convention. Under the new UK Charities Act 2006 all charities must be for 'public benefit' to be recognized as charities, but it is clear from the consultation paper of the Charities Commission[245] that the public worship will no longer be needed.

In the cases discussed so far, the state had to make decisions on allocations and exemptions to religious organizations, so a decision *had* to be made whether to differentiate between different religious organizations. Even this decision has to avoid judgments of value of religions. *A fortiori*, in cases in which government of its own initiative and not in a fulfilment of a prescribed function decides to take a stand on religious groups, such a value judgment is completely unwarranted. As will be seen, however, it is not always easy to differentiate between value judgment by government of religions themselves, which breaches government neutrality, and value judgment of religious organizations that is warranted by their social activities.

In the *Universelles Leben* case,[246] the applicant association complained about a government publication that referred to it as a 'sect', claiming the pejorative labelling infringed its religious freedom under Article 9. The European Commission decided the application inadmissible, citing the European Court's decision in *Otto-Preminger-Institut*[247] that those who manifest religious belief must be prepared to face criticism of that belief. The Commission concluded that the state may convey criticism of religions, so long as it does not amount to indoctrination, and that in this case the publication had no adverse repercussions on the religious freedom of the association.

But criticism of religion by a state is not the same as criticism by individuals. A religion must accept criticism from individuals or other religions. However, the state has limitations, it must act neutrally towards all beliefs, and certainly not express opinions against any of them. Of course, if the religious organization conducts harmful activities, the state must warn against these specific harmful activities. In the absence of such specific proven activity, the state cannot legitimately pass a value judgment on religion.

Indeed, the reasoning in a later decision of the European Court, *Leela Förderkreise v. Germany*,[248] is closer to this approach. The European Court determined that certain pejorative terms could not be used by the state to describe a religious movement, although it did not prohibit the use of the term 'sect'.

In *American Family Association*,[249] a US Circuit Court made finer distinctions in adjudicating a similar matter of government criticism of religion. A city council issued a resolution condemning the stand of several organizations, including Christian organizations, on homosexuality and encouraging media outlets to ban their advertisements on the matter. The organizations argued that by this, government was veering from neutrality on matters of religion. The majority on the Court decided that the message was about a specific issue, not about the religion itself, and distinct from it. Thus, it was permissible. 'Defendants' actions had a plausible secular purpose, did not have the primary effect of inhibiting religion and did not create excessive entanglement with religion', opined the Court. The dissenting judge, however, read the resolution as attributing responsibility to the religious organizations for anti-gay hate crimes, and thus as a condemnation of their religious belief. In principle however, rather than in application in the particular case, the positions of the majority and dissent are close and preferable to that of the European Commission. The state may, and sometimes must, take a stand on public issues that religions also take a stand on, such as health, education and discrimination. But the neutral state should take a stand on specific actions by religions, and not about a religion as such.[250] The dissent reminds us that this is a thin line, but, nonetheless, one that should be observed.

3.8 Conclusion

Whatever status states have granted to religion or religions, they have not been and will not be able to avoid conflict between opposing demands of religious freedom. This is true whether they have an established state religion or not, whether they require religions to be registered or not. In particular, these are conflicts between communities, between factions of communities or between communities and individuals within them.

A consistent and principled manner of addressing these conflicts requires recognizing the right of freedom of religion as an individual right. Communal rights are derived from them, and cannot supersede them. Some rights must be allocated to groups, but they still are individual rights. If group religious rights are given primary or equal recognition (in relation to individual rights), the state is faced with decisions in which it has to define the group and choose one among competing leaderships. Such decisions of the state are, in themselves, an intrusion of the state into religious affairs, which itself is an infringement of religious freedom.

Primacy of religious freedom as an individual right means, that individual self-determination is the decisive factor in allocation of group rights and privileges. So, although the state cannot avoid intruding in religious conflicts, in the sense that it must decide for one side or another, it should do so according to this principled approach. For international law to intervene in the constitutional structure of the state is controversial. Restriction on exercise of state sovereignty is inherent to international human rights law, but as seen in this chapter, regarding religious freedom the intervention goes to the heart of constitutional structure and state identity. Nevertheless, and perhaps precisely because of the political agenda behind states' position towards religion, international law should mandate protection of this individual right.

Notes

1 W. C. Durham, 'Perspectives on religious liberty: a comparative framework', in J. D. van der Vyver and J. Witte (eds), *Religious human rights in global perspective Vol. II – Legal perspectives*, The Hague: Martinus Nijhoff Publishers, 1996, 1.
2 I use the terms 'established church' and 'established religion' interchangeably. As most of the debate on the position of religion in the state has focused on Christian states, I continue to use the phrase 'state-church', but the legal positions discussed refer equally to other state-established religions.
3 Such as in Yemen (Article 3 of the 1994 Constitution), and in some states in Nigeria (see the 1999 Federal Constitution: Art. 275). Establishment of Sharia Court of Appeal; Art. 276 Appointment of Grand Kadi and Kadis of the Sharia Court of Appeal of a State; Art. 277 Jurisdiction; Art 278 Constitution; Art. 279 Practice and Procedure, available at http://nigeria.gov.ng/NR/rdonlyres/D38CF776-EE00-48DF-A09D-C06FE29997DA/0/NigerianConstitution.pdf (accessed 11 December 2009).
4 Iran has a republican constitutional structure with a legislative authority (*majlis*), but all enactments of the *majlis* are submitted to the Council of Guardians for inspection of their conformity to the tenets of Islam before they can become law (Article 94 of the 1979 Constitution). The executive branch is headed by a president, whose candidacy must likewise be approved by the *majlis* (Article 110 of the 1979 Constitution) (C. Mallat,

The renewal of Islamic law: Muhammd Baqer as-Sader, Najaf and the Shi'i International, Cambridge: Cambridge University Press, 1993).

5 The Constitution, Article 27, states that the King must be 'an adherent of Aryan Culture and the Hindu Religion'.

6 K. Gilbert, 'Women and family law in modern Nepal: statutory rights and social implications', *New York University Journal of Law and Politics,* 24, 1992, 729.

7 The possible conflict is with Convention on the Elimination of All Forms of Discrimination Against Women (adopted 18 December 1979) 1249 UNTS 13, Articles 2(b),(d), and (f).

8 Similar liberal states with a state-church are Norway, Denmark, Sweden, and Iceland.

9 In the United Kingdom, the head of the state is the head of the Church (the monarch is the Supreme Governor of the Church of England), as first established by Supremacy of the Crown Act 1534 (Repealed), and every monarch is required to join the Church of England, and marry a member of that religion (The Act of Settlement 1701). Other manifestations of the Establishment of Church are the membership in the House of Lords of Church of England Archbishops and Bishops (See: L. Leeder, *Ecclesiastical law handbook,* London: Sweet & Maxwell, 1997, 13), the appointment by the monarch of bishops and archbishops upon the advice of the Prime Minister, and the legislation of Measures of the General Synod of the Church of England, enacted pursuant to the Church of England Assembly (Powers) Act 1919, which is an Act of Parliament, constituting primary state legislation in the UK. In 1998 it was reported that the UK government is planning to amend the Act of Settlement, removing the bar on Catholics from taking the throne. See http://www.guardian.co.uk/world/2008/sep/25/anglicanism.catholicism1 (accessed 11 December 2009).

10 Currently, calls for disestablishment of the Church of England are heard from the Church and even (informally) the General Synod itself. A recent poll showed 48% of the UK population favour ending the existing link between state and Church, and only 36% wish to maintain it (A. Travis, 'Support grows for splitting church and state link', *The Guardian,* 23 January 2002).

11 On the UK and Church of England, see W. H. Mackintosh, *Disestablishment and liberation: the movement for the separation of the Anglican Church from state control,* London: Epworth Press, 1972. On the Orthodox Church see S. Runciman, *The Orthodox churches and the secular state,* Sir Douglas Robb Lectures, Auckland: University of Auckland, 1970.

12 Following in this matter the Krishnaswami Report: A. Krishnaswami, *Study in the matter of religious rights and practices – report of the Special Rapporteur of the Sub-Commission on Prevention of Discrimination and Protection of Minorities,* New York: United Nations, 1960. (See also: B. Dickson, 'The United Nations and freedom of religion', *International and Comparative Law Quarterly,* 44, 1995, 327–357.)

13 UN Doc A/8330 App. III (1971).

14 General Comment 22, CCPR/C/21/Rev.1/Add.4, 1993, para. 9 states only that: '[t]he fact that a religion is recognized as a state religion or that it is established as official or traditional or that its followers comprise the majority of the population, shall not result in any impairment of the enjoyment of any of the rights under the Covenant.'

15 See also: CCPR/3 (1982) (consideration by the Human Rights Committee of the initial report by Morocco).

16 The former Special Rapporteur, Elizabeth Odio Benito did not reach a conclusion as to whether legal arrangements such as establishment per se lead to intolerance, although she recognized that establishment does amount to certain discrimination. (E. Odio Benito, *Elimination of all forms of intolerance and discrimination based on religion or belief,* New York: United Nations, 1989, 20.)

17 *Darby v. Sweden* (1991) 13 EHRR 774 ECtHR.

18 J. Morsink, *The Universal Declaration of Human Rights: origins, drafting and intent,* Philadelphia: University of Pennsylvania Press, 1999, 263.

19 Comm. No. 195/1985 *Delgado Páez v. Colombia* CCPR/A/45,40/1990.
20 UN Doc. A/49/40 vol. I (1994) 31 at paras. 158 and 162.
21 Comm. No. 694/1996 *Waldman v. Canada*, CCPR/C/67/D/694/1996, at para 10.4.
22 *Darby v. Sweden* (1991) 13 EHRR 774 ECtHR.
23 *Canea Catholic Church v. Greece* (1999) 27 EHRR 21 ECtHR.
24 In cases such as: *Darby v. Sweden* (1991) 13 EHRR 774 ECtHR; App. No. 27008/95 *Williamson v. UK* EComHR.
25 See W. C. Durham, 'Perspectives on religious liberty: a comparative framework', in J. D. van der Vyver and J. Witte (eds), *Religious human rights in global perspective Vol. II – Legal perspectives*, The Hague: Martinus Nijhoff Publishers, 1996, 1.
26 Agreements of states with the Catholic Church reported to the study commissioned by Sub-Commission on Prevention of Discrimination and Protection of Minorities in 1989 were those of: Bolivia, Colombia, Italy, Argentina, Austria, Dominican Republic, Ecuador, El-Salvador, France, Federal Republic of Germany, Haiti, Hungary, Libya, Malta, Monaco, Morocco, Paraguay, Peru, Philippines, Poland, Portugal, Spain, Switzerland, Tunisia, Venezuela, Yugoslavia. (E. Odio Benito, *Elimination of all forms of intolerance and discrimination based on religion or belief*, New York: United Nations, 1989.)
27 In Spain, the Concordat was concluded concurrently to the framing of the 1979 constitution. Article 16(3) of the Constitution states that: 'No religion shall have a state character. The public powers shall take into account the religious beliefs of Spanish society and maintain the appropriate relations of cooperation with the Catholic Church and other denomination.' On the Spanish process of secularization of the Constitution see: J. A. Santo Paz, 'Perspectives on religious freedom in Spain', *Brigham Young University Law Review*, 2001, 669.
28 The Lateran Pact of 1929 between Italy and the Vatican preceded the 1948 Italian Constitution, Church and State were further separated by the 1985 Concordat replacing the Lateran Pact. The separation is enshrined in Article 7 of the Constitution (1947) which states:

(1) The State and the Catholic Church shall be, each within its own order, independent and sovereign.
(2) Their relations shall be regulated by the Lateran Pacts. Such amendments to these Pacts as are accepted by both parties shall not require the procedure for Constitutional amendment.

29 In Peru, the 1980 Concordat approved by Decreed Law 23211 preceded the 1989 secular constitution, which 'recognizes the Catholic church as an important element in the history, culture and moral formation of Peru'. This displaced the stronger reference in the 1933 constitution which 'protects' the Catholic faith, which, in turn, displaced the even stronger relationship in the 1920 constitution which declared that 'the nation shall profess the Roman Catholic Apostolic religion'.
30 Italy: See Article 8 of the Italian Constitution:

(2) Religious denominations other than Catholic shall have the right to organize themselves according to their own by-laws provided that they are not in conflict with the Italian legal system.
(3) Their relations with the State shall be regulated by law on the basis of agreements with their respective representatives.

Spain has agreements with the Evangelical, Islamic and Jewish communities establishing their legal status: Law 24/1992 Approving the Agreement of Cooperation between the State and the Federation of Evangelical Religious Entities of Spain; Law 25/1992 Approving the Agreement of Cooperation between the State and the Federation of Israelite Communities of Spain; Law 26/1992 Approving the Agreement of Cooperation between the State and the Islamic Commission of Spain, all agreements concluded pursuant to Article 7 of the General Act on Religious Freedom.

31 Their amendments do not require further constitutional implementation. Article 7(2) of the Italian Constitution.

32 Judgment no. 125/1957, See: D. L. Certoma, *The Italian legal system*, London: Butterworths, 1985, 121.

33 In Luxembourg, the Constitution, Article 22, states that: 'The State's intervention in the appointment and installation of heads of religions, the mode of appointing and dismissing other ministers of religion, the right of any of them to correspond with their superiors and to publish their acts and decisions, as well as the Church's relations with the State shall be made the subject of conventions to be submitted to the Chamber of Deputies for the provisions governing its intervention.' The HRC, in its concluding observations on the Luxembourg state report, UN Doc. A/48/40 vol. I (1993) 30, para. 134, expressed concern over discrimination against religions that had not entered into a covenant with the state, and therefore were not supported by the state.

34 This followed the demise of the colonels' rule.

35 See S. Mews (ed.), *Religion in politics*, Harlow: Longman, 1989, 88. This occurred at a time of growing integration into (liberal) Europe. On newer initiatives to further secularize the state, see Y. Stavrakakis, 'Religion and populism: reflection on the "politicised" discourse of the Greek Church', Discussion Paper No. 7, May 2002, The Hellenic Observatory, The European Institute, The London School of Economics, available at http://www.lse.ac.uk/collections/hellenicObservatory/pdf/StavrakakisDiscussionPaper.pdf (accessed 8 December 2009).

36 By 'secularity', I will refer to a variety of constitutional arrangements of states that do not endorse religion. The term 'secularism' has been used by some states to define their specific constitutional principle, I will use this term when discussing them.

37 See Chapter 2.

38 Article 26, and see J. A. Santo Paz, 'Perspectives on religious freedom in Spain', *Brigham Young University Law Review*, 2001, 669, 684.

39 Article 27.

40 J. A. Santo Paz, 'Perspectives on religious freedom in Spain', *Brigham Young University Law Review*, 2001, 669, 685; J. Martinez-Torrón, 'Freedom of religion in the case law of the Spanish Constitutional Court', *Brigham Young University Law Review*, 2001, 711.

41 Santo Paz, Ibid., 669.

42 The 1967 Law of Religious Freedom.

43 Article 16(3) of the Spanish Constitution states: 'No religion shall have a state character. The public powers shall take into account the religious beliefs of Spanish society and maintain the appropriate relations of cooperation with the Catholic Church and other denominations.'

44 Articles 27 and 130 of the Constitution prohibited religious vows and monastic orders, prohibited religions from owning charitable organisations, restricted public worship outside churches, voided the legal effect of religious oaths, stated that Churches had no legal personality, regulated the number of ministers, prohibited political voting of ministers, forbade ministers form criticizing laws or authorities, prohibited religious publications from commenting on public matters and prohibited political meetings in churches.

45 The 1917 Constitution, Article 24.

46 See J. A. Vargas, 'Freedom of religion and public worship in Mexico: a legal commentary on the 1992 federal act on religious matters', *Brigham Young University Law Review*, 1998.

47 Article 130.

48 See R. Hernandez-Forcada, 'The effect of international treaties on religious freedom in Mexico', *Brigham Young University Law Review*, 2002, 301, 307.

49 Argentina had likewise progressed through tumultuous relations of the state with the Vatican, exercising severe state control during most of the 20th century up until an

agreement of separation of Church and state in 1966, followed by the constitutional provision (Article 2) stating 'The Federal Government supports the Roman Catholic Apostolic religion.' See G. N. Floria, 'Religious freedom in the Argentine Republic: twenty years after the Declaration on the Elimination of Intolerance and Religious Discrimination', *Brigham Young University Law Review*, 2002, 341.

50 The Turkish Constitution, Article 24, declares that: 'Everyone shall have the right to freedom of conscience, faith and religious belief', and that 'No one may exploit or abuse religion, religious feelings or things held sacred by religion in any manner whatsoever with view to causing the social, economic, political or legal order of the State to be based on religious precepts, even if only in part, or for the purpose of securing political or personal influence thereby.' See further N. Oktem, 'Religion in Turkey', *Brigham Young University Law Review*, 2002, 371.

Other predominantly Muslim states that are constitutionally secular are: Senegal, Burkina Faso, Chad, Mali, Niger, Azerbaijan, Kyrgyzstan, Tajikistan, and Turkmenistan.

51 For a hermeneutic analysis of Turkish Secularism – *Laiklik* – see: A. Davison, *Secularism and revivalism in Turkey*, New Haven: Yale University Press, 1998; see also Chapter 4.

52 The Constitution of Turkey, Article 24.

53 *Kalac v. Turkey* (1997) 27 EHRR 552 ECtHR.

54 Ibid.

55 *Refah Partisi (The Welfare Party) v. Turkey* (2002) 35 EHRR 3 (Chamber decision); (2004) 37 EHRR 1 (Grand Chamber decision) ECtHR.

56 The *Refah* party rose to power in the 1980s and 1990s. In the 1994 general election it won 19% of the popular vote. A coalition government was formed with Mrs. Ciller's (secular) True Path Party. Some Turkish commentators championed the legitimacy of the party, which, although religious, chose to oppose secularism through participation in the democratic political process (N. Gole, 'Authoritarian secularism and Islamic politics: the case of Turkey', in A. R. Norton, *Civil society in the Middle East*, Leiden: Brill, 1995, 1). (Since the ruling a more moderate Islamic party, AKP, which embraced democratic principles, was elected to power in Turkey in November 2002.)

57 *Refah Partisi (The Welfare Party) v. Turkey* (2002) 35 EHRR 3 (Chamber decision).

58 *Refah Partisi (The Welfare Party) v. Turkey* (2004) 37 EHRR 1 (Grand Chamber decision) ECtHR.

59 French Constitution, Article 2.

60 The Law Concerning the Separation of Church and State, of 9 December 1905, D. 1906. 4. 6.

61 H. Astier, 'Secular France mulls mosque subsidies', *BBC News Online*, 20 January 2003. Nevertheless, the Government partially funded the establishment of the country's oldest Islamic house of worship, the Paris mosque, in 1926. (US Department of State International Religious Freedom Report 2002 – France, available at http://www.state.gov/g/drl/rls/irf/2002/13938.htm (accessed 8 December 2009).)

62 For a description of jurisprudence concerning the establishment clause of the 1st amendment to the US constitution see: G. Gunther, *Constitutional law*, 12th edn, New York: Foundation Press, 1999, 1503–1537. Description of the ever-widening religious diversity in the US, see J. Stein, 'Religion/religions in the United States: Changing perspectives and prospects', *Indiana Law Journal* I, 75, 2000, 37.

63 By barring Congress from making laws 'prohibiting exercise' of religion.

64 By barring Congress from making laws 'respecting an establishment of religion'.

65 This tension exists both at the federal level and at the level of the states. In *Everson v. Board of Education* 330 US 1 (1947) the US Supreme Court applied the First Amendment Establishment Clause to the states, through the Fourteenth Amendment. (Discussion of the way the case led to acceptance of the Establishment Clause's application to the states, see I. C. Lupu, 'Government messages and government money: *Santa Fe, Mitchell v. Helms* and the arc of the Establishment Clause', *William and Mary*

Law Review, 42, 2001, 771, 790). See also *Board of Education of Kiryas Joel Village School District v. Grumet* (512 U.S. 687 (1994)) in which the Everson principle was applied.

66 See G. R. Stone, L. M. Seidman, C. R. Sunstein, M. V. Tushnet and P. S. Karlan, *Constitutional law*, 6th edn, Aspen: Aspen, 2009, 1477–1502.

67 In such cases as *Muller v. Allen*, 463 US 388 (1983); *Aguilar v. Felton*, 473 US 402 (1985), *Mitchell v. Helms*, 530 US 793 (2000).

68 *Rosenberger v. University of Virginia*, 515 US 819 (1995).

69 N. Ashibe, 'The US constitution and Japan's constitutional law', in L. W. Beer (ed.), *Constitutional systems in late twentieth century Asia*, Seattle: University of Washington Press, 1992, 128.

70 Article 20(2).

71 Article 20(3).

72 Article 89.

73 Under the 19th-century Meiji Constitution, which recognized religious freedom for the first time, the imperial Shinto religion was nonetheless given an overarching position and was posited as a non-religious unifying force (T. Kawai, *Freedom of religion in comparative constitutional law with special reference to the UK, the US, India and Japan*, unpublished PhD Thesis, University of London, 1982).

74 Case (O) No. 902 of 1982; Minshu vol. 42, No. 5, p. 277.

75 Case (O) No. 902 of 1982; Minshu vol. 42, No. 5, p. 277.

76 Case (Gyo Tsu) No. 156 of 1992.

77 Including a groundbreaking ceremony at a municipal gymnasium. Case (Gyo-Tsu) No. 69 of 1971; Minshu vol.31, No. 4, at 533.

78 *Kohno v. Hiramatsu*, 56 MINSHŪ 1204 (Sup. Ct., July 9, 2002); *Higo v. Tsuchiya*, 56 MINSHŪ 1204 (Sup. Ct., Jul. 11, 2002). See further S. Matsui, 'Japan: the Supreme Court and the separation of church and state', *International Journal of Constitutional Law*, 2004 2(3), 534–545.

79 Article 137 of the Weimar Constitution was incorporated into the Basic Law through Article.140 of the Basic Law (Grundgesetz). Article 137(1) states that there will be no state-church. Article 4 of the Basic Law guarantees freedom of religion and belief. (Further see: S. Michalowski, L. Woods, *German constitutional law: the protection of civil liberties*, Aldershot: Ashgate, 1999, 187.)

80 Thus, prayers are allowed in state schools outside lessons, based on voluntary participation (*School Prayers Case* 52 BverfGE 223 (1979)), but display of crucifixes in classrooms is not permitted, as pupils have no similar possibility of avoiding it (*Crucifix in Classrooms Case* 93 BverfGE 1 (1995)).

81 Pursuant to the Weimar Constitution, Art. 137(5).

82 Section 3.2.

83 App. no. 30814/06.

84 *Buscarini v. San Marino* (1999) 30 EHRR 208 ECtHR.

85 This will be further discussed in Chapter 4.

86 (Adopted by the International Law Commission 2001) UN Doc. A/56/10.

87 *Rommelfanger v. Germany* (1989) 62 DR 151 EComHR.

88 *Costello-Roberts v. UK* (2001) 31 EHRR 1 ECtHR.

89 While the case did not involve Article 9, it can be seen as signalling the Court's approach to the applicability of Convention rights to non-state bodies.

90 See the German Constitutional Court's decision (of 4 June 1985) in the *Rommelfanger* case, that within the Catholic Church an employee has only a core free speech right.

91 Previously Article 25.

92 *X v. Sweden* (1979) 16 DR 68 EComHR. Also: *Omkarananda v. Switzerland* (1979) 25 DR 105 EComHR; *Iglesia Battisti et al. v. Spain* (1992) 72 DR 256 EcomHR. Previously, the Commission did not recognize that non-natural persons have rights under Article 9, in *Church of X v. UK* 12 YB 306. The question confronting the Commission was whether NGOs could claim a right to freedom of religion, conscience or belief.

93 L. Lehnof, 'Freedom of religious association: the right of religious organizations to obtain legal entity status under the European Convention', *Brigham Young University Law Review*, 2002, 561.

94 Saying the Church possesses and exercises rights 'in its own capacity as a representative of its members': *X v. Sweden* (1979) 16 DR 68 EComHR.

95 *X v. Denmark* (1976) 5 DR 157 EComHR.

96 See e.g. App. No. 72881/01, *The Moscow Branch of The Salvation Army v. Russia*; App. No. 48107/99 *Sâmbăta Bihor v. Romania*.

97 M. Evans, *Religious liberty and international law in Europe*, Cambridge: Cambridge University Press, 1997, 287, fn. 22.

98 *Finska forsamlingen I Stockholm and Hautaniemi v. Sweden* (1977) 23 EHRR CD 170 EComHR.

99 Now Article 34.

100 The applicant was one such parish that complained against the prescribed translation of liturgy into Finnish.

101 Not necessarily of the Church of Sweden, which under the Swedish 1992 Church Act (Kyrkolag 1992:300) has fairly limited characteristics of a state-church.

102 App. No. 27008/95 *Williamson v. UK* EComHR, as well as App. No. 12356/86 *Karlsson v. Sweden* EComHR; *Knudsen v. Norway* (1985) 42 DR 247 EComHR.

103 *Holy Monasteries v. Greece* (1994) 20 EHRR 1 EctHR.

104 *Parochial Church Council of the Parish of Aston Cantlow v. Wallbank* [2004] 1 AC 546, [2003] UKHL 37.

105 See opinions of Lord Nichols, Lord Hope, Lord Scott.

106 By Lord Hope (para. 49).

107 *Tyler v. UK* (1994) 77 DR 81 EComHR.

108 Art. 6(1): 'In the determination of his civil rights and obligations or of any criminal charge against him, everyone is entitled to a fair and public hearing within a reasonable time by an independent and impartial tribunal established by law.'

109 *König v. Germany* (1978) 2 EHRR 170 ECtHR.

110 See further: P. Van Dijk and G. J. H. van Hoof, *Theory and practice of the European Convention on Human Rights*, 3rd edn, The Hague: Kluwer, 1998, 394–406.

111 *Le Compte v. Belgium* (1982) 4 EHRR 1 ECtHR.

112 *H. v. Belgium* (1988) 10 EHRR 339 ECtHR.

113 *Pellegrin v. France* ECHR 1999-VIII 210 ECtHR.

114 App. No.63235/00, *Vilho Eskelinen v. Finland*, ECtHR.

115 Compare the American Convention on Human Rights, Article 8(1).

116 The Ecclesiastical Jurisdiction Measure 1963 (as amended by the Clergy Discipline Measure 2003) prescribes censures that may be pronounced when an ecclesiastical offence has been established. Decisions of ecclesiastical judges possess the status of law. However, whether review by civil court of the censures pronounced is possible is unsettled (N. Doe, *The legal framework of the Church of England*, Oxford: Clarendon Press, 1996, 217).

117 *R. v. Chief Rabbi ex p Wachmann* [1992] 1 WLR 1036, QB.

118 *Datafin v. City Panel on Takeovers and Mergers* [1987] QB 815.

119 *R. v. London Beth Din ex p Bloom* [1998] COD 131, QB.

120 See: T. M. Franck, *The power of legitimacy among nations*, New York: Oxford University Press, 1990; T. M. Franck, 'The emerging right to democratic governance', *American Journal of International Law* 86, 1992, 46; S. Marks, *The riddle of all constitutions: international law, democracy, and the critique of ideology*, New York: Oxford University Press, 2000.

121 B. Schanda, 'Religious freedom issues in Hungary', *Brigham Young University Law Review*, 2002, 405, 425.

122 *Jones v. Wolf*, 443 US 595 (1979).

123 *R. v. Imam of Bury Park Mosque ex p Ali* [1994] COD 142, CA.

124 App. No. 12356/86 *Karlsson v. Sweden* EComHR; *Knudsen v. Norway* (1985) 42 DR 247 EComHR; *X v. Denmark* (1976) 5 DR 157 EComHR.

125 *Rommelfanger v. Germany* (1989) 62 DR 151 EComHR. The applicant claimed a breach of his freedom of expression (Article 10), but it seems that, equally, there was a breach of his religious freedom, as the reliance on church doctrine prohibited him from expressing his ethical beliefs.

126 App. No. 12356/86 *Karlsson v. Sweden* EComHR.

127 App. No. 27008/95 *Williamson v. UK* EComHR.

128 Priests (Ordination of Women) Measure 1993 (No. 2).

129 See: App. No. 12356/86 *Karlsson v. Sweden* EComHR.

130 Priests (Ordination of Women) Measure 1993 (No. 2).

131 See: S. Bates, 'Gay bishop forced out by Lambeth Palace', *The Guardian*, 7 July 2003.

132 *Da Silva Mouta v. Portugal* (2001) 31 EHRR 47 ECtHR; *Frette v. France* ECHR 2002-I 34 ECtHR; App. No. 43546/02, *Case of E.B. v France*, ECtHR.

133 2000/78/EC of 27 November 2000, OJ 2000 L303/16.

134 Article 3.

135 Council Directive 2000/78/EC of 27 November 2000 establishing a general framework for equal treatment in employment and occupation O J L 303, 02/12/2000 pp. 16–22.

136 Section 13 (1): 'If a court's determination of any question arising under this Act might affect the exercise by a religious organisation (itself or its members collectively) of the Convention right to freedom of thought, conscience and religion, it must have particular regard to the importance of that right.'

137 Article 137(3) of the Weimar Constitution, which is incorporated into the Basic Law through Article 140.

138 In Article 48(2) of the Basic Law, which protects elected members from obstruction in accepting or exercising their office.

139 42 BverfGE 312 (1976).

140 70 BverfGE 138, 162–72 (1985).

141 70 BverfGE 138, 172 (1985).

142 *Sherbert v. Verner*, 374 US 398 (1963).

143 *Employment Division v. Smith*, 494 US 872 (1990).

144 For a compelling history of *Smith*, the man and the case, see G. Epps, *To an unknown god: religious freedom on trial*, New York: St. Martin's Press, 2001.

145 42 USC § 2000bb (1994).

146 In so far as it intruded on powers of the states.

147 *City of Boerne v. Flores, Archbishop of San Antonio* 521 US 507; 117 S. Ct. 2157 (1997).

148 Thus, a city ordinance specifically tailored to ban ritual slaughter of animals practiced by one religion, the Santria religion, did not survive the Supreme Court's scrutiny (*Church of the Lukumi Babalu Aye v. City of Hialeh* 508 US 520 (1993)).

149 *Gonzales v. Centro Espirita* 546 US 418 (2006).

150 *Bryce v. Episcopal Church of Colorado*, 289 F.3d 648 (10th Cir. 2002).

151 Generally on worker's rights within Churches, see D. Laycock, 'Towards a general theory of the religion clauses: the case of church labor relations and the right to church autonomy', *Columbia Law Review* 81, 1981, 1373, 1397.

152 See *EEOC v. Roman Catholic Diocese*, 213 F.3d 795, (4th Cir. 2000); *Gellington v. Christian Methodist Episcopal Church*, 203 F.3d 1299 (11th Cir. 2000); *Combs v. Central Tex. Annual Conference of the United Methodist Church*, 173 F.3d 343, (5th Cir. 1999).

153 *EEOC v. Catholic University of America*, 83 F.3d 455 at 462 (D.C. Cir. 1996).

154 *Petruska v. Gannon University* 462 F.2d 294 (3d Cir. 2006); *Dolquist v. Heartland Presbytery* 342 F. Supp. 2d 996, 1001 (D. Kansas 2004).

155 *EEOC v. Roman Catholic Diocese*, 213 F.3d 795, 800 (4th Cir. 2000).

156 *Alicea-Hernandez v. Catholic Bishop of Chicago*, 320 F.3d 698 (7th Cir. 2003).

157 Section 702, 42 U.S.C. Section 2000e-1.

158 *Corporation of the Presiding Bishop v. Amos*, 483 US 327 (1987).

159 *Corporation of the Presiding Bishop v. Amos*, 483 US 327 (1987).
160 *Rojas v. Fitch*, 127 F.3d 184 (1st Cir. 1997).
161 *EEOC v. Catholic University*, 83 F.3d 455, 460 (D.C. Cir. 1996).
162 App. No. 20402/92 *Spetz v. Sweden* EComHR.
163 Apps nos. 412/03 and 35677/04 *Holy Synod of the Bulgarian Orthodox Church v. Bulgaria*.
164 However, such schism in the religious community might justify civil law measures enacted by the state as to property allocation between the Churches (App. no. 52336/99 *Griechische Kirchengemeinde München und Bayern E.V. v. Germany* (dec.)).
165 See later discussion of improper use of minimum numbers of members for state registration of religions.
166 *Commack Self-serv v. Weiss* 294 F.3d 415 (2nd Cir. 2002).
167 *Cha'arei Shalom Ve'zedek v. France* ECHR 2000-VII 73 ECtHR.
168 Ibid., Cf. the dissenting opinion.
169 Y. Sheleg, 'In Germany, they're asking: Who's a Jew?', *Haa'retz English Edition*, 20 January 2003.
170 BVerwG 7 C 7.01 (Judgment of 28 in February 2002).
171 See below.
172 E.g. in Russia, the 1997 Law on Freedom of Conscience and Religious Associations.
173 E.g. in China, see: E. Kolodner, 'Religious rights in China: a comparison of international human rights law and Chinese domestic legislation', *Human Rights Quarterly*,16, 1994, 455.
174 See e.g. App. no. 184/02 *Kuznetsov v. Russia*.
175 In Bulgaria – The Denominations Act 2002; Georgia – a draft Law on Religion; Turkmenistan – The 1996 Law on Religion; in Belarus - 2002 Law on Religion. For a critical discussion of these laws, see *Problems of religious freedom and tolerance in selected OSCE states*, Report to the OSCE Supplementary Meeting on Freedom of Religion or Belief, Vienna, 17–18 July 2003, available at http://www.ihf-hr.org/viewbinary/viewdocument.php?doc_id=4723 (accessed 8 December 2009).
176 Bundesgesetzblatt 19/1988.
177 At least 20 years, 10 of which as a confessional community within the meaning of the law.
178 At least 0.2% of the population.
179 The law further discriminates between religions by creating a category of 'confessional communities', who do not share the rights of recognized religions, based on irrelevant criteria of membership size and length of time of operation.
180 App. no. 72881/01.
181 Similar decisions in which the Court found refusal to register ill founded in the particular case and therefore a breach of the applicants' religious freedom but with no scrutiny of the registration requirement itself: App. no. 952/03 *Biserica Adevărat Ortodoxă din Moldova v. Moldova*; App. no. 18147/02 *Church of Scientology v. Russia*, in which the Court viewed the refusal of Russia to register the Church as arbitrary and unlawful in the particular instance, and so in breach of Article 11 (freedom of association) read in light of Article 9. In App. No. 12282/02, *Cârmuirea Spirituală a Musulmanilor din Republica Moldova v. Moldova*, the European Court found that the registration requirement that included a demand to provide information on the fundamental principles of a religion may be justified in order to determine whether the religion seeking recognition was dangerous to a democratic society, and was compatible with Article 9.
182 *Metropolitan Church of Bessarabia v. Moldova* (2002) 35 EHRR 13 ECtHR.
183 The political background the case was that the government of Moldova was aligned with Russia and of the Church of Bessarabia with Romania.
184 These were prohibited to non-registered religions by sections 35 and 44 of the Moldovan Religious Denominations Act (see paragraph 129 of the Court opinion).

185 App. no. 40825/98, *Religionsgemeinschaft der Zeugen Jehovas v. Austria*, ECtHR (decided 31 July 2008).

186 This decision led to additional decisions in which refusal to recognize a religious society because it did not fulfil the registration criteria was deemed discriminatory (App. no. 76581/01, *Verein der Freunde der Christengemeinschaft v. Austria*, ECtHR) as was refusal to exempt from military service adherents of a non-registered religion where members of a registered religion would be exempted (App. no. 42967/98, *Löffelmann v. Austria*, ECtHR; App. no. 49686/99, *Gütl v. Austria*, ECtHR).

187 App. no. 39023/97, *Supreme Holy Council of the Muslim Community v. Bulgaria*, ECtHR.

188 *Metropolitan Church of Bessarabia v. Moldova* (2002) 35 EHRR 13 ECtHR.

189 *Kedroff v. St. Nicholas Cathedral*, 344 US 94 (1952).

190 The Religious Corporations Law of New York.

191 App. No. 30985/96 *Hasan and Chaush v. Bulgaria* ECtHR.

192 The Treaty of Lausanne from 1923, following the treaty of Athens of 1913, whose provisions were incorporated into Greek law in 1923. See: Kriari-Catrianis, I., 'Freedom of religion under the Greek Constitution', 47 *Revue Hellenique de Droit International* (1994).

193 See Chapter 1.

194 The Treaty of Athens, Article 11.

195 *Serif v. Greece* (2001) 31 EHRR 561 ECtHR.

196 See also App. No. 50776/99, 52912/99 *Agga v. Greece* ECtHR.

197 See the examples of India, Israel, Bangladesh and Sri Lanka discussed in Chapter 4. The effects on human rights of women of religious personal laws will be further discussed in Chapter 4.

198 See also Sudan, where conflict over accommodation of religious pluralism has been a basis of constitutional deadlock for the past 40 years. The 1985 Constitution states Islam to be the source of law, while the 1995 Asmara accords are premised on secularization. The Muslim community in the North is subject to *shari'a* personal and criminal law, while the South is subject to secular law. The *shari'a* system, however, affects both communities and both legal systems. The non-Muslim South is exempt from Islamic penal provisions, but this is a source of tension. For example, apostasy is a crime under Islamic law of the North, but the authorities of the South will be reluctant to extradite a Muslim apostate to the North (P. Nyot Kok, Lecture at the United States Institute for Peace meeting on 'religion, nationalism and peace in Sudan', 17 September 1997, Washington, DC).

199 D. J. Sullivan, 'Advancing the freedom of religion or belief through the UN Declaration on the Elimination of Religious Intolerance and Discrimination', *American Journal of International Law*, 82, 1988, 487, 514; F. Capotorti., *Study of the rights of persons belonging to ethnic, religious and linguistic minorities*, New York: United Nations, 1979, 155–156. This claim might also apply to religious freedom provisions in other international human rights instruments.

200 Sullivan, ibid.

201 See Chapter 2, fn. 12 and context.

202 D. J. Sullivan, 'Advancing the freedom of religion or belief through the UN Declaration on the Elimination of Religious Intolerance and Discrimination', *American Journal of International Law*, 82, 1988, 487, 518.

203 Under Article 13(1) of the Constitution.

204 *State of Bombay v. Narasu Appa Mali* AIR 1952 Bom 84; ILR 1951 Bombay 77. See further: V. P. Bharatiya, *Religion–state relationship and constitutional rights in India*, New Delhi: Deep and Deep, 1987.

205 The Bombay Prevention of Hindu Bigamus Marriages Act, 1946.

206 *Serif v. Greece* (2001) 31 EHRR 561 ECtHR.

207 *X v. Germany* (1975) 1 DR 64 EComHR [1975].

208 Pursuant to Law 1920/1921, Article 5, following the Treaty of Athens, 1913.
209 Law 1920/1921 Article 5 paragraphs 1 and 2. See: Kriari-Catrianis, I., 'Freedom of religion under the Greek Constitution', *Revue Héllènique de Droit International*, 47, 1994, 408.
210 Article 28.1 of the 1975 Greek Constitution mandates supremacy of international law (including the European Convention) over domestic laws.
211 Article 14 in conjunctions with other Articles such as Article 8 of the Convention. See Chapter 4.
212 *Refah Partisi (The Welfare Party) v. Turkey* [Judgment of the 3rd section, 2002], [Judgment of the Grand Chamber, 2004].
213 Ibid.
214 Ibid. If this reasoning will be accepted in interpretation of international human rights standards, it will mean that pluralist legal systems as exist in India or Israel will be seen to infringe religious freedom.
215 Ibid.
216 A. Parashar, *Women and family law reform in India: Uniform Civil Code and gender equality*, New Delhi: Sage Publications, 1992. Article 44 of the Constitution states that Indian legislators shall aim to establish a uniform civil code throughout India. This has not been achieved. Religious communities are governed by their own personal laws (Muslims, Christians, Zoroastrians, Jews and Hindus (including, for legal purposes, Buddhists and Sikhs)). India was aware of possible infringement of international standards, as it entered on its ratification of CEDAW a declaration regarding Articles 5(a) and 16(1) that it will abide by these provisions 'in conformity with its policy of non-interference in the personal affairs of any Community without its initiative and consent'. See further discussion in Chapter 4.
217 See Chapter 4.
218 *Stedman v. UK* [1997] 23 EHRR CD 168 EComHR.
219 *Konttinen v. Finland* (1996) 87-A DR 77 EComHR.
220 See also App. no. 55170/00 *Kosteski v. Macedonia*.
221 *Copsey v. WWB Devon Clays Ltd* [2005] EWCA Civ 932.
222 App. No. 16278/90 *Karaduman v. Turkey* EComHR; App. No. 18783/91 *Bulut v. Turkey* EComHR (religious students in a secular university), and by the European Court: App. No. 42393/98 *Dahlab v. Switzerland* ECtHR (religious teacher in a secular institution). These cases are discussed in Chapter 5.
223 *Larson v. Valente*, 456 US 228 (1982).
224 *Employment Division v. Smith*, 494 US 872 (1990).
225 508 US 520 (1993).
226 *Tenafly Eruv Association v. The Borough Of Tenafly* 309 F.3d 144 (3d Cir. 2002).
227 International Covenant on Civil and Political Rights, Article 2(1); In Europe: ECHR, Article 14.
228 International Covenant on Civil and Political Rights, Article 2(1); International Covenant on Social Economic and Cultural Rights Art 2(2).
229 Cf. Convention on the Elimination of all Forms of Discrimination against Women (adopted 18 December 1979) 1249 UNTS 13, Article 4(1).
230 *On the restitution of church property*, Decision 4/1993, (II.12) ABH. 48 (Constitutional Law Court), English translation in L. Sólyom and G. Brunner, *Constitutional judiciary in a new democracy*, Ann Arbor: University of Michigan Press, 2000, 246. See further discussion of the decision: B. Schanda, 'Religious freedom issues in Hungary', *Brigham Young University Law Review*, 2002, 405, 412–413.
231 Following the National Reconciliation Charter (the 'Taef Agreement', further see UN Doc. A/48/453 and E/C.12/1993/SR.14).
232 Article 24 states that:
The Chamber of Deputies is composed of elected members; their number and the method of their election is determined by the electoral laws in effect. Until such time

as the Chamber enacts new electoral laws on a non-confessional basis, the distribution of seats is according to the following principles:

a. Equal representation between Christians and Muslims.
b. Proportional representation among the confessional groups within each religious community.
c. Proportional representation among geographic regions.

233 Article G (a), the National Reconciliation Charter.
234 Lebanon's constitutional approach was not accepted by the Human Rights Committee. In its discussion of the Lebanese state report it expressed concern that every Lebanese citizen must belong to one of the religious denominations officially recognized by the Government, and that this is a requirement for eligibility to run for public office. It stated that this practice does not comply with the requirements of Article 25 of the Covenant (the right to vote and to be elected by universal suffrage) UN Doc. A/52/40 vol. I (1997) 53 at para. 353. Lebanon not only adopted a group-equality approach in its own constitution, but was an early proponent of group rights during the negotiation on the drafting of the UDHR, when such an approach did not hold sway. (J. Morsink, *The Universal Declaration of Human Rights: origins, drafting and intent*, Philadelphia: University of Pennsylvania Press, 1999, 274.)
235 Article 1: 'The State of Cyprus is an independent and sovereign Republic ... the President being Greek and the Vice-President being Turk elected by the Greek and the Turkish Communities of Cyprus respectively.'
Article 2: For the purposes of this Constitution:

(1) the Greek Community comprises all citizens of the Republic who are of Greek origin and whose mother tongue is Greek or who share the Greek cultural traditions or who are members of the Greek-Orthodox Church;
(2) the Turkish Community comprises all citizens of the Republic who are of Turkish origin and whose mother tongue is Turkish or who share the Turkish cultural traditions or who are Moslems.

236 Compare: an implied international endorsement of a group equality approach (on an ethnic basis) in Bosnia, in the Dayton Agreement, Annex IV, 35 ILM 170 (1996).
237 See: Northern Ireland Act 1998.
238 Police (Northern Ireland) Act 2000, Section 46.
239 *Walz v. Tax Commission*, 397 US 664 (1970).
240 1905 Law Concerning the Separation of Church and State.
241 This argument was relied on by the Finnish government to justify the funding of state-church parishes by Church tax (from which exemptions could be obtained) in its submission to the ECHR in *Kustannus oy vapaa ajattelija ab v. Finland* [1996].
242 Including a groundbreaking ceremony at a municipal gymnasium. Case (Gyo-Tsu) No. 69 of 1971; Minshu Vol.31, No.4, at 533.
243 See P. Luxton, *The law of charities*, Oxford: Oxford University Press, 2001, 46–49; *Gilmore v. Coates* [1949] AC 426, HL.
244 *Re Hetherington* [1990] Ch 1.
245 'Public benefit and the advancement of religion – draft supplementary guidance for consultation', The Charity Commission, 2008.
246 App. No. 29745/96 *Universelles Leben v. Germany* EComHR.
247 *Otto-Preminger-Institut v. Austria* (1995) 19 EHRR 34 ECtHR.
248 App. no. 58911/00 *Leela Förderkreise v. Germany*.
249 *American Family Association v. City and County of San Francisco*, 277 F.3d 1114 (9th Cir. 2002).
250 Except in such cases as the religion stands for one issue only, such as racism, to which the state is obliged to object.

4 Women and religious freedom

The protection of women's freedom of religion and belief is a paradigm test case of the conflict between religious freedom as a community right and the rights of individuals in that community. A core problem in the application of religious freedom is the inherent conflict between religious freedom, if it is given a group dimension, and women's right to equality and individual religious freedom. No international human rights instrument has, to date, comprehensively addressed or solved this difficult problem. While women's equality may be affected by claims of religious freedom in various contexts such as the workplace, this chapter will use examples mostly from the area of personal law, specifically marriage and divorce. The conflict in this area is not accidental. The doctrines of many religions have sought to regulate family life, deciding on the role of men and women within the family as one of the bases of the social structure that the religious doctrine sets up. Important inequalities in this area emanate from religion.

This chapter explains, first, why both the right to equality and the right to individual religious freedom of women should be seen as standing in conflict with community religious freedom (section 4.1). Then existing relative international legal protection of rights in this conflict are examined. I show that there exists a legal determination that posits women's individual rights above claims of group religious freedom (section 4.2). It will then be argued that the determination that group religious freedom cannot override women's individual rights should be upheld, but attention must be given to the complex problems this determination creates: Once a state acknowledges a right to religious freedom of communities and relegates legal powers to them, it is in practice more difficult for the state to implement rights of equality for women (section 4.2). The state may need to address discrimination of women in religious marriages even where there is no religious jurisdiction over personal law (section 4.3). However, not giving legal recognition to personal status systems of religious communities because they are discriminatory can result in further discrimination of women, which must be rectified (section 4.4). A clear, albeit far-reaching, consequence of recognizing the individual rights of women to equality and to freedom of religion and belief over any communal right of religious freedom is that religious institutions should not be able to curtail these rights of women even in their internal organization (section 4.5). Finally, the compatibility of institutional participation of religion in the law-making process that determines the rights of women, both at the national and international level, with religious freedom is questioned (section 4.6).

4.1 Introduction: the problem and existing international law

4.1.1 The conflict between group religious freedom and the religious freedom of women

It is not only women's right to equality that stands in conflict with a community right of religious freedom, but also women's individual right of religious freedom. Human rights instruments, following a liberal approach, speak of a right to 'manifest' and 'practice' religion or belief. For women, however, one of the most important aspects of freedom of religion may be the right to manifest their religious belief by being an equal member of a religious community or organization. Equality in the religious community is a religious freedom concern for women who choose to become, or remain, members of religious communities.[1] While the effect on equality of women by religions to which they belong has not traditionally been seen as a religious freedom concern, it is an important one from women's point of view.[2] The ability of women to belong to a faith of their choice, or, more often, a faith into which they were born and comprises their social and cultural connections, without being discriminated against, is vital to realizing their religious freedom. Application of feminist analysis to international law may be helpful in justifying this interpretation.[3] In the same way that MacKinnon argued that legal – and indeed human rights – concepts should be defined and addressed in ways that matter to women,[4] the scope of rights protected within the idiom of 'religious freedom' may thus have to be redefined.

The liberal approach to religious freedom, which mandates that everyone be allowed to choose their religion, but does not intervene in the 'private' realm of religions themselves, must be rejected in this context. What happens within and by religious communities should be of concern to international and national law.[5] Religious freedom is not about 'all or nothing' – either you choose to take part in a religion and must accept its inequalities, or you must cease to belong to that religion. For women, realizing religious freedom is often about realizing their freedom within religion.[6] The argument of voluntary choice, which resonates of the liberal tradition, 'you are free to leave the religion, therefore your liberty is not restrained', is flawed for various reasons that were discussed in this work.[7] This is particularly so for women who often cannot leave, or do not want to leave their religious community. This is so not only for economic reasons, as the economic disparity between men and women makes it difficult for women to leave, but unequal treatment and social status of women and girls in many cultures and religions, including in education and assigned gender roles, mean that they are effectively less able than men to exercise independence and exit their groups of origin.[8] Moreover, these women often have little influence over the rules of the community in which they live.

4.1.2 Guarantees of religious freedom of women in international documents

International covenants that guarantee freedom of religion and belief do not refer to specific rights of religion and belief of women. Neither does the 1981 UN Declaration on religion and belief do so. It is particularly surprising that this Declaration, proclaimed only two years after the adoption of the UN Convention on the Elimination of all Forms of Discrimination Against Women [CEDAW], has no mention of these concerns. Of course, most rights guaranteed in international documents are guaranteed to everyone, with no explicit mention of their applicability to women. But regarding religious freedom, because of the reasons just highlighted, there are particular causes for concern that, without specific mention, it would be interpreted in a way that would result in protection of the freedom of religion and belief of men but not of women.

CEDAW itself does not have any express provision dealing with discrimination of women on religious grounds, but it has several pertinent articles dealing with the elimination of practices based on the inferiority of either of the sexes,[9] right to vote and hold public office,[10] access to health care including family planning,[11] equality before the law,[12] and prohibition on discrimination in marriage.[13] The compliance of states with all these Articles may be affected by religious law, practice or tradition. Even a newer international document, the Beijing Declaration and Platform for Action, Fourth World Conference on Women,[14] does not refer to any effect of religion on women or even to women's rights in marriage.

As seen in Chapter 1, the 1981 Declaration, as well as newer proposed international documents, signal some shift towards adoption of group protection of religious communities. Such a shift in perception of religious freedom in international law, although it has not yet matured into a recognition of religious group rights, could potentially jeopardize the human rights of women, both their right to equality and their right to individual freedom of conscience and religion, for instance by the recognition of a right to a communal legal system without sufficient protection against discriminatory laws. These documents should be interpreted so as to include a right not to be discriminated against on the basis of sex by religious laws, practices, customs or institutions. No binding international instrument currently guarantees any such protection.

An important step was taken in General Comment 28 to the ICCPR,[15] adopted by the Human Rights Committee in 2000 as an updated General Comment on Article 3 (equality between men and women). It addresses the human rights concerns of equality between the sexes, including those raised by the right to freedom of religion. The GC states that 'Article 18 may not be relied upon to justify discrimination against women by reference to freedom of thought, conscience and religion.' An important premise of the General Comment is gleaned from paragraph 5, which asks that '[s]tate parties should ensure that traditional, historical, religious or cultural attitudes are not used to justify violations of women's right to equality before the law and to equal enjoyment of all Covenant rights.'[16]

The General Comment also addresses directly the conflict between women's equal rights under the convention and rights of minority members (including those of religious minorities) under Article 27 of the ICCPR. It determines that rights under Article 27 do not permit infringement of women's equality in enjoyment of rights.[17]

This approach can be supported by reference to Article 2 (non-discrimination) and Article 26 of the ICCPR (protection against discrimination in any field regulated and protected by public authorities).[18]

There exists a strong case for concluding that the prohibition of gender discrimination must be regarded as a norm of customary international law,[19] at least if the discrimination is systematic and state endorsed. Prohibition of similar discrimination on the basis of religion may also be customary law.[20] So, both these norms would obligate states, even if they had not ratified the relevant conventions or had entered reservations to the conventions on these issues. There is, however, no determination of the outcome, if these rights conflict, that is if one person's right to non-discrimination on the basis of gender is claimed to conflict with a right of a group to non-discrimination on the basis of religion (if such a right is recognized).

Prohibitions of discrimination on grounds of race are routinely recognized as *jus cogens*. Gender grounds of discrimination are less often argued to be norms of international law from which no derogation is permitted.[21] Neither is there evidence that discrimination on grounds of religion has attained such status.[22]

4.1.3 Reservations to convention provisions affecting non-discrimination in enjoyment of the right to religious freedom

The HRC has defined what are valid reservations to the ICCPR, in General Comment 24.[23] The Committee noted that human rights treaties differ from treaties that are mere exchange of obligations between states, in which they can reserve application of rules of general international law. Covenant provisions in human rights treaties that represent customary international law may not be subject to reservations. The Committee lists among these provisions, which represent customary law, the freedom of thought, conscience and religion. In General Comment 31[24] it clarifies that also Article 2 (non-discrimination) cannot be subject to reservation.[25] Thus, reservations to the ICCPR (on religious, or any other, grounds) cannot operate to deny these obligations. For the same reason the corresponding non-discrimination obligations in CEDAW (Articles 2, 7, 15, 16), at least to the extent that they protect the same rights as the ICCPR, should not be subject to reservations.

There is also a different basis for arguing that non-discrimination in enjoyment of rights on the basis of sex is not subject to reservations to CEDAW or the ICCPR, namely that they are incompatible with the object and purpose of the covenant,[26] as learned, respectively, from Article 2(a) of CEDAW[27] and from GC 28 to the ICCPR.

CEDAW General Comment to Article 16(2) notes with alarm the number of state parties that have entered reservations to Articles 2 and 16 based, inter alia, on cultural and religious beliefs and urges them to withdraw these reservations.[28] This in itself is a telling sign of the impact of religion on recognized human rights of women and should warrant further attention.

So, there is no clear hierarchy in international law between freedom of religion and equality on the basis of sex. The interpretation offered by the HRC in General Comment 28,[29] that freedom of religion cannot justify the limitation of equality between men and women, should serve as a starting point, but as will be seen, this raises a multiplicity of problems.

4.2 Application of discriminatory religious law through relegation to the religious communities

States give legal status to religious law by relegation of state authority to religious communities, usually in the area of family law. This legal structure directly pits the rights of religious communities against the rights of individuals, with specific implications for the rights of women in those instances in which the religious law is discriminatory to women. The clear direction of GC 28 is that a principle of religious freedom cannot override women's individual rights; however states find it particularly difficult, for political reasons, to intervene to reverse such discrimination, especially in the law of minority communities, as will be seen. It seems easier for states to assuage political group aspirations by conceding to religious groups' jurisdiction over the family, often compromising the rights of women, rather than risking a political confrontation and power struggle between subgroups in the state. In this case state practice regrettably does not support the General Comment of the Human Rights Committee, which remains *de lege ferenda*.

4.2.1 Religious tribunals and the right of women to equality before the law

The claim has been made that in international law the right to manifest religion or belief includes the right to observe and apply religious law in a community, including the right to establish and maintain religious tribunals.[30] As will be seen, this is cause for concern, as it potentially harms individual rights, and often among these the rights of women.

If such a community right is recognized, the question that follows is whether international human rights obligations apply to legal proceedings of religious courts, and specifically, in the context of this chapter, whether the right of women to equality before the law applies in those courts. Article 15 of CEDAW guarantees women equality before the law in civil matters. It has been questioned[31] whether the Article also applies to religious courts or to religious law administered by secular courts. While it would be advisable if future human rights documents would refer specifically to equality before religious courts, I think it is clear that if the religious court or law is authorized by the state, Article 15 applies, because, as far as international law is concerned, it *is* the state law.

Personal law can be relegated, by law, to the religious communities in different ways. In India, for example, a secular state, the personal law is the law of the individual's religious community,[32] and it is applied in the secular courts. In Bangladesh, a Muslim state,[33] personal law is the religious law of the individual's religious community. As in India, it is applied in the secular court system, in the Family Courts.[34] In Israel,[35] personal law is mostly that of the individual's religious community.[36] Religious tribunals have exclusive jurisdiction in certain instances and concurrent jurisdiction with secular courts in other instances.[37] Appellate religious courts are subject to limited judicial review by the (secular) Supreme Court of Israel. In Sri Lanka,[38] family law is communal, religious or customary,[39] but there is a separate jurisdiction only for the Muslim minority religious courts, which operate according to Muslim law,[40] and in which sit religious judges, known as *qazis*. Their judgments can be ultimately appealed to the (secular) Supreme Court of Sri Lanka. In these instances, the substantive law is the religious law, but the religious courts are subject to the general court system.

The CEDAW Committee saw an inherent conflict between religious law and jurisdiction, on one hand, and the equality provisions of CEDAW, on the other. For instance, on Israel it noted that: '[I]n order to guarantee the same rights in marriage and family relations in Israel and to comply fully with the Convention, the Government should complete the secularization of the relevant legislation, place it under the jurisdiction of the civil courts and withdraw its reservations to the Convention.'[41]

One of the dangers of adopting a principle of relegation is that the state may choose not to rely directly on religion as a reason to diverge from the international human rights norm, but on the relegation of state authority to the religious community. This can be seen in the reservations to CEDAW that emanate from religious reasons. These are of two types: the first, reservations that rely directly and explicitly on religious grounds. These are the reservations submitted by religious Islamic states or Muslim majority states (Bangladesh, Egypt, Iraq, Jordan, Libya, Saudi Arabia, Syria, Tunisia), subjecting some or all state obligations under the Convention to *shari'a* law.[42] The second are the reservations entered by India and Israel. These rely, for their justification, on a domestic legal principle of autonomy of religious communities in the sphere of family law.

4.2.2 Competing religious and secular sources of legal authority and protection of the rights of women

In these last mentioned legal systems, in which religious and secular legal systems operate side by side, the religious legal systems develop as a competing legal system with that of the state. The secular state views itself as the ultimate source of law, from which both the secular and the religious legal systems draw their authority. However, religious legal systems do not view the state as their source of authority, but see themselves as deriving their authority from a divine source. This competition has direct implications for the ability of the state to uphold its international obligations to safeguard human rights of women. This is evident, for example, in India and in Israel.

The demand in international law that states guarantee equality raises a question of the relationship between religious and secular law within the domestic system. Even in states where constitutional protection from discriminatory laws exists, religious law may be excluded from its ambit. In India, according to the constitution, 'laws in force' are void[43] if they are inconsistent with the constitutionally protected fundamental rights.[44] An early post-independence case[45] suggests the Bombay High Court viewed religious law as falling outside the ambit of 'laws in force' and therefore not void even if it is inconsistent with such rights.[46]

However, in 1995 in *Sarla Mudgal*[47] the Supreme Court of India ruled that personal laws operate by force of secular legislation, not religious authority. This determination was not made in order to test their constitutionality, but as a prerequisite to the Court's determination that they can be superseded by a Uniform Civil Code.[48] But, if religious personal law operates by force of secular law, this should open the way to argue that it also must be subject to constitutional review.

At the core of domestic conflicts between religious and secular legal systems, is a conflict of perception about the source and authority of law. The secular system views the formal source of religious law recognized by the state as state law. The religious system views its formal source as religion. Each of these two viewpoints has implications as to which higher legal norms religious law has to conform to, including domestic human rights legal provisions, and international human rights norms.[49] Among these are provisions of equality of women.

Just such a conflict arose in Israel. A decision of the Supreme Court, based on the application of the Equal Rights of Women Law, 1951 to religious courts, directed the religious courts to follow the principle of community property, which does not exist in Jewish law.[50, 51] The rabbinical courts did not accept this ruling, and it has brought a head-on collision between the religious courts and the Supreme Court. The religious courts viewed their own legitimacy as deriving purely from religious law, and saw themselves as unable to deviate from it. Thus, the judgment of the Supreme Court of Israel was not followed by the Great (appellate) Rabbinical Court.[52] A conference of Rabbinical Court judges announced that they will continue to ignore the direction to rule according to the Supreme Court direction on community property, and will refer only to Jewish law.[53] Indeed, even in the *Bavli* case itself, the Local Rabbinical Court ignored the direction of the Supreme Court.[54] The only effective solution that would guarantee protection of gender equality as recognized by the Supreme Court would be the abolition at least of non-consensual jurisdiction of religious courts in matters of family law.

4.2.3 Religious autonomy and women in minority groups

The relegation of personal law to religious communities is often particularly detrimental to minority women. States may find it especially difficult to intervene with anti-discriminatory legislative reforms in the law of minority religions. As will be seen, this is so in states with various different combinations of minority and majority religions. A delicate political balance between majority and minority will mean that the minority will be 'left alone' even when the state attempts to implement its obligations of equality in international law.

A legal system based on autonomy of religious communities might be even more reluctant to intervene in minority religious personal law that infringes women's rights than some outright religious states. In India, polygamy is prohibited for those religions in which a subsequent marriage for someone already married is void, but not when such a marriage is valid according to the applicable religious personal law, i.e. for Muslims.[55] As the Supreme Court of India in *Sarla Mudgal*[56] pointed out, even Muslim states (Iran, Islamic republics of the former Soviet Union, Morocco, Pakistan, Syria, Tunisia) have banned or restricted polygamy, while India, a secular republic with personal laws of religious communities, has not.

Constitutional equality provisions can be used to protect women in minority communities, but not without difficulty. In the landmark *Shah Bano* case,[57] the Indian Supreme Court ordered post-divorce maintenance payments under the (secular) Code of Criminal Procedure, generally unrecognized under Muslim Law beyond a period of three months, while also suggesting an interpretation of Muslim law allowing for the maintenance order.[58] Political uproar from the Muslim community caused the Indian Parliament to reverse the law in the Muslim Women (Protection of Rights on Divorce) Act 1986, which denies Muslim women the option of exercising their rights under the provisions of secular legislation. Thus, the Court's attempt to intervene in religious law proved politically unacceptable and was reversed by the political system. The Indian Supreme Court was finally called on to determine the constitutionality of the Muslim Women (Protection of Rights on Divorce) Act.[59] It decided that unless interpreted in a way that would benefit divorced Muslim women as much as the general law (the Criminal Procedure Code) benefited women of other religions, the Act would be contrary to constitutional guarantees of equal protection of the law and equality on the basis of religion.[60] Therefore it interpreted the Act expansively, so as to allow for maintenance payments to Muslim women.[61] The clash between two sources of law is clear. The state judicial system saw the religious law as part of state law, thus open to interpretation by judges. The religious authorities viewed interpretation of religious law as a matter of doctrine reserved for religious authorities. The clash is particularly strong when the religion is one of a minority community.

Bangladesh, a predominantly Muslim state, found it easier to intervene in Muslim personal law and harder to intervene in discriminatory Hindu personal law of the minority. Religious laws govern personal law issues such as marriage, child custody and property. Some provisions discriminatory to women still exist,[62] as was highlighted by CEDAW in concluding observations on Bangladesh's state report.[63] Some provisions of Muslim personal law had been modified, but, claimed the state representative, it would not be easy to modify Hindu personal law because of the complex religious issues involved.[64] This is a mirror image of the situation in India, a predominantly Hindu state, where it has proved easier for the state to modify by legislation Hindu personal law than the personal law of the Muslim minority (as seen for instance in the *Shah Bano* case). Indeed, Engineer comments that: 'The secular forces in that country [Bangladesh] have been demanding further changes in the Muslim personal law. It is, however, interesting to note that like the Muslim minority in India the Hindu minority in Bangladesh resists any change in its personal law. Thus, Hindu women in Bangladesh are still governed by age-old traditions and laws.'[65]

The case of Bangladesh (a Muslim majority/Hindu minority state), just as the case of India (a Hindu majority/Muslim minority state), shows that women in minority religions face a particular barrier from state intervention to protect their rights, no matter which is the state religion and which is the minority religion. The state plays a delicate political balance; it tries particularly to avoid conflict with minority groups that may see any intervention in the status quo of religious law as government encroachment. Thus, women's rights fall victim to a political balancing act.

The difficulty of the state in according equal rights to women once jurisdiction is granted to religious communities proves in Israel, as well, to be particularly great regarding minority communities. The Family Court Law, 1995, was amended in 2001, by the addition of Article 3(b1), which grants concurrent jurisdiction in matters of family law (except marriage and divorce) of Muslims and Christians to (civil) family courts. Until this amendment, all such matters were exclusively under the jurisdiction of religious courts. Among these are proceedings for spousal support. Jewish women have had the option since 1953 to initiate proceedings for spousal support in either religious or civil court.[66] The award of spousal support is consistently higher in family courts than in all religious courts, and religious courts do not follow a principle of community property.[67] Thus the outcome is less likely to be equitable to women in a religious court.[68] The women of minority religions were harmed by lack of political will to interfere in the religious autonomy of minority religious communities.[69] Even after the passage of the legislation, it remains to be seen whether women of minority religions will have the same accessibility to civil courts as those of the majority religion.[70] It also remains to be seen how the civil courts will interpret the religious law of minority religions, and whether they will be able, as outsiders to the religious community, to interpret it in a way compatible with women's equality.

The state may try to rectify human rights violations by religious law through directly applicable secular legislation. This too raises distinct problems if it is perceived as interference in the autonomy of minority religions. In Israel, secular legislation was sometimes, but not always, perceived this way by the Muslim minority legal system. The Muslim *qadis* have ignored the secular prohibition of underage marriage as grounds for divorce.[71] In other cases they accepted and even welcomed secular legislation, such as the introduction of legal principle of 'the best interest of the child'.[72]

Thus, in these four examples drawn from India, Bangladesh, Sri Lanka and Israel, relegation of personal law to religious communities has meant greater difficulty for the state law to rectify discrimination in personal law of minority women than of women of the majority religion.

These intractable problems would also point against recognition of a group right of religious freedom that includes exclusive, and possibly even concurrent, jurisdiction over personal law.

4.3 Discrimination in religious marriage not caused by the state

4.3.1 Registration of religious marriages by the state without religious jurisdiction over personal status

The last section dealt with states that accord some autonomous legal status to religious communities, and the implications thereof for women. There are adverse implications for women also where the state recognizes, although it does not aid, a religious discriminatory practice, in instances in which the state offers everyone a civil alternative to religious marriage.[73] If the state itself discriminates in marriage provisions, it is clearly breaching the provisions which mandate equality in marriage in international conventions to which it may be party, including the ICCPR (Article 23(4)), CEDAW (Article 16) and Protocol 7 of the European Convention (Article 5 of which mandates equality between spouses in marriage, in private law rights between them, in relation to their children, during marriage and in its dissolution).[74] It is less clear whether a state that recognizes religious marriages that have extra-legal discriminatory implications, breaches its obligations, even though the civil legal provisions that rule the marriage are not discriminatory.

It seems that the provisions mentioned earlier should apply in such a case as well. By relegating the role of arranging marriages to religious bodies, the state cannot 'privatize' it. Rather, the state must ensure that the religious marriages that it recognizes do not cause breaches of human rights, which it is internationally obligated to uphold. As the Home Secretary stated in the parliamentary debate on the UK Human Rights Act 1998,[75] when conducting marriages, the Church stands in place of the state and performs a function for civil society. Thus the Act would apply to churches in this role. So, also, should international human rights obligations.

A further example of the reluctance of states to intervene in the religious personal law of minority communities is seen in Sri Lanka.[76] A dual standard exists in the provision of minimum age of marriage.[77] In Sri Lanka the minimum age has been set to 18, except for Muslims, because of Muslim personal law, which does not provide a minimum age of marriage.[78] For Muslims, the Muslim Marriage and Divorce Act 1951 allows girls as young as 12 to marry without the permission of a *qazi*, and younger girls to marry with the *qazi*'s permission after any such inquiry as he may deem necessary. Likewise, polygamy is permitted, in certain circumstances, for Muslims.[79] Thus, a state that prohibits polygamy[80] and under-age marriages in its general laws, allows a minority religious community to operate a different law on these matters. Hence, women in a minority community are particularly adversely impacted on by relegation of personal law to a religious community.

Of course, even if the state did not recognize the registration of the marriage, the spouses would still be allowed to marry religiously, but would need to marry by civil registry as well, and only the civil marriage would be recognized by the state (as is the case, for instance, for Muslim marriages). In such a case, the state would not be seen as sanctioning a discriminatory marriage. Nevertheless, the discriminatory marriage would still be permitted to take place, the human rights implications of which will be discussed in the following section.

4.3.2 State attempts to rectify discrimination in religious marriage may not be enough to preserve equality

Because of the ingrained position of religion in many societies, even a conscious decision of the state not to recognize any religious law may not be enough to prevent discrimination to women caused by the application of internal religious law in the religious communities.

The existence of a non-discriminatory state secular system of family law may not suffice to guarantee that women's individual rights are not infringed by a religious system of law. If religious systems exist as unofficial systems of law, as part of the exercise of communal religious freedom, women's rights may be infringed in ways which the state may or may not be able to rectify.

In both the UK and USA, Jewish law is an unofficial system of law. In the UK, Jewish marriages are registered by the state;[81] in the USA, only civil marriages are registered. In both, state courts grant divorces. However, a divorce ordered by a civil court will not suffice for the parties to be considered divorced according to Jewish law. Both parties must be consenting parties to religious divorce (*get*).[82] Usually it is the husband who may be able to withhold the *get* from the wife. While the civil court can grant legal divorce, lack of a religious divorce will mean that the wife will not be able to remarry under Jewish law.

The civil law cannot rectify this, but laws in certain states in the USA as well as in the UK remove the possibility of the husband obtaining a civil divorce but leaving his wife effectively unable to remarry, by withholding the religious divorce. The New York state '*get* law', the most famous of these,[83] denies civil divorce to a petitioner absent a showing that the petitioner has removed 'all barriers to remarriage' of a spouse, including 'religious or conscientious restraint'. Similarly, the UK Divorce (Religious Marriages) Act 2002 states that when a marriage is entered according to Jewish or other religious usages, in divorce proceedings 'the court may order that a decree of divorce is not to be made absolute until a declaration made by both parties that they have taken such steps as are required to dissolve the marriage in accordance with those usages is produced to the court.'

In 1992 New York law was further amended[84] to allow the court to take into account refusal of one spouse to remove barriers to remarriage of the other spouse in the distribution of marital property and determination of maintenance. Stone[85] shows that the Jewish community supported the first provision, as it is not in conflict with Jewish law. The second provision, however, was controversial among the Jewish community due to a possibility that the imposition of financial penalties on a recalcitrant spouse creates a compelled divorce (*get me'useh*), which is invalid under Jewish law,[86] as there must be consent of both parties.[87] Currently there is no international legal requirement that states withhold granting civil divorce until all religious barriers to remarriage have been removed.

The unofficial system of law has implications for the lives of women within the religious community, which the state cannot always correct. Thus, even a clear determination that a community right of freedom of conscience and religion cannot prevail over the individual rights of women will not always have a possible practicable implementation. Women choose to belong to communities, or have no real choice but to do so, and abide by their internal rules. Providing an equal secular alternative may not be enough, application of fundamental human rights provisions to consequences of religious marriages may be needed.

4.4 Non-recognition of discriminatory religious marriages may further the discrimination of women

The decision to uphold individual rights over a community right of religious freedom is not straightforward to apply in practice even when the state decides not to relegate legal power to religions that discriminate on the basis of gender.

The decision of a state not to recognize a religious system of marriage, because it is incompatible with equality to women, can harm the individual rights of both women and men who, because of social and cultural preferences, use the unrecognized system. A preferable individual rights approach would consider, in each case, whether individual rights would be, on balance, furthered or harmed by the recognition of the marriage for the purpose under consideration.

Religious systems of law which are not part of the state legal system and whose legal acts are not recognized by the state's legal system may nonetheless have vital importance for people's lives, and indeed have legal consequences under state law. The existence of an unofficial religious legal system, and its impact on women, should thus be analysed as one of the effects of religion in the state that impact the lives of women.

4.4.1 Potentially polygamous marriages

Religious legal systems that have no official legal status, but have important legal consequences, which may be different for men and women, are evident, for instance, in regard to Muslim marriages in the UK[88] and in South Africa. While according legal validity to religious arrangements such as marriage may constitute a breach of equality for women, sometimes non-recognition of such marriages may have a discriminatory effect. This can be seen in a number of cases that reached the South African courts. In *Ryland v. Edros*,[89] the Supreme Court of South Africa decided that it could recognize a Muslim marriage, which is not a valid marriage under the South African Marriage Act,[90] as a valid contract. The Court considered a Muslim marriage as not *per se* contrary to public policy, even if potentially polygamous. In this case, the motivation for the ruling, it seems, was that the Court wanted to recognize the wife's property and financial rights after divorce. Not recognizing the marriage would have left her with nothing, on the dissolution of what was, de facto, a marriage. Thus, in this case, recognizing the religious marriage, even as a private law contract furthers the woman's right in the particular instance.[91] This is so, although general validation of Muslim religious marriages, even as a civil contract, is potentially harmful for women (as it validates marriages that are potentially polygamous).[92] We see, that non-recognition of a religious practice by the state has a legal effect, just as recognition has an effect. Non-recognition of discriminatory marriages by law in a society in which such marriages take place may still be discriminatory towards women.[93]

Another implication of non-recognition of Muslim religious marriages in South Africa arose in *Fraser v. Children's Court*.[94] The issue raised was the rights of biological parents regarding their required consent to the adoption of their child. The Act required the permission of both mother and father, when they were married, for a court decision to allow the child's adoption. But in the case of unmarried parents the mother's permission alone sufficed. The Act saw customary African unions, which are not recognized as legal marriages, as an exception requiring permission of both parents. But, it did not make the same exception for Muslim marriages, which are also not recognized as legal marriages. The Court found the distinction between customary unions and Muslim marriages discriminatory and thus in breach of Article 8 of the Interim Constitution. Thus, the Court found a way to rectify the result of non-recognition of Muslim marriages, for the purposes of adoption.

In an important recent case, *Daniels v. No*,[95] the Constitutional Court of South Africa recognized Muslim marriages for the purposes of intestate inheritance. But the reasoning of Judge Sachs and Judge Ngcobo were revealingly different. Judge Sachs viewed the word 'spouse' in the laws discussed in the case as including spouses of a Muslim marriage. Judge Sachs was careful to stress[96] that the decision 'eliminates a discriminatory application of particular statutes without implying a general recognition of the consequences of Muslim marriages for other purposes ... [T]he recognition which it accords to the dignity and status of Muslim marriages for a particular statutory purpose does not have any implications for the wider question of what legislative processes must be followed before aspects of the *shari'a* may be recognised as an enforceable source under South African law.' Sachs mentions in his decision the constitutional principle of 'non-sexism'.[97] He stresses that in a patriarchal society men find it easier to acquire property and the laws under question achieve substantial equality between men and women, from which women in Muslim marriages would not benefit if excluded from the law's ambit.

This rationale seemingly leaves room for non-recognition of Muslim marriages for those purposes in which such recognition would harm women's substantive equality with men.

Judge Ngcobo uses a seemingly broader base for his decision. He contrasts the new constitutional order against the old order under which cultures and laws of blacks were not recognized, and thus their marriages were not recognized. He cites the constitutional provision that guarantees freedom of religion,[98] which also permits 'marriages concluded under any tradition or a system of religion'.[99]

By its clear wording, the South African Constitution[100] *permits* recognition of religious marriages, but does not mandate such recognition. It is implied by Judge Ngcobo's opinion that such recognition may be warranted by the principle of religious freedom and religious equality. But if so, it is not clear if such recognition would have to be accorded to Muslim (or other religious) marriages even in instances where this would infringe women's equality.[101] Thus, both judges reach the same result, but while Judge Sachs' approach relies on the principle of non-discrimination of women, Judge Ngcobo's relies on a principle of religious freedom, which, without a qualification based on the individual right of non-discrimination between men and women, could lead to unwarranted results.[102]

4.4.2 Polygamous marriages

A similar dilemma is raised in regard to polygamous marriages. The principle that communal religious freedom cannot override women's right to equality would mandate prohibition of such marriages. But, if such marriages are ignored by the law, in some cases the rights of individuals, especially those of women, will be harmed.

International treaties do not directly forbid polygamy. However, the ICCPR, in Article 23(4), mandates equality between spouses. In General Comment 28, the HRC stated that polygamy is incompatible with equality of treatment with regard to the right to marry, as guaranteed by the ICCPR.[103] The same conclusion should be reached from CEDAW, which in Article 15 guarantees equality before the law, and in Article 16 guarantees equality in marriage, as indeed the CEDAW committee decided in General Comment 21.

Formerly, English courts refused to recognize polygamous unions. In *Sowa v. Sowa*,[104] the UK Court of Appeal decided that a potentially polygamous marriage did not entitle the wife to any remedies under matrimonial laws. The legal position was changed by the Matrimonial Causes Act 1973,[105] which permits the court to grant matrimonial relief (including orders regarding maintenance) in a polygamous marriage. As for the state's obligations, the position is different. In 1998 the Court of Appeal decided[106] that a polygamous wife is not entitled to a widow's benefit under the Social Security Act 1975.[107] This ruling raises a problem: validation of polygamous marriages is inimical to women's equality. But women who lived in polygamous marriages are doubly harmed by non-recognition of their rights under law – once by the marriage itself, and a second time by the withholding of widows' benefits. The result is particularly troublesome when the women concerned are in substantial need of economic assistance.

The Protocol to the African Charter on Human and Peoples' Rights on the Rights of Women in Africa[108] addresses this complexity. It states that 'monogamy is encouraged as the preferred form of marriage, and that the rights of women in marriage and family, including in polygamous marital relationships are promoted and protected.'[109] Other national and international bodies would do well to adopt similar standards.

A similar approach may be needed regarding not just polygamous marriages, but other unrecognized religious marriages. The African Women's protocol obligates the state parties to legislate that marriages must be recorded and registered,[110] not be polygamous,[111] and must be based on informed consent of the parties,[112] who are both over 18 years old.[113] They are meant to ensure, as far as possible in a social context of gender disparity, that women are equal and autonomous partners in the marriage. However, if religious marriages continue to take place in breach of these provisions, states may have to continue to recognize these as de facto marriages in order to guarantee rights of spouses, usually women, both between the spouses and towards the state, as seen in the *Daniels* decision.

4.5 Discrimination of women in internal religious affairs by religious institutions

The most far-reaching but logical conclusion of the adoption of a principle of superiority of gender equality over communal religious freedom, such as that adopted in GC 28, is that this principle will have to be employed even in doctrinal areas of religions, including the appointment of clergy.

4.5.1 Clergy who hold public office

The right of religious organizations to run their internal organization is perhaps the right that is most justifiably reserved to the community, with which international law will find it hardest to interfere. However, even under existing international law, barring women from serving as clergy who hold public office should be impermissible.

Where religious clergy are given public office by the state, or they are appointed by the state to hold office in which they exercise legal powers within religious communities, discrimination against women in their appointments should be considered a discriminatory act by the state itself. As such, it may run afoul of provisions of both CEDAW,[114] which guarantees the right to hold public office on equal terms, and the ICCPR,[115] which guarantees equality in access to public service. Article 3 guarantees all ICCPR rights to men and women on an equal basis. Although GC 28 does not refer specifically to the appointment of clergy or religious judges, its unambiguous language interpreting Article 3 leaves no room for exception, and means that even religious doctrine as to appointment of clergy cannot serve as justification for a breach of gender equality in appointments to public office.

An example of such appointments, in Israel, is the appointment by the state of two State Rabbis and City Rabbis.[116] In Israel, jurisdiction in matters of family law is given to state-appointed religious judges.[117] Women may not fill the posts of either state-appointed rabbis or religious judges.[118] The CEDAW committee has criticized Israel over the fact that women cannot become religious judges.[119]

This implies that the CEDAW committee holds the view that international human rights treaty obligations of states should be implemented in the appointment of religious judges even if this intervenes in religious doctrine. Alternatively, the state could abolish altogether the legal capacities of religious judges.

It is not clear if the same would apply to clergy appointed or funded by the state who do not hold a judicial role. It is more questionable if theirs can be considered a 'public office'. Judicial office is public office, as its holder executes a core function of the state. A clergyman who only performs religious service does not execute any such state function. However, if the clergy is appointed to office by the state, holds office in a state-church, or is paid as a civil servant, there is a strong argument to see the position such a clergy holds as a public office as well.

4.5.2 Clergy who do not hold public office

Even concerning the appointment of clergy who are not holders of public office, the state may have an obligation to prohibit gender discrimination. Under CEDAW, the parties are obliged to take appropriate measures to modify the social and cultural patterns of conduct of men and women, with a view to achieving the elimination of practices that are based on the idea of the inferiority or the superiority of either of the sexes or on stereotyped roles for men and women.[120] This is a fairly weakly worded – although unique – provision of an obligation on the state to attempt to effect change. Nevertheless, it means that the state must endeavour to eradicate culturally determined gender roles even in private religious organizations.

The argument for imposing a legal obligation of non-discrimination on private religious organizations becomes stronger the clearer the involvement of the state with the religious organization. If the religion is legally or financially established or supported by the state there will be a stronger reason for demanding that the state reverse the discriminatory practice. But there is a basis for arguing that the states must promote non-discrimination even in religious organizations in which it is not involved.

4.5.3 Discrimination in appointment to religious office as a concern for international law

There is further indication that discrimination against women within religions, even in areas which are at the core of religious doctrine, is an issue in which international law can legitimately intervene. The former UN Special Rapporteur, Elizabeth Odio Benito, suggested in her study to the Sub-Commission on Prevention of Discrimination and Protection of Minorities[121] that studies be undertaken about discrimination against women within churches and within religions, including discrimination in ceremonies and worship, in becoming ministers of religion and in having a part in the hierarchal organizations of religions. She calls for immediate attention to this issue by the UN and recommends that the Sub-Commission undertake this study. Her suggestion implicitly includes a determination that discrimination of women by religions is within the ambit of international human rights law. The UN has taken no further action on this.

Application of constitutional non-discrimination principles to religious organizations is also absent in most states. A state constitution, which takes an important step in this direction, is that of South Africa. In South Africa, the non-discrimination provision of the Constitution[122] has application for private actors, which would include religious bodies. Legislation which must be enacted in order to prohibit such discrimination by religious organization would certainly be controversial, raising objections such as those voiced by Van der Vyver, that a scenario in which 'the Roman Catholic Church might be constrained to justify its internal ruling before a secular tribunal smells of totalitarianism of the worst kind.'[123]

The European Court of Human Rights has dealt with this issue only indirectly, as we saw in Chapter 3. It ruled that where a state-church decided to ordain women clergy, a clergyman who did not approve could not claim his right to freedom of religion was infringed.[124] The question whether state-churches were obligated to ordain women clergy did not arise.[125]

Sometimes, it is precisely the establishment, the granting of legal status by the state, which exempts the institutions of the religious community from general law of non-discrimination on the basis of sex. In the UK, the Church of Scotland was granted jurisdiction over 'matters spiritual' in the Church of Scotland Act 1921.[126] In *Percy*,[127] an associate minister was demoted from her position by the Church following allegations of misconduct. She filed claim under the Sex Discrimination Act 1975, claiming that she was treated differently from male ministers. The Scottish Court of Session accepted the claim of the Church that the employment tribunal had no jurisdiction to entertain any complaint by the appellant of sex discrimination, since it was a question concerning an office in the Church[128] and was accordingly a 'matter spiritual'. It followed that the Church had the right, 'subject to no civil authority', to adjudicate finally on the matter and the employment tribunal had no jurisdiction. The decision was overturned in the House of Lords,[129] which decided that unlawful discrimination was a civil matter and not a 'spiritual matter' and so was not excluded from the jurisdiction of the employment tribunal.[130]

Here, in the decision of the Court of Session, the autonomy of the religious community to govern its institutions was given *a priori* precedence over the general law of non-discrimination in employment. This is precisely the type of preference of community over women's equality that GC 28 directs against. As was argued in Chapter 3, the constitutional structure of religion in the state has direct implications for the relationship between individual and group rights. These could have adverse implications for women, as exemplified in the ruling of the Court of Session in this case.

4.5.4 *Discrimination of women by religious and tax-exempt status*

State endorsement of discriminatory religious organizations occurs even where religious institutions are not directly funded by the state, but are indirectly subsidized by receiving tax-exempt status. It can be argued, that even such an indirect endorsement is impermissible: If these religious institutions discriminate against women, their tax-exempt status as charitable institutions should be removed,[131] for a similar reasoning to that used to deny tax-exempt status from private educational institutions which discriminate on the basis of race in the USA.[132]

It could, however, be argued, that there is a dividing line between impermissible direct state funding of discriminatory religious institutions, and permissible indirect funding via tax exemptions. Such an interpretation would recognize as legitimate a 'sphere of private support', arguing that since people are allowed to adhere to discriminatory religions, they should be allowed to donate to them.

Nevertheless, these last considerations justify a right of everyone to donate to a religion of their choice, but not a right to do so under tax-exempt conditions.

4.6 Secular legislation based on religious motives

The multiplicity of conflicts between women's equality and religious doctrines is not coincidental. They stem from the all-encompassing nature of religions as normative systems that organize private, as well as public, aspects of life. Since these systems were formulated historically in patriarchal societies, they often reflect those values. Thus, it must be asked, not only whether in particular cases reliance on religion infringes the rights of women, but whether, in principle, reliance on religious reasons for legislation should be seen as infringing religious freedom, among others, of women.

Secular legislation that infringes recognized human rights of women is, in many cases, based on religious motivation. Often there will be reasons based on social or cultural norms that have their grounding in religion, even if religion is no longer seen as their justification. Laws that have particular significance for the rights of women, such as those regarding rights of marriage, reproduction, abortion or contraception, will often be based on such social norms. International human rights law has, so far, not addressed this problem.

An important question is, whether such legislation can be said to infringe illegitimately the religious freedom of men and women who do not subscribe to those religious beliefs. In other words, the question raised is whether religious freedom is breached by the fact that secular legislation is based on religious motives, apart from any infringement of other rights which the law or policy might cause. This question has, in general terms, already been discussed in Chapter 2. While this question is relevant to both men and women whom such legislation affects, this chapter addresses specifically laws that affect women. The reason for raising this issue in regard to women's freedom of religion is that there may be different considerations regarding women. Even in democratic states, where women participate equally in the democratic process, their effective political power is often less than that of men, for various reasons (such as lack of influence and less than proportional representation within political parties), and so the product of the legislative process may not proportionately reflect their beliefs.[133] Also, even if both women and men choose, by majority vote, to institute law based on specific religious teaching, the law will reflect the underlying discriminatory attitude to women often embedded in religious norms.

4.6.1 Religious reasons for state legislation

The problem whether religious reasons for legislation are legitimate, especially where these are concerned with the private lives of men and women, is theoretically difficult, constitutionally fundamental, and politically loaded. Nowhere is this more so than in the case of regulation of abortion.

Because it is not yet clear whether there is a right of abortion in international law, it is important to examine the process by which domestic and international law and policy on this issue is made. Currently, a right over reproduction is not explicitly included in any of the main human rights instruments. CEDAW guarantees equal access to healthcare, including 'family planning',[134] a term deliberately left vague. GC 24[135] interprets that 'it is discriminatory for a State party to refuse to provide legally for the performance of certain reproductive health services for women. For instance, if health service providers refuse to perform such services based on conscientious objection, measures should be introduced to ensure that women are referred to alternative health providers.'

Access to contraception and abortion might be considered as included in Article 2 in conjunction with Article 1 of CEDAW (prohibition of discrimination), although this would entail a complex argument that lack of access to abortion constitutes 'distinction, exclusion or restriction made on the basis of sex', because lack of means of ensuring reproductive choice have vastly unequal consequences for men and women, thus perpetuating existing gender inequalities.[136]

Only the Protocol to the African Charter on Human and Peoples' Rights on the Rights of Women in Africa includes a specific obligation of state parties to protect reproductive rights of women, including authorizing abortion in cases of rape and when continued pregnancy endangers the mental and physical health of the mother or the life of the mother or the foetus or is the result of incest.[137] This is not a full right to abortion based on a perception of women's bodily autonomy, but rather a truncated right, based on what are perceived by society as fruit of crimes committed and danger to health.

The International Conference on Population and Development ('The Cairo Conference')[138] did not recognize a right to abortion. This was directly due to religious involvement in the discussions. The Vatican was one of the most active participants in the Cairo Conference, objecting to all references to human rights of abortion and contraception.[139] The Beijing Declaration and Platform for Action[140] suggests states not take punitive steps against women who have undergone abortions, but nowhere suggest that it is a right of women. The follow-up report[141] also does not suggest such a right.

While the question of abortion is usually argued as one of substantive rights, the process of the determination of these rights should also be considered. If a state or international policy is deemed in breach of religious freedom because of institutional religious involvement in its formulation, this adds a different reason to argue that prohibitions on abortions are in breach of human rights.

In the context of the debate on the constitutionality of prohibition of abortions in US law, Tribe has argued that whenever the views of organized religion play a dominant role in formulating an entire government policy, as is the case with abortion, it is an improper involvement of religion in the political process, violating the establishment clause of the First Amendment.[142] Later, however, in a move that is testament to the difficulty of this question, he shifted his stand, acknowledging that, in fact, religion could not be disentangled from the public debate on the issue.[143]

The influence of religion on the legislative process can be seen in the constitutional reform concerning abortion in Ireland.[144] In referendum on the issue, religious arguments played a pivotal role in supporting one side of the debate.[145] The CEDAW Committee criticized this influence of the Church on law and policy. The Committee noted in 1999,[146] that although Ireland is a secular state, the influence of the Church is strongly felt not only in attitudes and stereotypes but also in official state policy.[147] In particular, it noted, women's right to health, including reproductive health, is compromised by this influence.[148] While criticizing church involvement in legislation in a specific case, it seems that the Committee viewed the involvement of the Church in formulating state policy in a secular state as an institutional problem of human rights.[149]

However, religious involvement in referendum, as in Ireland, raises separate considerations. The use of religious arguments in a referendum is perhaps the most justifiable of all uses of religious arguments in policy making. As shown in Chapter 2, the strongest argument against use of religious reasons exists when these are used by public servants; these arguments are weaker against religious reasons for voting by individual citizens, such as voters in referendum. It is practically impossible to disallow the reliance of individual voters on religious reasons for their voting. Not only that, but the right of free speech includes the right of the voters to hear and consider any religious message before voting, as well as the right of the religious speakers to impart such a message. Thus, while institutional religious involvement in deciding the rights of women is problematic, it may not be easy to justify its prohibition.

There is, however, a strong, although not conclusive, case for claiming that women do have a right of access to abortion under international law.[150] If so, regardless of the legitimacy of using religious reasons for the decision to vote for or against abortions, a law that prohibits abortions could be attacked on substantive human rights grounds.

The argument that the right to freedom of religion and belief includes a right that the state will not legislate secular laws based on religious norms was raised, but not examined, in a case of the European Court of Human Rights. In *Johnston*,[151] the European Court concluded that Article 12 of the European Convention (the right to marry) does not include a right to divorce and neither does Protocol 7 to the Convention and, further, that neither is such a right included in Article 8 (protection of family life).[152] Johnston claimed as well that lack of a divorce provision breached his rights under Article 9, as the inability to live with his new partner as married man and wife was against his conscience. The Court summarily dismissed this claim, saying Johnston's freedom to have and manifest his convictions was not in issue. The law in Ireland has changed since the ruling.[153]

Malta is now the only state under the jurisdiction of the European Court that has no divorce provision, and to which this case is directly applicable.[154] However, the Court's analysis of religious freedom is still relevant. It viewed freedom of conscience as limited to the right to manifest convictions. The European Court interpreted narrowly the concept of religious freedom. It did not raise the question whether the state, by mandating a system of marriage and divorce that conforms to one religious creed, impinges on the freedom of religion and conscience of those who do not subscribe to that belief.

Lack of divorce provisions impinges on the liberties of both men and women, but its effect on men is different from its effect on women. In a social structure in which most marital unions are dominated by men, through unequal financial power and traditional gender roles, lack of divorce provisions constitutes a breach of equality for women, as well as a breach of freedom of conscience for both men and women.

When a state shapes the lives of men and women, constricting them through laws based on religious doctrine, a question of religious freedom is raised. This is true, of course, not just regarding lack of divorce, but regarding any other legal arrangement that is based on religious doctrine.

As discussed in Chapter 2, a contrary argument can be made, that, in keeping with liberal conceptions, channeling religious motives into the political system through democratic participation is not only legitimate, but also has a positive public value. However, women have historically been, and mostly still are, excluded from the formulation of religious doctrine. So, the legitimation of religious motives for legislation discriminates against women in the legislative process, apart from any discrimination that may be manifested in the resulting legislation.

4.6.2 Religious reasons for international norms

A comparable situation to the use of religious reasons in legislation arises when religious reasons underpin a state's international obligations, or when religious reasons or religious institutional involvement influence the formulation of international documents. Because religions typically espouse a comprehensive value system of gender differentiation, their involvement will entail a systematic influence on the development of international law in regard to the rights of women. The Catholic Church is in a legally unique position to influence such developments,[155] because of its centralized structure and its status in international law.[156] Other religions may also exert influence through states.

An example of how religious obligations might influence the creation of international law is seen in the opposition by some of the delegates of proposals for the inclusion in the Universal Declaration of Human Rights of equal rights of men and women to contract or dissolve a marriage. These were delegates of states bound by laws based on Concordats with the Church, which created obligations in respect of religious marriage and divorce. These would not permit them to accept the proposed text.[157] The right was finally mentioned in Article 16, which states that men and women are 'entitled to equal rights as to marriage, during marriage and at its dissolution'.[158] The reliance on the Concordats in the negotiations, however, suggests that pre-existing international law treaties, which had already absorbed much of religious tenets (in this case, of Catholic doctrine) had already shaped the constitutional structure of the rights of men and women in states.

An example of institutional religious involvement in the formulation of international documents relating to the rights of women occurred when the Vatican was one of the most active participants in the Cairo Conference, objecting to all references to human rights of abortion and contraception.[159] The Holy See stated in a reservation to the final document of the Cairo Conference that it understood that the document does not affirm a new international right to abortion.[160] The Vatican also participated in the 1995 UN Beijing Conference on Women,[161] but lobbied China to ban reformist Catholic groups, which support women's equality, from participating in it.[162]

The influence of religious bodies on formulation of international law affecting women's freedom of conscience and religion is evident also in the Rome Statute for the International Criminal Court.[163] The statute includes several gender-specific offences. Important in its implication of religious attitudes is the offense of forced pregnancy, in Article 7(2)(f): '"Forced pregnancy" means the unlawful confinement of a woman forcibly made pregnant, with the intent of affecting the ethnic composition of any population or carrying out other grave violations of international law. This definition shall not in any way be interpreted as affecting national laws relating to pregnancy.' The wording was controversial, as the inclusion of the limitation that the woman was 'forcibly made pregnant' means that confinement of a woman who is pregnant by consensual sex will not be a crime under the statute. The limitation was included at the behest of the Vatican.[164]

Thus, institutional religious involvement in formulating international human rights documents (or documents which affect human rights) is problematic. The strongest argument against this involvement is in the case of direct involvement of religious organizations. A somewhat weaker argument exists where states rely on religious arguments. After all, it may be argued that every party to the drafting process brings with it some preconceived ideological notion, and a religious approach is no less legitimate than any other. However, the nature of institutional religious involvement is different where the rights of women are at issue, as religions have not just a preset conception on particular issues but a comprehensive and non-negotiable set of conception about gender roles.

4.6.3 Religious determinations and individual conscience

In theory, it is possible to argue that a communal religious determination should never prevail over individual choice. However, it is not always easy to decide where an aggregate of individual rights ends and a communal policy mandating one religious belief begins. Rights of religious freedom are pitted against each other when doctors, nurses or hospitals refuse to perform abortions. The health service professional does not wish to perform an act against his or her religious beliefs, but the woman seeking abortion is being denied this medical service for religious reasons, which do not form any part of her belief. This becomes a critical problem where most doctors or hospitals in her area refuse to perform this procedure. The CEDAW Committee viewed this as an infringement of women's reproductive rights, stating that if health service providers refuse to perform such services based on conscientious objection, measures should be introduced to ensure that women are referred to alternative health providers.[165] The CEDAW committee thus expressed its concern at the refusal, by some hospitals in Croatia, to provide abortions on the basis of conscientious objection of doctors.[166]

An individual doctor relies on individual religious freedom in refusing to perform the abortion, a right typically recognized.[167] A central policy of the state based on the same reasons, even if democratically decided, would be an imposition of group values over individual rights. A confluence of doctors or hospital administrations, all manifesting their religious beliefs to abstain from performing abortions, falls somewhere between the two. Thus, some cases cannot be categorized neatly as either a clash of rights, or an imposition of a religious belief of a group on an individual. Here, there cannot be a principled determination but, rather, each case must be decided on an ad hoc basis.

4.7 Conclusion

As has been argued in Chapters 2 and 3, religious freedom should be viewed as an individual right, which a derivative right of the community cannot overcome. So, a claim of community religious freedom cannot override the individual freedom of religion or belief of women within religious communities. The same reasoning would lead to the conclusion that no right of community religious freedom can override the right of non-discrimination between the sexes. These conclusions match those of the UN HRC in GC 28. However, this chapter has raised some of the complexities that this determination creates: states delegate jurisdiction in matters of personal law to religious communities, and so their ability to intervene and uphold principles of equality is weakened, particularly within minority communities. Thus, women who are members of minorities are harmed twice. However, even if religious personal status is not accorded legal recognition, unofficial marriage and divorce still exist. Non-recognition of these might, again, lead to double discrimination of women (and in some cases men), once within the religious marriage and a second time by non-recognition of the marriage by the state. A suggested approach could be one of determination in every legal situation, whether individual rights would be harmed or furthered by recognition of the partnership as a marriage for the particular determination of a legal right. While such an approach lacks certainty and forseeability, as spouses will not know their rights until a judicial determination is made, it is better than either alternative of blanket recognition of discriminatory religious marriages or non-recognition. As has been seen, regarding Jewish law, there may be a limit as to the ability of the law to intervene in the discriminatory outcome of extra-legal religious marriages. A principle that views gender equality above communal religious freedom will have to address two further controversial questions: that of the legitimacy of institutional religious participation in the lawmaking process at the national and international level, and that of the discrimination of women in the internal practice of religious organizations.

Notes

1 On the impact of different religions on women's human rights, see C. W. Howland, *Religious fundamentalism and the human rights of women*, New York: St. Martin's Press, 1999; A. Rahman, 'Religious rights versus women's rights in India: a test case for international human rights law', *Columbia Journal of Transnational Law*, 28, 1990, 473; A. An-Na'im, 'The rights of women and international law in the Muslim context', *Whittier Law Review*, 9, 1987, 491.

2 For a claim that international human rights law based on a liberal conception of freedom largely excludes women, sees S. Wright, 'Economic rights, social justice and the state: a feminist reappraisal', in D. Dallmeyer (ed.), *Reconceiving reality: women and international law*, Washington, DC: American Society of International Law, 1993, 117, 129.

3 For a discussion of the applicability of feminist theories to international law, see H. Charlesworth and C. Chinkin, *The boundaries of international law: a feminist analysis*, Manchester: Manchester University Press, 2000; H. Charlesworth, C. Chinkin and S. Wright, 'Feminist approaches to international law', *American Journal of International Law*, 85, 1991, 613.

4 C. MacKinnon, *Feminism unmodified: discourses on life and the law*, Cambridge, MA: Harvard University Press, 1987.

5 On how states can be accountable in international law for non-state infringements of women's rights, see R. Cook, 'Accountability in international law for violation of women's rights by non-state actors', in D. Dallmeyer, *Reconceiving reality: women and international law*, Washington, DC: American Society of International Law, 1993, 93; C. Romany, 'State responsibility goes private: a feminist critique of the public/private distinction in international human rights law', in R. Cook, *Human rights of women: national and international perspectives*, Philadelphia: University of Pennsylvania Press, 1994, 85.

6 Feminists, among others, pointed out that the liberal conception of freedom was framed in negative terms, as absence of constraint, rather than in positive terms, as the opportunity for self-realization: E. Frazer and N. Lacey, *The politics of community: a feminist critique of the liberal-communitarian debate*, Hemel Hempstead: Harvester-Wheatsheaf, 1993, 60.

7 See discussion in Chapter 3.

8 See S. Muller Okin, 'Is multiculturalism bad for women?', in J. Cohen, M. Howard and M. C. Nussbaum (eds), *Is multiculturalism bad for women?*, Princeton: Princeton University Press, 1999; A. Shachar, *Multicultural jurisdictions: cultural differences and women's rights*, Cambridge: Cambridge University Press, 2001; S. Muller Okin, ' "Mistresses of their own destiny": group rights, gender and realistic rights of exit', *Ethics* 112, 2002, 205.

9 Convention on the Elimination of all forms of Discrimination against Women (adopted 18 December 1979) 1249 UNTS 13, Article 5.

10 CEDAW, Article 7.

11 CEDAW, Article 12.

12 CEDAW, Article 15.
13 CEDAW, Article 16.
14 Adopted 15 September 1995, UN Doc. A/CONF.177/20 and A/CONF,177/20/ Add. 1.
15 CCPR/C/21/Rev.1/Add.10.
16 The relation between CEDAW and the ICCPR should also be a matter for concern. Coherence should be sought in the interpretation of UN human rights conventions. Such concerns would lead to question Saudi Arabia's ratification of CEDAW in October 2000 subject to a reservation that '[i]n case of contradiction between any term of the Convention and the norms of Islamic law, the Kingdom is not under obligation to observe the contradictory terms of the Convention.' The reservation seems to go directly against GC 28 to the ICCPR to which Saudi Arabia is not a party. But GC 28 would reinforce the interpretation that the reservation is contrary to the object and purpose of CEDAW itself.
17 Paragraph 32 of the General Comment states that:
   [T]he rights which persons belonging to minorities enjoy under Article 27 of the Covenant in respect of their language, culture and religion do not authorize any State, group or person to violate the right to the equal enjoyment by women of any Covenant rights, including the right to equal protection of the law. States should report on any legislation or administrative practices related to membership in a minority community that might constitute an infringement of the equal rights of women under the Covenant (Comm. No. 24/1977, *Lovelace v. Canada*, Views adopted July 1981) and on measures taken or envisaged to ensure the equal right of men and women to enjoy all civil and political rights in the Covenant. Likewise, States should report on measures taken to discharge their responsibilities in relation to cultural or religious practices within minority communities that affect the rights of women.

18 Also relevant is the ICESCR, Article 3, which guarantees equal enjoyment of economic, social and cultural rights.
19 The Restatement [Third] of the Foreign Relations of the United States § 702 Cmt. 1 (1987) states that freedom from gender discrimination as state policy, in many matters, may already be a principle of international law (702 comment (l)). However, this is only if discrimination is a matter of state policy, not if these are acts of individuals which are not condoned by state; see also H. Charlesworth and C. Chinkin, 'The gender of *jus cogens*', *Human Rights Quarterly*, 15, 1993, 63, 83; the authors refer to the Opinion of Judge Ammoun in the International Court of Justice decision *Legal Consequences for States of the Continued Presence of South Africa in Namibia (South-West Africa) Notwithstanding Security Council Resolution 276* [1970] ICJ Reports 4, for the argument that the right to equality, codified in the UDHR, is a pre-existing customary norm.
20 The Restatement [Third] of the Foreign Relations of the United States § 702 Cmt. 1 (1987) states that there exists a strong case that systematic discrimination on grounds of religion is violation of customary law (702 comment (j)). See also D. J. Sullivan, 'Gender, equality and religious freedom: toward a framework for conflict resolution', *New York University Journal of International Law & Policy* 24, 1992, 795, 798.
21 H. Charlesworth and C. Chinkin, 'The gender of *jus cogens*', *Human Rights Quarterly*, 15, 1993, 63, 70.
22 The Restatement [Third] of the Foreign Relations of the United States § 702 Cmt. 1 (1987) does not list either religious discrimination or gender discrimination as *jus cogens* (comment (n)), although noting that international law in this area is developing and may already be more comprehensive than noted.
23 CCPR/C/21/Rev.1/Add.6.
24 CCPR/C/21/Rev.1/Add.13.
25 U.N. Doc. HRI/GEN/1/Rev.1 at 26 (1994. See also GC 18, on non-discrimination (1989).

26 Convention on the Elimination of all Forms of Discrimination Against Women (adopted 18 December 1979) 1249 UNTS 13, Article 28. See also: The Vienna Convention on the Law of Treaties, 1155 UNTS 331, Article 19(c), and the ICJ decision in *Reservations to the Genocide Convention* [1951] ICJ Reports, 15.

27 A claim raised in the objections to the reservations.

28 CEDAW General Comment 21, adopted 4 February 1994, UN Doc. A/47/38.

29 CCPR/C/21/Rev.1/Add.10.

30 F. Capotorti, *Study of the rights of persons belonging to ethnic, religious and linguistic minorities*, New York: United Nations, 1979, implies that religious marriages should be recognized. He mentions that some states recognize entire systems of personal status, but he does not raise problem of gender discrimination. Capotorti claims that preservation of customs and legal traditions forms part of protection of minorities, although notes that 'some argue' that these must be subject to the state's moral and social policy. See also D. J. Sullivan, 'Gender, equality and religious freedom: toward a framework for conflict resolution', *New York University Journal of International Law & Policy*, 24, 1992, 795, 805 fn. 29; T. Meron, *Human rights lawmaking in the United Nations: a critique of instruments and process*, Oxford: Clarendon, 1986, 155–156.

31 D. J. Sullivan, 'Advancing the freedom of religion or belief through the UN Declaration on the Elimination of Religious Intolerance and Discrimination', *American Journal of International Law*, 82, 1988, 487, 516.

32 In India, a complicated set of laws governs personal law of different religious denominations. A codification of the various personal laws began during colonial rule, and continued after independence. For instance, the Hindu Marriage Act, 1955 codifies Hindu Law; the Constitution sanctioned the Shari'at Act, 1937, as the prevailing Muslim Personal law (January 26, 1950), with few reforming Acts such as the Dissolution of Muslim Marriages Act, 1939 giving the wife a right to dissolution of the marriage in certain cases. Indian Divorce Act 1869 and Indian Christian Marriage Act 1872 govern Christians; the Parsee Marriage and Divorce Act, 1956, govern Parsees.

33 According to Article 2A added in the 1988 amendment to the Constitution.

34 The Family Courts Act 1985.

35 Defined as a 'Jewish and democratic state' in two of its basic laws (Basic Law: Freedom of Vocation and Basic Law: Human Freedom and Dignity).

36 The Palestine Order in Council 1922–1947, (which remains in force from the pre-independence period) states in Section 47 that some matters of personal law are subject to religious law, whether civil or religious courts have jurisdiction. These matters are defined in Section 51, mainly matters of marriage, divorce and alimony and maintenance.

37 In Israel, the Rabbinical Courts Jurisdiction (Marriage and Divorce) Law, 1953, Art. 1, grants exclusive jurisdiction to Rabbinical (religious) Courts in matters of marriage and divorce of Jews. In other matters, such as spousal alimony, the Rabbinical court has concurrent jurisdiction with the civil courts (Art. 4). The Druze Courts Law, 1962 Art. 4 grants exclusive jurisdiction to Druze religious courts in marriage and divorce of Druze. The Shari'a Courts have exclusive jurisdiction over personal status matters: marriage and divorce, child custody and support, paternity, alimony and maintenance of Muslims (The Palestine Order in Council 1922-1947, The Procedure of the Muslim Courts Act, item 7).

38 A state, which, in Article 9 of the Constitution, accords Buddhism a foremost place.

39 See D. C. Jayasuriya, *Law and social problems in modern Sri Lanka*, New Delhi: Sterling Publishers, 1982, 37–53.

40 According to the Muslim Marriage and Divorce Act 1951.

41 Concluding Observations of the CEDAW Committee: Israel (adopted 12/08/97) UN Doc. A/52/38/Rev.1, Part II paras. 132–183. Israel expressed its Reservation to Article 7(b) concerning appointment of women to serve as judges of religious courts where this is prohibited by the laws of any of the religious communities in Israel.

42 At the 1987 GA Third Committee discussion on reservations to CEDAW, Iraq and Egypt both justified their reservations on the sovereign right of States to choose their

political, economic and social system without the interference of others (Egypt, A/C.3/42/SR.26 par. 9; Iraq, A/C.3/42/SR.29 par. 29. See L. Lijnzaad, *Reservations to UN Human Rights Treaties – ratify and ruin?*, Dordrecht: Martinus Nijhoff Publishers, 1995, 333).

43 Under Article 13(1) of the Constitution.

44 Included in Part III of the Constitution.

45 *State of Bombay v. Narasu Appa Mali* AIR 1952 Bom 84; ILR 1951 Bombay 77.

46 For a dictum to the same effect by the Indian Supreme Court, see *Krishna Singh v. Mathura Ahir* AIR 1980 SC 707.

47 *Sarla Mudgal v. Union of India* AIR 1995 SC 1531; 1995 SCC (3) 635.

48 The Court urged the government to conform to Article 44 of the Constitution, which states that the State shall endeavour to secure a uniform civil code throughout the territory of India, and legislate the UCC. The CEDAW committee noted, in its consideration of India's state report in 2005 that the central government is of the opinion that the country is not ready to adopt a uniform civil code on the heterogeneous groups. However, the Committee welcomed the government's attempts to consider each of the personal laws independently to make these gender equal by repealing the discriminatory provisions (CEDAW/C/IND/2-3 para. 4).

49 Compare Elon, who argues that in Israel, although Jewish law in matters of marriage, divorce and child support has been incorporated by blanket reference, its formal source in Israeli law must be considered the secular legislature which incorporated it and not a religious source (M. Elon, *Jewish law: history, sources, principles*, Philadelphia: The Jewish Publication Society, 1994, 1757).

50 HCJ 1000/92 *Bavli v. Great Rabbinical Court* 48 (2) PD 221.

51 A principle of equal ownership of property during marriage and at its dissolution is included in General Comment 21 paras. 30–33 to CEDAW, interpreting CEDAW Article 16(1)(h). This principle is unrecognized not only in religious legal systems. Although existing in most European systems and US states, it is also not recognized in UK law. It was considered and rejected by the Law Commission in 1978 (see Law Com. No 86 (Third Report on Family Property)). The Matrimonial and Family Proceeding Act 1984 did not change from the existing legal regime of separation of assets.

52 As can be seen in HCJ 2222/99 *Gabbai v. Great Rabbinical Court* 54 (5) PD 401.

53 M. Shava, *The personal law in Israel*, 4th edn, Tel Aviv: Modan, 2001, 786.

54 Case (Tel Aviv Local Rabbinical Court) 884/99 *Bavli v. Bavli*.

55 Section 494 of the Penal Code, as interpreted in *Sarla Mudgal v. Union of India* AIR 1995 SC 1531; 1995 SCC (3) 635. See also *Muhamma Latheef v Nishat* (2003 (2) Kerala Law Times (KLT) (short notes) 100 [case no. 130], in which the Kerala High Court held that bigamy (in a Muslim marriage) amounts to mental cruelty to the first wife, entitling her to a decree for dissolution of marriage (R. Hoque and M. Khan, 'Judicial activism and Islamic family law: a socio-legal evaluation of recent trends in Bangladesh', *Islamic Law and Society*, 14, 2007, 204.)

56 *Sarla Mudgal v. Union of India* AIR 1995 SC 1531; 1995 SCC (3) 635.

57 *M. A. Khan, v. Shah Bano Begum* 1985 SCC 556.

58 Ruling that in case the woman is unable to maintain herself after the period of *iddat*, she is entitled to have recourse to Section 125 of the Code of Criminal Procedure.

59 In Writ Petition (civil) 868 /1986 *Latifi v. Union of India* (decided 28/09/2001), available at http://judis.nic.in (accessed 14 December 2009).

60 Articles 14 and 15 of the Constitution. It could be argued that not only would Muslim women have been treated unequally on the basis of religion, had the maintenance provisions not applied to them, as the Indian court ruled, but on the basis of sex as well. In a society in which married women generally do not work outside their home and do not earn money, some form of financial compensation upon divorce is necessary to redress at least somewhat the inequality created between the former husband and wife. Absence of any post-divorce financial payment to the wife, in disregard of her

contribution to the marriage, would fall far below the standard set by Article 16(1)(h) of CEDAW as interpreted in para. 32 of CEDAW General Comment 21, which demands that in distributing property upon dissolution of marriage, financial and non-financial contributions of the spouses should be accorded the same weight.

61 See further examples of the difference between reform of Hindu personal law and the personal law of minority religions, which Parashar attributes to political calculation, in A. Parashar, *Women and family law reform in India: Uniform Civil Code and gender equality*, New Delhi: Sage Publications, 1992, Chapter 4.

62 For Muslims, mainly the Muslim Family Law Ordinance, 1961. It permits polygamy under certain conditions, but it is a restricted option. It recognizes unilateral divorce (*taleq*) where it is revocable, and permits limited grounds for divorce by the wife. The Government of Bangladesh is considering a draft uniform family code which offers further reforms to the Muslim Family Ordinance, for instances providing women with broad grounds for divorce. Hindu personal law allows polygamy by the husband (which is outlawed in India for Muslims). Hindu personal law does not recognize a woman's right of inheritance. See: *Human rights in Bangladesh – a study of standards and practices*, Dhaka: Bangladesh Institute of Law and International Affairs, 2001, 72.

In *Jesmin Sultana* v *Mohammad Elias* ((1997) 17 BLD 4), the only case in which the courts have ruled on this issue, the High Court of Bangladesh ordered the repeal of s. 6 of the Muslim Family Laws Ordinance 1961 and the imposition of provisions banning polygamy. However, the Appellate Division overturned the High Court Division's ruling ((1999) 19 BLD (AD) 122) admonishing the lower court for intervening in the matter. In *Dilruba Akter v A. H. M. Mohsin* ((2003) 55 DLR (HCD) 568), the court took a more modest step, imposing a penalty on the husband for entering into a second marriage without written permission of the Arbitrary Council as required by the Muslim Family Laws Ordinance.

63 Concluding Observations of the CEDAW Committee: Bangladesh (adopted 01/02/93) A/48/38, paras. 248–326.

64 The legal situation as described by Lailufar Yasmin in 'Law and order situation and gender-based violence: Bangladeshi perspective' (Regional Centre for Strategic Studies, Policy Studies 16 Ch. 4: http://www.rcss.org (accessed 11 January 2009)), is that Hindu women are still governed by the ancient Shastric law. Laws of the colonial period too remain, as they were not revised after independence, specifically, the Hindu Widows Remarriage Act 1856, Hindu Women's Right to Property Act of 1937 and the Hindu Women's Right to Separate Residence and Maintenance Act of 1946. Hindu women in Bangladesh do not have a right to divorce but can have a right to live separately. Hindu law does not make marriage registrations compulsory. Hindu women's inheritance of property is very restricted.

65 A. Engineer, 'Bangladesh showing the way', *The Hindu*, 14 May 2001.

66 Rabbinical Courts Judgment Law (Marriage and Divorce), 1953, Article 4.

67 HCJ 9734/03 *A. v. Great Rabbinical Court* (decided 21.10.2004).

68 In societies in which, in marriages, wives still provide more of the home work and husbands more of the paid employment, some redress of inequality between spouses upon divorce is achieved by ordering of support payments (or other financial compensation). So, realistic amounts of support payments may be considered a measure to redress inequality of women.

69 In other instances the Israeli legislation intervened, affecting Muslim minority religious law: Unilateral repudiation of marriage against the wishes of the wife is an offence according to Art. 181 of the Penal Law, 1977. Polygamy is prohibited (for members of all religions) by Article 176 of the Penal Law, 1977. B. Shoughry-Badarne, *International law, personal status and the oppression of women: the case of Muslim women in Israel*, unpublished LL.M. thesis, American University, Washington, DC, 2001, claims, however, that the law is ineffectively enforced despite a high incidence of polygamous marriages among the Beduin Muslim community.

70 Layish notes, that even when Muslim women have a choice of secular jurisdiction more favourable to them, such as in matters of inheritance, they prefer litigation in the Shari'a Court due to social and religious pressures. See A. Layish, 'The status of the Muslim women in the Sharia Courts in Israel', in F. Raday, C. Shalev and M. Liban-Kooby (eds), *Women's status in Israeli law and society*, Tel Aviv: Shocken, 1995, 364.

71 The Age of Marriage Act, 1950, Article 3.

72 A. Layish, 'The status of the Muslim women in the Sharia Courts in Israel', in F. Raday, C. Shalev and M. Liban-Kooby (eds), *Women's status in Israeli law and society*, Tel Aviv: Shocken, 1995, 364.

73 The HRC has opined that, 'the right to freedom of thought, conscience and religion implies that the legislation of each State should provide for the possibility of both religious and civil marriages. In the Committee's view, however, for a State to require that a marriage, which is celebrated in accordance with religious rites, be conducted, affirmed or registered also under civil law is not incompatible with the Covenant' (General Comment 19 para. 4 to the ICCPR).

74 Protocol No. 7 to the 1950 European Convention for the Protection of Human Rights and Fundamental Freedoms, ETS 117, (entered into force 1 November 1988). It has not been ratified by the UK.

75 *Hansard* HC vol. 312 Col 1017 (20 May 1998).

76 Sri Lanka has a Buddhist majority, while there are also Hindu and Christian minorities. The problem discussed only exists regarding Muslim personal law.

77 CEDAW prohibits the betrothal and marriage of a 'child' (in Article 16(2)), but does not specify what age is considered a child. The UN Recommendation on Consent to Marriage, Minimum Age for Marriage and Registration of Marriage (GA Res. 34/180 December 18, 1979) refers to 'no less than fifteen' and makes an exception only where a 'competent authority' has decided it is in the interests of intended spouses (Compare: the minimum Age, 18, in the Protocol to the African Charter on Human and People's Rights on the Rights of Women in Africa, Art. 6(b)).

78 See Concluding Observations of the CEDAW Committee: Sri Lanka. 07/05/2002.A/57/38 (Part I), paras. 256–302.

79 Under the Muslim Marriage and Divorce Act 1951.

80 See D. C. Jayasuriya, *Law and social problems in modern Sri Lanka*, New Delhi: Sterling Publishers, 1982.

81 The Marriage Act 1949 Section 26(1)(d).

82 M. Elon, *Jewish law: history, sources, principles*, Philadelphia: The Jewish Publication Society, 1994, 1754–1755, fn. 9.

83 New York Domestic Relations Law para. 253 amended in 1983. A similar Federal law was enacted in Canada: Canada Divorce Act 1985 section 21.1, Ch.18, I Statutes of Canada (1990). The Supreme Court of Canada in *Bruker v. Marcovitz* 2007 SCC 54 ruled, (by a 7-2 majority), that a Jewish man must pay his ex-wife damages to compensate her for losses arising from his refusal to provide her with a Jewish divorce as he had contractually agreed. The Australian Law Reform Commission, in its report, 'Multiculturalism and the law', *ALRC Report No 57*, 1992, proposed similar legislation. In Australia, the Family Court in *Gwiazda v Gwiazda* No. M10631 of 1992 (unreported, see G. Segal, 'The inter-operation of religious and secular legal systems in the Australian context', *Justice*, 7, 2001, 8, 11, ordered, by using its injunctive power, a wife who refused to accept the get, to appear before the Beth Din in Melbourne. (So-called 'Gwiazda Orders' are now to order a party to appear in front of Beth Din and accept/receive a get.)

84 By sec. 236 part B.

85 S. L. Stone, 'The intervention of American law in Jewish divorce: a pluralist analysis', *Israel Law Review* 34, 2000, 170.

86 M. Elon, *Jewish law: history, sources, principles*, Philadelphia: The Jewish Publication Society, 1994, 1754–1755, fn. 9.

87 S. Maidment Kershner, '*Agunot:* new solutions from old sources', *New Law Journal*, 151, 2001, 720, 720–721, 730 examines the use of action for damages in tort by the wife from whom the *get* is withheld in the USA, and the possibility of such action in the UK.

88 S. Bano, 'Shari'a Courts in relation to divorce within Muslim communities in Britain' lecture delivered at the conference: Gender and cultural diversity – European perspectives, 17 October 2003, London School of Economics, London.

89 *Ryland v. Edros* 1997 (2) SA 690 (CC); 1997 (1) BCLR 77.

90 The Marriage Act 1961.

91 Where third party interests are involved the situation is more complex. Indeed in *Amod v. Multilateral Motor Vehicle* 1997 (12) BCLR 1716 (D) the Muslim marriage was held not to give the widow any rights as a 'wife' of the deceased against the insurer.

92 Indeed, prior to this decision, in *Ismail v. Ismail* 1983 (1) SA 1006 (A) the Appellate Division rejected a claim for maintenance based on a Muslim marriage, ruling that such a marriage was potentially polygamous and could not enjoy ad hoc recognition, being against public policy.

93 See further: C. Rautenbach, 'Gender equality and religious family laws in South Africa', *Queensland University of Technology Law and Justice Journal*, 3, 2003, 1, who cites South African statutes specifically including as beneficiaries spouses in unofficial religious marriages including the Special Pensions Act and the Demobilisation Act.

94 *Fraser v. Children's Court* 1997 (2) SA 218 (CC).

95 *Daniels v. No* 2004 (7) BCLR 735 (CC).

96 Ibid., at para. 26.

97 Ibid., at para. 22, citing Section 1(b) of the Constitution.

98 The Constitution, Section 15.

99 Section 15(3)(a).

100 Section 15 (3)(a): 'this Section does not prevent legislation recognising – (i) marriages concluded under any tradition or a system of religion.'

101 Article 15(3), however, would mean that it could not, as such recognition would have to be consistent with the other provisions of the Constitution. (See also J. Van der Vyver, 'Constitutional perspectives on Church-State relations in South Africa', *Brigham Young University Law Review*, 1999, 935, 659–664.)

102 In July 2003, the South African Law Reform Commission also addressed the matter of Muslim marriages in a report to the Minister of Justice along with proposed draft legislation for the Muslim Marriages Act, which, due to public concern, has not reached the legislative stage.

103 Para. 24.

104 *Sowa v. Sowa* [1961] p. 70.

105 Matrimonial Causes Act 1973, Section 47.

106 *Bibi v. Chief Adjudication Officer* [1998] 1 FLR 375, [1998] 1 FCR 301. See discussion of previous cases: C. Hamilton, *Family, law and religion*, London: Sweet & Maxwell, 1995, 73.

107 But for income-related benefits, there is an allowance for a second wife in a polygamous marriage. See Section 121 and 147(5) Social Security Contributions and Benefits Act 1992 (as amended by the Private International Law (Miscellaneous Provisions) Act 1995 Sch, para. 4); Income Support (General) Regulations 1987 reg 18; Family Credit (General) Regulations 1987 reg 46; *Din v. National Assistance Board* [1967] 2 QB 213, [1967] 1 All ER 750. See further N. Lowe and G. Douglas, *Bromley's Family Law*, London: Butterworths, 1998, 51.

108 Adopted by the African Union, 11 July–August 13, 2003.

109 Article 6(c).

110 Article 6(d).

111 Article 6(c).

112 Article 6(a).

113 Article 6(b).

114 Article 7(b).

115 Article 25(c).
116 Pursuant to the Chief Rabbinate Law, 1980 and the Jewish Religious Services Law, [combined version] 1971.
117 See Shari'a Courts (Verification of Appointments) Law, 1965; Druze Courts Law, 1962; Rabbinical Courts Jurisdiction (Marriage and Divorce) Law, 1953 regarding, respectively, Muslim, Druze and Jewish Courts.
118 Israeli law exempts these posts from the general provision of equality in appointment to public posts (Equal Rights of Women Law, 1953, Article 7(c)).
119 CEDAW Concluding Observations on Israel's State Report: Israel, A/52/38/Rev.1 part II (1997) 87. Israel has, in fact, submitted a reservation to Article 7(b) precisely on this point.
120 Article 5(a).
121 E. Odio Benito, *Elimination of all forms of intolerance and discrimination based on religion or belief*, New York: United Nations, 1989, 54.
122 Article 9(4): 'No person may unfairly discriminate directly or indirectly against anyone on one or more grounds in terms of subsection (3). National legislation must be enacted to prevent or prohibit unfair discrimination.' (The grounds in subsection (3) include gender.)
123 J. Van der Vyver, 'Constitutional perspectives on Church-State relations in South Africa', *Brigham Young University Law Review*, 1999, 935, 668.
124 App. No. 27008/95 *Williamson v. UK* EComHR. See also App. No. 12356/86 *Karlsson v. Sweden*. EComHR; *Knudsen v. Norway* (1985) 42 DR 247 EComHR.
125 For the position of the Catholic Church see the Congregation for the Doctrine of the Faith, Declaration Inter Insigniores on the question of the Admission of Women to the Ministerial Priesthood (October 15, 1976): AAS 69 (1977), 98–116, which denies the possibility of the ordination of women, a position repeated in the Ordinatio Sacerdotalis (22 May, 1994) of John Paul II (see the Vatican website at http://www.vatican.va (accessed 14 December 2009).
126 Section 3.
127 In the Scottish Court of Session: *Percy v Employment Appeal Tribunal Order and Judgment* [2001] ScotCS 65. In the House of Lords: *Percy v Church of Scotland* [2005] UKHL 73.
128 In terms of Article IV of the Declaratory Articles contained in the Schedule to the Church of Scotland Act 1921.
129 *Percy v. Church of Scotland* [2005] UKHL 73.
130 See also, following this ruling *New Testament Church of God v. Stewart* [2007] IRLR 178.
131 R. Cook, 'Accountability in international law for violation of women's rights by non-state actors', in D. Dallmeyer, *Reconceiving reality: women and international law*, Washington: American Society of International Law, 1993, 93, 107.
132 *Bob Jones University v. US*, 461 US 574 (1983).
133 See CEDAW GC 23 'Women in political and public life' (adopted 1997) UN Doc. A/52/38; R. Cook and B. Dickens, 'Human rights dynamics of abortion law reform', *Human Rights Quarterly*, 25, 2003, 1, 44.
134 Article 12(1).
135 (Adopted 1999), UN Doc. A/54/38/Rev. 1, Chapter 1.
136 See R. Cook, 'Women's rights: a bibliography', *New York University Journal of International Law and Politics*, 24, 1992, 857, 680.
137 Protocol to the African Charter on Human and People's Rights on the Rights of Women in Africa, Article 14(2)(c).
138 Paragraph 8.25, Program of Action of the International Conference on Population and Development, 13 September 1994, UN Doc. A/CONF. 171/13.
139 See M. K. Eriksson, *Reproductive freedom in the context of international human rights and humanitarian law*, The Hague: Martinus Nijhoff Publishers, 2000, 187.
140 Fourth World Conference on Women, 15 September 1995, A/CONF.177/20 and A/CONF,177/20/Add. 1 Chapter IV paragraph 107 (k).

141 Report of the ad hoc committee of the whole of the twenty-third special session of the General Assembly, 2000 (UN Doc. A/S-23/10/Rev.1).

142 L. Tribe, 'Forward: toward a model of roles in due process of life and law', *Harvard Law Review*, 87, 1973, 1, 18–25.

143 L. Tribe, *American constitutional law*, 2nd edn, Minola: Foundation Press, 1988, 1349–1350.

144 For discussion, see D. Dooley, 'Gendered citizenship in the Irish Constitution', in T. Murphy and P. Twomey (eds), *Ireland's evolving constitution: 1927–1997*, Oxford: Hart, 1998, 121.

145 Previously the Eighth Amendment of the Constitution Act, 1983 acknowledged 'the right to life of the unborn, with due regard to the equal right to life of the mother'. The Thirteenth Amendment (1992) provided that 'Article 40.3.3° (the right to life of the unborn) would not limit freedom to travel between Ireland and another state', and the Fourteenth Amendment (1992) provided that 'Article 40.3.3° (the right to life of the unborn) would not limit freedom to obtain or make available information relating to services lawfully available in another state'. The latest, 2002, constitutional referendum on abortion sought to amend Article 40 to limit the cases in which a woman could legally obtain an abortion, so that medically necessitated permitted abortions would exclude danger to the women's life from suicidal intent. The amendment was rejected. See further the referendum committee website: http://www. refcom.ie (accessed 14 December 2009).

Although the Fifth Amendment (1972) removed from the Constitution the special position of the Catholic Church, Church involvement in constitutional debates remained influential. On the religious institutional religious involvement backing the failed 2002 amendment see C. Parkin, 'Papal support for abortion law amendment', *Press Association Ireland*, 2 March 2002; 'Ireland decides, the Pope supports Ahern on Abortion', *The People* (Ireland), 3 March 2002.

146 CEDAW Concluding Observations on the second and third periodic reports of Ireland 1999, A/54/38/Rev.1, para. 180.

147 On Church involvement in lawmaking in Ireland see also: G. Whyte, 'Some reflections on the role of religion in the constitutional order', in T. Murphy and P. Twomey (eds), *Ireland's evolving constitution: 1927–1997*, Oxford: Hart, 1998, 51.

148 In its 2005 report, the CEDAW committee again voiced concerns over Ireland's restrictive abortion laws. (CEDAW Concluding comments: Ireland (2005), paras. 38–39).

149 No substantial determination as to the existence of a right of abortion has been made under the European Convention. *Open Door and Dublin Well Women v. Ireland* (1992) 15 EHRR 244 ECtHR raised the issue indirectly. It dealt with an injunction banning dissemination of information in Ireland on abortion clinics outside Ireland. The Court decided the case on the issue of freedom of expression and made no determination as to whether a right of access to abortion is included within Convention rights. In App. No. 51792/99 *Tokarczyk v. Poland* EctHR, the Court decided that the conviction of the applicant for arranging abortions did not infringe his rights under Article 10. The question whether women had a right of access to abortions again remained unanswered. In *H v. Norway* (1992) 73 DR 155 EComHR, the Commission, asked to rule on a potential father's right in connection with an abortion, left broad discretion to the state on this issue, avoiding again a clear statement on the existence and permissible limitations of a woman's right. In *Tysiąc v. Poland* (application no. 5410/03) the Court decided that where the law permitted abortion to save the life or health of the pregnant woman, as it did in Poland, an uncertain procedure that caused severe anxiety to the women was in breach of Article 8 of the Convention. Again, no determination was made as to whether recognition of a right to abortion in these circumstances was required.

150 See Section 5 above.

151 *Johnston v. Ireland* (1986) 9 EHRR 203 ECtHR.

152 Neither does the ICCPR, which does mandate, however, in Article 23, paragraph 4, that states parties shall take appropriate steps to ensure equality of rights and responsibilities of spouses as to marriage, during marriage and at its dissolution.

153 The Irish Referendum on Divorce on 24 November 1995 had been carried. Consequent to the constitutional amendment, the Family Law (Divorce) Act 1996 came into force on 27 February 1997.

The Irish Constitution, Article 41(3) as amended the 1995, states that:

(1) The State pledges itself to guard with special care the institution of Marriage, on which the Family is founded, and to protect it against attack.

(2) A court … may grant a dissolution of marriage where… (i)… the spouses have lived apart from one another for … at least four years during the five years, (ii) there is no reasonable prospect of a reconciliation … (iii) such provision as the Court considers proper … will be made for the spouses, any children of either or both of them and any other person prescribed by law, and (iv) any further conditions prescribed by law are complied with.

(3) No person whose marriage has been dissolved under the civil law of any other State but is a subsisting valid marriage under the law for the time being in force within the jurisdiction … [=of Ireland] shall be capable of contracting a valid marriage within that jurisdiction during the lifetime of the other party to the marriage so dissolved.

154 After legislation of a divorce law in Chile in March 2004, the Philippines is the only other state with no divorce provisions. The Catholic Church was influential in all three states in opposition to divorce legislation. See CBC-Canada Radio, 'Chilean divorce law passed', 3 November 2004.

155 For the position of the Catholic Church on many issues pertinent to the rights of women, see the Report on the Holy See submitted by Abdelfattah Amor, Special Rapporteur on Freedom of Religion and Belief, E/CN.4/2000/65 of 15 February 2000.

156 The Holy See is a permanent subject of general international law. It concludes international treaties on the basis of full equality on behalf of the State of the City of the Vatican or on its own behalf (J. L. Kunz, 'The status of the Holy See in international law', *American Journal of International Law*, 46, 1952, 308). The Vatican, through the Holy See on its behalf, carries out activities, which in international law are traditionally assigned to states. Besides Concordats, the Vatican is signatory to other international treaties, it has diplomatic relations with states, and has a UN permanent observer status (S. W. Bettwy, 'US–Vatican recognition: background and issues', *Catholic Lawyer*, 29, 1984, 225, 236).

157 See AC.2/SR.6/ p.4 (M. Amado of Panama) quoted in J. Morsink, *The Universal Declaration of Human Rights: origins, drafting and intent*, Philadelphia: University of Pennsylvania Press, 1999, 122. Subsequent Concordats loosened state obligations in this area considerably: for instance, the 1984 Concordat with Italy (see D. L. Certoma, *The Italian legal system*, London: Butterworths, 1985, 123) and the 1979 Concordat with Spain (see J. Martinez-Torrón, 'Freedom of religion in the case law of the Spanish Constitutional Court', *Brigham Young University Law Review*, 2001, 711, 728–729).

158 Likewise, the ICCPR states in Article 23 (4) that 'States Parties to the present Covenant shall take appropriate steps to ensure equality of rights and responsibilities of spouses as to marriage, during marriage and at its dissolution.'

159 See M. K. Eriksson, *Reproductive freedom in the context of international human rights and humanitarian law*, The Hague: Martinus Nijhoff Publishers, 2000, 187.

160 UN Doc. A/CONF. 171/13 p.147. The Holy See is party to some UN human rights treaties: CERD, CRC and CAT (the Convention against Torture, 1465 UNTS 85) but not CEDAW, ICCPR or the ICSECR.

161 See further C. W. Howland, 'The challenge of religious fundamentalism to the liberty and equality rights of women: an analysis under the UN Charter', *Columbia Journal of Transnational Law*, 35, 1997, 271, 296.

162 See: J. Preston, 'UN Summit on women bars groups: China, Vatican block opponents admission', *Washington Post*, 17 March 1995, A36.

163 Adopted 17 July 1998, UN Doc. A/CONF.183/9.

164 See B. C. Cedant, 'Gender-specific provisions in the International Criminal Court', in F. Lattanzi and W. A. Schabas (eds), *Essays on the Rome Statute of the International Criminal Court*, Naples: Ripa Fagnano Alto, 1999.

165 CEDAW GC 24, A/54/38/Rev.1, Part 1, 1999, para. 11.

166 CEDAW Concluding Observations on Croatia, A/53/38/Rev.1 part I (1998) 10 at para. 109; See also CEDAW Concluding Observations on Italy, A/52/38/Rev.1 part II (1997) 106 at para. 353.

167 Compare section 38(1) of the UK Human Fertilisation and Embryology Act 1990 exempting any person objecting to the activities covered by the Act from any duty to participate in them.

5 Children, education and religious freedom

The right of the child to religious freedom is unique. The right of the child as individual stands in potential conflict with interest in the child's religious upbringing by several communities to which it belongs: the family, the state, and sometimes the child's religious community. This chapter examines how children are affected by the conflict between individual and group perceptions of religious freedom, problems that current international law instruments fail to solve. The chapter concludes that, under the guise of a right of the child, various group and individual interests have been protected by international law, and the only principled way of protecting the child's religious freedom is through careful separation of individual rights from other social interests.

Article 14 of the Convention on the Rights of the Child[1] [CRC] guarantees the child's right to freedom of religion.[2] The conflicting claims surrounding religious freedom become evident when it is observed that most of the reservations to the CRC are of three types, all connected to religious perceptions of the child: reservations to Article 14, the right of religious freedom,[3] reservations to articles of the Convention regarding adoption or family planning,[4] and reservations to the entire Convention, based on the dominance of religion in the state.[5] Most of these are reservations by Islamic states, although the Holy See also has entered broad reservations based on religion.[6] It is questionable whether such broad reservations to the Convention are valid, as indeed some of the signatories to the Convention have declared.[7]

An overarching provision of the CRC, Article 5, establishes that all Convention rights differ from the rights accorded to adults, in that the child's parents, and sometimes members of the extended family or community,[8] retain the right and duty to provide, in a manner consistent with the evolving capacities of the child, appropriate direction and guidance in the exercise by their children of their Convention rights.[9]

Freedom of religion of the child is, however, subject to a further qualification. Article 14 refers specifically to the obligation on states to respect the rights and duties of parents to provide direction to their child. Parental rights are mentioned in regard to freedom of religion; they are not mentioned in articles regarding other rights of the child, such as rights of expression, assembly and privacy.[10] Why this difference? If the reason is the relative immaturity of the child to make his or her own decisions and exercise autonomous choice, this reason applies to many other rights. However, regarding religion, parents are seen as having a right to shape their child's identity. In this it differs from freedom of speech or freedom of assembly of the child. Religion has a long-term relational aspect, distinct from its individual-liberty aspect, which these liberty rights do not have. If religious freedom is about belonging to a group, then the child's immediate group, the family, has a recognisable interest in maintaining group cohesion, at least while the child is still part of that group. Rights that have only an individualistic-liberty aspect but no identity aspect, such as freedom of expression or association, do not contain a similar protected interest – of fostering familial identity – for the parents.

5.1 Choice of religion

The right to choose one's religion is a defining aspect of the individualistic view of religious freedom. The group identity view of religious freedom, however, seeks to protect and foster existing religious cultures. Both views accept that individuals have a right to change their religion. However, liberals and communitarians view the value of such change, and therefore the legitimate legal barriers upon exercise of this right, differently. Liberals see value in change itself, namely in the exercise of personal choice; communitarians value the continuation of religious traditions while not opposing the option of change. Therefore, communitarians argue for barriers that foster the community by making such change more difficult. Children's right to change religion are limited by both perceptions for different reasons and to different extents. Liberals limit the child's right in accordance with the developing capabilities of exercise of personal autonomy. Communitarians limit the exercise of the child's right in order to enable a fostering of identity.[11]

The conflict between religious community and individual rights was evident during the drafting process of the CRC. Article 14 was modelled on Article 18 of the ICCPR. During the negotiations, there was broad consensus on the child's right to religious freedom. As with the inclusion of a general right to change religion in the Universal Declaration, so too in the CRC negotiations some Islamic states objected to the inclusion of a right of the child to change his or her religion, because such a right conflicts with the laws of Islam.[12] This was problematic: the right to adopt a religion was already conferred without limit of age in the ICCPR, so its exclusion from the CRC could be viewed as an elimination of an existing right. In one of the submissions that raised this objection,[13] the representative of Bangladesh reasoned that the right of the child to change religion would conflict with what was to become Article 18 of the CRC – the principle that parents have primary responsibility for the upbringing of the child.

In the end, no mention was made of the child's right to choose religion.[14] This may be seen as a lacuna, a question open to interpretation in light of Article 18 of the ICCPR, rather than a decision that such a right does not exist. International law does not establish a minimum age below which the child is unable to adopt a religion of his or her choice. In international law there has not, apparently, been a direct legal challenge of a child against his or her parents regarding the right to practice religion.[15]

Exclusion of the right to change religion undermines the core of religious freedom as an individual right. Freedom, of any sort, means a right to choose. Without choice, it is almost impossible to speak of religious freedom. The child is tied into an identity decided for him or her, thus significantly limiting his or her freedom. The only, minimal, meaning the right retains is as a limitation on government from interfering with the identity the child acquired at birth.

5.2 The child's religion in situations of change of family

The child's religious identity, usually given at birth, is a product of social and legal mechanisms constituting group choice. The child's religious identity is determined from, or even before, its birth. This determination is recognized and given legal protection in certain cases. A newborn child clearly cannot choose his or her religion. So, it may be asked what is being protected: a right of the child or an interest of the community it was born into?

Generally, the child's religious identity bestowed on it by its parents is unquestioned. As long as the parents agree on the child's religion, no question is asked as to whether the choice of religion is in the best interest of the child (as long as it does not cause neglect). Only in cases of parental disagreement does the legal system ask if the religious choice of either parent stands in conflict with their child's best interests. Indeed, when one parent converts, the state may be prone to side with the parent who holds the religion into which the child was born.[16]

When prospective adoptive parents[17] are both of a different religion than the birth religion of the child, the question arises even more acutely:[18] should children be adopted or fostered by parents of a different religion?[19] Are those who oppose cross-religion adoptions protecting the child's interest to remain in his/her religion, or the group interest to maintain its membership? With a child old enough to understand his or her religious affiliation, it is understandably in the interests of the child not to add change of religion to the overwhelming change of the adoption itself. But an argument has been raised also against inter-religious adoption of infants, akin to the argument raised against inter-racial adoption. Generally, such arguments are voiced against adopting from a minority or disadvantaged racial or religious group. The argument can be seen as protecting an individual right – protecting the child from being denied its heritage – but should perhaps be seen as protecting a group interest of self-preservation. Such a group interest may stand in direct conflict with the interests of the child in a speedy adoption. For example, US federal law firmly opposes racial matching in adoption by prohibiting reliance on race to delay or deny adoptive placement by federally funded agencies.[20] There is no similar prohibition on matching religious background in adoption.

International legal regulation, found in the CRC (Article 20(3)), mandates that, in placement of children, whether for adoption or foster care, due regard is to be given to the child's ethnic, religious, cultural and linguistic background. Article 8 specifically mentions a right of the child to preserve his or her identity.

Article 3 demands that the best interests of the child be a primary consideration in all actions concerning children. However, there is no clear indication as to how these provisions are to be translated into practice regarding adoption. Specifically, who can decide on the exercise of the child's right to identity: the parents, the adoption agency, the courts? And where is the child's right to identity to be placed among other considerations?

The UN Declaration on the Elimination of All Forms of Intolerance and of Discrimination Based on Religion or Belief in Article 5(4) states that in the case of a child who is not under the care either of his parents or of legal guardians, due account shall be taken of their expressed wishes or of any other proof of their wishes in the matter of religion or belief, the best interests of the child being the guiding principle. There are no clearer international norms.

In the UK, until the Children Act 1975, consent to adoption could be given subject to a condition concerning the religion in which the child would be brought up. Even when a mother had reconsidered, after the placement of her child, and asked for the child to be returned to her so she could place the child with an agency of her religion, the Court of Appeal held that the court must give effect to the religious choice of the parent.[21] This reflected a common law rule that parents (originally the father, or the mother of an illegitimate child) have a natural right to determine the religion of their children.

Following the 1972 report of the Houghton Committee, the Children Act 1975 abolished this possibility. The subsequent Adoption Act 1976 provided (in s. 7) that an agency shall, in placing a child, have regard, insofar as is practicable, to any wishes of the child's parents or guardians as to the religious upbringing of the child. Today, the Adoption and Children Act 2002 requires the adoption agency duly to consider the child's religious persuasion, racial origin and cultural and linguistic background (see s. 1(5)), although the paramount consideration is the child's welfare, and any delay in placing the child must be borne in mind as likely to prejudice the child's welfare (see s. 1(2), and (4)). A similar approach is taken by the UK Children Act 1989, which applies in other matters regarding the upbringing of the child (such as placement of children in foster homes by local authorities). Section 1(1) mandates that the welfare of the child shall be a paramount consideration. Section 22(5)(c) mandates that a local authority give due consideration to the child's religious persuasion, racial origin and cultural and linguistic background.

Even prior to the 2002 Adoption and Children Act, English courts have taken into consideration the prospective adopted children's religious, and other, background. If there are suitable adopters of the requested religion, they will be preferred. But the English courts have seen the welfare of a child as a consideration that can prevail over the religious convictions of the parents/parent if there are no suitable adopters of the required religion. For instance, in *Re C (Adoption: Religious Observance)*[22] the High Court accepted that parents' religious wishes should be taken into account, but their wishes should be weighed against the child's need for a stable, loving environment and other emotional, cultural and religious needs. The legitimacy of the consideration of religious background itself was not questioned.

It is unquestioned by the courts, in the cases that will be discussed, and indeed follows the statute, that a child, even a baby who is clearly not yet attached to any religion, should preferably be placed with a family of his or her religion of origin. There is no discussion in case law of why this is so, or what interest is served by including this consideration.

The effect of such as consideration can be beneficial, but can also sometimes be detrimental to the child. In some cases in which there is difficulty in finding religiously matching adopters, the child remains in foster care, delaying or even preventing adoption. This was the case in *Re E (An Infant)*,[23] in which wardship proceedings were at issue. A previous decision had accepted the mother's religious belief that the child must be brought up in a family of a particular religion as a valid reason for her refusal to consent to adoption (hence the wardship proceedings). Even though the case concerned a baby a few months old, the court held that great significance should be given to the wishes of the mother as to the religious upbringing of her child, but not when the child's welfare required otherwise (as in the case at hand). Thus, wardship was continued. But, because of the previous ruling, the child could not be adopted, which, other than for reasons of religion matching, would have been the preferable option for the child's welfare. Apart from the practical consequences of recognition of parents' refusal to agree to a cross-religion adoption, there appears to be a lack of clarity as to what rights are involved. In *Re P (A Minor) (Residence Order: Child's Welfare)*,[24] a daughter with Down's syndrome, of Orthodox Jewish parents, was placed with a non-practising Christian foster family. In deciding whether to vary the residence order, Butler-Sloss LJ cited as the primary consideration the welfare of the child. In this case, the child's need for a settled life outweighed the religious considerations. But through the balancing of considerations an important question arose, whether the insistence of the parents that the child would be placed only with a Jewish family was meaningful, as her capacity to understand her religious affiliation was not expected ever to surpass that of a 10-year old. This factor led the lower court to reject the parents' challenge to the placement, finding that she was unlikely to have any real perception of her Jewish heritage. The Court of Appeal accepted this reasoning (although mostly its decision was based on the other factors weighing heavily in favour of the placement). However, it can be asked, why should it matter at all, as a consideration for placement, whether a child will be able to understand (in the future) his or her religious affiliation? If the right invoked in support of this consideration is a right of the child to enjoy his or her religious affiliation, then a placement of a small child for adoption is never an exercise of this right, as there is no exercise of choice involved. This is true of any small child, whether he or she will be able in the future to understand his or her religious identity or not, as it is an identity which was chosen for him or her. By the same token, if what is invoked is a right of the parents that their child will continue to bear their religious identity, then placement within their religion is always an exercise of this right, whether or not the child will ever be able to understand this identity.

In *Re P*, Ward LJ, concurring, agreed with the analysis of Butler-Sloss LJ, which weighed religion as one factor in determining the welfare of the child. He added to the welfare analysis a rights analysis, mentioning that children have rights in international conventions ratified by the United Kingdom. The conventions 'may not have the force of law but, as international treaties, they command and receive our respect', he said, referring specifically to Article 14 of the Convention on the Rights of the Child (guaranteeing freedom of religion). He called it 'a right to practise one's parents' religion'. There is a confusion in this rights analysis between the rights of the child and the rights of the parents. The assumption that the child, who is not choosing the religion of his or her adoptive parents, is in some way exercising his or her own right by being given the opportunity to practise his or her parents' religion, is telling. In fact, what is protected in this case is an interest of the biological parents to have their children brought up in their religion, even when they will be raised in a different family. This may be an interest worthy of protection or even of recognition as an independent right, but it is certainly not a right protected by the Convention, which protects rights of children. But there is a pivotal difference between adoption into a family of a different race and adoption into a family of a different religion. Parents could bring up a child within a racial/cultural identity different from their own, more or less successfully, as the case may be. But religion has to be believed in. Parents could respect the different religion of the child, but they could not play the parental role inherent in the doctrines of many religions, unless they themselves believed in it. This problem is shown by the *Re E*[25] case: it was suggested by the unsuccessful prospective adopters, who now wanted to be granted custody of the child, that they would bring the child up according to the Roman Catholic faith, even though they were secular, of Jewish descent. This proposal was understandably rejected by the court, which saw the inevitable meaning of placement with this family, namely that the child would not be raised as a Catholic.[26]

It would be better to acknowledge the existence of an argument supporting matching that is separate from any measure of psychological adjustment in adoption. This argument is based on a claim of a right of belonging to a defined community, whether defined by religion or by race. This raises two further distinct questions: whether such a right is conceptually possible and whether it exists within international human rights law, and criticisms on both counts have been raised earlier. Such an argument could also be construed as an argument for a right of the parents or of the community to which the child was born. Sometimes, it may be legitimate to consider group interests in adoption placement, particularly in cases where the survival of the group is at stake.

Protection of religious identity is rarely protection of the exercise of individual choice. Religion is usually assigned at birth: it is determined more by heredity than by any process of conscious choice. What is protected is affiliation usually, determined not even by an active choice of parents but by their own membership in a religious group. This is seen most clearly when the retention of original religious identity is stretched to its limit – in the case of adoption. In this case, the child no longer belongs to a particular religion as part and parcel of belonging to the birth family. The social perception that values retaining the child's religion in adoption protects neither choice nor family connections, but a predetermined identity.

5.3 Right to religious education: protection of right of child or of community?

Religious identity is determined at birth but fostered through education. Education influences the way individual choices are made. Religious education has thus always been a subject of importance in international law.

Guarantee of education in conformity with the child's religion is one of the first issues in which international law has dealt not only with domestic state policy, but also with the conduct of the family unit itself. It is worthwhile exploring the considerations implied by international instruments, especially whether these are considerations regarding the right of the child or the protection of community interests.

Initially state obligations regarding religious education were not based on the child's rights or even parents' rights, but were intended to protect and preserve the relevant minority. The particular interest in children's education was a product of minority communities' wish to guarantee the continued existence of their religious minority community into the next generation.

Protection of religious education in international law began in instruments protecting groups, and predates the 1948 watershed of individual rights. The Minority Treaties[27] included a guarantee of religious education. For instance, the 1919 Minorities Treaty between the Principled Allied and Associated Forces and Poland[28] committed Poland to equal funding for the educational, religious and charitable causes of minorities. The Permanent Court of International Justice[29] opined that the prohibition of privately owned schools by the Albanian constitution was a breach of Albania's obligations towards religious and linguistic minorities.

A similar minority protection guarantee in the inter-war era – a provision regarding children's religious education – was included in the Anglo-Irish treaties. The Articles of Agreement for a Treaty between Great Britain and Ireland[30] establish that Ireland would not endow any religion or restrict free exercise or affect the child's right to attend publicly financed schools without receiving religious education.[31] Article 44.2.4 of the 1937 Irish constitution guarantees the right of any child to attend school without receiving religious instruction. In this case, too, the religious education provision in a treaty concluded between two states was aimed at protection of the Protestant minority rather than the child's rights, as other rights of children are not mentioned or protected by it.

Even in the post-1948 era of individual human rights, the right to choose religious or moral education was only gradually recognized as an individual right of the child. First it was only recognized as a right of the parents, and only later of the child itself. Under the ICCPR,[32] states undertake to 'have respect for the liberty of the parents and, when applicable, legal guardians, to ensure the religious and moral education of their children in conformity with their own convictions'. The same wording is used in Article 13(3) of the International Covenant on Economic, Social and Cultural Rights. Van Bueren[33] argues that the omission of the child's own right to religious freedom was due to oversight rather than conscious exclusion.

It is more likely, however, that this approach follows the Universal Declaration, which views the child's religious education as a right of the parents rather than of the individual child. Indeed, such a right accorded to the child would be incompatible with that of the parent. Article 26(3) of the Universal Declaration states: 'Parents have a prior right to choose the kind of education that shall be given to their children.' While this Article does not refer specifically to religious education, it is clearly one of the important choices protected by it.[34] Its phrasing resulted from a conscious ideological choice of the drafters to offset state power over education by giving parents the pre-emptory choice over the *kind* of education their children receive. In this context, it is notable that during the drafting negotiations, the proponents of this phrase, such as Dr Malik of the Lebanon, stressed the need to take control of education out of the hands of states, where dictators could use it to teach against the principles enshrined in the Declaration, much as Hitler used the state education system to inculcate Nazi principles.[35] This rationale reflects the fear that the state will provide an education that will teach pupils not to respect human rights. It ignores the possibility that the child's parents will choose private education, including religious education, which will go against the human rights principles of the Declaration. The child is not mentioned as a bearer of rights, but rather a power balance is sought between the state, which can and must provide compulsory education,[36] and the parents, who have a prior right of choice of education.

Similarly, the 1981 Declaration on the Elimination of All Forms of Intolerance and of Discrimination Based on Religion and Belief declares the child's right to access to education in accordance with the wishes of his or her parents or guardians, the best interests of the child being the guiding principle.[37] Thus, the parents are given initial legal control over the child's religion. The only limitations on the practices of the child's religious upbringing are that they not be injurious to the child's health or development.[38] By giving the parents the right to organize the life of the family in accordance with their religion or belief,[39] the 1981 Declaration recognizes the family as an autonomous religious group headed by the parents. Unequivocal recognition of the child's own rights was finally given in the CRC, which includes the child's rights to religious freedom[40] and education.[41]

As in international documents, the right to choose religious education as a right of the parents is also espoused in some national constitutions.[42]

The European Convention for the Protection of Human Rights and Fundamental Freedoms and its jurisprudence bring into sharp relief the problems of assigning to parents the right to choose religious education for their child. The European Convention recognizes in Protocol 1(2) that: '[T]he state shall respect the right of parents to ensure such education and teaching in conformity with their own religious and philosophical convictions.'[43]

Since no mention is made of the child's right regarding his or her education, it is not the right of the child that is encapsulated in Protocol 1(2) but the right of the parents. Here, as with the similar provisions enshrining parental choice in religious education, it may be suggested that the right is accorded to parents because they are seen as agents of the religious community to which they belong.

Although a Church or religious community cannot claim to be victim of infringement of Protocol 1(2),[44] this does not exclude the possibility that parents who do so will act as agents of their religious communities.[45]

The Charter of Fundamental Rights of the European Union attempts to affect a balance between the parents' right and the constraint of democratic principles.[46] Again, the voice of the child is not heard.

The right to choose education according to religious and philosophical convictions should be framed in legal documents as a right of the child himself or herself and not as a right of the child's parents. Normally, this right can be exercised by the parents on behalf of children too young to make a rational choice by themselves. The exercise of this right will, of course, shift to the child in accordance with his or her evolving capacities. However, because it is the right of the child, parents should not be allowed to exercise it on the child's behalf in all cases, and the courts should prefer an option that ensures the child's continuing religious freedom.

Why parents should not always be allowed to exercise this choice can be seen in the US Supreme Court decision *Wisconsin v. Yoder*.[47] The Supreme Court, by majority decision, affirmed the rights of members of the Amish religious community to refrain from sending their children to school after the age of 14, an age younger than that mandated by law for compulsory school attendance (which was 16).[48] The decision was based on the petitioners' right to religious freedom. The Court viewed the conflict as one between state and parents, ignoring a potential conflict of interest between parents and the child. Under the right to religious freedom, the US Supreme Court allowed the community to maintain its future membership by making it harder for young people with less education to leave. The state itself has a social interest, distinct from that of the children and from that of the Amish community, in providing children with the sort of education that will allow them to become socially responsible citizens.[49] By choosing to protect the religious freedom of the parents, the Court fosters and protects the community at the expense of (individual) children's liberty: the wishes of parents and community were furthered at the cost of the child's choice of education.[50]

The right to choose education is given to parents, in fact, as they are seen as representatives of the religious groups to which they belong, likely to send their children to schools of the same group, thus maintaining group membership. In contrast, if children (at least older children) are given a right to choose, overriding the decision of their parents, they may be more likely to opt out of the group into which they were born.[51]

A broader conceptual problem is raised by this discussion. Human rights generally guarantee various aspects of the individual's autonomy, choice and freedom of action. It is not clear, then, how a human right can guarantee an individual's right over someone else's choices and actions. A right to respect for family life, accorded in the Universal Declaration to the Family,[52] comes close to this as it has a relational aspect, but it is still not a right over another's actions or choices. (Compare the ICCPR, which phrases this as an individual's right to family life.[53])

5.4 What sort of education is compatible with religious freedom?

What sort of education should the state provide? Assuming that the state is acting in the best interest of its citizens' children, what education should the state choose to provide? Should it provide a choice between religious and secular education, or should it provide only secular education? International law, as we have seen, requires, at a minimum, that parents have a choice of private religious education for their children. However, in a liberal state, it might be argued that no religious education should be given to children, despite their wishes or those of their parent. Even if the child chooses his or her religious education, he or she will be unduly influenced in his or her choice by his or her parents. Therefore, non-religious education is the only 'clean slate' on which the child will grow up to become a free-thinking citizen, who will make up his or her own mind as to choice of religion in the future.[54]

However, making a neutral choice is, of course, making a choice. There may be a difference, but not a great one, between non-religious education (education that is neither religious nor secular) and 'not religious' education (secular education).[55] Children who study in a secular school, even one that is not anti-religion, are more likely to accept a secular outlook in the future.

The liberal neutrality approach may encounter another obstacle. Students do not come to school as *tabula rasa*. Even when the school sets out to provide a neutral educational setting, students may change it by exercising religious behaviour or expression. If the school tries to restore the neutral setting by limiting students' expression, it risks infringing the students' religious freedom.

Liberals wish to provide children with a neutral education, but encounter the problem of defining neutrality in education. Can we choose neutrality in education as a meta-value, without choosing neutrality as a value in itself?[56] Can neutrality be imparted as a negative capability – do not be prejudiced against any religious viewpoint, rather than a positive capability – be neutral in your religious and philosophical convictions?[57]

It can be argued that such a meta-value, or negative capability, can be taught, but not at a very young age. In order to grow up as full individuals, according to this argument, the child should first be given an affiliation, whether national or religious. It is not advisable or even possible to raise a child with no sense of identity. Similarly, we can teach the child not to accept stereotypical gender roles and to accept different sexual orientations, but it would seem impossible not to instil in the child some gender role, rather than a completely neutral gender identity.

The view that religion is constitutive of the person is central to a strong version of the communitarian critique of liberalism. A softer version of the communitarian argument against liberal neutral education can be summarized by Nagel's[58] claim that liberal theory is non-neutral, because it discounts conceptions that depend on interpersonal relations. These conceptions, it can be added, are ever present in the children's environment.

This conclusion can also be reached through a different argument, namely that the family as a group has rights. O'Neill[59] has commented on the tension between the child's rights and family rights. He sees the approach of liberal individualism as unsatisfactory when it comes to the intra-family relationship and suggests instead a mode of family covenant. Although he does not deal with the role of religion in the family covenant, it seems that religious cohesion might play an important part in this covenant. Even strict liberals will be hard pressed to accept that there is no importance in familial religious cohesion, although, from a liberal standpoint, this may not have enough importance to trump individual choices.

While the practical translation of a child's rights will be different than those of an adult, and should be constrained within family boundaries, I see no compelling reason to reject *in principle* the liberal model of individual rights in regard to children. Neither do I see a reason to reject it in regard to a child's freedom of religion.

5.5 Community religious education and individual human rights

Do students have a right to religious freedom in a denominational school? Individual rights stand in potential conflict with an institution, which is an exercise of community autonomy. It should be asked whether, in this case, group or individual right should prevail.

5.5.1 Schools as public entities

Due to the nature of education, educational establishments can never be considered simply as private law organizations. As schools provide a public service, they should be seen as institutions that are subject to at least some of the same human rights provision as state entities. Even private schools are entities of a public nature operating in the public sphere, and therefore have to accord human rights to their students.[60]

Problems arise when the rights of students conflict with the claims of religious educational institutions to religious autonomy, or their wish to exercise religious rights as a community. The UNESCO Convention against Discrimination in Education 1960 prohibits, in Article 1, discrimination on the grounds of religion, among other grounds. However, in Article 2(b) it exempts from its definition of discrimination, among others:

> The establishment or maintenance, for religious or linguistic reasons, of separate educational systems or institutions offering an education which is in keeping with the wishes of the pupil's parents or legal guardians, if participation in such systems or attendance at such institutions is optional and if the education provided conforms to such standards as may be laid down or approved by the competent authorities.

The Privy Council has recently interpreted this Convention as leaving the decision up to the state. Religious schools can discriminate in admissions on religious grounds without breaching the Convention. But, commensurate with the Convention, a state may decide to prohibit such discrimination.[61] In the case under discussion, Mauritius prohibited religious discrimination in the Constitution.[62] Therefore, the Privy Council decided that state-funded Catholic secondary schools could not allocate places so as to create a majority of Catholic students. Due to the restriction in the state Constitution, the schools' intention to preserve their religious ethos was not a permissible justification for discrimination in admission.

The interpretation given by the Privy Council to international law, letting the state determine whether to permit discrimination in religious schools, means that UK law, which allows publicly funded religious schools to preserve their religious character through special admission arrangements,[63] does not fall foul of international standards. Such recognition by the state of the legitimacy of attempts by schools to maintain their religious character, even at the expense of discrimination of individual pupils, is permitted under this interpretation of existing international law. However, such an exemption of religious schools from non-discrimination is problematic, because allowing religious schools to accept only students of their own community, as they define it, makes the state an accomplice to discrimination.

The UK Supreme Court has, however, dealt differently with one type of religious discrimination by schools. In *R. (E) v. Governing Body of JFS*[64] the court, by majority decision decided that a religious school is exempt from prohibitions on discrimination on the grounds of religion under the Equality Act 2006 (s. 50(1)(a)), but not from the prohibition on discrimination on the grounds of race (which includes ethnic and national origins) under the Race Relations Act 1976. Under the rules of the Chief Rabbi of the UK (and indeed the doctrine of Orthodox Judaism) only a child of a Jewish mother (by birth or Orthodox conversion) is deemed Jewish, and will be given priority in admission. Jews were seen by the Court as a racial group (defined by ethnicity and additionally by conversion) as well as a religious group. The school's decision to exclude a student from priority admission based on his mother's non-Jewish ethnicity was seen by the Court of Appeal as discrimination on racial grounds, thus impermissible. The Court says that the school may give priority based on the Jewish faith but not ethnicity.

In Judaism, membership is defined through ethnicity rather than through faith. The decision means that the school cannot give priority to members of the Jewish religion as it defines them. This decision lends support to an individualistic view of religious freedom. The individual student, who defines himself as Jewish and whose family views itself as Jewish, is not left outside the school due to a community definition of membership of the religion.

The decision should lead to an examination of the legal standards permitting exemption of religious schools from the prohibition on religious discrimination. Faith schools should not be able to discriminate on the basis of race or on the basis of religion. In some religions, such as Judaism, these happen to coincide, in other religions they do not. But the assumption that religion as a basis for exclusion is different from race is problematic. If a student views himself or herself as belonging to a religion, state-aided schools should not be permitted to exclude them, whether by an ethnic test or by a belief test.

States must allow private religious education, but have no obligation under the ICCPR to fund religious schools. This is generally so, although the Human Rights Committee left open the possibility that the ICCPR entails, in certain situations, an obligation to provide some public funding for private schools.[65] (One may suppose that the case of a community that would cease to exist without state aid is one such a situation.) However, if schools of one religious denomination are funded by the state, then, under the ICCPR, other religions are entitled to funding, too.[66] A denial of funding in such circumstances would breach both Article 18(4) and Article 26 (the right to equal and effective protection against discrimination).

In *Re the School Education Bill of 1995 (Gauteng)*,[67] the Supreme Court of South Africa rejected the argument that there is an affirmative obligation on the state to provide community schools (in this case based on common language, but similar reasoning applies to religious schools).[68] The Court read the South African Constitution in conformity with international law as providing only a right to set up such schools without state interference. Judge Sachs, in his concurring opinion enquired further as to how this constitutional interpretation could reconcile the right to have schools based on common culture with the constitutional and international law prohibition against discrimination: What is provided for, he says, 'is not a duty on the state to support discrimination, but a right of people, acting apart from, but in practicable association with the State, to further their own distinctive interests'.[69]

But Judge Sachs' analysis shows that there is a problem: setting up and funding community schools, whether religious or linguistic, which accept only students of their own community, can be considered tantamount to discrimination by the state. This argument can be taken a step further: if setting up and funding a discriminatory institution makes the state an accomplice in discrimination, so does according such institutions a right to exist. This problem has not been dealt with in international law, and has resulted in different solutions in national laws.

A solution to the problem of maintaining both principles – choice of religious schools and non-discrimination – is for states to require that all religious schools not discriminate in admission against students of other religions, and allow the latter to be absent from religious education. This solution was attempted in Ireland, which demanded that publicly funded church schools clearly announce the hours for religious education, so students could choose not to attend. But this arrangement failed in practice: in reality it became impossible to attend a publicly funded church school without receiving religious education.[70]

5.5.2 *The argument of voluntary participation*

Is there an argument that private religious schools *should* be exempt from anti-discrimination norms? One oft-used argument in favour of exemption of private schools (and sometimes even public schools) from the obligation to respect religious freedom is that the student chose voluntarily to attend, and so must abide by the rules set by the institution. Two cases show how this argument has been deployed, one regarding a student in private education, the other regarding a student in public education.

In the *Wittman*[71] case in South Africa, a pupil had opted to attend a private denominational school. Therefore, a South African court reasoned, the religious school is not required to respect the student's choice regarding manifestation of religion and belief. By choosing to attend the private school, reasoned the Court, the student voluntarily agreed to abide by its regulations, including mandatory attendance in religious instruction and prayers. The Court acknowledged the existence of a right not to attend religious activities in schools,[72] but concluded that the right does not apply when choosing to attend a private school, and that this right was thus waived in this case.

The argument of voluntary participation has also been used with regard to public schools. The US courts have produced a long line of cases trying to decide the permissible forms of religious expression in public schools that do not contravene the US constitutional principle of separation of church and state. In *Lee v. Weisman*,[73] the Supreme Court decided that school graduation ceremonies in which clergymen offered prayers breached the establishment clause of the First Amendment and therefore were unconstitutional. The argument that attendance at the ceremony was voluntary was rejected. Although the students could excuse themselves from attending, it is not voluntary in any meaningful sense, because not attending would deprive them of participation in an important occasion recognizing their educational achievement.

The argument of voluntary participation is more convincing with regard to private schools than public schools. The public provision of education for every child, without discrimination, is the obligation of the state. The public school must treat all equally. In contrast, in the case of private religious schools, there is some merit in the argument of voluntary participation. Private schools may have been founded to uphold a particular community heritage. However, the school's right to maintain its religious tradition is not absolute.

Two considerations can be advanced in support of the child's rights in a religious school. The first is that a child in an educational establishment, whether attending by compulsion or voluntarily, contributes to the social and religious environment as much as he or she absorbs from it. Wanting to be part of a school does not mean leaving your beliefs at home. The right of the school to maintain the original religious outlook of its founders must be balanced against the students' religious outlook and convictions. It is important to recognize that the school is a developing institution: the student body, and the changes in the culture and religion of the students over the years, legitimately shape the school as much as its preset rules.

The second consideration is that of factors specific to each case: whether the school serves a unique minority or a majority community, whether is it funded by the state, and whether the student has other equivalent educational opportunities. When the student claiming a breach of religious freedom is part of a minority or when the church school has benefited from preferential state funding, the right of the student should be paramount to the school's autonomy. Where there is a majority faith or a faith that operates a predominant number of schools, it should be treated differently from a minority faith. Members of a minority or disadvantaged religious group must have equal access to good educational institutions, which will generally, in such cases, belong to the faith of the majority. In such a case, equal access means access without impediments to the student's religious freedom, and the individual right should outweigh the interest of cultivating religious group identity (of the 'strong' religious group).

5.6 Religious freedom of teachers

An issue closely linked to the child's right of religious freedom in schools is that of a teacher's right of religious freedom in both denominational and non-denominational schools. If there is a right to have denominational schools, this has direct implications on discrimination of potential employees on a religious basis. Should the general principle of non-discrimination in employment apply to denominational schools?

In the UK, the provisions of the Schools Standards and Frameworks Act 1998 answer this question. Section 60 allows a foundation or voluntary school which has a religious character (i.e. a privately established but state supported religious school)[74] to hire teachers whose religious opinions are in accordance with the tenets of the religion of the school[75] in preference to other teachers, and permits termination of employment of a teacher whose conduct is incompatible with the precepts, or with the upholding of the tenets, of the religion.[76, 77]

This contrasts with the Employment Equality (Religion or Belief) Regulations 2003 that apply in the case of workers who are not teachers, and provide much narrower exemptions from the provisions of non-discrimination. The Regulations state that non-discrimination rules in hiring do not apply where there is a genuine occupational requirement for an employer holding a particular religious ethos,[78] or, for any other employer, a genuine and determining occupational requirement.[79] Department of Trade and Industry guidelines[80] suggest, for instance, that belonging to a certain religion may be a legal requirement for carers in a religious care home, but not for maintenance workers.

Elsewhere, unnecessarily broad exemptions apply to schools and hospitals. The UN Human Rights Committee criticized Ireland's Employment Equality Act, which exempts hospitals and schools directed by religious organizations from the duty not to discriminate on religious grounds even, in certain cases, in employing persons whose functions are not religious. This, the Committee concluded, may result in discrimination contrary to Article 26 of the ICCPR.[81]

The EU Council Directive Establishing a General Framework for Equal Treatment in Employment and Occupation[82] allows, in Article 4(2), states to exempt from its provision of non-discrimination those 'occupational activities within churches and other public or private organisations the ethos of which is based on religion or belief … where, by reason of the nature of these activities or of the context in which they are carried out, a person's religion or belief constitute a genuine, legitimate and justified occupational requirement'. It remains to be seen what precise interpretation will be given to this exemption.

Clarke,[83] discussing the situation in Ireland, has argued that there should be neither a right to have schools that exclude teachers or students of other religions nor a right to receive state funding. In Ireland, such schools are run by the Catholic Church. Clarke likens a right to state aid for schools excluding teachers or students of other religions to the establishment of publicly funded hospitals for Catholics only. He claims that this would obviously be repugnant even though there are other hospitals for non-Catholics. This approach views schools as providing a public service, whatever their ownership, and argues that rules governing public institutions should apply to them.

But there is a difference between a school and a hospital. A school can be said to have the formation of group identity as one of its legitimate objectives. The same cannot be said of a hospital. There is no recognized right to have a denominational hospital, but there is a right to attend a religious school. This factor may crucially provide a difference between regulation of employment in church schools and employment in church hospitals.

An approach that seeks to accommodate the conflicting rights of religious education and non-discrimination in employment should balance the rights of teachers with the legitimate aim of the school in fostering identity and should not give schools carte blanche for excluding non-adherents. The determination whether it is legitimate for a denominational school to discriminate in hiring depends on factors such as whether it is a school of a majority or minority community, whether there are other schools in the area, and whether the school is state-financed.

5.7 Community religious schools and equality of female children

Whether community schools are subject to obligations of religious freedom is controversial. It is even more controversial whether denominational schools must respect the principle of gender equality, even if it conflicts with their religious ethos. This is a crucial question to which international law gives no clear answer. A well-recognized principle regarding discrimination is that separate education is inherently unequal.[84] However, a prohibition on gender segregation in religious education[85] will have devastating implications on most organized religious education systems. In fact, one of the main reasons that religious communities maintain their own schools, and that parents want to send their children to such schools, is in order to ensure sex-separate education.

The UNESCO Convention against Discrimination in Education 1960 sets down binding international rules purporting to combat discrimination in education.[86] Rather than setting a coherent rule, these articles show the problematic standards of equality that are applied to religion and gender. Starting with a broad anti-discrimination statement which includes religion and gender, the Convention reverts immediately to a separate-but-equal standard for gender.[87] This standard, which would not be acceptable under the Convention for any other basis of segregation, is deemed acceptable by the Convention in the context of sex segregation.

Separate educational systems based on linguistic or religious differentiation are also permitted, but only if participation in such schools is optional. As in other international human rights documents, the UNESCO Convention makes this contingent on the wishes of the parents, not the child.[88] Sex-separate education is permitted even when no other option is offered by the state.

The final document of the International Consultative Conference on School Education in Relation with Freedom of Religion and Belief, Tolerance and Non-Discrimination, convened by the then UN Special Rapporteur on religious intolerance, Abdelfattah Amor,[89] also prevaricated and gave no guidance on how educational equality (especially with regard to gender) should be weighed against parental wishes. It deemed that states should promote 'the awareness of gender aspects, with a view to promoting equal chances for men and women',[90] but also declared that 'the role of parents ... is an essential factor in the education of children in the field of religion or belief; and that special attention should be paid to ... supporting parents to exercise their rights and fully play their role in education in the field of tolerance and non-discrimination.'[91] Thus, no clear guidance is given as to whether parental choice or gender equality should be paramount.

5.8 Wearing of headscarves: a conflict of group and individual values

A test case of the conflict between religious community, parental choice and gender equality in education, involving many of the issues discussed in this chapter, is that of the restrictions on the wearing of headscarves by Muslim students and teachers, raising political as well as legal issues, issues the determination of which will define the limits of religious freedom.

5.8.1 Four states – four cases

In order to understand the correlation between religious freedom, equality and the legal status of religion in the state in the context of this issue, I compare decisions in four different constitutional settings: In France, a state which is constitutionally secular with a Christian majority Muslim students in public schools are members of a minority; in the UK, a Muslim student in a state school; in Israel, a Jewish-majority state a student who is a member of the Muslim minority in a private Christian minority school; in Turkey, a secular state with a Muslim majority Muslim student in higher education.[92]

In France, in 1989, citing the principle of laicity, a state school prohibited the wearing of headscarves by female students and expelled them for refusing to abide by this rule. The Council of State advised the Minister for National Education, in an advisory opinion, that '[t]he wearing, by students, of tokens expressing their religious affiliation is not, by itself, incompatible with the principle of laicity. However, this liberty would not permit pupils to flaunt, in a conspicuous fashion, symbols of religious affiliation which, by their very nature, by the conditions under which they are worn ... would constitute an act of pressure, proselytism or propaganda.'[93] The decision then enumerates cases in which this would be forbidden, including circumstances in which such expression would infringe on the dignity or the liberty of other pupils in the school. Later rulings by the Council of State, which struck down complete bans on the wearing of headscarves, narrowed, by way of interpretation, the broad language of the decision, and clarified that a ban would be justified only in extreme cases.[94]

After years of public turmoil regarding this issue, the Stasi Committee,[95] appointed by then President Chirac, recommended that pupils not be allowed to wear 'ostentatious' religious or political symbols, citing specifically headscarves, large crosses and the *kippa*, while discrete religious symbols should be allowed. The law subsequently enacted[96] prohibits the wearing of 'symbols by which pupils ostensibly manifest their religious affiliation' in public schools, high schools and colleges.[97] The policy was eventually deemed by the European Court of Human Rights not to be an infringement of students' Article 9 rights.[98]

In the UK, *R. (Begum) v. Denbigh High*[99] dealt with a matter of a student wishing to wear a *jilbab* (full covering) to school. The House of Lords decided that it was within the legitimate discretion of the head teacher to decide as she did on a school uniform that, in her estimation, was acceptable by mainstream Muslims but in a way that did not threaten or pressure others as the *jilbab* may have.

In Israel, Mona Jabarin, a Muslim girl, petitioned the Supreme Court after she was refused admittance to a Christian school based on her insistence on wearing a headscarf.[100] In Israel, this problem was even more complex than in France or the UK: here, a member of one religious minority (Islam) wished to attend a school of another religious minority (Christianity) in a state with a Jewish majority. The school agreed to accept a student from outside its religious community, but asked that it abide by its dress rules. Should the state interfere? In this case, it did not. The court rejected the student's petition, relying on the autonomy of the denominational school.

The final case, the matter of students wearing headscarves in Turkey, has been ruled on twice by the organs of the European Convention on Human Rights. First, it arose before the European Commission of Human Rights in *Karaduman v. Turkey*.[101] In this case, a university student, not a child, was refused a university degree certificate until she submitted a photograph of herself in which she was not wearing a headscarf, in conformity with the university's disciplinary regulations. Her claim of breach of religious freedom (in contravention of Turkish and international law) was dismissed by the domestic court and she applied to the European Commission, claiming a violation of her right to religious freedom, in contravention of Article 9 of the European Convention. The Commission declared the complaint inadmissible, accepting a state principle of secularism as justifying the ban.

In the more recent case in the European Court, *Şahin v. Turkey*,[102] the university policy of prohibiting the wearing of headscarves was again called into question by a student. The Court dismissed the application, but its analysis differed from that offered in *Karaduman*. The Court did not rely on the principle of secularism, *in itself*, as a justification of the state's restrictions on religious expression, but saw the application of the secularism principle in the case to be justified under the public order qualification in Article 9(2) of the Convention. Specifically, the Court saw equality between the sexes and preventing social pressure on *other* female students to wear the headscarf as justifying the Turkish ban.

In all these jurisdictions, the various courts and policy makers did not uphold the religious freedom of the student above countervailing policy considerations. I proceed to examine the reasons for these decisions, and whether they can be justified.[103]

5.8.2 Religious freedom as individual right

From a liberal-individualistic view of religious freedom, three principal criticisms can be levelled at the reasoning deployed by the courts and decision makers.

5.8.2.1 Religious freedom includes free religious expression

The freedom to express religious beliefs, as with any other manifestation of the freedom of expression, must include the freedom to express such beliefs in a conspicuous manner, even in a manner that may be seen as flaunting religious symbols. Both the decisions of the French Council of State and the subsequent French legislation, which entail that students may wear religious symbols but not ostensibly manifest them, fall short of this requirement. In the context of a school, as opposed to the general public forum, it is reasonable that a more restrictive interpretation be given to freedom of speech. The right to proselytize, for instance, although included in the right to freedom of religion, may legitimately be subject to some restriction in the school context. A school is a compulsory educational institution. Children are sent to school by their parents on the understanding that they are there to study, not to be preached to and converted to a different religion or a different form or orthodoxy of their own religion. However, the wearing of religious apparel, in itself and without proof of further harm, cannot be considered an act of proselytism or pressure which justifies its prohibition. In the UK case, *Begum*, there was a factual argument that pressure existed on female pupils in the school. This is different from an a priori assumption that apparel entails pressure, and must be proved.

In the *Karaduman* and *Şahin* decisions, the ban on headscarves is less justified in this respect. The Turkish cases concern university students, not children. These are educated adults, albeit young adults, making their own decisions and studying among other young adult students. A prohibition on religious expression in a university, which relies on the effect or pressure the religious expression may have on other students, is less justified than a similar decision in a school setting.

5.8.2.2 *Voluntary participation in a public activity does not amount to a waiver of rights*

A second justification for dismissing the headscarf wearers' claim, which is to be questioned, is that of 'voluntary choice'. This reason was used by the European Commission in the *Karaduman* case. The Commission decided that, by choosing to study at a secular university, the student submitted to the university's rules. The reliance on the 'voluntariness' of enrolment begs two questions.[104] The first is factual: could the student have obtained her science degree at a non-secular institution of comparable calibre? The student may have had no comparable choice. The second question is normative: must a student submit to secular rules just because she chose to study at a higher educational institution?[105] The student's claim in this case is especially strong as she attended a public university. The student chose to take part in a public educational activity, training to be a scientist, a contributing, creative member of society. In weighing the student's religious freedom against the university code, it appears that the code should be changed so that she is given equal access to education, rather than her human right be impaired in order to uphold the university's code.[106]

Of course, a student's right to religious freedom can be subject to legitimate limitations. It might be that succumbing to students' demand to wear religious dress will create a religious atmosphere in the university, which the other students may find pressurizing and may impair the open liberal atmosphere that the university seeks to provide to its students. However, this is a separate justification that must be proved.

One of the judges in the English *Begum* case, Lord Hoffmann,[107] relied on an 'argument of voluntariness' to dismiss the pupil's arguments. The pupil chose not to move to another school, he reasoned, and so her rights were not infringed. Lord Hoffmann relied on the European Court cases that expound this argument: *Kalac* and *Chaarei Shalom*. I criticize these decisions in Chapter 2, and for the same reasons Lord Hoffmann's reasoning in the *Begum* case is to be questioned. A pupil has a right to religious freedom at every school; it is the state that must justify why she is denied the exercise of this right at her particular school. Proximity of another school, which reasonably accommodates her beliefs, *might* be a reasonable justification, but the onus should be on the school to show that it is a reasonable and proportional interference with her right.[108]

5.8.2.3 *A principle of secularity*

A third justification, which does not tally with religious freedom as an individual right, is that raised in *Karaduman*, the implied acceptance by the European Commission of the Turkish state's principle of secularity as justifying the demand for conformity with a secular dress code. A different approach has emerged in *Şahin*. This is a more critical approach. The Court did not rely merely on the state's invocation of a principle of secularism, but cited the reasons that justify its application in this case despite its impact on religious freedom, namely the political and social situation in Turkey and its effect on other university students.

The constitutional character of the state should not justify a breach of religious freedom if it is otherwise illegitimate. In cases before the European Court and Commission, Turkey has repeatedly argued it needs to protect the principle of secularity in order to maintain democracy.[109] The Commission, in *Karaduman*, noted that secular universities may ensure that fundamentalist religious movements do not disturb public order in universities, or pressure students who do not practise religion. That is a legitimate government concern, if proved, and should be distinguished from reliance on a principle of secularity as such.

The European Court, in *Şahin v. Turkey*, reaffirmed the determination in *Karaduman*, namely that the ban is a legitimate restriction of religious freedom. However, it analysed the pressures exerted on other students to dress religiously, as well as the political and social context in which extremist political movements seek to impose religious precepts, as analysed in *Refah Partisi*, rather than simply affirming the principle of secularism. It viewed, in the political context, the steps taken under the principle of secularity as proportionately furthering the legitimate aims of gender equality and a secular way of life. The Court relied on a principle encountered during its previous rulings on matters of state and religion: it viewed the relationship between state and religion as an issue on which national determination will be given particularly wide berth within the margin of appreciation. This is a group conception interpretation of religious freedom, in this case, paradoxically upholding a secularist stance.

In *Dogru v. France*,[110] the European Court returned to the reliance on the principle of secularism used in *Karaduman*. The Court in *Dogru* rejected the application of a pupil who was prohibited from wearing a headscarf to a state school. Although the Court relies on, but never fully explains, a health and safety justification for interference by the state, the Court mostly relies again on the principle of secularism. But this principle in itself should not justify infringement of religious freedom, in the same way as a principle of a state-church would not justify such infringement. It may be that the infringement is justified on grounds listed in Article 9(2), but that needs to be shown by the state.

A principle of secularity may also offend the liberal principle of neutrality. Such a principle can be neutral on its face but discriminatory in practice. A law, such as that in France, which bans wearing religious symbols and clothing, may ban a practice that is compulsory in one religion but not compulsory in another. Prohibition of religious dress cannot be justified by arguments that such dress is 'provocative', that the institution was voluntarily entered into or that the state is constitutionally secular, but it can be justified by being proved as harm to other students. So it is in public institutions, but is this different in a private denominational school?

5.8.3 Religious freedom of the student or religious autonomy of the community?

Where the student attends a school of a minority community, an argument can be made for upholding the religious freedom of the community, an argument that does not arise in state schools. There is clear social value in fostering cultural and educational institutions of minority religious communities. Such schools can lose their value as a meaningful expression and preservation of the community if they are not allowed to maintain their internal rules as decided on by the community.

The Israeli Court dismissed the student's petition because the school in question was a private denominational school, and not a state school. The court preferred the autonomy of the religious (Christian) community to the religious freedom of the individual (Muslim) child. (One of the three judges on the panel commented that he would have reached the same conclusion in a case of a state school.[111])

Should there be a difference of treatment between a state school and a private denominational school in the need to respect individual religious freedom? One is a public institution and the other a private institution. However, at least basic human rights should apply to private institutions operating in the public sphere. The public/private divide is not clear cut. For instance, in the Israeli case, the denominational school was publicly funded, as occurs in some other states.

It appears that an institution open to general public enrolment should be seen as a semi-public institution, which must treat the participants in its activities with equal respect for their rights, unless this directly contradicts the religious principles of the institution. This is similar to arguing that a religious hospital must treat all its patients with equal respect for their rights, although it might be exempt from providing abortions. Wearing a headscarf does not stand in such direct contradiction to principles of a Christian school as to justify its outright prohibition.

It is a difficult case, as the justification for having denominational schools is precisely to allow them to depart from the general liberal norms. The communitarian approach would recognize the right of the religious community to set its own rules. However, there are strong reasons to insist that all religious communities respect basic human rights (including freedom of religion), at least in all their public institutions that are not of an inherently religious character.

Institutions of religious communities can be separated into core religious institutions used solely for religious service (such as mosques, synagogues, churches), a middle level of institutions (such as religious schools), which provide a social service and do not play a part in religious services but have a purpose of furthering a certain religious outlook, and a third rank of institutions (such as religious hospitals), which provide a public service, motivated by religious imperatives, but which do not themselves serve a religious purpose. Institutions of the first level are justified in demanding adherence to their dress code even in contravention of individual religious freedom; institutions at the third level are not. Institutions at the middle level are justified in overriding individual choice of religious dress only when it directly contradicts their religious ethos.

5.8.4 Equality of female students

Defending the custom of wearing a headscarf, especially by reliance on human rights arguments, raises serious questions as to the obligation of states to positively promote non-discrimination of women. The practice of wearing a headscarf for women, in both Jewish and Muslim society, is repressive to women.[112] It instils unequal values of modesty in behaviour and dress for men and women. It inculcates inequality between the sexes and marginalizes young women in society from a young age.[113] Wearing a scarf for religious reasons *is*, therefore, different from other signs of religious affiliation, such as a Sikh *pugri* (turban) or Jewish *kippa*. Upholding a student's right to wear a headscarf is really promoting the right of her family and society to instil values of inequality from childhood. This is an example of the problem discussed earlier, whereby acknowledging rights to religious behaviour in the education system legitimizes practices that reinforce discriminatory views, in contravention of human rights norms. International law mandates that states counter such customs, even when practised in the private sphere[114] and, of course, in state schools, which are public institutions.

However, there is a strong counterargument. It has been argued by cultural feminists and others that, in her society, a headscarf may help a woman preserve her freedom.[115] The actual outcome in the Israeli case was that, after her case was dismissed, Mona attended an inferior school. Allowing the wearing of a headscarf would have, in reality, permitted Mona to attend a top school and get a top education. In this case, a discriminative practice can lead to better educational choices, which will ultimately advance equality for the girl.

However, acknowledging such a practice as a protection for women serves to reinforce the discriminatory attitude that made it necessary in the first place. Hassan[116] argues that the purpose of the veil was to make it safe for women to go about their work without sexual molestation, but Muslim societies have used the pretext of protecting the chastity of Muslim women to put them behind veils, shrouds and locked doors. The goal of the law should be to eradicate discriminatory social attitudes. But, in the short run, ignoring the fact that prohibiting discriminatory practices may limit women's access to education and work outside the home will only harm women.

One solution is to consider ways to empower girls, both legally and socially, to make their individual religious choices, rather than accept the choices of the religious community. For example, the Stasi Committee recommended that immigrant students (particularly girls) should be informed that over the age of 16 they can apply for French citizenship without parental consent, and that they would be able to continue their studies without parental consent.

The social context cannot be ignored. In Turkey, a state that has opted for a secular regime, Islam is a majority religion, as it is in Tunisia, where there are also prohibitions on wearing headscarves in schools.[117] In these cases, the state is trying to prevent the advancement of fundamentalist attitudes of its own majority religion. In the case of a student from a minority religion (such as the cases in France), other considerations arise. The actions of a government curtailing manifestations of a minority religion should be subject to more rigorous scrutiny than the actions of a government curtailing the manifestation of a majority religion, as there is more cause for concern that only the specific manifestations of belief of the minority religion will be curtailed.

In the English *Begum* decision, the Court appears to have adopted the approach that the matter is best left to the discretion of the school's authorities (per Lord Bingham), as this was a sensitive matter and the school found a way of accommodating mainstream Muslim dress. The case notes many factual indications of pressure on other students to adhere to the more severe religious dress, but this crucial and legitimate consideration in favour of the school's decision was not a major consideration in most of the judges' opinions. The social context was also, rightly, considered by some of the judges as a consideration for upholding the school's decision. Lord Foscott pertinently noted the arrival of the pupil with her brothers at school, when first wearing the *jilbab*, which suggests the dress did not reflect her own choices.[118] But it was only Baroness Hale who based her justification of the school's action on the need to educate children, who are not yet capable of making their own choices, in a climate of sexual equality.

General principles that mandate a preference for individual rights, developed in the discussion of other issues in this study, are applicable also to headscarf disputes. There is no justification for overriding individual religious rights even when confronting provocative speech, even where participation is voluntary, and even within state institutions of a constitutionally secular state. Only clear evidence of a direct threat to the religious freedom of others should be sufficient to curtail the religious freedom of headscarf wearing students. It is harder to argue for religious dress freedom within community religious institutions, but even there, individual religious freedom must be respected unless there is an overriding justification. It is legitimate, even mandated by international human rights law, to protect gender equality, a right no less important than religious freedom. However, the benefits and harm of a prohibition on discrimination for the promotion of gender equality must be assessed in each social context.

5.9 Teachers' headscarves and religious freedom in employment[119]

The wearing of headscarves in schools raises similar, but somewhat different, considerations when the wearers are teachers. The European Court has decided that prohibiting a teacher in a state elementary school from wearing a headscarf was a permissible limitation of religious freedom under Article 9(2) of the ECHR in the case of *Dahlab*.[120] The Court accepted that the wearing of a headscarf might have some proselytizing effect, because, in the Court's estimation, it appears to be imposed on women by a precept, which, the Court assumed, is laid down in the Koran, and is hard to square with the principle of gender equality. In the Court's opinion, wearing of an Islamic headscarf was incommensurate with the tolerance, respect for others, equality and non-discrimination that all teachers in a democratic society must convey to their pupils.

This begs the question what cultural and religious differences are permissible. The Court based its decision on the impressionable age of the primary school pupils. Of course, attitudes are learned through observations at an early age. However, the teacher did not manifest lack of tolerance to other religions or attempt to proselytise. The Court accepted as given the liberal model of a school that presents a homogenous front to the pupils. It did not suggest the alternative model where toleration is learned through variety. The first model in effect further ghettoises minority communities and minority women, as they will simply refrain from teaching in state primary schools.

The European Court had followed a much more robust approach in a case which dealt with political ideology rather than religion, in the matter of *Vogt*.[121] A teacher was dismissed from a state school because of her Communist party membership. The Court agreed that the state policy of refusing positions in the civil service to employees who were members of a political party that pursued aims 'incompatible with the democratic constitutional systems' served a legitimate aim, but its application must be balanced with the right of freedom of expression of the teacher. Where the teacher had not expressed undemocratic views within or even outside the school, her membership of a party that held such views could not in itself justify the dismissal as necessary in a democratic society.[122] In the *Dahlab* case, no such particularized attempt at balancing the employee's right against the danger to her pupils was undertaken by the court.

The German Constitutional Court in the *Case of the headscarf of the schoolteacher*[123] ruled, by a majority vote, that the ban by a *Land* on the wearing of headscarves by teachers in public schools was illegal. The ban restricted three rights guaranteed by the basic law: equality in eligibility for public office,[124] eligibility to hold public office without regard to religious affiliation,[125] and religious freedom.[126] A restriction on rights guaranteed by the basic law cannot be imposed without a basis in legislation. There was no basis in law for the banning of headscarves, and therefore the ban was unconstitutional. However, the Court ruled that the *Land* could legislate such a ban, subject to constitutional limitations, which would be a permissible restriction of religious freedom, commensurate with Article 9 of the European Convention. For a ban to pass constitutional muster, the legislator would have to consider the religious makeup of the population, the tradition of the schools and the intensity of religious feelings in the area.

The three dissenting judges argued that a public servant voluntarily accepts a limited scope of basic rights by aligning himself with the state. Thus, teachers have lesser protection of their rights than parents and students. This is justified because as public servants they are given power over the citizen. A corollary of this power bestowed by the state on the public servant is the acceptance of a limitation of rights. So, the *Land* could ban this behaviour of the teacher even absent enabling legislation (such legislation being, in any case, forbidden by the basic law).

In France, such a prohibition, based on the identification of someone fulfilling a role on behalf of the state with the state itself, is extended beyond schools to public institutions. French Justice Minister Dominique Perben barred a woman from a court jury for wearing a headscarf, arguing that the Muslim scarf worn by the juror at a trial was contrary to the principle of impartiality. He stated he did not want open signs of religious commitment in French courts.[127] The Stasi Committee similarly noted that the Minister of Justice objected to a female lawyer appearing in court with a veil.

Barring the wearing of a headscarf for jury duty is, in some ways, a more serious breach of individual religious freedom than barring it for teachers. It is the individual's ability to take part in the legal system while adhering to his or her religion that is being compromised. Not only that, but Muslim defendants and litigants have a right, as does any other citizen, that members of their community be equally represented on the justice system that decides their legal fate.

The wearing of headscarves has been restricted not just in the public but also in the private sphere. In the *Case of the headscarf of a shop worker*,[128] the German Constitutional Court did not accept the petition of a shop worker who claimed that her employer's ban on her wearing a headscarf to work violated her religious freedom, guaranteed by Article 4(1) of the basic law, because her religion forbade her from appearing in public without the scarf. The Court relied on Article 12(1) of the basic law, which guarantees freedom of vocation to both the employer and the employee. Private persons (such as the employer) are not subject to obligations of the basic law, so the shop has no obligation to allow her to wear the scarf. Neither does the shop have an obligation to accommodate her needs, for example, by letting her work in a back room.

The French Stasi Committee[129] has likewise decided that the law ought to allow private enterprises to restrict shop workers wearing headscarves from dealing with customers. This seems a particularly groundless limitation of personal freedom. While the wearing of headscarves by teachers can reasonably be argued to influence their pupils, entrusted by their parents to the education system, no similar influence can be said to be exerted by shop workers. The intolerance of customers to minority workers dressed according to their religion is precisely the discrimination that international human rights law seeks to uproot.

The EU Council Directive Establishing a General Framework for Equal Treatment in Employment and Occupation,[130] which member states needed to implement by 2 December 2003,[131] prohibits, among others, indirect discrimination, which includes use of apparently neutral provisions which would put a person of a particular religion or belief at a disadvantage unless justified by a legitimate aim achieved by appropriate and necessary means.[132] This applies both in public and private employment. It is surprising that the Stasi Committee ignored the existence of this directive, as at least arguably, it applies to such dress prohibitions. Although the aims the prohibitions attempt to achieve are legitimate, whether the means are appropriate and necessary is doubtful.

Further international instruments should require states to guarantee religious freedom in the private sector in those areas that affect individuals most, such as employment. It is difficult to view this as an issue of contractual freedom. Clearly, workers need to accept the posts available to them, and should not be made to choose between such positions and their religious freedom.[133]

5.10 Conclusions

International law has, for a long time, protected religious freedom and religious choice as a right of the family, rather than a right of the child. It was a right of the parents, seen as agents of their religious community, which was upheld against the state. Even today, international law prevaricates between recognising a right of the child and protecting a right of the parents over the child's religious education.

Religious freedom as a right of the child must be better protected in the school. Children should be regarded as bearers of rights of religious freedom within the school, whether they (or their parents on their behalf) have chosen to attend public or private schools. Such freedom may be restricted according to legitimate needs within the school, but cannot be infringed merely on the basis that the student attends the school. Indeed, learning to exercise individual choice is an important lesson for schools to teach.

Teachers, as well as students, must be seen as individuals with a right to freedom of religion and conscience, which they do not 'check at the door' as they enter the education system. However, their freedom can be legitimately restricted to a greater extent than that of students in order to preserve the rights of others.

This chapter examined the duality of religious freedom at its inception. It showed that what is perceived as an exercise of individual choice and free will is in most cases determined at birth, fostered by education and seldom changed even when the child ceases to be a child. The formation of identity is thus largely attributable to the group. Largely, but not solely. It is the ability to maintain individualistic-critical facilities towards group religious identity, as well as the identity of minority religions, which must be protected through the legal system.

Notes

1 Convention on the Rights of the Child (adopted 20 November 1989) 1577 UNTS 3.
   See S. Langlaude, *The right of the child to religious freedom in international law*, The Hague: Martinus Nijhoff Publishers, 2007.
   See also G. Van Bueren, *Child rights in Europe: convergence and divergence in judicial protection*, Brussels: Council of Europe, 2008; note in particular pp. 77ff.
2 Similarly, the African Charter on the Rights and Welfare of the Child, OAU Doc. CAB/LEG/24.9/49 (1990), (entered into force November 29, 1999) Article 9, guarantees that:
   1. Every child shall have the right to freedom of thought conscience and religion.
   2. Parents, and where applicable, legal guardians shall have a duty to provide guidance and direction in the exercise of these rights having regard to the evolving capacities, and best interests of the child.
   3. States Parties shall respect the duty of parents and where applicable, legal guardians to provide guidance and direction in the enjoyment of these rights subject to the national laws and policies.

3 Reservations to Article 14: Algeria, Bangladesh, Iraq, Jordan, Kiribati, Malaysia, Morocco, Poland (child's rights to be exercised with respect for parental authority), Singapore (right to be exercised with respect for authority of parents, schools and those entrusted with care of the child).
4 Egypt, Syria, UAE (reservation to adoption provision); Holy See (reservation to 'family planning', parental rights (concerning Articles 13, 14, 15, 16 and 28)).
5 Broad reservation based on state religion: Afghanistan, Brunei Darussalam, Djibouti, Iran, Kuwait, Maldives, Mauritania, Qatar, Saudi Arabia.

6 The Holy See entered reservations to Article 24 (regarding 'family planning') and a reservation (regarding Articles 13, 14, 15, 16 and 28) interpreting the articles of the Convention in a way which safeguards the primary and inalienable rights of parents, in particular concerning education (Articles 13 and 28), religion (Article 14), association with others (Article 15) and privacy (Article 16).

7 See objections to reservations by Austria, Denmark, Finland, Germany, Ireland, Italy, Netherlands, Norway, Portugal, Slovakia and Sweden.

8 When 'provided for by local custom'.

9 See also Poland's declaration in respect of Articles 12–14, which provides that children's rights of free speech, religious freedom, association, privacy and the right to be heard on matters affecting them are exercised with respect for parental authority 'in accordance with Polish customs and traditions'.

10 Although M. G. Flekkoy and N. H. Kaufman, *The participation rights of the child: rights and responsibilities in family and society*, London: Jessica Kingsley Publishers, 1997, 34, point out that the parents' right is only 'to provide direction' to the child, and not to determine the child's religion.

11 The formation of identity is itself a right of the child protected by the Convention on the Rights of the Child (adopted 20 November 1989) 1577 UNTS 3, Article 8.

12 S. Detrick and J. E. Doek, *The United Nations Convention on the Rights of the Child: a guide to the 'travaux preparatoires'*, Dordrecht: Martinus Nijhoff Publishers, 1992, 26.

13 UN Doc. E/CN.4/1986/39 Annex IV p. 2.

14 S. Detrick and J. E. Doek, *The United Nations Convention on the Rights of the Child: a guide to the 'travaux preparatoires'*, Dordrecht: Martinus Nijhoff Publishers, 1992, 26.

15 J. E. Coons, 'The religious rights of children', in J. D. van der Vyver and J. Witte (eds), *Religious human rights in global perspective, Vol. I – religious perspectives*, The Hague: Martinus Nijhoff Publishers, 1996, 157, 159. G. Van Bueren, *International law on the rights of the child*, The Hague: Kluwer, 1998, 158, points out that the Human Rights Committee asked Norway whether views of 12 year olds were considered when joining or resigning from the Church of Norway (UN Doc A/36/40), thus indicating, that in the Committee's view this was an age at which children should have such choice.

16 Such an Austrian law prohibiting a parent, without the consent of the other parent, from bringing up children in a faith different from that held by the parents at the time of the marriage, or different from the religion in which the children had previously been brought up, was examined by the European Court of Human Rights in *Hoffman v. Austria* (1993) 17 EHRR 293 ECtHR. The Court found that the law in question impermissibly subjected each parent to different treatment on the basis on his or her religion, violating Article 14 in conjunction with Article 8 of the ECHR.

17 See also cases such as *J v. C*, H L, [1969] 2 W.L.R. 540, where the child's foster parents were required to raise him in the Catholic faith (the faith of his natural parents).

18 See further A. Scolnicov, 'The child's right to religious freedom and formation of identity', *International Journal of Children's Rights*, 15(2), 2007, 251.

19 For example: the Israeli Adoption Law, 1981, Article 5 states that there is no adoption but by a parent of the same religion as the child. (However, this can be bypassed, as Article 13A(c) of the Legal Capacity and Guardianship Law, 1962 allows for the conversion of the child to the religion of the adoptive parent.)

20 The Multiethnic Placement Act 1994, as amended by the Interethnic Adoption Provisions 1996, 42 USCA 1996b. However, E. Bartholet, 'Private race preferences in family formation', *Yale Law Journal*, 107, 1998, 2351, 2354, claims that permissible 'cultural competence' considerations are in fact used for racial matching.

21 *Re Carroll* [1931] 1KB 317.

22 [2002] 1 FLR 1119.

23 [1964] 1 WLR 51.

24 [2000] Fam. 15.

25 See note 12.

26 The Court nevertheless approved the custody of the Jewish couple in this case.
27 See discussion of the Minority Treaties in Chapter 1.
28 Treaty Series, No. 8 (1919). Treaty reprinted in J. Robinson et al., *Were the minority treaties a failure?*, New York: Institute of Jewish Affairs, 1943, Appendix I.
29 *Minority Schools in Albania* (advisory opinion) PCIJ Rep. (ser. A/B) No. 4 (1935).
30 6 December 1921. Documents on Irish Foreign Policy Vol. I, 1919–1922 NAI DE 2/304/1.
31 Article 16.
32 Article 18 (4).
33 G. Van Bueren, *International law on the rights of the child*, The Hague: Kluwer, 1998, 159.
34 J. Morsink, *The Universal Declaration of Human Rights: origins, drafting and intent*, Philadelphia: University of Pennsylvania Press, 1999, 267.
35 Ibid.
36 Universal Declaration of Human Rights, Article 26(1).
37 Declaration on the Elimination of All Forms of Intolerance and Discrimination Based on Religion or Belief, UNGA Res. 36/55 (adopted 25 November 1981), Article 5(2).
38 Article 5(5).
39 Article 5(1).
40 Article 14.
41 Article 28.
42 E.g., in Cyprus, Article 18 of the 1960 Constitution provides the right of parents to bring up their children according to their own convictions. However, the Constitution of Malta, Article 2, specifically decrees that '[R]eligious teaching of the Roman Catholic Apostolic Faith shall be provided in all State schools as part of compulsory education.'
43 The African Charter on the Rights and Welfare of the Child makes the same point more vaguely, demanding in Article 9(3), on religious freedom of the child that 'States Parties … respect the duty of parents and where applicable, legal guardians to provide guidance and direction in the enjoyment of these rights subject to the national laws and policies.'
44 App. No. 34614/97 *Scientology Kirche Deutschland v. Germany* EComHR.
45 At least in one case, this brought about a strange result. In App. No. 36283/97 *Keller v. Germany* (1998) 25 EHRR CD 187 EComHR the Commission ruled that Scientologist parents, who claimed their rights under of Protocol 1(2) were violated by a government leaflet to schools targeting Scientology, were not victims under Article 25 of the Convention. This was because the leaflet was directed against the religion and not the individual parents. It seems that, between *Scientology Kirche* and *Keller*, parents, children and communities whose religion is targeted by the government all remain without remedy. It follows from the conjunction of these two cases that Protocol 1(2) does not give children any rights. The religious community is not a right holder under Protocol 1(2), and parents cannot claim to be victims of a breach of Protocol 1(2) unless they are specifically targeted by the state (usually a hostile government policy will be directed at a religion and not individual parents). So there is no victim of a Protocol 1(2) violation when the state publishes literature against the education of one particular religion.
46 Charter of Fundamental Rights of the European Union, Article 14: 'The freedom to found educational establishments with due respect for democratic principles and the right of parents to ensure the education and teaching of their children in conformity with their religious, philosophical and pedagogical convictions shall be respected, in accordance with the national laws governing the exercise of such freedom and right.'
47 *Wisconsin v. Yoder*, 406 US 203 (1972).
48 The right to choose religious education as an alternative to public schooling was recognized in US law in the earlier Supreme Court decision *Pierce v. Society of Sisters* 268 US 510 (1925).
49 D. De Groot, 'The liberal tradition and the constitution: developing a coherent jurisprudence of parental rights', *Texas Law Review*, 78, 2000, 1278, 1310–1314.

50 Indeed, Justice Douglas, in partial dissent, noted the potential conflict between the interests of the parents and the children. (Ibid., at 242.)

51 See also the UK decision in *R. v. Secretary of State forEducation and Science ex p. Talmud Torah Machzikei Hadass School Trust* and analysis, in A. Scolnicov, 'The child's right to religious freedom and formation of identity', *International Journal of Children's Rights*, 15(2), 2007, 251, 264.

52 Universal Declaration to the Family, Article 16(3).

53 Ibid., Article 17. See also Article 8 of the European Convention on Human Rights and Fundamental Freedom (adopted 4 November 1950) 213 UNTS 221.

54 In Comm. No. 40/1978 *Hartikainen v. Finland*, CCPR/C/OP/1/1984 at 74, the UN Human Rights Committee decided that state requirement that every school pupil will receive some instruction in religion or ethics, when the parents are given a choice to accept the school instruction or to opt for outside instruction of their choosing, does not breach Article 18(4) of the ICCPR.

55 For an argument that secular education inevitably prejudices the child against religion, see R. Ahdar, 'The child's right to a godly future', *The International Journal of Children's Rights*, 10, 2002, 89.

56 See Waldron's analysis of the different meanings of neutrality within liberal theory, in J. Waldron, *Liberal rights: Collected papers, 1981–1991*, Cambridge: Cambridge University Press, 1993, 143–167.

57 Compare a discussion of first and second order neutrality in P. De Marneffe, 'Liberalism, liberty, and neutrality', *Philosophy and Public Affairs*, 19, 1990, 253.

58 T. Nagel, 'Rawls on Justice', in N. Daniels (ed.), *Reading Rawls: critical studies of 'A theory of justice'*, Oxford: Oxford University Press, 1975, 9.

59 J. O'Neill, *The missing child in liberal theory*, Toronto: Toronto University Press, 1994, 63.

60 See: *Costello-Roberts v. UK* (2001) 31 EHRR 1 ECtHR.

61 *Bishop of Roman Catholic Diocese of Port Louis v. Tengur* (Mauritius) [2004] UKPC 9.

62 In section 3.

63 The School Standards Act 1998, section 91.

64 [2009] UKSC 15.

65 Comm. No. 191/1985 *Blom v. Sweden* CCPR/C/32/D/191/1985; Comm. Nos. 288, 299/1988 *Lundgren and Hjord v. Sweden* CCPR/C/67/D/694/1996.

66 Comm. No. 694/1996 *Waldman v. Canada*, CCPR/C/67/D/694/1996. But see the Supreme Court of Canada's decision, which was the basis of this communication and ruled that there was no breach of religious freedom where only schools of one religion were funded, because of their special legal status in the state: *Adler v. Ontario* [1996] 3 SCR 609; (1996) 140 DLR (4th) 3.

67 1996 (4) BCLR 537 (CC); [1996] 3 CHLRD 310.

68 Schools based on common race were made an exception to the right to establish community schools in the School Education Act. However, the inherent danger in the permitted categories is that common culture or religion could overlap with racial discrimination, and basing institutions on these grounds could be an indirect way to discriminate racially.

69 Per J. Sachs, at para. 77.

70 D. M. Clarke, 'Education, the state and sectarian schools', in Murphy and Twomey (eds), *Ireland's evolving constitution*, Oxford: Hart, 1998, 65, 74.

71 *Wittman v. Deutscher Schulverein* 1999 (2) BCLR 92 (T); 1998 (4) SA 423 (T).

72 Based on Section 14(2) of the Interim Constitution, currently Section 15 of the Constitution. See also J. Van der Vyver, 'Constitutional perspectives on Church-State relations in South Africa', *Brigham Young University Law Review*, 1999, 935, who claims that the school could have been seen as an organ of the state (at fn. 105).

73 *Lee v. Weisman* 505 U.S. 577 (1992).

74 See definition in Schools Standards and Frameworks Act 1998, section 20.

75 Section 60(5)(a)(i).

76 Section 60(5)(b).

77 In Ireland, see *Flynn v. Power* [1975] IR 648, in which termination of employment of a teacher in Catholic schools whose personal life the school saw as departing from the school values was held not to constitute unfair dismissal.

78 Employment Equality (Religion or Belief) Regulations 2003, Regulation 7(3).

79 Regulation 7(2).

80 'Religion or belief in the workplace – a guide for employers and employees', available at http://www.acas.org.uk (accessed 8 December 2009) at 13.

81 Concluding Observations on Ireland's State Report: Ireland, ICCPR, A/55/40 vol. I (2000) 61 at para. 443.

82 2000/78/EC of 27 November 2000.

83 D. M. Clarke, 'Education, the state and sectarian schools', in Murphy and Twomey (eds), *Ireland's evolving constitution*, Oxford: Hart, 1998, 65, 70–71.

84 See, e.g., on grounds of race: *Brown v. Board of Education*, 347 US 483 (1954).

85 Such as that implied by the prohibition on gender discrimination in religious schools in the D. Shelton and A. Kiss, 'A draft model law on freedom of religion, with commentary', in J. D. van der Vyver and J. Witte Jr., *Religious human rights in global perspective Vol. II – legal perspectives*, The Hague: Martinus Nijhoff Publishers, 1996, 559.

86 UNESCO Convention against Discrimination in Education 1960. The relevant articles read:

Article 1

1. For the purpose of this Convention, the term 'discrimination' includes any distinction, exclusion, limitation or preference which, being based on race, colour, sex, language, religion, political or other opinion, national or social origin, economic condition or birth, has the purpose or effect of nullifying or impairing equality of treatment in education and in particular:

(a) Of depriving any person of or group of persons of access to education of any type or at any level.

(b) Of limiting any person or group of persons to education of an inferior standard.

(c) Subject to the provision of Article 2 of this Convention, of establishing or maintaining separate educational systems or institutions for persons or groups of persons; or

(d) Of inflicting on any person or group of persons conditions which are incompatible with the dignity of man.

2. ... [T]he term education refers to al types and levels of education ...

Article 2

When permitted in a State, the following situations shall not be deemed to constitute discrimination, within the meaning of Article 1 of this convention:

(a) The establishment or maintenance of separate educational systems or institutions for pupils of the two sexes, if these systems or institutions offer equivalent access to education, provide a teaching staff with qualifications of the same standard as well as school premises and equipment of the same quality, and afford the opportunity to take the same or equivalent courses of study;

(b) The establishment or maintenance, for religious or linguistic reasons, of separate educational systems or institutions offering an education which is in keeping with the wishes of the pupil's parents or legal guardians, if participation in such systems or attendance at such institutions is optional and if the education provided conforms to such standards as may be laid down or approved by the competent authorities, in particular for education of the same level;

(c) The establishment or maintenance of private educational institutions, if the object of the institutions is not to secure the exclusion of any group but to provide educational facilities in addition to those provided by the public authorities, if the institutions are conducted in accordance with that object, and if education provided conforms with such standards as may be laid down or approved by the competent authorities, in particular for education of the same level.

87 Article 2(a).

88 Article 2(b).

89 Madrid, 23–25 November 2001, available at: http://www.unhchr.ch/html/menu2/7/b/cfedu-home.html (accessed 14 December 2009).

90 Article 7(d).

91 Article 9.

92 The issue of wearing of headscarves by female students is contentious in other multi-religious societies. For instance, some Japanese public schools prevented the wearing of headscarves, relying on a rule that religious clothing is not allowed to be worn in public schools. See K. Boyle and J. Sheen (eds), *Freedom of religion and belief: a world report*, London: Routledge, 1997, 214. In Singapore, Muslim girls who wore scarves (*tudungs*) were suspended from public schools. The government claimed its policy was aimed at maintaining racial harmony between the country's ethnic Chinese majority and Muslim Malay minority. See BBC News, 'Third schoolgirl suspended over scarf', 11 February 2002. In Holland a ban on a student wearing a headscarf to school has recently been lifted only in the face of imminent legal action (J. Sparks, 'Girl in head-scarf goes centre stage in Dutch election', *The Sunday Times*, 11 January 2003). In Spain, a state school in El Escorial refused to allow a student to wear a *hijab*. The school's decision was supported by the Education Minister, who argued that the *hijab* was not 'a religious symbol but a sign of discrimination against women': E. Daly, 'Split in row over girl's veil', *The Observer*, 17 February 2002. In Belgium, a recent local ban on headscarves has prompted legal proceedings. See http://www.nrc.nl/international/Features/article2370136.ece/Headscarf_ban_a_slap_in_the_face_for_Flemish_Muslims (accessed 14 December 2009).

93 Advice of 27 November 1989, cited in A. An-Na'im, 'Human rights and Islamic identity in France and Uzbekistan: Mediation of the local and the global', *Human Rights Quarterly*, 22, 2000, 906, 920.

94 *Kherouaa and others, November 2, 1992* in *Public Law*, 1993, 198, and see discussion in Poulter, 'Muslim headscarves in school: contrasting legal approaches in England and France', *Oxford Journal of Legal Studies*, 17, 1997, 43.

95 'Le rapport de la commission Stasi sur la laïcité', 'The report of the Stasi committee on secularity', *Le Monde*, 12 December 2003.

96 Law no. 2004–228 of 15 March 2004.

97 In 2010 the French National Assembly has passed a bill banning wearing a *burqua* in all public places. The bill would become law if approved by the Senate (http://www.bbc.co.uk/news/10611398)

98 App. No. 27058/05 *Dogru v. France* [2008] ECtHR.

99 *R. (Begum) v. Denbigh High* [2006] UKHL 15. See also A. Scolnicov, 'A dedicated follower of (religious) fashion', *Cambridge Law Journal*, 64, 2005, 527–530 discussing the Court of Appeal's decision *R. (on the application of SB) v. Headteacher and Governors of Denbigh High School* [2005] EWCA Civ 199. See also *R. (On the application of X) v. The Headteacher of Y School* [2007] EWHC 298 (Admin) which essentially follows the ruling and reasoning of the House of Lords in *Begum*.

100 HCJ 4298/93 *Jabarin v. the Minister of Education* PD 48 (5) 199.

101 App. No. 16278/90 *Karaduman v. Turkey* EComHR; a similar case is App. No. 18783/91 *Bulut v. Turkey* EComHR.

102 App. 44774/98 *Şahin v. Turkey* EctHR [2004].

103 Legal determinations regarding international human rights law in this matter have also been made in other states. For instance, in Trinidad and Tobago, in *Sumayyah Mohammed (a minor) v. Lucia Moraine* [1196] 3 LRC 475; 2 CHRLD 276 (High Court Decision of 17 Jan 1995) a Muslim student was not allowed to wear *hijab* in a publicly funded

Catholic secondary school, contrary to the school uniform rules. The court found the school's decision not discriminatory on the grounds of religion and not in violation of freedom of religion, as the relevant Education Act was deemed not to apply to manifestation of belief. Although an interpretation of domestic law, this interpretation contradicts international legal norms, which clearly protect all aspects of manifestation of religion. The Court ultimately accepted the student's claim on reasons of administrative law, as it found the decision of the school an unreasonable exercise of discretion.

104 For a discussion of voluntariness in European Commission of Human Rights decisions, see C. Evans, *Freedom of religion under the European Convention on Human Rights*, Oxford: Oxford University Press, 2001, 130–131.

105 For further discussion of the normative question whether, when there is an adequate alternative, a religious objector should be required to choose between the facility which is compatible with his beliefs or remaining in the same facility, or whether there is a duty to accommodate religious beliefs in every facility, see S. Leader, 'Freedom and futures: personal priorities, institutional demands and freedom of religion', *Modern Law Review*, 70, 2007, 713.

106 M. Minow, *Making all the difference*, Ithaca: Cornell University Press, 1990, 287, remarks on a correlative issue of free speech, that: '[L]egal arguments can be made both to restrict and to extend students' First Amendment rights in light of the school's mission to socialize young people … and to inculcate the habits of good citizenship. … [S]peech may be restricted to guard against disorder. But we might ask can its restriction be justified to maintain a particular order.'

107 Per Lord Hoffmann, paras. 53–55.

108 A legal avenue which presents a different approach in English law is seen in *Watkins-Singh, R. (on the application of) v. Aberdare Girls' High School* [2008] EWHC 1865 (Admin), in which the Divisional Court accepted a *discrimination* claim for refusal to let a student wear religious dress to school based on the Race Relations Act.

109 See *Kalac v. Turkey* (1997) 27 EHRR 552 ECtHR; *Refah Partisi (The Welfare Party) v. Turkey* (2002) 35 EHRR 3 (Chamber decision), (2004).

110 App. No. 27058/05 *Dogru v. France* [2008] ECtHR.

111 HCJ 4298/93 *Jabarin v. Minister of Education* 48(5) PD 199, 204, per J. Goldberg.

112 See: M. Rafiq Khan, *Socio-legal status of Muslim women*, London: Sangam Books, 1993, 59, arguing that veiling is a reminder to Muslim women that their place is in the home (relying on a quote from the *Qur'an* (24:31)).

113 See F. Mernissi, *Women and Islam*, Oxford: Basil Blackwell, 1991, in which the author argues that through misinterpretation of Mohamed's teaching women have become veiled, secluded and marginalized objects rather than subjects. See also F. Mernissi, *Beyond the veil*, Cambridge: Cambridge University Press, 1975.

114 Convention on the Elimination of all Forms of Discrimination against Women (adopted 18 December 1979) 1249 UNTS 13, Article 5.

115 S. Poulter, 'Muslim headscarves in school: contrasting legal approaches in England and France', *Oxford Journal of Legal Studies*, 17, 1997, 43, 69.

116 R. Hassan, 'Rights of women within Islamic communities', in J. van der Vyver and J. Witte Jr. (eds), *Religious human rights in global perspective*, The Hague: Martinus Nijhoff Publishers, 1996, 361, 382.

117 This was criticized by the CRC Committee: CRC/C/15/Add.181 (2002) at paras. 29.

118 See my suggestion elsewhere that the court of first instance should have appointed separate representation for her at trial: A. Scolnicov, 'A dedicated follower of (religious) fashion', *Cambridge Law Journal*, 64, 2005, 527–530.

119 See additionally a survey of state practices in relation to wearing of the female Islamic dress (generally referred to as the *hijab*), or any feature of this dress such as the headscarf (*khimar*), face veil (*niqab*) and the head-to-toe all enveloping garment (*jilbab*) in the education and employment areas. See M. Ssenyonjo, 'The Islamic veil and freedom

of religion, the rights to education and work: a survey of recent international and national cases', *Chinese Journal of International Law*, 6, 2007, 653–710.

120 App. No. 42393/98 *Dahlab v. Switzerland* ECtHR.

121 *Vogt v. Germany* (1995) 21 EHRR 205 ECtHR.

122 But see also the earlier case *Kosiek v. Germany* (1987) 9 EHRR 328 ECtHR.

123 BVerfG, 2BvR 1436/02, decided 3.6.2003 (German Constitutional Court website: http://www.bverfg.de/entscheildungen/rs2030603_2bvr143602.html) (accessed 14 December 2009).

124 Basic law, Article 33(2).

125 Article 33(3).

126 Article 4.

127 BBC News, 'French juror barred for headscarf', 25 November 2003.

128 BVerfG, 1 BvR 792/03, decided 30.7.2003 (German Constitutional Court Website: http://www.bverfg.de/entscheidungen/rk20030730_1bvr079203.html) (accessed 14 December 2009).

129 'Le rapport de la commission Stasi sur la laïcité', 'The report of the Stasi committee on secularity', Le Monde, 12 December 2003.

130 2000/78/EC of 27 November 2000 OJ 2000 L303/16.

131 Article 18.

132 Article 2(a).

133 This, of course, does not preclude limitations resulting from health and safety or similar concerns.

6 Religious freedom as a right of free speech

Religious freedom was analysed in Chapter 2 as a right that can be understood through two conceptions: as a right of expression and as a right of identity. This duality is related, though not identical, to that between an individual perception and a community perception of the right to religious freedom, and is evident in the legal regulation of this right. It is particularly evident in legal regulations that place limits on expression. In these cases, how the right to religious freedom is conceived will determine the boundaries of this right.

This study argued that religious freedom should be construed first and foremost as an individual right. In Chapter 2, the individual right was related to the expressive-critical aspect of religious freedom, and the community right to its identity aspect. However, both aspects inform the right to religious freedom to a certain extent even in its construction as an individual right, and this chapter explores some of the implications of this balance on the regulation of religious speech.

In this chapter, it will argued that contrary to the view that religious speech should be subject to community choices, it must be viewed as a matter for individual choice just as any other speech. The degree of protection accorded to religious speech should not be any less than that accorded to other kinds of political speech. For the same reason, the right to religious freedom must include a right to receive religious speech. The right of free religious speech should be accorded on the basis of equality between religions. As will be shown, seemingly neutral procedural regulations can be used illegitimately to effect discrimination in protection of religious speech against unpopular religions.

The distinction between religion as expression and religion as identity is utilized in the present chapter to examine four types of regulation that limit religious speech, and to enquire as to their justification: First, those offences that prohibit proselytism and the justifications offered for them will be examined, arguing that, under the guise of protection of individual religious autonomy, the prohibition of proselytism serves also as a means of religious group self-preservation. Next, imposition of penalties by the religious group itself on members whose religious speech it views as unacceptable is examined. It will be argued that even such internal sanctions cannot be left solely to group autonomy and determination, but that the state and international law must require religious groups to respect a certain degree of free speech of their members. I then consider prohibition of religious speech when such speech is labelled blasphemous. I demonstrate that this offence protects religion as identity at the expense of the protection of religion as expression, a price that strikes an unacceptable balance of rights. Last, I turn to a most important area of regulation of religious speech and speech concerning religion under current debate: the prohibition of religious hate speech. I argue that an understanding of the dual nature of religious freedom as a right which protects both identity and expression would lead to regulation of speech that is unique and different from regulation of other types of hate speech.

6.1 Free speech and religion – preliminary issues

6.1.1 The degree of protection of religious speech – a matter for community resolution?

Religious speech is speech, and therefore is protected by the right of free speech[1] (in addition to the right of religious freedom). But does it merit higher, lower or equal protection relative to other speech because of its religious character?

The European Court of Human Rights in *Wingrove*[2] stated that there is a wider margin of appreciation available to states when regulating speech in the realm of morals and, especially, religion than when restricting political speech or debating matters of public interest.[3] This exemplifies a 'hands-off' treatment of international human rights law when courts confront religious choices made by the state.[4] But speech relating to morals and religion *is* political speech. It is speech that relates to society and its values; indeed, it is speech that shapes society. It is a factor in the market place of ideas. Under the approach that leaves wider discretion regarding religious speech to the state, one kind of political speech is thereby treated differently from others. The implications of this point beyond this case are discussed in this chapter.

6.1.2 Right to receive religious speech

The view of religion as speech has other implications too. The conception of religious freedom as an expressive-individualistic right, the purpose of which is to foster critical debate, implies a right to receive views about religion as well as to impart them. Therefore, the religious freedom that is restricted by limitations on religious speech is both that of those who impart the speech and of those who wish to receive the speech. This is true, for instance, when speech is censored for religious reasons.

However, the Inter-American Court of Human Rights in *The Last Temptation of Christ* case[5] analysed this aspect of religious freedom differently. The applicants claimed that their ability to receive information was impaired by a ban on the screening of the film *The Last Temptation of Christ*. The Court decided that their right to freedom of thought and expression, guaranteed by Article 13 of the American Convention on Human Rights, was infringed, because the right includes freedom to receive information. It saw, however, no infringement of Article 12, the right to freedom of religion and belief, because, it reasoned, no one's right to practise, change or disseminate his or her religion or belief was impaired by the ban.[6]

But freedom of religion encompasses also a right of the individual to be inquisitive and critical about religion. In fact, such a view of religious freedom was one of the original justifications of this right.[7] In this view, just as freedom of expression includes the freedom to receive information, so freedom of religion and belief includes the right to receive information relating to religion, both advocating religions and criticizing them. The Court regrettably followed a narrower interpretation, encompassing only the actions of practice, manifestation and change of religion without the freedoms that allow the individual to make rational choices about religion.

6.1.3 *Equality of protection of the right to religious speech*

Protection of religious freedom of expression, as well as any other aspect of religious freedom, must be accorded equally. However, how equality should be assessed is a matter for debate. The different perceptions of equality are brought into relief in the examination by the European Commission, in *Choudhury v. UK*,[8] of the offence of blasphemy in the UK. (This offence has now been repealed, as will be discussed later.) Because this offence in the UK applied only to Christianity, the applicant's requests to UK authorities to prosecute Salman Rushdie and the publishers of his book *The Satanic Verses* for blasphemy were dismissed.[9] The applicant claimed that his rights under Article 9 of the European Convention were breached, since the UK authorities did not protect his religion from blasphemy. The European Commission decided that there was no interference with the applicant's freedom of religion, which does not include a right to any specific form of proceedings against those who offend the sensitivities of an individual or group. Because no right under Article 9 was breached, there was also no violation of Article 14, which only arises in connection with discrimination of Convention rights.

The Commission seems right in not viewing the lack of blasphemy proceedings as a breach of religious freedom. However, the Commission's interpretation of what constitutes discrimination in protection of religious freedom is remiss. If a state decides to offer a certain means of protection of religious freedom, even such as is not mandated by Article 9, whether the measure discriminates against the applicant should be assessed according to the protection of religious freedom that the state in fact offers to other religions. The request for the application of the blasphemy prohibition to another religion should have been denied only because ordering such a prohibition would be incommensurate with the religious freedom of others.

There are wider implications of this interpretation of discrimination in religious freedom. It would follow from *Choudhury* that only a limited ambit of protection is offered by Article 14 in conjunction with Article 9. The state is required only not to discriminate in according the minimum standard mandated by Article 9. Any further protection it offers to religious freedom on a discriminatory basis is not a violation of the Convention. A preferable interpretation would accord equality not just in the minimum provision demanded by Article 9, but also in the actual implementation of the right of religious freedom by the state.

6.1.4 Discrimination in the right to religious speech by seemingly neutral procedural regulations

Not only substantive regulation, but procedural restriction can also impede freedom of religion. In particular, seemingly neutral provisions applicable to all religions escape legal censure, but may in fact impact some religions more than others (whether intentionally or not) with a discriminatory result. How such procedural restrictions escape legal censure can be seen in the European Court decision in *Manoussakis*.[10] The case concerned a Greek law requiring prior state authorization for use of premises for religious worship. Such authorization was denied to Jehovah's Witnesses. The European Court[11] decided that the law was incompatible with Article 9 in so far as it allowed ministerial discretion for authorization beyond the formal conditions laid down in the law. However, the ruling should have given a broader protection to religious freedom: any law limiting where worship may take place (beyond health and safety regulations which apply to all public buildings) is an unjustified infringement of religious freedom. It is the state that must justify why a restriction should be permitted. Furthermore, formal conditions, even seemingly neutral ones, are likely to impact minority religions and unpopular religions adversely. Indeed, in this case, this was exemplified by the demand of the law that 50 families submit the request, a demand that was harder for smaller religions to meet, as hinted at by Judge Martens (in a concurring opinion). An approach more critical of state regulation would have better served the protection of religious freedom.

The danger inherent in state authorities laying down seemingly neutral provisions that adversely impact minority or unpopular religions is highlighted by a recent decision of the US Supreme Court.[12] It held that a town ordinance making it a misdemeanour to engage in door-to-door advocacy without first registering with the mayor and receiving a permit violated the First Amendment as it applied to religious proselytizing and to distribution of handbills. The Court stated that '[i]t is offensive –not only to the values protected by the First Amendment, but to the very notion of a free society – that in the context of everyday public discourse a citizen must first inform the government of her desire to speak to her neighbours and then obtain a permit to do so.' Thus, under US law, even procedural regulation, with no discretion as to the substance of the speech, is not permitted. The Court noted that the seemingly neutral technical provision in fact disproportionately impacts religious groups such as Jehovah's Witnesses, which lack financial resources and so rely on door-to-door canvassing to proselytize.

When dealing with regulations impacting religious freedom, two contrasting legal approaches applicable to cases of restrictions on religious freedom, including religious speech, are apparent. The first is content with the formal equality and general applicability of the regulation, while the second approach looks at whether the seemingly formal regulation has a disparate impact on small religions, which lack relevant resources. This second approach better protects religious freedom.

6.2 Restrictions on proselytism as protection of community identity

The relationship between the competing conceptions of religious freedom as an individualistic-deliberative right and as a right that protects identity as part of the community (or even the cohesiveness of the community itself) is reflected in the legal regulation of proselytism. The right to change religion is internationally recognized as included in the right to religious freedom.[13] The right to convince others to change their religion is more controversial. In international instruments, it is specifically mentioned only in the American Convention,[14] but it is generally recognized as part of religious freedom.[15] A study of its limitations is instructive in understanding this right.

To justify restrictions on proselytism, two arguments, compatible with a liberal point of view, are deployed: prevention of coercion and prevention of undue influence.[16] Prohibition of coercion to change religion is justified, as coercion negates free will. The argument of undue influence is more problematic. There is a fine line between effecting a change of religion that is devoid of free will (through coercion) and the legitimate right to convince others to change their religion within the free market place of ideas. It seems that previously UN studies have not sufficiently acknowledged this distinction, but have, rather, permitted prohibition of both.[17]

The former Special Rapporteur to the Sub-Commission on Prevention of Discrimination and Protection of Minorities, Elisabeth Odio Benito, recommended in her study[18] that states adopt provisions against coercion to change religion. Prevention of coercion to change religion is legitimate and, indeed, warranted government policy. However, Odio Benito did not consider the greater danger to religious freedom inherent in the potential use by governments of such legislation for persecution of unpopular minority religions that proselytise, even absent proof of use of coercion.

The earlier work of Special Rapporteur Arcot Krishnaswami in his study on religious rights commissioned by the Sub-Commission on Prevention of Discrimination and Protection of Minorities[19] included a proposal that 'no one should be subjected to coercion or to improper inducements likely to impair his freedom to maintain or change his religion or belief.'[20] However, what comprises improper inducements is, of course, a matter of broad interpretation, and such a broad prohibition is open to misuse by the state.

The Special Rapporteur on Freedom of Religion or Belief, Asma Jahangir, in her 2005 Interim report[21] was more sensitive in her approach to the danger to religious freedom inherent in prohibitions on inducement to conversion, as well as that of coercion to convert.[22]

On a principled level, it may be questioned whether such prohibitions in fact protect individual autonomy or rather maintain the cohesiveness of the community.[23]

Four different examples of state prohibition on proselytism exemplify this last point. In the *Kokkinakis* case,[24] the European Court found Greek anti-proselytism law,[25] which prohibited exertion of influence upon religious belief by moral or material support, or by appeal to someone of low experience or intellectual faculties, to be compatible with Article 9.[26] In Germany, the Constitutional Court decided, in the *Tobacco Atheist* case,[27] that the denial of parole to a prison inmate who tried to bribe other inmates with tobacco to forswear their religion, did not breach Article 4 of the basic law (which guarantees religious freedom). This, reasoned the Court, was because the right to proselytize exists only when not exploiting a harsh situation of others, which is inconsistent with their dignity.[28]

Based on an apparently similar justification of unfair inducement, Israel's penal law includes offences of offering another person monetary or material compensation to effect his religious conversion,[29] accepting such compensation from another for a religious conversion,[30] and causing the religious conversion of a minor.[31] In 2001, France passed a law 'aimed at strengthening the prevention and the repression against cults and sects',[32] creating a criminal offence of abusing a state of ignorance or weakness, leading the person to an act or an abstention which is seriously harmful to him.[33] This applies not only to minors or persons of diminished legal capacity (in which case the law is undoubtedly a justified restriction), but also to 'persons in a state of psychological or physical subjection resulting from serious pressures exercised', a less clear and more controversial category. Depending on its interpretation, this definition could mean different things. Under a broad interpretation, this could even include pressures that are equivalent to high-pressure sales techniques.

Seemingly, restrictions on proselytism are justified as even liberals exclude some classes of people from full autonomy. These restrictions are based on an objection to the use of manipulative techniques to cause someone to change their religion. However, use of the same manipulative techniques on people who are already members of the religion (or other ideological group), including children, in order to maintain their membership, is not considered illegal. Thus, welfare provisions for members of a church would not be illegal, but provision of the same services for outsiders would be. This shows that behind a façade of individual-based reasoning, the prohibitions are predicated on a view of religious freedom as a group identity right. So, breaking this identity in a way incompatible with full autonomy is seen as harmful, but maintaining identity through similar means is not.

Article 9 does not protect improper proselytism such as the offering of material or social advantage, stated the European Court in *Larissis v. Greece*.[34, 35] But religious institutions routinely offer material and social advantages to their own members in order to keep them as members. It is only when religions do so in conversion of others that states interfere. If the object is to protect individuals from undue influence, why do prohibitions exist in one case but not the other? Possibly what is protected is more the group to which the individuals belong, rather than the individuals themselves.

There is yet another consideration: as we have seen, prohibitions on proselytism have been enacted regarding the use of material inducements or exertion of influence on people whose capacities or circumstances render them vulnerable. All are forms of manipulation regarded as improper. But manipulation is a constant element in interactions between people in society. Prohibitions apply almost only to conversion of *religious* beliefs; manipulation of other ideas and beliefs in similar circumstances (ranging from political persuasion and election campaigning to the inducement to purchase products, by means including PR and advertising) generally remains legal, and even desirable in a society predicated on a free marketplace of ideas. This distinction between change of religious beliefs and change of any other belief lacks any coherent justification. This further points to the conclusion that prohibitions on proselytism are, in fact, intended to protect and foster existing religious identities rather than individual autonomy.

This criticism applies to laws prohibiting proselytism of adults. Prohibitions on inducing children to convert are justified, based on the widely shared perception that it is easier for adults to manipulate children's beliefs. Indeed, calls for stricter regulation of commercial advertising targeted at children follow the same approach. Differential treatment regarding adults, protecting them from manipulation of religious beliefs but not from manipulation of other categories of beliefs and ideas, hints that states which prohibit conversion for a pecuniary interest are protecting groups from 'poaching' members rather than the individual aspect of religious freedom. Thus, under an individual-based conception of religious freedom, many restrictions on proselytism are unjustifiable.[36]

6.2.1 Restrictions on proselytism in the private sphere

Restrictions on religious speech, including proselytism, are not only imposed by the state. Private bodies may impose restrictions that are no less onerous, especially against small and unpopular religions. In a recent case in Israel,[37] a newspaper refused to carry an advertisement for a book advocating the religious beliefs of Messianic Jews, claiming that this advertisement would offend parts of its readership. While the majority of the District Court held that a private newspaper was under no legal obligation to enter into contract with potential advertisers, the dissenting judge argued that a newspaper may not discriminate on the grounds of religious belief in deciding which advertisements to publish.

Such an interpretation of the obligations of a newspaper, a private body, to respect human rights, especially in a small market with a limited number of newspapers, would preserve the freedom of religious speech of unpopular minorities. Absent such protection, dominant religious groups could curtail the right of minorities to propagate their religion through private action, as effectively as government can curtail it through legal restrictions.

This is yet another area where private actors can effectively harm religious freedom. Granted that any restriction on private actors would have to take into account their rights, particularly when imposition on the freedom of the press is involved, the interpretation of the right of religious freedom in national laws and international law should move beyond the traditional ambit of protection of religious freedom only in the public sphere.

6.3 Freedom of religious speech and sanctions within a religious group

Indisputably, everyone has a right in international law to leave a religious group[38] and expound views different from its teachings. But an important question is what sort of sanctions the religious group itself may impose against those it considers heretics. Religious groups employ a variety of sanctions ranging from purely social sanctions to termination of employment (of employees), stripping of the body's assets, initiation of applicable civil legal proceedings, and excommunication. If a group is allowed to maintain its religious identity, it must have some means of doing so; however, the freedom of religious speech of its members is curtailed if they know that sanctions may be imposed on them for speaking their mind and expressing their beliefs. Such expression is also the way for religions to develop, conduct internal debate and discussions, and manifest the true beliefs of their members.

Apostasy and heresy present a conflict between the right of individuals to believe what they choose and the right of the religious group to promulgate its own religious doctrine. Sullivan[39] believes this presents an open question in international law. She argues that if religious and secular authorities overlap and try to suppress the expression of belief by alleged heretics by stripping them of secular privileges or property rights, the right of the individual prevails. It is clear from this position that she believes there is an 'inner-religious' sphere in which the group should prevail, for example, permitting the group to impose religious sanctions on individuals, even excommunication of such members. There is a strong argument for non-involvement of the law in such internal doctrinal matters, allowing for a community right of religious freedom. However, individuals may have arguments for the recognition of their human rights within religious communities and institutions, as explained in Chapter 3. Even religious sanctions against individual members may have to withstand a test of compliance with certain human rights provisions.

Forbidding individuals that a religion considers heretics from claiming that they belong to that religion is an infringement of their religious freedom, as guaranteed by Article 1 of the 1981 Declaration.[40] This interpretation favours the rights of the individual or splinter group over the dominant group. If this right is recognized against the group itself and not just as a right against the state and its sanctions,[41] then this will be a right against religious sanctions emanating from religious dogma, and not a right against the secular actions of the state. The decisions of who is considered a member and what is regarded as heresy are part of every religion's doctrine, and thus are issues in which legal intervention will most directly jeopardize religious freedom. However, the need to promote debate and discussion within religions, and to protect the rights of those who engage in such debate, would favour this interpretation of religious freedom.

This raises an important question: to what extent can the state, and indeed international law, legitimately interfere in the inner workings of a religious group. The activities which are at the inner core of a religious group – the interpretation of religious doctrine, appointment of clergy and the conduct of worship – are those in which state intervention directed at upholding the rights of individual members is hardest to justify. But even within this inner core of the religious group religious freedom and equality of individual members should be maintained. The conflict between religious doctrine and the legal protection of rights is at the heart of intense controversies such as appointment of female and gay clergy and the right of dissenting clergy to voice their opinions. An individualistic approach to religious freedom means that religious organizations should not be a barrier to protection of individual rights. However, the ambit of what might be justified limitations of these rights would be broader in direct matters of religious doctrine than in other aspects of life organized by religious communities.

6.4 Prohibition of blasphemous speech derives from an identity perception of religious freedom

The discussion thus far has focused on the legality of sanctions within a religion. However, those views and beliefs to which religious groups object are sometimes prohibited by the state itself. A state can protect a religious group's view of its own religion, inhibiting individual religious expression, through an offence of blasphemy. As will be seen, how religious freedom is conceptualized, as an expressive-critical right or as an identity right, will be determinative of the legitimacy of this prohibition. A critical-expressive approach leads to the conclusion that this offence should be eliminated. An identity approach will tend to support the legitimacy of this prohibition.[42] The offence, originally based on identification of religion with the state, has found new identity-based justifications, such as protection of feelings of all believers and a particular justification based on the protection of minority religions. A balance must be struck between the critical and expressive conceptions, which would mandate against blasphemy offences but would permit certain hate speech prohibitions (discussed further later).

An examination of the offence of blasphemy in the UK highlights these considerations. While this offence has been recently abolished in the UK,[43] and is no longer commonly utilized in most other liberal democracies,[44] its analysis is instructive.

In Ireland, the question of blasphemy and freedom of speech directed against religion arose again with the passing of the 2009 Defamation Act, which in section 36 criminalizes the publication or utterance of blasphemous material (abusive or insulting to matters held sacred by any religion).

As will be seen, the identity conception of religious freedom has been given greater weight than the expressive-critical conception, even in the discussion of abolition of the offence.

6.4.1 Prohibition of blasphemy as protection of the state

Originally, the offence of blasphemy had as its object the protection of the state through the protection of the established religion, a symbol of the state. The prohibition of blasphemy protected the official faith, irrespective of whether affront to feelings was caused.[45] Historically,[46] blasphemy law in the UK was closely related to the crime of sedition, since the Crown was both the head of state and head of the Church: attacks on God and on the established religion were viewed as attacks on the social order.[47] As Sir Hale ruled in *Taylor's Case*: 'For to say religion is a cheat, is to dissolve all those obligations whereby the civil societies are preserved, and the Christianity is parcel of the laws of England; and therefore to reproach the Christian religion is to speak subversion of the law.'[48] The King's Bench stated in *Rex v. Woolston*[49] that 'the Christian religion is established in this Kingdom and therefor would not allow any books to be writ, which should tend to alter that establishment.'[50] So, it is not surprising that even Christian non-Anglican denominations were protected only to the extent that their beliefs were common to those of the established Church.[51] If the justification of the offence of blasphemy is like that of sedition – namely, the prohibition of an act that unravels the social order – then once there is no longer an essential connection between one religion and the basic order of society, the offence is bereft of justification.

This interpretation of the crime of blasphemy is echoed in the judgment of the Supreme Court of Ireland in *Corway v. Independent Newspapers*.[52] In that case, an appeal against judgment dismissing a plaintiff's motion to commence private criminal prosecution for blasphemous libel, under the Defamation Act 1961, against a newspaper that ran a cartoon portraying the Eucharist in an insulting light was rejected. The Court reasoned that the Irish blasphemy cases (the latest from 1855) based the crime on the principle that protection of Christianity, the established religion, was inseparable from protection of the state. Once Ireland disestablished its Church (in 1869), the offence could not survive.[53] The 2009 Defamation Act has now changed the legal position so that saying something abusive or insulting to matters held sacred by a religion with intent to cause outrage is a criminal offence.

6.4.2 Protection of religious feelings

Today, the more common justification given for prohibiting blasphemy, one that relies on the terms of liberal theory, is not the protection of religion itself but of the rights of others, namely the protection of religious feelings. Relying on such a justification, a majority of the European Court of Human Rights in *Otto-Preminger-Institut*[54] decided that forfeiture of a film following criminal prosecution for 'disparaging religious doctrine', defined as expression 'likely to cause justified indignation', was not in violation of Article 10 of the European Convention.[55] The majority argued that the right to freedom of religion, enshrined in Article 9, includes a right to respect for the religious feelings of members of a religious group, which must be balanced against the right of the individual to criticize religion (protected by Article 10).[56]

The majority of the Court relied on the identity aspect of religious freedom to include protection of religious feelings in Article 9.[57] The majority opinion stated that while members of religious groups cannot expect to be exempt from criticism or even denial of their faith, some methods of opposing religious beliefs can be thought to inhibit those who hold such beliefs from exercising their religious freedom, and the state may take measures to protect them.[58] Indeed, in this extreme situation, restricting freedom of religion for some maximizes freedom of religion for all. However, the Court moved from arguing that speech, which inhibits believers from exercising their religious freedom, can be legitimately prohibited, to acknowledging a broader general right to respect for religious feelings not dependent on the showing of any such inhibition, as was the case here. The Court stated that gratuitously offensive remarks about the religious opinions of others 'do not contribute to any form of public debate capable of furthering progress in human affairs'.[59] But the Court failed to consider that while harm, strife and conflict were historically initiated by such remarks, equally great intellectual debate has been achieved by precisely such offensive remarks.

6.4.3 Protection of minorities

A different argument for retention of the offence of blasphemy (and for its extension to the protection of all religions in the UK (the offence protected only the majority religion)) has been offered by Parekh:[60] a majority religion does not need the protection offered by an offence of blasphemy, but minority religions do because of their vulnerability in the face of the majority. This view can be criticized, especially in the context in which it was expressed, that of the Salman Rushdie case.[61] Rushdie is a member of a minority religious group in the UK. The protection, which Parekh suggested for minority religions to protect them from the majority, would work in this case against Rushdie, a member of the minority itself. His right to criticize his own community would be curtailed: protection of the community would override the individual rights of a member of the community. This is an unwarranted solution. The protection of religious minority members, rather than the dogma of the religion, which should be open to criticism, can be achieved by other means such as prohibitions on hate speech, which will be discussed later.

6.4.4 The UK Parliamentary Select Committee Report

The offence of blasphemy, last successfully prosecuted in the UK in 1977,[62] has now been abolished.[63] However, an analysis of the offence is instructive and the history leading up to its abolition will be briefly recounted. Following a 1985 report by the Law Commission,[64] which concluded that the offence should be repealed, and a similar recommendation by the UN Human Rights Committee,[65] in 2002, the House of Lords appointed a Select Committee 'to consider and report on the law relating to religious offences'. The Report[66] did not offer a conclusion regarding the law of blasphemy, but offered several possible options for reform which will be discussed later.[67] The report, in its approach to religious freedom, mostly encompasses the identity aspect of religious freedom rather than its expressive-critical aspect, as will be seen in the following discussion.

In its analysis of the law under the Human Rights Act 1998,[68] the Committee saw in the prohibition a contravention of freedom of expression (Article 10) and of the obligation not to discriminate in the application of the right to religious freedom (Articles 9 to 14). It thus looked at the equality of protection of religious freedom of the members of groups, which the blasphemy laws either did or did not protect. The Report did not consider religious freedom as a critical-expressive right, the religious freedom of the blasphemer, which is impaired by blasphemy laws.

The Select Committee suggested three options for reform the offence of blasphemy, without choosing between them: 'leave as is', repeal, or replace with a broader offence.[69] The reasoning behind each of the approaches reveals more of a community-identity approach than an expressive-critical approach to religious freedom. One reason for the first option, leaving the law unchanged,[70] was that blasphemy law was part of the legal fabric; this reasoning underscores the law's constitutional heritage and national identity, which should be tampered with only for weighty reasons. This is a viewpoint that sits squarely within the community perception of the right to religious freedom.

Under the reasons in support of the 'repeal' option,[71] the Report stressed that the common law offence of blasphemy was discriminatory as it protected only one religion. The Report also stated that the most serious deficiency of the blasphemy offence is that UK courts had interpreted the offence as one of strict liability. The Report did not directly ask, however, whether any offence of blasphemy would be commensurate with respect for religious freedom. An expressive-critical approach would raise this question and answer it by noting that a blasphemy offence is incommensurate with the right to religious freedom.

Under the option of replacement of the offence with a broader, non-discriminatory provision,[72] the Report suggested the use of the Indian Penal Code provisions as a starting point, particularly Article 295A, which states:

> Whoever, with deliberate and malicious intention of outraging the religious feelings of any class of citizens of India, by words, either spoken or written, or by signs or by visible representations or otherwise, insults or attempts to insult the religion or religious beliefs of that class, shall be punished with imprisonment … or with a fine, or with both.

The Indian Supreme Court viewed this Article as commensurate with the Indian Constitution's provisions of freedom of speech and freedom of religion.[73] The Indian approach, as the Report itself noted, is based on the uppermost consideration of preventing religious strife in a particular political context. The Report envisioned problems with such a law, namely potential misuse for political prosecutions (which it did, however, see as unlikely to occur in the UK) and the difficulty of defining hurt to religious feelings.

Yet the more basic objection should stem from a view of religious freedom that sees the value of this right in the freedom to criticize and debate issues of religion and belief. Even deliberately insulting speech is not necessarily without merit; some effective conveying of religious ideas for and against religions is deliberately provocative and insulting. There is, however, speech that effectively silences, through propagation of hate or intimidation, members of a religious group from expressing their own voice and enjoying their rights as equal citizens. This speech should be more narrowly defined and is better addressed through prohibitions on hate speech.

6.5 Prohibition of religious hate speech: striking a balance between the identity and expressive perceptions of religious freedom

The duality of protection of expression and protection of identity inherent in religious freedom is also key to understanding and constructing an offence of religious hate speech. Religious hate speech has a unique character different from other hate speech. This becomes apparent through analysis of international and domestic lawmaking and legal decisions regarding this offence. The analysis that follows also highlights those considerations that must be kept in mind when restraining speech, restrictions which are the subject of current legal controversy.

6.5.1 Existing international protection

The different UN human rights conventions take different approaches to hate speech. The UN Convention on the Elimination of All Forms of Racial Discrimination [CERD] applies to hate speech based on race, colour, descent, nationality or ethnic origin, but not religion. It mandates a much broader prohibition than the ICCPR, Article 20(2) of which mandates that: 'Any advocacy of national, racial or religious hatred that constitutes incitement to discrimination, hostility or violence shall be prohibited by law.' This provision stands in conflict with rights enshrined in Articles 18 (freedom of religion) and 19 (freedom of speech), or, put another way, Article 20 carves out a sphere of speech and religion which is not protected by Articles 18 and 19. What restrictions are permitted (and, indeed, mandated) by Article 20 on Article 18 and Article 19 rights is left unclear. CERD, in Article 4(a), mandates that state parties prohibit not just incitement to hatred and discrimination, but also the dissemination of ideas based on racial superiority. Regarding religion, it would not be possible to proscribe theories of superiority without severely curtailing the expressive aspect of religious freedom, as the essence of many religions is a claim that they are the true religion and that other religions are false.[74]

The decisions of the Human Rights Committee offer some, but not much, guidance, as they lack a principled approach. In some cases the solution to the balance of rights is clear cut, as there is legitimate reason to curtail the expressive aspect of religious freedom. *Ross v. Canada*[75] concerned a Canadian teacher who lost his teaching position for publishing anti-Semitic writings. The Human Rights Committee justified the restriction of Ross's rights by the protection of the rights and freedoms of others under Articles 18 and 19, including their right to have an education in the public school system free from bias, prejudice and intolerance. The reasoning in this case is understandable and justifiable. The case does not concern a regular exchange of speech between adults, but an adult, a teacher, in a position of authority vis-à-vis children. The ambit of freedom of religious expression should be much narrower in such a situation than it is in the adult market place of ideas.

Regarding speech targeted at adults, the case is more complicated. In *J.R.T.*,[76] the HRC found that Canada did not breach the author's Article 19 rights, because Canada complied with Article 20(2). In that case, indeed, the speech was inciting, especially when set against the historical context of anti-Semitism; its subject was a religious group and not religious ideas and was legitimately prohibited. But the HRC gave no guidance as to whether or how it attempted to balance Article 19 against Article 20(2).[77]

The EU Council Framework Decision on Combating Racism and Xenophobia[78] defines racism and xenophobia[79] as: 'the belief in race, colour, descent, religion or belief, national or ethnic origin as a factor determining aversion to individuals or groups'. It mandates that states criminalize intentional conduct of public incitement to violence or hatred for a racist or xenophobic purpose or to any other racist or xenophobic behaviour that may cause substantial damage to individuals or groups concerned,[80] as well as public insults or threats towards individuals or groups for a racist or xenophobic purpose.[81]

The EU has so far failed to adopt the Framework Decision mainly due to fears that the Decision could be used to restrict political and expressive rights.[82] This is a danger regarding criminalization of any speech that may be regarded as racist or xenophobic, but it is a particular danger regarding religious speech, which is often used to express political ideas that may be unduly classified as racist or xenophobic.

In 2007, the Parliamentary Assembly of the Council of Europe adopted Recommendation 1805 on blasphemy, religious insults and hate speech against persons on grounds of their religion.[83] This Recommendation set a number of guidelines for member states in view of Articles 9 and 10 ECHR. In 2008, the Venice Commission issued a report on blasphemy, religious insult, and incitement to religious hatred.[84] The report concluded that 'it is neither necessary nor desirable to create an offence of religious insult' (and 'the offence of blasphemy should be abolished', a conclusion also reached in Recommendation 1805).

The lack of clear guidance in international law on religious hate speech prompts a closer examination of how states have dealt with this issue.

6.5.1.1 *National treatment*

In the UK, the Racial and Religious Hatred Act was passed in 2006 after much controversy. A proposal to extend the offence of incitement to racial hatred was accepted in the Anti-Terrorism, Crime and Security Bill 2001 but was subsequently dropped. It was, however, included in the Religious Offences Bill 2002, and reintroduced in the Serious Organised Crime and Police Bill 2004.[85] Incitement to racial hatred was already a criminal offence under the Race Relations Act 1965 and Part III of the Public Order Act 1986. Under the latter Act, it is an offence to use threatening, abusive or insulting words or behaviour or display written material that is threatening, abusive or insulting and which is intended or is likely to stir up racial hatred.[86] The House of Lords Select Committee, in its report on the proposed Religious Offences Bill,[87] did not reach a conclusion as to whether there needs to be any additional legal protection 'either for believers as a class, or for the objects connected with their beliefs'. However, the Racial and Religious Hatred Act 2006, subsequently introduced and passed by Parliament, broadened the offence in the Public Order Act to cover religious hatred (Section 29B). 'Religious hatred' is defined as hatred directed against a group of persons defined by reference to religious belief or lack of religious belief. In contrast with the existing racial hatred offence, however, the new religious hatred offence can only be committed if the actor *intended* to cause religious hatred; in comparison, the existing offence can be committed where the actions are *likely* to cause racial hatred.

Section 29J was added in final stages of drafting to pacify vocal opposition to the bill in Parliament, especially in the House of Lords. It is entitled 'Protection of Freedom of Expression' and reads: 'Nothing in this Part shall be read or given effect in a way which prohibits or restricts discussion, criticism or expressions of antipathy, dislike, ridicule, insult or abuse of particular religions or the beliefs or practices of their adherents, or of any other belief system or the beliefs or practices of its adherents, or proselytising or urging adherents of a different religion or belief system to cease practising their religion or belief system.'

6.5.2 Religious hate speech should be treated differently from other hate speech

While laws against religious hatred and intolerance have a laudable purpose, such laws may impermissibly contravene both freedom of religion and freedom of expression. Special Rapporteur Odio Benito[88] lists approvingly states that have laws penalising acts of intolerance and discrimination based on religion or belief, and recommends that all states adopt similar laws. However, she does not attempt to distinguish between laws that legitimately prevent incitement and laws that themselves contravene religious freedom and freedom of expression by preventing legitimate religious speech.[89] A fine but crucial line must be drawn between the two. Where such a line must be drawn has been the subject of much controversy within state practice and juridical debate, as well as within the limited international case law on the subject.

The legitimacy of limitations on hate speech as restrictions of free speech has been much debated.[90] The debate has centred on hate speech targeting race. But religious hate speech differs from racial hate speech, a point that has not received much attention. Treating religious and racial hate speech in the same way does not sufficiently protect religious freedom. When religious freedom is involved, its dual character must be taken into account. A religion consists of a group of people whose identity it helps to define. But a religion also consists of ideas. There is potential social benefit in speech against Catholicism or anti-Catholicism, for example, but not against members of those groups. There is no similar differentiation regarding racial hate speech. There is simply no possible social benefit arising from speech against 'blacks' as 'blacks', and there is no such thing as speech against the idea of 'blackness'.[91]

The difference between the two types of speech, that targeting ideas and that targeting groups, can be understood by comparison to other possible categories of hate speech. In the landmark case *R.A.V. v. City of St. Paul*,[92] the US Supreme Court ruled on the constitutionality of a St Paul ordinance that banned offensive speech on the basis of race, colour, creed, religion, or gender. It held the ordinance was invalid because it constituted content discrimination:[93] it did not ban speech on other possible bases such as political affiliation, union membership, or homosexuality. 'The First Amendment does not permit [the city] to impose special prohibitions on those speakers who express views on disfavored subjects', reasoned the Court. The law was deemed to be unconstitutional because the prohibition was based on the *subject* of the speech.[94]

Interestingly, although the case dealt with racial hate speech, the Court criticized the ordinance by using an example from discourse about religion. Under the ordinance, stated Justice Scalia, for the majority:[95] 'One could hold up a sign saying, for example, that all "anti-Catholic bigots" are misbegotten; but not that all "papists" are, for that would insult and provoke violence "on the basis of religion".' Under the ordinance, the Court reasoned, speech against a religion would be prohibited, but speech against those who oppose religion would not. Thus, the Court saw the ordinance as constituting not just content discrimination but also impermissible and unconstitutional viewpoint discrimination.

Indeed, one-sided prohibitions on speech concerning religion, which apply to some sides of the debate but not to others, are an unacceptable limitation of free speech and freedom of religion. Furthermore, any prohibition that stifles speech concerning whose religious beliefs are right or wrong, even in insulting terms, is an unwarranted limitation on the critical-expressive aspect of religious freedom, one of the key justifications of this right.[96] Legislation against religious hate speech should follow an approach that distinguishes between permissible offensive speech against ideas and impermissible offensive speech against people *qua* members of a religious group. Some hints of such an approach can be discerned in Justice Stevens' concurring opinion, in which he argues that the St Paul ordinance is not discriminatory because it does not bar hurling fighting words based on conflicting ideas, but does bar anyone from hurling such words based on the recipient's race, colour, creed, religion or gender.

Contrary to the reasoning of the Court, I would argue that political affiliation and union membership are different from race, creed and gender. Speech against political affiliation and union membership targets views (which should be permissible), while speech against race, colour or gender targets groups or inherent characteristics (which should, under certain conditions, be impermissible). Religion can belong to both categories: speech against religion can be either against a religious view or against a religious group of people, making it harder to distinguish between speech that should be permissible and speech that should not. In the case of the former, freedom to use offensive speech against religious beliefs may have a social benefit. In the discussion of a Canadian law prohibiting speech likely to expose a person to hatred or contempt because of his religion (among other grounds),[97] Greenawalt rightly points out that some religious views deserve hatred and contempt, such as religious racist views. This law was the subject of the *Taylor*[98] case in the Supreme Court of Canada. The Court decided that the law was not a restriction of freedom of expression intolerable in a free and democratic society.[99] However, the dissent argued that the scope of the prohibition was too broad and invasive, catching more expressive conduct than can be justified. The use of the words 'hatred' and 'contempt', argued the dissent, are vague, subjective and susceptible of a wide range of meanings, extending the scope of the law to cover expression presenting little threat of fostering hatred or discrimination and even reaching speech that is, in fact, anti-discriminatory.[100] There was no defence in the law under discussion regarding honest religious disagreement – Greenawalt believes the Court should have noted this.

I would put the criticism more broadly: religions consist, on the one hand, of views and, on the other, of people whose identity is defined by belonging to them. Any prohibition on religious hate speech should be approached with this differentiation between speech against ideas and speech against a group of people in mind so as to prohibit the latter but not the former. When speech is religiously motivated, the decision as to what comprises permissible speech must consider not only freedom of expression but also freedom of religion, especially so if the offending speech is claimed to be inherent to the practice of religion, such as reading or publishing sacred texts which contain the offending speech. In *Alba v. The State of Israel*,[101] the Supreme Court of Israel denied an appeal against the appellant's conviction for incitement to racism[102] for publishing an article, presuming to rely on an interpretation of religious texts, claiming that, under Jewish law, the killing of non-Jews was a lesser offence than the killing of Jews. Alba had relied on the problematic statutory defence of quotation of religious scripture.[103] The majority judges did not accept the defence, as they found the publication a misleading presentation of Jewish scripture showing a clear intent to incite to racism.

But the defence itself is problematic: why should speech that constitutes reiteration of existing religious doctrine be treated differently from other hate speech? Either all hate speech prohibitions should be subject to determination of intent, or they should not be. Why should religious speech be acceptable where other speech would not be? Under the classification suggested in this chapter, which makes speech inciting against religious ideas permissible but speech inciting against people based on their religion impermissible, speech such as Alba's would not be protected merely by virtue of its religious sources.

A much broader prohibition of religious speech aimed at maintaining peaceful relations between communities is evident in the approach of the Supreme Court of India. In the *Hindutva*[104] cases, the Indian Supreme Court ruled that the prohibition on seeking votes using religious grounds[105] falls under a legitimate public order exception to the constitutional free speech guarantee,[106] relying on India's constitutionally determined secular character for the assertion that such expression is against decency and propriety in a secular society.[107] Toleration between religious communities was seen as paramount to any consideration of free expression. The Court viewed the principle of a secular society, and indeed the attempt to maintain tolerance between religions, as justifying a displacement of religious speech from the public-political arena in its most crucial process – democratic elections. It is suggested that the complete prohibition on religious election speech goes beyond the legitimate aim of maintaining religious tolerance. Only speech actually provoking hatred and strife between religions should be prohibited.

6.6 Conclusions

It has been seen that viewing religious freedom as an expressive-individualistic right has important consequences for analysing the permissible limitations of this right in cases of religious speech. It has been argued that, under an individualistic approach, the protection of religious speech would be equal to that of other political speech (while under a community approach more would be left to the determination of the state). Under the individualistic-expressive-critical view religious freedom protects not just the speaker but also the willing recipient of the speech.

An examination of proselytism has revealed that the limitations placed on proselytism, though explained as protection of personal autonomy, in keeping with an individualistic perception of religious freedom, may be due more to a conception of this right that tries to maintain the identity of the proselytized or even the identity and cohesiveness of the group itself. In weighing the balance between the free exchange of religious ideas and the preservation of existing religious identity, an individualistic-expressive conception of the right would see more value in the former, while the community conception would see more value in the latter. An individualistic-expressive approach would thus limit restrictions on proselytism to those that impair individual autonomy and negate free choice, in the same way that other types of persuasive speech are regulated.

An individualistic-expressive approach would see value in speech considered blasphemous by a religious group. This would mean not only that the state could not restrict such speech, but also that it might have to protect the individual even from sanctions by the religious community. The question of religious sanctions within the group directly confronts the religious freedom of the group with that of the individual. The group approach would favour allowing the group its own sanctions, including expulsion, against those it considers to veer from its doctrine. An expressive-individualistic approach would seek to implement human rights even regarding sanctions within the group. This would be an extreme implementation of the individualistic-expressive approach, as it would mean that the group would not have unlimited discretion even in the application of its own doctrine.

The view of religious freedom as a right that protects both the expression of ideas and the equality of members of all religions in the public sphere would lead to a treatment of hate speech regulation that would differentiate between speech about ideas and speech about members of religious groups.

Notes

1   Recognized in all major human rights instruments, including: Article 19(2) International Covenant on Civil and Political Rights (adopted 16 December 1966) 999 UNTS 171

(ICCPR), and Article 10 European Convention on Human Rights and Fundamental Freedom (adopted 4 November 1950) 213 UNTS 221 (ECHR).

2 *Wingrove v. UK* (1996) 24 EHRR 1 ECtHR.

See similarly App. no. 42571/98 *I.A. v. Turkey*: 'A State may therefore legitimately consider it necessary to take measures aimed at repressing certain forms of conduct, including the imparting of information and ideas, judged incompatible with respect for the freedom of thought, conscience and religion of others (It is, however, for the Court to give a final ruling on the restriction's compatibility with the Convention).'

3 This approach led the Court, by majority vote, to accept censorship of a film bound to outrage some Christian believers, as it viewed the restriction of free speech (Article 10(2), ECHR) as a legitimate protection of the religious freedom of others. See also App. no. 64016/00 *Giniewski v. France*. In App. no. 44179/98 *Murphy v. Ireland* however, the Court stressed that 'supervision [by the Court] can be considered to be all the more necessary given the rather open-ended notion of respect for the religious beliefs of others and the risks of excessive interferences with freedom of expression under the guise of action taken against allegedly offensive material.'

4 Compare the discussion of the deference accorded to state policy in issues concerning religion in the Charter of Fundamental Rights of the European Union in Chapter 1.

5 Judgment of February 5, 2001, *Olmedo-Bustos v. Chile*, Inter-American Court of Human Rights (Ser. C) No. 73 (2001).

6 The American Commission, which brought the case to the Court, thought that Article 12 had been breached.

7 See discussion in Chapter 2.

8 *Choudhury v. UK* [1990] 12 HRLJ 172.

9 *R. v. Chief Metropolitan Magistrate, ex p Choudhury* [1991] 1QB 429 [1991] 1 All ER 306, QB.

10 *Manoussakis v. Greece* (1996) 23 EHRR 387 ECtHR.

11 Ibid.

12 *Watchtower Bible & Tract Society of New York v. Village of Stratton* 536 U.S. 150 (2002); 122 S.Ct. 2080.

13 E.g., ICCPR, Article 18 (right to adopt religion of choice); the American Convention on Human Rights, OAS TS No. 36, at 1 (adopted 22 November 1969) 1114 UNTS 123, Article 12(1) (prohibiting impairment of the right to change religion).

14 Article 12(1) refers specifically to a right to disseminate religion or belief.

15 Under the ECHR *Kokkinakis v. Greece* (1994) 17 EHRR 397 ECtHR. See also *Larissis v. Greece* (1999) 27 EHRR 329 ECtHR.

16 See also P. M. Taylor, 'The questionable grounds of objections to proselytism and certain other forms of religious expression', *Brigham Young University Law Review*, 2006, which criticizes a third justification offered for prohibitions on proselytism – that of respect for the rights of others.

17 Although HRC General Comment No. 22 makes clear that there is no distinction between coercion to convert and coercion to adhere to a religion, both are prohibited under Article 18 of the ICCPR. It states, in paragraph 5:

Article 18.2 bars coercion that would impair the right to have or adopt a religion or belief, including the use of threat of physical force or penal sanctions to compel believers or non-believers to adhere to their religious beliefs and congregations, to recant their religion or belief or to convert.

Available at http://www.unhchr.ch/tbs/doc.nsf/%28Symbol%29/9a30112c27d1 167cc12563ed004d8f15?Opendocument (accessed 8 December 2009).

18 E. Odio Benito, *Elimination of all forms of intolerance and discrimination based on religion or belief*, New York: United Nations, 1989, 26.

19 A. Krishnaswami, *Study in the matter of religious rights and practices - report of the Special Rapporteur of the Sub-Commission on Prevention of Discrimination and Protection of Minorities*, New York: United Nations, 1960.

20 Rule 1(3) of his 16 proposed rules.

21 UN Doc. A/60/399.

22 She has opined that:

> [A]ny form of coercion by State and non-State actors aimed at religious conversion is prohibited under international human rights law, and any such acts have to be dealt with within the remit of criminal and civil law. Missionary activity is accepted as a legitimate expression of religion or belief and therefore enjoys the protection afforded by Article 18 of ICCPR and other relevant international instruments. Missionary activity cannot be considered a violation of the freedom of religion and belief of others if all involved parties are adults able to reason on their own and if there is no relation of dependency or hierarchy between the missionaries and the objects of the missionary activities.
>
> … [C]ertain forms of "unethical" conversion are not per se contrary to international standards. Moreover, while some of these acts may not enjoy protection under human rights law, they should not as a result necessarily be seen to constitute a criminal offence …[C]ases of alleged "unethical" conversion be addressed on a case-by-case basis, examining the context and circumstances in each individual situation and dealt with in accordance with the common criminal and civil legislation … [T]he adoption of laws criminalizing in abstracto certain acts leading to "unethical" conversion should be avoided, in particular where these laws could apply even in the absence of a complaint by the converted person.

Available at http://www2.ohchr.org/english/issues/religion/docs/A_60_399.pdf (Paragraphs 67–68) (accessed 8 December 2009).

23 Several justifications of proselytism in particular instances have been offered which rely explicitly on the maintenance of community identity, for example, Makau Wa Mutua's approach that indigenous African religions are not equipped to deal with missionary religions, and so state action against external religions is justified (M. Wa Mutua, 'Limitation on religious rights', in J. D. van der Vyver and J. Witte (eds.), *Religious human rights in global perspective, Volume II – Legal perspectives*, The Hague: Martinus Nijhoff Publishers, 1996, 417). T. Földesi, 'The main problems of religious freedom in Eastern Europe' in J. D. van der Vyver and J. Witte (eds.), *Religious human rights in global perspective Vol. II – Legal perspectives*, The Hague: Martinus Nijhoff Publishers, 1996, 243, who argues that after years of communism and state-sponsored secularism in Eastern Europe giving some legal protection to the historical church by restrictions on proselytizing religions from the outside is justified. Lerner argues for a right of the community against the right of those who wish to proselytize based on a right to privacy, recognized in Article 17 of the ICCPR, although this would seem to be a right that can only be a right of individuals (N. Lerner, *Religion, beliefs and international human rights*, Markinoll: Orbis Books, 2000, 117). These justifications remain outside the present discussion, which deals with the ostensibly liberal individualistic justifications, which, as will be seen, also indirectly protect community cohesiveness.

24 *Kokkinakis v. Greece* (1994) 17 EHRR 397 ECtHR.

25 Law no. 1672/1939 (Section 2) makes it an offence to engage in 'proselytism', defined as: 'an attempt to intrude on the religious beliefs of a person of a different religious persuasion (eterodoxos), with the aim of undermining those beliefs, either by any kind of inducement or promise of an inducement or moral support or material assistance, or by fraudulent means or by taking advantage of his inexperience, trust, need, low intellect or naïvety'.

26 Even though it found a breach of the Convention in its application in the particular case.

27 12 BverfGE 1 (1960).

28 See D. P. Currie, The *constitution of the Federal Republic of Germany*, Chicago: University of Chicago Press, 1994, 253.

29 Section 174A, the penal law, 1977.

30 Section 174B, the penal law, 1977.
31 Section 368, the penal law, 1977.
32 Law No. 2001-504 of 12 June 2001.
33 Section 20, amending Section 223-15-2, the French Criminal Code.
34 *Larissis v. Greece* (1999) 27 EHRR 329 ECtHR, para. 45.
35 The holding of the Court, however, which dealt with proselytizing without material inducement, seems right to differentiate between a military context, in which it did not view a Greek conviction for proselytising as an infringement of Article 9, and the civilian context, in which it viewed the ban as infringing Article 9.
36 Criminalization of the acceptance of material remuneration by the convert (Section 174B of the Israel penal law, 1977, as described earlier) may be an even clearer infringement of religious freedom. Everyone has a right to change religion. A prohibition on accepting remuneration for doing so is a limitation of this right. It may be justified as a paternalistic limitation, prohibiting people from becoming victims of exploitation, but in its broad scope it may be an impermissible protection of the group rather than a permissible protection of the individual.
37 Civ. App. (Jerusalem) 3060/02 *Stern v. Palestine Post* (decided 18.11.2003).
38 UDHR Article 18, (the right to change religion). This provision was omitted from the ICCPR, ICESCR, and the 1981 Declaration, which, however, does not derogate from existing rights (see Chapter 1). So, apostasy laws, which exist in some Islamic states, such as Sudan, forbidding Muslims from changing their religion, are clearly in contravention of international norms. This right is explicitly recognized in CCPR General Comment No. 22, para. 5.
39 D. J. Sullivan, 'Advancing the freedom of religion or belief through the UN Declaration on the Elimination of Religious Intolerance and Discrimination', *American Journal of International Law*, 82, 1988, 495.
40 A. Krishnaswami, *Study in the matter of religious rights and practices – Report of the Special Rapporteur of the Sub-Commission on Prevention of Discrimination and Protection of Minorities*, New York: United Nations, 1960, 38, and A. V. Ribiero, *Implementation of the Declaration on the Elimination of All Forms of Intolerance and of Discrimination based on Religion or Belief*, New York: United Nations, 1987, 15, cited by D. J. Sullivan, Ibid.
41 This was the case in Pakistan, following the legislation of the Anti-Islamic Activities of the Quadiani Group, Lahori Group and Ahmadis (Prohibition and Punishment) Ordinance, 1984, which prohibits members of the Ahmadia from calling themselves Muslims. In *Zaheer-ud-din v. The State* 1993 SCMR 1718, the constitutional validity of the Ordinance was upheld by Pakistan's Supreme Court (over a dissent which thought it breached religious freedom). The Court majority opinion was based on the rationale of a 'religious trademark', that a prohibition on the Ahmadi from calling themselves by a title that already belonged to others was not a breach of their religious freedom. For a criticism of the decision, see M. Lau, 'The case of *Zaheer-ud-din v. The State* and its impact on the fundamental right to freedom of religion', *Yearbook of Islamic and Middle Eastern Law*, 1, 1994, 565.
42 Any approach consistent with rudiments of human rights protection would be opposed to the kind of blasphemy provisions such as those included in Sections 295-B, C and 298-A, B and C of the Pakistan Penal Code. These mandate life term or death sentences, are used to violate religious freedom are not proportionate and serve no legitimate purpose (in addition to the breach of human rights inherent in the death penalty for any offence).
43 The common law offences of blasphemy and blasphemous libel were abolished by s. 79 of the Criminal Justice and Immigration Act 2008. See also the Racial and Religious Hatred Act 2006.
44 An offence of blasphemy, or similar offences, exist in other states, including democratic states, such as Austria (Articles 188 and 189, the Penal Code), Denmark (Paragraphs 140 and 266b, the Penal Code), Finland (Section 10 of Chapter 17, the

Penal Code), Greece (Articles 198, 199, and 201, the Penal Code), Italy (Articles 402–406, the Penal Code), and the Netherlands (Article 147, the Penal Code). These are mostly not in use. The analysis of the former English offence illustrates the principles involved.

In many other liberal democracies, blasphemy is not an offence. In the USA, following *Burstyn v. Wilson* 343 U.S. 495 (1952) prosecutions for blasphemy (under state blasphemy laws) would violate the US Constitution, although some state blasphemy laws remain, unenforceable, on the books (such as Chapter 272 of the Massachusetts General Laws, Section 36).

45 D. Shelton and A. Kiss, 'A draft model law on freedom of religion, with commentary', in J. D. van der Vyver and J. Witte Jr., *Religious human rights in global perspective Vol. II – Legal perspectives*, The Hague: Martinus Nijhoff Publishers, 1996, 559.

46 History of the crime of blasphemy in Europe, see A. Cabantous, *Blasphemy: Impious speech in the West from the 17th to the 19th century*, trans. E. Rauth, New York: Columbia University Press, 2001.

47 R. C. Post, 'Cultural heterogeneity and law: pornography, blasphemy, and the First Amendment', *California Law Review*, 76, 1988, 306.

48 *Taylor's Case* 86 Eng. Rep. 189, 1 Vent. 293 (K.B. 1676).

49 *Rex v. Woolston* 94 Eng. Rep. 112, 1 Barn. K.B. 162 (1729).

50 Ibid., 113.

51 The Law Commission Working Paper No. 79: Offences against religion and public worship 5–6 (1981).

52 *Corway v. Independent Newspapers* [1996] IEHC 27; [1999] 4 IR 484, discussed in S. Ranalow, 'Bearing a constitutional cross: examining blasphemy and the judicial role in *Corway v. Independent Newspapers*', *Trinity College Law Review*, 2000, 95.

53 Similarly, in Italy, Articles 402–406 of the Penal Code prohibit offence to the state religion. The repeal of the law proclaiming Catholicism to be the official state religion in Italy apparently means that these provisions are no longer in force. A different provision, Article 724, prohibits insult to any religion.

54 *Otto-Preminger-Institut v. Austria* (1995) 19 EHRR 34 ECtHR.

55 This followed similar reasoning by the European Commission in an earlier case, *Lemon v. UK* (1982) 5 EHRR 123 ECtHR. S. Leader, 'Blasphemy and human rights', *Modern Law Review*, 46, 1983, 340, argues that the Commission should not have recognized a right of citizens not to be offended in their religious beliefs, as only fundamental rights explicitly mentioned in the Convention are 'rights of others' which may justify limitation on free speech. In *Handyside v. UK* (1979–80) 1 EHRR 737 ECtHR, dealing with speech that did not address religion, the European Court offered a test of balance of interests under the European Convention when offensive speech is involved.

56 The dissenting opinion (of Judges Palm, Pekkanen and Makarczyk) was that a right to protection of religious feelings is not included in the Article 9 right to freedom of religion. The opinion states that it is legitimate for the state to curtail offensive anti-religious speech only when it is violent or abusive. The dissent argues that the applicants can rely on both Article 10 and Article 9, as freedom of religion and belief includes a right to express views critical of the religious opinions of others.

57 Richards argues that such protection of group identity interests, as were recognized in this case, inevitably implicates the court in deciding who are the groups and what are the beliefs that are owed respect, and it will tend to adopt the views of the dominant religious groups on these questions (D.A.J. Richards, *Free speech and the politics of identity*, Oxford: Oxford University Press, 1999).

58 *Otto-Preminger-Institut v. Austria* (1995) 19 EHRR 34 ECtHR, para. 47.

59 Ibid., para. 49.

60 B. Parekh, 'Equality in a multicultural society', in J. Franklin (ed.), *Equality*, London: Institute for Public Policy Research, 1997, 145.

61 See description of some of the public discussion and consequences of the Rushdie affair in R. L. Able, *Speaking respect, respecting speech*, Chicago: University of Chicago Press, 1998, 21–43.

62 *R. v. Lemon* [1979] AC 617, [1979] 1 All ER 898, HL. This was the subject of a failed application to the European Court (*Lemon v. UK* (1982) 5 EHRR 123 ECtHR).

63 Even if a criminal offence is rarely, or even never, used for prosecution by the state, its existence may have other legal implications, e.g. its use for a private prosecution. Another such use was as a basis for a request for an injunction against an exhibition in Australia, which was ultimately denied. (*Pell v. Council of Trustees of the National Gallery of Victoria*, [1998] 2 VR 392 (Supreme Court of Victoria), see Casenote, *Melbourne University Law Review* 22, 1998, 217.)

64 'Offences against religion and public worship', Law Com.145, 1985 (HMSO, London).

65 Concluding observations on state report of UK, ICCPR, A/55/40 vol. I (2000), 47.

66 House of Lords Select Committee Report on Religious Offences in England and Wales, 10 April 2003, Volume I, HL Paper 95–I.

67 The Report was initiated following the Religious Offences Bill, but ultimately dealt with a wider scope of subjects, including the question of the offence of blasphemy raised by the Law Commission's 'Offences against religion and public worship' report, Law Com.145, 1985 (HMSO, London) and by the 'incitement' clause which was omitted from the Anti-Terrorism Crime and Security Act 2001 (see further M. M. Idriss, 'Religion and the Anti-Terrorism, Crime and Security Act 2001', *Criminal Law Review*, 2002, 890).

68 Select Committee Report in Annex 3.

69 Ibid., 13–18.

70 Ibid., 13.

71 Ibid., 14.

72 Ibid., 15. This option was suggested by Lord Scarman in *R. v Lemon* [1979] AC 617, 658.

73 *Ramji Lal Modi v. State of Uttar Pradesh*, AIR 1957 SC 622; 1957 SCR 860.

74 As discussed in Chapter 2.

75 Comm. No. 736/1997 *Ross v. Canada* CCPR/C/70/D/736/1997.

76 Comm. No. 104/1981 *J.R.T. and the W.G. Party v. Canada* CCPR/C/18/D/104/1981. The author of the communication whose telephone services were curtailed by the Canadian authorities posted pre-recorded messages denouncing 'the dangers … of international Jewry leading the world into wars, unemployment and inflation and the collapse of world values and principles'. (This communication concerned the same individual and party as the Canadian Supreme Court Case: *Canada (Human Rights Commission) v. Taylor* [1990] 3 S.C.R. 892 discussed in the next section.)

77 Some further guidance can be gleaned from the decision of the HRC in Comm. No. 550/1993 *Faurisson v. France* CCPR/C/58/D/550/1993, which addresses Article 19, but the reasoning of which is applicable also to Article 18. The assessment of incitement is made in regard to the historical context. Thus, Holocaust denial constitutes incitement against Jews, legitimately prohibited according to all Committee members. But a French law, the 'Gayssot Act', which amends the Law on the Freedom of the Press of 1881, Section 24, was deemed overbroad by the concurring Committee members, as it would prohibit bona fide research connected with matters decided by the Nüremberg Tribunal, and thus would contravene Article 19.

78 Proposal for a European Union Framework Decision on Combating Racism and Xenophobia (2002) OJ C75E/269. See also http://europa.eu/legislation_summaries/justice_freedom_security/combating_discrimination/l33_en.htm (accessed 8 December 2009). To view online, see http://www.consilium.europa.eu/ueDocs/cms_Data/docs/pressData/en/jha/93741.pdf (accessed 8 December 2009).

79 Article 3(a).

80 Article 4(a).

81 Article 4(b).
82 The press release following the 2794th Council meeting, in Luxembourg in April 2007 stated that:

'The Council reached a general approach on a Framework Decision on Racism and Xenophobia.

The text will be adopted once some parliamentary scrutiny reservations have been lifted and the text has been revised by the legal linguistic group.' See http://www.consilium.europa.eu/ueDocs/cms_Data/docs/pressData/en/jha/93741.pdf (accessed 8 December 2009).

83 Available at http://assembly.coe.int/Main.asp?link=/Documents/AdoptedText/ta07/EREC1805.htm (accessed 8 December 2009).
84 Available at http://www.venice.coe.int/docs/2008/CDL-AD(2008)026-e.pdf (accessed 8 December 2009).
85 Section 119.
86 Sections 18–19.
87 House of Lords Select Committee Report on Religious Offences in England and Wales, 10 April 2003, Volume I, HL Paper 95–I.
88 E. Odio Benito, *Elimination of all forms of intolerance and discrimination based on religion or belief*, New York: United Nations, 1989, 25.
89 Indeed, fear of allowing over-broad restrictions apparently caused the omission of provisions regarding a duty to prohibit hate speech (religious among others) from the Constitution of the Republic of South Africa, 1993, after it was initially included in the ANC draft Bill of Rights issued in 1990 (in *South African Journal on Human Rights*, 7, 1991, 110). See E. Neisser, 'Hate speech in the new South Africa: constitutional considerations for a land recovering from decades of racial repression and violence', *South Africa Journal of Human Rights*, 10, 1994, 336.
90 For a few interesting positions in the vast theoretical literature on this issue, see C. Sunstein, *Democracy and the problem of free speech*, New York: The Free Press, 1993, Chapter 6; R. C. Post, 'Racist speech, democracy and the First Amendment', in H. L. Gates et al. (eds), *Speaking of race, speaking of sex*, New York: New York University Press, 1994, 115; O. Fiss, *The irony of free speech*, Cambridge, MA: Harvard University Press, 1996, especially 16–22.
91 In some states, such as Brazil, racial hate speech laws have been interpreted to include religious groups (see Superior Tribunal de Justiça HC 15155/RS (decided, 18/12/2001)). In the UK, the judicial interpretation in *Mandla v. Dowell Lee* [1983] 2 AC 548, [1983] 1 All ER 1062, HL (which dealt with discrimination, not with hate speech) according to which the Race Relations Act 1976 would encompass some religious groups but not others, was one of the motivations for legislation broadening the prohibitions of the Race Relations Act to cover religious groups, as discussed in this chapter.
92 *R.A.V. v. City of St. Paul* 505 US 377 (1992).
93 In any case, the ordinance was deemed over-broad by all the Justices as it was not limited to a prohibition of 'fighting words', utterances that convey almost no exposition of ideas and whose value is clearly outweighed by their harm, so as to except them from First Amendment protection. (See *Chaplinsky v. New Hampshire*, 315 US 568 (1942); *Beauharnais v. Illinois*, 343 US 250 (1952)).
94 The conclusion from *R.A.V.* is that the only way a US state can legislate against hate speech is by prohibiting injurious speech based on any group affiliation, or any injurious speech (so as not to run afoul of the Court's prohibition on content discrimination). Indeed, in *Virginia v. Black* (538 US 343 (2003)), a statute that prohibited one type of hate speech (cross burning) for whatever reason was held constitutional by the Supreme Court. It reasoned that as long as the prohibition does not discriminate as to the content of the speech, a state may choose to prohibit only those forms of intimidation that are most likely to inspire fear of bodily harm.
95 Per Justice Scalia, *R. A. V. v. City of St. Paul* 505 US 377, 392.
96 See discussion in Chapter 2.

97 The law prohibited 'to communicate telephonically … any matter that is likely to expose a person or persons to hatred or contempt by reason of the fact that that person or those persons are identifiable on the basis of a prohibited ground of discrimination'. The prohibited grounds of discrimination include (though are not restricted to) race, national or ethnic origin, colour and religion.

98 Canadian Supreme Court Case: *Canada (Human Rights Commission) v. Taylor* [1990] 3 S.C.R. 892.

99 Ibid., 939–940.

100 Ibid., 955–961.

101 Crim. App. 2831/95 *Alba v. The State of Israel*, 50 (5) PD 221.

102 Article 144B of the penal law, 1977 creates an offence of publication with intent to incite to racism. The different treatment of religious hate speech is clear in Israeli law: in addition to the offence of publication with intent to incite to racism there is an offence of incitement to racism (Article 144A), for which no specific intent is required. However, this broader offence is limited to grounds of race, colour or ethnic-national origin, but not religion.

103 Article 144C(b) of the penal law, 1977 states that publication of quotations from scripture and prayer books or practice of religious ceremony will not be considered as constituting the offence of incitement to racism, unless they were done with an intention to incite.

104 *Dr. Ramesh Yeshwant Prabhoo v. Prabhar Kashinath Kunte* (1996) 1 SCC 130; AIR 1996 SC 1113; [1996] 3 CHRLD 343.

105 Articles 123(3) and (3A) of the Criminal Code.

106 Article 19(2) of the Constitution.

107 India is defined in the preamble to its Constitution as a secular state. Its secular character is reinforced in Article 28(1), which guarantees that: 'No religious instruction shall be provided in any educational institution wholly maintained out of State funds.' This extreme position against the involvement of the state with institutionalized religion is evident only in states with marked church state separation, such as the USA.

7   Conclusion

Religions, which pre-date the state as a source of power, seemed to be on the wane with the emergence of modernity, but in today's world the conflicts surrounding religion, state, human rights, individuals and collectives, and national and international law are as prominent as ever. In a recent analysis of ongoing armed conflicts worldwide, out of 16 major armed conflicts ongoing in 2009, about half were attributable, at least partially, to a religious cause.[1] Crucially, since 2001 the conflict with al-Qaeda could be added to this list. The role of religion in the modern world has, however, been largely overlooked by international lawyers. It is of paramount importance that freedom of religion, and its limitations, be defined and protected in a coherent manner by international law.

This study has developed an argument for the preference of religious freedom as an individual right over religious freedom as a group right. Its first objective was to point out a crucial conflict between these two conceptions and delineate its many facets, some of them in areas in which the conflict may not have been initially anticipated. The second objective was to persuade that, in this conflict, individual rights should prevail. Throughout the discussion, it has been seen that, although a preference of individual rights over group rights raises considerable problems, a preference of group rights raises problems, both theoretical and practical, which are even harder to surmount.

7.1 Theoretical conclusions

Religious freedom can and should be interpreted as an individual right, and as a group right only if derived from individual rights and not overriding them. This is the main conclusion of this study.

7.1.1 Conceptual argument as to the existence of group rights

7.1.1.1 Group rights are incommensurate with the concept of human rights

The purpose of human rights is to protect men and women from the power of the collective, monopolized by the state (Chapter 2). Therefore, to use the concept of human rights merely to transfer power from the state to groups within the state empties this concept of all meaning. So, there could not be a right of the group itself that overrides individual rights. Thus, there could only be a group right of religious freedom in the sense of an aggregate of individual rights.

Even when dealing with the most nuclear group, the family, the right of the family group cannot be substituted for a right of the individual child (Chapter 5).

7.1.2 Arguments as to the dual character of the right of religious freedom

7.1.2.1 The dual character of religious freedom and the right of the individual both to belong to, and dissent from the group, must be upheld

In the theoretical exposition (Chapter 2) it was argued, based, among other things, on the justifications given to religious freedom in liberal theory, that this right has two aspects. It is a right that protects the ability to express and criticize. It is also a right that protects identity and, therefore, equality. It is a right of doing and of being.

The evolving politics of identity, which centre on nationality, race, ethnicity and religion, have resulted in a shift to the protection of the identity aspect of religious freedom (Chapter 1). But both aspects of this right need to be maintained and protected: the identity aspect, which is connected to belonging to a community, and the expressive-critical aspect, connected to individuality (especially individual stances against the community).

This duality, between right of identity and right of expression, was shown in Chapter 6 to be key to the analysis of religious speech and its legitimate boundaries. It was shown that individual religious speech, including speech which criticizes the group the speaker belongs to, or a group the speaker does not belong to, can only be effectively protected through an individualistic perception of this right.

7.1.3 Arguments as to why individual rights should supersede group rights, even if group rights are recognized

7.1.3.1 On entering a religious group, 'you do not leave your rights at the door'

Because religion is part of one's identity, individuals should not be made to choose between participation in religious activities, communities and institutions, and their basic rights, such as freedom of speech and non-discrimination. It is the meaningful participation in religious life sought by members and workers as a manifestation of their religious freedom that calls for guarantees of rights by the state. Therefore, religious communities and organizations should themselves be required to respect rights of individuals.

This argument was developed and nuanced in Chapter 3. If religious organizations are to exist, they clearly must be able to put certain demands on their members, under certain conditions. Human rights within the organization will be interpreted according to context, but this does not mean that members waive their rights when entering the religious organization.

7.1.3.2 *The public character of religions mandates respect for individual rights*

Religions have a public, as well as private, character and so must accord individual rights in their public activities. This is true especially of state established religions, but also in a lesser measure of all religions. A religious organization cannot be said to be a wholly private affair. For example, religious schools, as providers of education, fulfil a role of the state. Educational institutions that belong to one religious denomination may have obligations to respect certain human rights of all students (Chapter 4). Institutions of religious communities are also employers. As such, they must have human rights obligations towards their employees. As seen in Chapters 3 and 4, religions control important aspects of personal life through marriage, divorce and family status. This too is an exercise of authority relegated by the state. Even when personal law is exercised by the religious community without recognition of the state, it is exercising state-like authority as far as the members affected are concerned. Religions in this case cannot be considered purely private institutions. Even towards members who dissent from the group, the religious group should not be considered to have unlimited discretion as to sanctions, in disregard of human rights (Chapter 6).

The classical-liberal distinction between the public realm and the private realm is particularly unhelpful in the realization of individual religious freedom. Religious freedom is often curtailed by actors and arrangements operating in the private sphere, not least by religious communities and religious organizations themselves, acting towards their own members or others. Traditionally, human rights law has addressed the public realm, the abuse of citizen's rights by the state. To advance religious freedom, however, it must go beyond these boundaries and address abuse of individual rights by the group as sanctioned by the state.

7.1.3.3 *There is no effective voluntary choice and so individual freedom must be respected both within and without groups*

Freedom of religion must be redefined to include both freedom to choose, manifest and practice religion, as stated in many existing international and national instruments, and freedom within religious organizations and communities. If individuals' freedoms within religions are restricted, this impairs their right both to choose religions and to remain within their chosen religion. Religious freedom of both those who are unable effectively to leave a religion and those who may not wish to do so is breached. Especially harmed are socially weaker members within the religious communities (such as children, dissenters – who may be considered blasphemers and apostates by their religion – and women in some societies).

However, religions, which are social constructs, are defined by their set of rules. Some imposition of rules within community institutions must be acceptable, as long as the ability to leave the religious group is granted.

Exclusive jurisdiction over matters of personal law should not be accorded to a religious community to which individuals may not have chosen to belong. As argued in Chapters 3 and 4, even where there is a choice, the state cannot deem its citizens to have waived their religious freedom merely by the fact of belonging to a religious group.

7.1.3.4 *Equal protection of members of minorities can and should be achieved through a conception of individual rights*

A strong argument encountered for recognition of group rights was that, in order to accord meaningful, rather than formal, equal treatment, the relevant social context should be taken into account. Specifically, it should be recognized that the existing social and legal framework is geared towards the majority religion. I agreed with these assumptions, but argued that this can be taken into account within the individual conception, by according substantive rather than formal equality. This may entail differential treatment of minority and majority religions, in order to achieve substantive equality.

Furthermore, analysis of rights that takes social context (majority/minority status) into account would mean that sometimes individuals should even have a right of religious freedom against religious groups of which they are not members. The religious freedom of children of minority religions may be adversely impacted both within the state school system and within the school system of another religious group. While it is legitimate for schools of both kinds to have regulations, religious freedom of students should be protected in schools of both kinds, taking into account factors such as majority/minority status of the pupil and the difference between private and public schools.

In fact, as seen mainly in Chapter 4, state principles of group autonomy, or simply majority/minority politics, may cause states to avoid intervening within minority religious communities in order to protect rights of individuals in those communities, even more than they avoid interference within the majority religious community. This has been exemplified in regard to rights of women in religious communities, in several states, each with a different religious composition.

It was shown that an important influence on religious freedom, the status of religions in the state, particularly established religions, has been largely ignored by international law. While arguing for an individual rights approach, this work has not ignored the importance of religion in forging ties that form social, communal and national identity. For this reason, an established state religion, in states in which there is one, while necessarily constituting some form of group preference, cannot be dismissed outright as illegitimate. However, the fact that there is a state religion should put on the state an onus of proving that no further discrimination is caused to members of minority religions, other than that inherent in the fact that one religion is considered a state religion and others are not.

7.1.4 *Argument as to further problems of religious freedom created by recognition of religious group rights in the state*

7.1.4.1 *According religious group rights involves the state in evaluation of the social worth of religious groups, thereby breaching state neutrality*

For the implementation of laws that accord group rights, often the state must accept one determination of the group and its representative leadership. This is frequently unacceptable to subgroups, dissenting leaders or individuals within the group. Any determination by the state between competing claims means it will not remain neutral. Group determination is not only misguided in principle, but is also problematic in application. The definition of the group causes the state to breach its neutrality. Even when the state is neutral, it is called on to make decisions that include value judgments on religions. According rights to groups adds further difficulties as it calls on the state to make legal determinations predicated on value judgments between subgroups and regarding group leadership.

This argument is qualified. In some cases, it was shown in Chapter 3, it is simply not possible to accord the right to individuals. Such for example, is allocation of funding to religions. It would not be possible to let each member decide what should be done with the funding, and so some form of group determination is unavoidable.

The conclusion of this work must be qualified in other ways as well. In some cases there was shown to be a moral justification for putting the peaceful relations within a mixed community above individual religious equality. In such a case, a group basis for equality could be used (proportional representation of the communities) rather than an individual basis (equal treatment regardless of a person's religion).

However, while these, and other, more complex considerations must be taken into account, they do not detract from the conclusion of the course of argument presented, namely that religious freedom must be understood as an individual right.

7.2 Some practical implications

The analysis suggested in this work has highlighted some of the important areas deficient in the protection of religious freedom. Two important areas of life have been left outside the scope of legal protection due to the classical liberal distinction between the public sphere, in which human rights are protected, and the private sphere, in which they are not. One of these is the workplace; another is the family.

In the workplace, human rights must be protected from private, as well as public, actors. This area has traditionally escaped the notice of human rights law, which has protected rights from the power of the state. However, here the distinction between the public and the private is not conducive to the protection of human rights. The place of work has become one of the important areas in which people spend much of their lives and so it exerts a strong influence on their lives, as much, if not more than the state. This status of the workplace as lying between the public and the private spheres was highlighted in Chapter 3 (regarding the rights of employees in workplaces with various degrees of religious affiliation) and in Chapter 5 (in the discussion of teachers and other public and private sector employees).

The ILO Discrimination (Employment and Occupation) Convention (No. 111) forbids discrimination in the workplace on various grounds, including religion. As shown, however, the question what constitutes discrimination on grounds of religion is much more complicated than it is on other grounds such as race or colour, precisely because of the individual and group claims made on this right. More detailed instruments are important. One such instrument is the EU Council Directive Establishing a General Framework for Equal Treatment in Employment and Occupation.[2] Other regional and international bodies should inquire into the adoption of similar detailed instruments protecting religious freedom and guaranteeing equal treatment in the workplace.

The other area explored in this study, in which religious freedom is harmed by the private/public distinction in the applicability of human rights law, is that of the family. Here too, traditionally, human rights law has not addressed infringements emanating from private actors, notably the family. Family law often implements religious perceptions. This shapes, to a large extent, the perception of women's role in the family and the community.

Women's religious freedom should be integrated into the mainstream of discourse on religious freedom and into any future legal instruments on religious freedom. The determinations of the Human Rights Committee in General Comment 28 should be implemented by states. The different UN human rights conventions, particularly the ICCPR, the ICESCR, and CEDAW should be interpreted according to the same principles as those elucidated in GC 28, so that equality of women guaranteed by these instruments could not be subject to restrictions or reservations based on religion.

Some more specific recommendations arose out of this discussion: The Human Rights Committee and the CEDAW Committee should call on signatory state parties in which personal law is religious law to legislate a secular non-discriminatory system of personal law.

International human rights law does not sufficiently protect rights of women within unofficial unions that are unrecognized by the state law (whether religious marriages, other unofficial marriages, or cohabitation). Such unions should be legally protected. This means ad hoc recognition of these unions as equal to marriages, in those instances in which rights of the spouses will be furthered and not harmed by the recognition.

A critical analysis of the influence of religion on the legal interpretation of gender roles in the state should also lead to a re-evaluation of the law regarding sexual orientation and the recognition of the need for specific international legal standards in this area.[3] Similarly to their role in defining gender roles, religions have played a role in defining morality and deviancy of sexual orientation. Both in the case of gender roles and in the case of sexual orientation, such definitions emanating from religious sources have been incorporated into the law.

Investigation of the right of the child to religious freedom has revealed a disparity between the assertion that a right of the child to religious freedom is protected and the underlying assumptions reflected in legal reality, which protects choices of parents, communities and states. It should be recognized that existing formulations in international instruments of the rights of parents to choose the religious education of the child should be understood as a right derivative of that of the child, a right to exercise the right for the immature child, who is the ultimate bearer of his own right to religious freedom.

Future international instruments that guarantee religious choice in education should include protection of gender equality. This is particularly so, as religious education is often sex segregated. While care must be taken not to deter parents from sending female children to schools, progress should be made, by education and by legal provisions, to elimination of sex disparity in education due to religious perceptions.

The analysis in this work of the oversight of the dual nature of the right of religious freedom has pointed to the unique way it should be protected in the marketplace of ideas. Incitement to religious hatred should be prohibited, but only through legislation that carefully circumscribes the ambit of protection and guards freedom of religious speech. International instruments which deal with religious hatred should differentiate between religious and other bases of hate speech, tailoring the provisions of religious hate speech to allow for expression attacking religious views but not expressions attacking members of religious groups.

It is important to develop legal means to prevent religions and religious organizations from infringing human rights. A crucial question is whether religions can be subjects of international law. There are clearly great difficulties in according legal personality to religions in international law: they are non-state entities, they operate in the spiritual realm and many do not have a clear institutional structure to which responsibility for violations can be imputed. However, the idea is not without basis. As has been seen, religions, through their representatives or through the actions of states, are already participants in the formation of international and national law, affecting human rights.[4]

Of course, religions vary greatly. It is easier to make the theoretical argument, as well as to delineate the practical application with regard to large religions with well-recognized, state-like institutions, than with regard to small, diffuse religions. The Catholic Church is the paradigmatic case for application of these international legal norms. It already takes part, directly and indirectly, in the formulation of international norms. These considerations will need to be taken into account in the discussion of the possibility for expansion of international human rights law and its application to religious bodies.

The political participation of religious parties that espouse undemocratic principles was explored (in Chapter 2). It was shown that, in addition to the considerations present regarding limitations on undemocratic parties that are not religious, religious freedom is a consideration that must be taken into account when limiting the political participation of such parties.

7.3 A few final words

This discussion can be placed within the broader debate on democratic liberalism in international law. Proponents of democratic liberalism in international law argue that the individuals who constitute the state must give their consent to the government in order to legitimize its actions at the international level,[5] and that only following a democratic process will validate a state's exercise of power. International lawyers of this school have also argued for linkage of the legitimacy of governments to observance of human rights as well as to participatory democracy.[6] The argument for democratic liberalism has been criticized, on various grounds, among them the potential harm of dividing the world into Western and non-Western states,[7] and that democratic liberalism accepts as legitimate only one view of religion and its place in the public sphere.

The role of religion in the international public sphere has become a focal point of attention for scholars of international relations. The study of law should explore the legal aspects of this debate. Huntington, in two influential articles,[8] argued that world politics are entering a new phase in which fundamental conflicts will not be between nation-states, or even ideological or political rivals, but between civilizations. These are differentiated from each other by their history, language, culture, tradition, and, most importantly, religion.[9]

This argument has caused considerable backlash. Among others, Ajami[10] counters Huntington's claims by arguing that modernity and secularism are on the rise even in non-Western states, which, according to Huntington's paradigm, should be on the opposite side of the culture clash to the Western world. He cites Algeria, India and Turkey as examples in which middle classes held off religious-traditionalist turns. It has been seen that this is a 'glass half full' description of situations that could equally be described, as 'the glass half empty'. In Algeria, democratic election rights were suspended as a way for the secular state to fend off a religious challenge to the democratic system (see Chapter 1). In Turkey, too, religious freedom is restricted in order to maintain separation of religion and state (see Chapters 3 and 5). In India, broad laws restricting religious speech have been recently used to curb fostering of religious strife (see Chapter 6). The conflict between religious and secular forces in these societies may have a price in civil liberties.

The study of religious freedom and human rights has particular importance for today's international society. Only a principled international approach, applied without prejudice, can protect religious freedom worldwide.

Notes

1   According to data compiled by the Stockholm International Peace Research Institute, *Yearbook 2001: armaments, disarmament and international security*, Oxford: Oxford University Press, 2001.

2   Council Directive 2000/78/EC of 27 November 2000 establishing a general framework for equal treatment in employment and occupation OJ L 303, 02/12/2000, 16–22.

3   Compare E. Heinze, *Sexual orientation – a human right: an essay on international human rights law*, Dordrecht: Martinus Nijhoff Publishers, 1995.

4 This has been shown in Chapter 4 in the context of women's religious freedom, but is true also in other areas in which religions have an important influence on daily life.

5 T. M. Franck, *The power of legitimacy among nations*, New York: Oxford University Press, 1990; T. M. Franck 'The emerging right to democratic governance', *American Journal of International Law*, 86, 1992, 46.

6 See, for instance, S. Marks, *The riddle of all constitutions: international law, democracy, and the critique of ideology*, New York: Oxford University Press, 2000.

7 T. Carothers, 'Empirical perspectives on the emerging norm of democracy in international law', *Proceedings of the American Society of International Law*, 1992, 261; further discussion, S. Marks, *The riddle of all constitutions: international law, democracy, and the critique of ideology*, New York: Oxford University Press, 2000, 46.

8 S. P. Huntington, 'The clash of civilizations?', *Foreign Affairs*, 1993, 22; S. P. Huntington, 'The west: unique, not universal', *Foreign Affairs*, 1996, 28.

9 While initially Huntington lists all these defining characteristics of civilization, his discussion refers almost exclusively to religions.

10 F. Ajami, 'The summoning', *Foreign Affairs*, 72, 1993, 2. This is one of a number of responses to Huntington that were published in this issue of *Foreign Affairs*.

Bibliography

Abe, M., 'The Buddhist view of human rights', in A. An-Na'im, *Human rights and religious values: an uneasy relationship?*, Amsterdam: Rodopi, 1995.

Able, R.L., *Speaking respect, respecting speech*, Chicago: University of Chicago Press, 1998.

Ackerman, B.A., *Social justice in the liberal state*, London: Yale University Press, 1980.

Ahdar, R., 'The child's right to a godly future', *The International Journal of Children's Rights*, 10, 2002, 89.

Ajami, F., 'The summoning', *Foreign Affairs*, 72, 1993, 2.

Alston, P. (ed.), *People's rights*, Oxford: Oxford University Press, 2001.

An-Na'im, A., 'The rights of women and international law in the Muslim context', *Whittier Law Review*, 9, 1987, 491.

——, 'Human rights in the Muslim world', *Harvard Human Rights Journal*, 3, 1990, 13.

——, *Towards an Islamic reformation: civil liberties, human rights and international law*, Syracuse: Syracuse University Press, 1990.

—— (ed.), *Human rights in cross-cultural perspective*, Philadelphia: University of Pennsylvania Press, 1992.

——, 'Human rights and Islamic identity in France and Uzbekistan: mediation of the local and the global', *Human Rights Quarterly*, 22, 2000, 906.

Arvin, P., *Buddhist politics: Japan's Clean Government Party*, The Hague: Martinus Nijhoff Publishers, 1971.

Ashibe, N., 'The US constitution and Japan's constitutional law', in L.W. Beer (ed.), *Constitutional systems in late twentieth century Asia*, Seattle: University of Washington Press, 1992.

Astier, H., 'Secular France mulls mosque subsidies', *BBC News Online*, 20 January 2003.

Audi, R., 'The separation of church and state and the obligations of citizenship', *Philosophy and Public Affairs*, 1989, 259.

Australian Law Reform Commission, 'Multiculturalism and the law', ALRC Report No. 57, 1992.

Baldwin, G.H., 'Clergy lead attack on weapons export bill', *The Times*, 4 February 2002.

Bano, S., 'Shari'a courts in relation to divorce within Muslim communities in Britain' lecture delivered at the conference: Gender and cultural diversity – European perspectives, 17 October 2003, London School of Economics, London.

Barnes, T., 'Ireland's divorce bill: traditional Irish and international norms of equality and bodily integrity at issue in a domestic abuse context', *Vanderbilt Journal of Transnational Law*, 31, 1998, 617.

Barry, B., *Liberty and justice*, Oxford: Clarendon, 1990.

Bartholet, E., 'Private race preferences in family formation', *Yale Law Journal*, 107, 1998, 2351.

Bates, S., 'Gay bishop forced out by Lambeth palace', *The Guardian*, 7 July 2003.

BBC News, 'French juror barred for headscarf', 25 November 2003.

——, 'Third schoolgirl suspended over scarf', 11 February 2002.

Beck, G., 'Human right adjudication under the ECHR between value pluralism and essential contestability', *European Human Rights Law Review*, 2, 2008, 214–244.

Bederman, D.J., *International law in antiquity*, Cambridge: Cambridge University Press, 2001.

Bedjaoui, M., 'The right to development', in M. Bedjaoui, *International law: achievements and prospects*, UNESCO, Norwell: Martinus Nijhoff Publishers, 1991.

Beer, L.W. (ed.), *Constitutional systems in late twentieth century Asia*, Seattle: Washington University Press, 1992.

Berlin, I., *Four essays on liberty*, Oxford: Oxford University Press, 1969.

Berkovits, B., 'Get and talaq in English law: reflections on law and policy', in C. Mallat and J. Connors (eds), *Islamic family law*, London: Center of Islamic and Middle East Law, 1990.

Bettwy, S.W., 'US–Vatican recognition: background and issues', *Catholic Lawyer*, 29, 1984, 225.

Bharatiya, V.P., *Religion – state relationship and constitutional rights in India*, New Delhi: Deep & Deep, 1987.

Boyle, K. and J. Sheen (eds), *Freedom of religion and belief: a world report*, London: Routledge, 1997.

Buergenthal, T. and J.R. Hall, *Human rights, international law and the Helsinki Accord*, Montclair: Allanheld Osmun, 1977.

Cabantous, A. (trans. E. Rauth), *Blasphemy: impious speech in the west from the 17th to the 19th century*, New York: Columbia University Press, 2001.

Capotorti, F., *Study of the rights of persons belonging to ethnic, religious and linguistic minorities*, New York: United Nations, 1979.

Carothers, T., 'Empirical perspectives on the emerging norm of democracy in international law', *Proceedings of the American Society of International Law*, 1992, 261.

CBC-Canada Radio, 'Chilean divorce law passed', 3 November 2004.

Cedant, B.C. 'Gender-specific provisions in the International Criminal Court', in F. Lattanzi and W.A. Schabas (eds), *Essays on the Rome Statute of the International Criminal Court*, Naples: Ripa Fagnano Alto, 1999.

Certoma, D.L., *The Italian legal system*, London: Butterworths, 1985.

Charlesworth, H. and C. Chinkin, 'The gender of *jus cogens*', *Human Rights Quarterly*, 15, 1993, 63.

——, *The boundaries of international law: a feminist analysis*, Manchester: Manchester University Press, 2000.

Charlesworth, H., C. Chinkin and S. Wright, 'Feminist approaches to international law', *American Journal of International Law*, 85, 1991, 613.

Ching, J., *Confucianism and Christianity – a comparative study*, Tokyo: Kodansha International, 1977.

Chinkin, C., 'Reservations and objections to the Convention on the Elimination of all Forms of Discrimination Against Women', in J.P. Gardner (ed.), *Human rights as general norms and a state's right to opt out – reservations and objections to human rights conventions*, London: British Institute of International and Comparative Law, 1997.

Clapham, A., *Human rights in the private sphere*, Oxford: Clarendon Press, 1993.

Clarke, D.M., 'Education, the state and sectarian schools', in T. Murphy and P. Twomey (eds), *Ireland's evolving constitution: 1927–1997*, Oxford: Hart, 1998.

CNN, 'Scalia questions Catholic anti-death penalty stance', 5 February 2002.

Congregation for the Doctrine of the Faith, 'Declaration Inter Insigniores on the Question of the Admission of Women to the Ministerial Priesthood', AAS 69 1977, October 15 1976, 98–116.

Cook, R., 'Women's rights: a bibliography', *New York University Journal of International Law and Politics*, 24, 1992, 857.

——, 'Accountability in international law for violation of women's rights by non-state actors', in D. Dallmeyer, *Reconceiving reality: women and international law*, Washington: American Society of International Law, 1993.

—— and B. Dickens, 'Human rights dynamics of abortion law reform', *Human Rights Quarterly*, 25, 2003, 1.

Coons, J.A. 'Book review: *Freedom of religion: a world report, ed. K. Boyle and J. Sheen*', *The American Journal of Comparative Law*, 49, 2001, 161.

Coons, J.E., 'The religious rights of children', in J.D. van der Vyver and J. Witte (eds), *Religious human rights in global perspective, Vol. I – religious perspectives*, The Hague: Martinus Nijhoff Publishers, 1996.

Cranston, M., 'John Locke and the case for toleration', in S. Mendus and D. Edwards (eds), *On toleration*, Oxford: Clarendon Press, 1987.

Currie, D.P., *The constitution of the Federal Republic of Germany*, Chicago: University of Chicago Press, 1994.

Daly, E., 'Split in row over girl's veil', *The Observer*, 17 February 2002.

Davison, A., *Secularism and revivalism in Turkey*, New Haven: Yale University Press, 1998.

De Bary, W.T., *Confucianism and human rights*, New York: Columbia University Press, 1998.

De Groot, D., 'The liberal tradition and the constitution: developing a coherent jurisprudence of parental rights', *Texas Law Review*, 78, 2000, 1278.

De Marneffe, P., 'Liberalism, liberty, and neutrality', *Philosophy and Public Affairs*, 19, 1990, 253.

De Zayas, A.M., 'International judicial protection of peoples and minorities', in C. Brolmann, R. Lefeber and M. Zieck (eds), *Peoples and minorities in international law*, Dordrecht: Martinus Nijhoff Publishers, 1992.

Detrick, S. and J.E. Doek, *The United Nations Convention on the Rights of the Child: a guide to the 'travaux préparatoires'*, Dordrecht: Martinus Nijhoff Publishers, 1992.

Dickson, B., 'The United Nations and freedom of religion', *International and Comparative Law Quarterly*, 44, 1995, 327–357.

Doe, N., *The legal framework of the Church of England*, Oxford: Clarendon Press, 1996.

Dombrowski, D.A., *Rawls and religion: the case for political liberalism*, Albany: State University of New York Press, 2001.

Donnelly, J., 'In search of the unicorn: the jurisprudence and politics of the right to development', *California Western International Law Journal*, 15, 1985, 473.

Dooley, D., 'Gendered citizenship in the Irish Constitution', in T. Murphy and P. Twomey (eds), *Ireland's evolving constitution: 1927–1977*, Oxford: Hart, 1998.

Durham, W.C. 'Perspectives on religious liberty: a comparative framework', in J.D. van der Vyver and J. Witte (eds), *Religious human rights in global perspective Vol. II – legal perspectives*, The Hague: Martinus Nijhoff Publishers, 1996.

Dworkin, R., 'Liberalism', in S. Hampshire (ed.), *Public and private morality*, Cambridge: Cambridge University Press, 1978.

——, *Taking rights seriously*, London: Duckworth, 1994.

Edge, P., *Legal responses to religious difference*, The Hague: Kluwer Law International, 2002.

Edwards, J., 'Collective rights in the liberal state', *Netherlands Quarterly of Human Rights*, 17, 1999, 259.

Elon, M., *Jewish law: history, sources, principles*, Philadelphia: The Jewish Publication Society, 1994.

Elshtain, B., 'State imposed secularism as a potential pitfall of liberal democracy', at the conference: Religious liberty and the ideology of the state, Prague 2000, available at http://www.becketfund.org/other/Prague2000/Elshtainpaper.html (accessed 8 December 2009).

Engineer, A., 'Bangladesh showing the way', *The Hindu*, 14 May 2001.

Epps, G., *To an unknown god: religious freedom on trial*, New York: St. Martin's Press, 2001.

Eriksson, M.K., *Reproductive freedom in the context of international human rights and humanitarian law*, The Hague: Martinus Nijhoff Publishers, 2000.

Evans, C., *Freedom of religion under the European Convention on Human Rights*, Oxford: Oxford University Press, 2001.

Evans, M., *Religious liberty and international law in Europe*, Cambridge: Cambridge University Press, 1997.

——, 'The UN and freedom of religion: the work of the Human Rights Committee', in R.J. Ahdar (ed.), *Law and religion*, Burlington and Aldershot: Ashgate, 2000.

Fernandez, D.L., 'Religious minorities in Spain: minority religions, social change and freedom of conscience', CESNUR International Conference 2002, Salt Lake City, Utah, June 2002, available at http://www.cesnur.org (accessed 8 December 2009).

Fiss, O., *The irony of free speech*, Cambridge, MA: Harvard University Press, 1996.

Fitzgerald, P.J., *Salmond on jurisprudence*, 7th edn, London: Sweet & Maxwell, 1966.

Flekkoy, M.G. and N.H. Kaufman, *The participation rights of the child: rights and responsibilities in family and society*, London: Jessica Kingsley, 1997.

Floria, J.G.N., 'Religious freedom in the Argentine Republic: twenty years after the Declaration on the Elimination of Intolerance and Religious Discrimination', *Brigham Young University Law Review*, 2002, 341.

Földesi, T., 'The main problems of religious freedom in Eastern Europe', in J.D. van der Vyver and J. Witte (eds), *Religious human rights in global perspective Vol. II – legal perspectives*, The Hague: Martinus Nijhoff Publishers, 1996.

Forfar, D., 'Individuals against the state? The politics of opposition to the re-emergence of state shinto', in I. Neary (ed.), *Case studies on human rights in Japan*, Surrey: Japan Library, 1996.

Fox, G.H. and G. Nolte, 'Intolerant democracies', *Harvard International Law Journal*, 36, 1995, 41.

——, 'Intolerant democracies', in R.B. Roth and G.H. Fox (eds), *Democratic governance and international law*, Cambridge: Cambridge University Press, 2000.

Franck, T.M., *The power of legitimacy among nations*, New York: Oxford University Press, 1990.

——, 'The emerging right to democratic governance', *American Journal of International Law*, 86, 1992, 46.

Frazer, E. and N. Lacey, *The politics of community: a feminist critique of the liberal-communitarian debate*, Hemel Hempstead: Harvester-Wheatsheaf, 1993.

Ghai, Y., 'Human rights and interethnic claims', *Cardozo Law Review*, 21, 2000, 1093.

Gilbert, K., 'Women and family law in modern Nepal: statutory rights and social implications', *New York University Journal of Law and Politics*, 24, 1992, 729.

Glaser, N., 'Individual rights against group rights', in W. Kymlicka (ed.), *The rights of minority cultures*, Oxford: Oxford University Press, 1995.

Glendon, M.A., 'Religious freedom and the original understanding of the Universal Declaration of Human Rights', at conference: Religious liberty and the ideology of the state, Prague 2000, available at http://www.becketfund.org/other/Prague2000/Glendon Paper.html (accessed 8 December 2009).

Gole, N., 'Authoritarian secularism and Islamic politics: the case of Turkey', in A.R. Norton, *Civil society in the Middle East*, Leiden: Brill, 1995.

Gombrich, R., *Theravda Buddhism*, London: Routledge, 1988.

Gomez, L., *An introduction to object relations*, London: Free Association Books, 1997.

Goodstein, L., 'Churches on right seek right to back candidates', *The New York Times*, 3 February 2002.

Gray, J., *Liberalism*, 2nd edn, Bristol: Open University Press, 1995.

——, *The two faces of liberalism*, Cambridge: Polity, 2000.

Greenawalt, K., 'Religion as a constitutional concept', *California Law Review*, 72, 1984, 753.

——, *Religious convictions and political choice*, New York: Oxford University Press, 1988.

——, *Private consciences and public reasons*, New York: Oxford University Press, 1995.

——, 'Religion and American political judgement', *Wake Forest Law Review*, 36, 2001, 401.

Grotstein, J.S. and D.B. Rinsley (eds), *Fairbairn and the origins of object relations*, New York: Guilford Press, 1994.

Gunther, G., *Constitutional law*, 12th edn, New York: Foundation Press, 1999.

Gutmann, A., 'Communitarian critics of liberalism', *Philosophy and Public Affairs*, 14, 1985, 308.

—— (ed.), *Multiculturalism*, Princeton: Princeton University Press, 1994.

Habermas, J. *[Between facts and norms]: contributions to a discourse theory of law and democracy*, Oxford: Polity, 1996.

Haksar, V., *Equality, liberty and perfectionism*, Oxford: Oxford University Press, 1979.

Hamilton, C., *Family, law and religion*, London: Sweet & Maxwell, 1995.

Hammer, L.M., *The international human right to freedom of conscience*, Aldershot: Ashgate, 2001.

Hampton, J., *Political philosophy*, Boulder, CO: Westview Press, 1997.

Harris, B., 'Should blasphemy be a crime? The 'Piss Christ' case and freedom of expression', *Melbourne University Law Review*, 22, 1998, 217–230.

Hassan, R., 'Rights of women within Islamic communities', in J. van der Vyver and J. Witte Jr. (eds), *Religious human rights in global perspective*, The Hague: Martinus Nijhoff Publishers, 1996.

Hayek, F.A., *The constitution of liberty*, London: Routledge & Kegan Paul, 1960.

Heinze, E., *Sexual orientation – a human right: an essay on international human rights law*, Dordrecht: Martinus Nijhoff Publishers, 1995.

Hernandez-Forcada, R., 'The effect of international treaties on religious freedom in Mexico', *Brigham Young University Law Review*, 2002, 301.

Higgins, R., 'Comments', in C. Brolmann, R. Lefeber and M. Zieck (eds), *Peoples and minorities in international law*, Dordrecht: Martinus Nijhoff Publishers, 1992.

Hoffmann (Lord), 'The universality of human rights', *Law Quarterly Review*, 125, 2009, 416–432.

House of Lords Select Committee Report on Religious Offences in England and Wales, 10 April 2003, Volume I, HL Paper 95–I.

Howard, R.E. and J. Donnelly, 'Human dignity, human rights and political regimes' in J. Donnelly, *Universal human rights in theory and practice*, Ithaca: Cornell University Press, 1989.

Howland, C.W., 'The challenge of religious fundamentalism to the liberty and equality rights of women: an analysis under the UN Charter', *Columbia Journal of Transnational Law*, 35, 1997, 271.

——, *Religious fundamentalism and the human rights of women*, New York: St Martin's Press, 1999.

Human rights in Bangladesh – a study of standards and practices, Dhaka: Bangladesh Institute of Law and International Affairs, 2001.

Hunter, J.D., 'The challenge of modern pluralism', in J.D. Hunter and O. Guinness (eds), *Articles of faith, articles of peace: the Religious Liberty Clause and American public philosophy*, Washington: Brookings Institution, 1990.

Huntington, S.P., 'The clash of civilizations?', *Foreign Affairs*, 1993, 22.

——, 'The west: unique, not universal', *Foreign Affairs*, 1996, 28.

Idriss, M.M., 'Religion and the Anti-Terrorism, Crime and Security Act 2001', *Criminal Law Review*, 2002, 890.

Introvigne, M., 'Freedom of religion and belief in the Christian/western world', introductory lecture at the conference organized by the International Humanist and Ethical Union, 4 May 2001, available at http://www.cesnur.org/2001/mi_osli_en.htm (accessed 8 December 2009).

Janis, M.W. (ed.), *The influence of religion on the development of international law*, Dordrecht: Martinus Nijhoff Publishers, 1991.

Jayasuriya, D.C., *Law and social problems in modern Sri Lanka*, New Delhi: Sterling Publishers, 1982.

Johnson, D., 'Cultural and regional pluralism in the drafting of the UN Convention on the Rights of the Child', in M. Freeman and P. Veerman (eds), *The ideologies of children's rights*, Dordrecht: Martinus Nijhoff Publishers, 1992.

Kawai, T., *Freedom of religion in comparative constitutional law with special reference to the UK, the US, India and Japan*, unpublished PhD Thesis, University of London, 1982.

King, P., *Toleration*, London: Allen & Unwin, 1976.

Kingsbury, B., 'Competing structures of indigenous people's claims', in P. Alston (ed.), *People's rights*, Oxford: Oxford University Press, 2001, 69.

Knights, S., *Freedom of religion, minorities and the law*, Oxford: Oxford University Press, 2007.

Kolodner, E., 'Religious rights in China: a comparison of international human rights law and Chinese domestic legislation', *Human Rights Quarterly*, 16, 1994, 455.

Kramnick, I. (ed.), *The portable Enlightenment*, New York: Penguin, 1995.

Kriari-Catrianis, I., 'Freedom of religion under the Greek Constitution', *Revue Héllènique de Droit International*, 47, 1994, 397.

Krishnaswami, A., *Study in the matter of religious rights and practices – report of the Special Rapporteur of the Sub-Commission on Prevention of Discrimination and Protection of Minorities*, New York: United Nations, 1960.

Kunz, J.L., 'The status of the Holy See in international law', *American Journal of International Law*, 46, 1952, 308.

Kuppe, R., 'The three dimensions of the rights of indigenous peoples', *International Criminal Law Review*, 11(1), 2009, 103–118.

Kymlicka, W., *Liberalism, community and culture*, Oxford: Oxford University Press, 1989.

——, *Multicultural citizenship: a liberal theory of minority rights*, Oxford: Clarendon Press, 1995.

——, 'The internationalization of minority rights', *International Journal of Constitutional Law*, 6(1), 2008, 1–32.

Langlaude, S., *The right of the child to religious freedom in international law*, The Hague: Martinus Nijhoff Publishers, 2007.

Lau, M., 'The case of *Zaheer-ud-din v. The State* and its impact on the fundamental right to freedom of religion', *Yearbook of Islamic and Middle Eastern Law*, 1, 1994, 565.

Lauterpacht, H. (ed.), *Oppenheim's international law*, Vol. I, London: Longman, 1948.

Law Commission Working Paper No. 79, 'Offences against religion and public worship', 5–6, 1981.

Laycock, D., 'Towards a general theory of the religion clauses: the case of church labor relations and the right to church autonomy', *Columbia Law Review*, 81, 1981, 1373.

Layish, A., 'The status of the Muslim women in the shari'a courts in Israel', in F. Raday, C. Shalev and M. Liban-Kooby (eds), *Women's status in Israeli law and society*, Tel Aviv: Shocken, 1995.

'Le rapport de la commission Stasi sur la laïcité', 'The report of the Stasi committee on secularity', *Le Monde*, 12 December 2003.

Leader, S., 'Blasphemy and human rights', *Modern Law Review*, 46, 1983, 338.

——, 'Freedom and futures: personal priorities, institutional demands and freedom of religion', *Modern Law Review*, 70, 2007, 713.

Leeder, L., *Ecclesiastical law handbook*, London: Sweet & Maxwell, 1997.

Lehnof, L., 'Freedom of religious association: the right of religious organizations to obtain legal entity status under the European Convention', *Brigham Young University Law Review*, 2002, 561.

Lerner, N., 'Religious human rights under the United Nations', in J. van der Vyver and J. Witte Jr. (eds), *Religious human rights in global perspective Vol. II – legal perspectives*, The Hague: Martinus Nijhoff Publishers, 1996.

——, *Religion, beliefs and international human rights*, Markinoll: Orbis Books, 2000.

Leuprecht, P., 'Minority rights revisited', in P. Alston (ed.), *People's rights*, Oxford: Oxford University Press, 2001.

Lijnzaad, L., *Reservations to UN human rights treaties – ratify and ruin?*, Dordrecht: Martinus Nijhoff Publishers, 1995.

Locke, J. (trans. J.W. Gough), *A letter on toleration*, Oxford: Clarendon Press, 1968.

—— (ed. M. Goldie), *Two treatises of government*, London: Everyman, 1993.

Lowe, N. and G. Douglas, *Bromley's Family Law*, London: Butterworths, 1998.

Lupu, I.C., 'Government messages and government money: *Santa Fe*, *Mitchell v. Helms* and the arc of the Establishment Clause', *William and Mary Law Review*, 42, 2001, 771.

Luxton, P., *The law of charities*, Oxford: Oxford University Press, 2001.

MacIntyre, A., *After virtue*, 2nd edn, Notre Dame: University of Notre Dame Press, 1984.

MacKinnon, C., *Feminism unmodified: discourses on life and the law*, Cambridge, MA: Harvard University Press, 1987.

Mackintosh, W.H., *Disestablishment and liberation: the movement for the separation of the Anglican Church from state control*, London: Epworth Press, 1972.

Macklem, P., 'Minority rights in international law', *International Journal of Constitutional Law*, 6(3/4), 2008, 531–552.

Maclear, J.F., *Church and state in the modern age: a documentary history*, New York: Oxford University Press, 1995.

Maidment Kershner, S., '*Agunot*: new solutions from old sources', *New Law Journal*, 151, 2001, 720.

Mallat, C., *The renewal of Islamic Law: Muhammd Baqer as-Sader, Najaf and the Shi'i International*, Cambridge: Cambridge University Press, 1993.

Marks, S., *The riddle of all constitutions: international law, democracy, and the critique of ideology*, New York: Oxford University Press, 2000.

Martin, J.P., 'Religion, human rights and civil society: lessons from the seventeenth century for the twenty first century', *Brigham Young University Law Review*, 2000, 933.

Martinez-Torrón, J., 'Freedom of religion in the case law of the Spanish Constitutional Court', *Brigham Young University Law Review*, 2001, 711.

Matsui, S., 'Japan: the Supreme Court and the separation of church and state', *International Journal of Constitutional Law*, 2(3), 2004, 534.

Mayer, A.E., 'Universal versus Islamic human rights: a clash of cultures or a clash with a construct?', *Michigan Journal of International Law*, 15, 1994, 307.

McConnell, M.W., 'The origins and historical understanding of free exercise of religion', *Harvard Law Review*, 103, 1990, 1409.

McDonald, M., 'Should communities have rights – a reflection on liberal individualism', in A. An-Na'im (ed.), *Human rights in cross-cultural perspective*, Philadelphia: University of Pennsylvania Press, 1992.

McDougall, W.A., 'Religion in world affairs: introduction', *Orbis*, 42, 1998, 159.

Mernissi, F., *Beyond the veil*, Cambridge: Cambridge University Press, 1975.

——, *Women and Islam*, Oxford: Basil Blackwell, 1991.

Meron, T., *Human rights lawmaking in the United Nations: a critique of instruments and process*, Oxford: Clarendon, 1986.

Mews, S. (ed.), *Religion in politics*, Harlow: Longman, 1989.

Michalowski, S. and L. Woods, *German constitutional law: the protection of civil liberties*, Aldershot: Ashgate, 1999.

Mickelson, K., 'How universal is the Universal Declaration?', *University of New Brunswick Law Journal*, 47, 1998, 19.

Miller, D. (ed.), *The Blackwell encyclopedia of political thought*, Oxford: Blackwell, 1991.

Minow, M., *Making all the difference*, Ithaca: Cornell University Press, 1990.

Morris, N., 'Blasphemy law to be consigned to history', *The Independent*, 15 November 2001.

Morsink, J., *The Universal Declaration of Human Rights: origins, drafting and intent*, Philadelphia: University of Pennsylvania Press, 1999.

Muller Okin, S., 'Is multiculturalism bad for women?', in J. Cohen, M. Howard and M.C. Nussbaum (eds), *Is multiculturalism bad for women?*, Princeton: Princeton University Press, 1999.

——, '"Mistresses of their own destiny": group rights, gender and realistic rights of exit', *Ethics*, 112, 2002, 205.

Mutua, M. Wa, 'Limitation on religious rights', in J.D. van der Vyver and J. Witte (eds), *Religious human rights in global perspective Volume II – legal perspectives*, The Hague: Martinus Nijhoff Publishers, 1996.

Nagel, T., 'Rawls on justice', in N. Daniels (ed.), *Reading Rawls: critical studies of 'A theory of justice'*, Oxford: Oxford University Press, 1975.

Neisser, E., 'Hate speech in the new South Africa: constitutional considerations for a land recovering from decades of racial repression and violence', *South Africa Journal of Human Rights*, 10, 1994, 336.

Nettheim, G., '"Peoples" and "populations" – indigenous peoples and the rights of peoples', in J. Crawford (ed.), *The rights of peoples*, Oxford: Clarendon, 1988.

Newman, J., *On religious freedom*, Ottawa: University of Ottawa Press, 1991.

Nielsen, J.S., 'Contemporary discussions on religious minorities in Islam', *Brigham Young University Law Review*, 2002, 353.

Nozick, R., *Anarchy, state, and utopia*, Oxford: Blackwell, 1974.

Nsereko, D.D., 'Religion, the state and law in Africa', *Journal of State and Church*, 28, 1986, 269.

Oberleitner, G., 'Monitoring minority rights under the Council of Europe's Framework Convention' in P. Cumper and S. Wheatley (eds), *Minority rights in the 'new' Europe*, The Hague: Martinus Nijhoff Publishers, 1999.

Odio Benito, E., *Elimination of all forms of intolerance and discrimination based on religion or belief*, New York: United Nations, 1989.

Oktem, N., 'Religion in Turkey', *Brigham Young University Law Review*, 2002, 371.

O'Neill, J., *The missing child in liberal theory*, Toronto: Toronto University Press, 1994.

Ordinatio Sacerdotalis, 22 May 1994 of John Paul II, available at http://www.vatican.va/ (accessed 8 December 2009).

Paine, T., *The rights of man. Part I*, in B. Kuklick (ed.), *Thomas Paine – political writings*, Cambridge: Cambridge University Press, 1989.

Panikkar, R., 'Is the notion of human rights a western concept?', *Diogenes*, 120, 1982, 75.

Parashar, A., *Women and family law reform in India: uniform civil code and gender equality*, New Delhi: Sage, 1992.

Parekh, B., 'Equality in a multicultural society', in J. Franklin (ed.), *Equality*, London: Institute for Public Policy Research, 1997.

——, *Rethinking multiculturalism: cultural diversity and political theory*, Basingstoke: Palgrave, 2000.

Parkin, C., 'Papal support for abortion law amendment', *Press Association Ireland*, 2 March 2002.

Pentassuglia, G., 'Evolving protection of minority groups: global challenges and the role of international jurisprudence', *International Criminal Law Review*, 11(2), 2009, 185–218.

The People (Ireland), 'Ireland decides, the Pope supports Ahern on abortion', 3 March 2002.

Perry, M.J., *Religion in politics: constitutional and moral perspectives*, Oxford: Oxford University Press, 1997.

——, 'Why political reliance on religiously grounded morality does not violate the Establishment Clause', *William and Mary Law Review*, 42, 2001, 663.

Pollis, A. and P. Schwab, 'Human rights: a western construct with limited applicability' in A. Pollis and P. Schwab (eds), *Human rights: cultural and ideological perspectives*, New York: Praeger, 1980.

Post, R.C., 'Cultural heterogeneity and law: pornography, blasphemy, and the First Amendment', *California Law Review*, 76, 1988, 297.

——, 'Racist speech, democracy and the First Amendment' in H.L. Gates et al. (eds), *Speaking of race, speaking of sex*, New York: New York University Press, 1994.

Poulter, S., 'Muslim headscarves in school: contrasting legal approaches in England and France', *Oxford Journal of Legal Studies*, 17, 1997, 43.

Preston, J., 'UN summit on women bars groups: China, Vatican block opponents admission', *Washington Post*, 17 March 1995.

Problems of Religious Freedom and Tolerance in Selected OSCE States, Report to the OSCE Supplementary Meeting on Freedom of Religion or Belief, Vienna, 17–18 July 2003, available at http://www.ihf-hr.org/viewbinary/viewdocument.php?doc_id=4723 (accessed 8 December 2009).

'Public benefit and the advancement of religion – draft supplementary guidance for consultation', The Charity Commission, 2008.

Rafiq Khan, M., *Socio-legal status of Muslim women*, London: Sangam Books, 1993.

Rahman, A., 'Religious rights versus women's rights in India: a test case for international human rights law', *Columbia Journal of Transnational Law*, 28, 1990, 473.

Ranalow, S., 'Bearing a constitutional cross: examining blasphemy and the judicial role in *Corway v. Independent Newspapers*', *Trinity College Law Review*, 2000, 95.

Rautenbach, C., 'Gender equality and religious family laws in South Africa', *Queensland University of Technology Law and Justice Journal*, 3, 2003, 1.

Rawls, J., *Political liberalism*, New York: Columbia University Press, 1993.

——, *A theory of justice*, 2nd edn, Cambridge, MA: Harvard University Press, 1999.

——, and J.B. Herman, *Lectures on the history of moral philosophy*, Cambridge, MA: Harvard University Press, 2000.

Raz, J., *The morality of freedom*, Oxford: Clarendon, 1988.

'Religion or belief in the workplace – a guide for employers and employees', available at http://www.acas.org.uk (accessed 8 December 2009).

Rentelin, A.D., *International human rights: universalism vs. relativism*, Newbury Park: Sage, 1990.

Ribiero, A.V., *Implementation of the Declaration on the Elimination of All Forms of Intolerance and of Discrimination based on Religion or Belief*, New York: United Nations, 1987.

Richards, D.A.J., *Free speech and the politics of identity*, Oxford: Oxford University Press, 1999.

Robinson, J., et al., *Were the minority treaties a failure?*, New York: Institute of Jewish Affairs, 1943.

Roland, A., *In search of self in India and Japan: towards a cross-cultural psychology*, Princeton: Princeton University Press, 1988.

Romany, C., 'State responsibility goes private: a feminist critique of the public/private distinction in international human rights law', in R. Cook, *Human rights of women: national and international perspectives*, Philadelphia: University of Pennsylvania Press, 1994.

Rousseau, J.J., *The social contract*, Harmondsworth: Penguin Books, 1968.

—— (trans. M. Cranston), *Discourse on the origin of inequality*, Harmondsworth: Penguin, 1984.

Runciman, S., *The Orthodox churches and the secular state*, Sir Douglas Robb Lectures, Auckland: University of Auckland, 1970.

Sadurski, W., 'Rights and moral reasoning: an unstated assumption – a comment on Jeremy Waldron's "Judges as moral reasoners"', *International Journal of Constitutional Law*, 7(1), 2009, 25–45.

Sandel, M., 'Freedom of conscience or freedom of choice', in J. Hunter and O. Guinness (eds), *Articles of faith, articles of peace*, Washington: Brookings Institute, 1990.

——, *Liberalism and the limits of justice*, Cambridge: Cambridge University Press, 1998.

Sanders, T.G., *Protestant concepts of church and state – historical backgrounds and approaches for the future*, New York: Holt, Rinehart & Winston, 1964.

Santo Paz, J.A., 'Perspectives on religious freedom in Spain', *Brigham Young University Law Review*, 2001, 669.

Schanda, B., 'Religious freedom issues in Hungary', *Brigham Young University Law Review*, 2002, 405.

Scolnicov, A., 'A dedicated follower of (religious) fashion', *Cambridge Law Journal*, 64, 2005, 527.

——, 'Religious law, religious courts and human rights within Israeli constitutional structure', *International Journal of Constitutional Law*, 4(4), 2006, 732.

——, 'The child's right to religious freedom and formation of identity', *International Journal of Children's Rights*, 15(2), 2007, 215.

——, 'Multi-religious societies and state legal systems: religious marriages, the state and implications for human rights' in T. Wilhelmsson (ed.), *Private law and the many cultures of Europe*, The Hague: Kluwer Law International, 2007, 405.

——, 'Women and religious freedom: a legal solution to a human rights conflict?', *Netherlands Human Rights Quarterly*, 4, 2007, 569.

Shachar, A., *Multicultural jurisdictions: cultural differences and women's rights*, Cambridge: Cambridge University Press, 2001.

Shava, M., *The personal law in Israel*, 4th edn, Tel Aviv: Modan, 2001 (in Hebrew).

Shaw, M., *International law*, 5th edn, Cambridge: Cambridge University Press, 2003.

Sheleg, Y., 'In Germany, they're asking: who's a Jew?', *Haa'retz English Edition*, 20 January 2003.

Shelton, D. and A. Kiss, 'A draft model law on freedom of religion, with commentary', in J.D. van der Vyver and J. Witte Jr., *Religious human rights in global perspective Vol. II – legal perspectives*, The Hague: Martinus Nijhoff Publishers, 1996.

Shougry-Badarne, B., *International law, personal status and the oppression of women: the case of Muslim women in Israel*, unpublished LL.M. thesis, American University, Washington, DC, 2001.

Sieghart, P., *The international law of human rights*, New York: Oxford University Press, 1983.

Simpson, A.W.B., *Human rights and the end of empire*, Oxford: Oxford University Press, 2001.

Smart, N., *The philosophy of religion*, New York: Oxford University Press, 1979.

Sólyom, L. and G. Brunner, *Constitutional judiciary in a new democracy*, Ann Arbor: University of Michigan Press, 2000.

Sparks, J., 'Girl in headscarf goes centre stage in Dutch election', *The Sunday Times*, 11 January 2003.

Ssenyonjo, M., 'The Islamic veil and freedom of religion, the rights to education and work: a survey of recent international and national cases', *Chinese Journal of International Law*, 6, 2007, 653.

Stavrakakis, Y., 'Religion and populism: reflection on the "politicized" discourse of the Greek Church', Discussion Paper No. 7, May 2002, The Hellenic Observatory, The European Institute, The London School of Economics, available at http://www.lse.ac.uk/collections/hellenicObservatory/pdf/StavrakakisDiscussionPaper.pdf (accessed 8 December 2009).

Stein, S.J., 'Religion/religions in the United States: changing perspectives and prospects', *Indiana Law Journal*, 75, 2000, 37.

Steiner, H.J. and P. Alston, *International human rights in context: law, politics, morals*, 2nd edn, Oxford: Oxford University Press, 2000.

Stockholm International Peace Research Institute, *Yearbook 2001: Armaments, disarmament and international security*, Oxford: Oxford University Press, 2001.

Stone, G.R., L.M. Seidman, C.R. Sunstein, M.V. Tushnet and P.S. Karlan, *Constitutional law*, 6th edn, Aspen: Aspen, 2009, 1477–1502.

Stone, S.L., 'The intervention of American law in Jewish divorce: a pluralist analysis', *Israel Law Review*, 34, 2000, 170.

Stout, J., *The flight from authority: religion, morality, and the quest for autonomy*, Notre Dame: University of Notre Dame Press, 1981.

Sullivan, D.J., 'Advancing the freedom of religion or belief through the UN Declaration on the Elimination of Religious Intolerance and Discrimination', *American Journal of International Law*, 82, 1988, 487.

——, 'Gender, equality and religious freedom: toward a framework for conflict resolution', *New York University Journal of International Law & Policy*, 24, 1992, 795.

Sunstein, C., *Democracy and the problem of free speech*, New York: The Free Press, 1993.

Tahzib, B., *Freedom of religion or belief – ensuring effective international legal protection*, The Hague: Martinus Nijhoff Publishers, 1996.

Taylor, C., *The sources of the self: the making of modern identity*, Cambridge: Cambridge University Press, 1989.

——, 'Religion in a free society', in J.D. Hunter and O. Guinness (eds), *Articles of faith, articles of peace*, Washington: The Brookings Institution, 1990.

——, 'Multiculturalism: examining the politics of recognition', in A. Gutmann (ed.), *Multiculturalism*, Princeton: Princeton University Press, 1994.

Taylor, P.M., *Freedom of religion: UN and international human rights law and practice*, Cambridge: Cambridge University Press, 2005.

Taylor, P.M., 'The questionable grounds of objections to proselytism and certain other forms of religious expression', *Brigham Young University Law Review*, 2006, 811.

Tesón, F., 'The Kantian theory on international law', *Columbia Law Review*, 92, 1992, 53.

Thornberry, P., *International law and the rights of minorities*, Oxford: Clarendon Press, 1990.

——, *Minorities and human rights law*, Minorities Rights Group, 1991.

——, *Indigenous peoples and human rights*, Manchester: Manchester University Press, 2002.

Travis, A., 'Support grows for splitting church and state link', *The Guardian*, 23 January 2002.

Tremlett, G., 'Poverty, ignorance and why 17 women face jail for abortion', *The Guardian*, 18 January 2000.

Tribe, L., 'Forward: toward a model of roles in due process of life and law', *Harvard Law Review*, 87, 1973, 1.

——, *American constitutional law*, 2nd edn, Minola: Foundation Press, 1988.

US Department of State International Religious Freedom Report 2002 – France, available at http://www.state.gov/g/drl/rls/irf/2002/13938.htm (accessed 8 December 2009).

Van Bueren, G., *International law on the rights of the child*, The Hague: Kluwer, 1998.

——, 'Child rights in Europe: convergence and divergence in judicial protection', Brussels: Council of Europe, 2008.

van der Burg, C., 'Traditional Hindu values and human rights', in A. An-Na'im (ed.), *Human rights and religious values: an uneasy relationship?*, Amsterdam: Rodopi, 1995.

Van der Vyver, J., 'Constitutional perspectives on church–state relations in South Africa', *Brigham Young University Law Review*, 1999, 935.

Van Dijk, P. and G.J.H. van Hoof, *Theory and practice of the European Convention on Human Rights*, 3rd edn, The Hague: Kluwer, 1998.

Vargas, J.A., 'Freedom of religion and public worship in Mexico: a legal commentary on the 1992 federal act on religious matters', *Brigham Young University Law Review*, 1998, 421.

von Bernstorff, J., 'The changing fortunes of the Universal Declaration of Human Rights: genesis and symbolic dimensions of the turn to rights in international law', *European Journal of International Law*, 19(5), 2008, 903.

Waldron, J., *Liberal rights: collected papers, 1981–1991*, Cambridge: Cambridge University Press, 1993.

——, 'Inalienable rights', *Boston Review* 24, 1999, available at http://bostonreview.net/BR24.2/Waldron.html (accessed 8 December 2009).

——, 'Judges as moral reasoners', *International Journal of Constitutional Law*, 7(1), 2009, 2–24.

Walters, F.P., *A history of the League of Nations*, Vol. 1, Oxford: Oxford University Press, 1952.

Weithman, P.J., 'The separation of church and state: some questions for Prof. Audi', *Philosophy and Public Affairs*, 1991, 52.

——, 'Religious reasons and the duties of membership', *Wake Forest Law Review*, 36, 2001, 511.

Wellman, C.H., 'Liberalism, communitarianism and group rights', *Law and Philosophy*, 18, 1999, 37.

Whyte, G., 'Some reflections on the role of religion in the constitutional order', in T. Murphy and P. Twomey (eds), *Ireland's evolving constitution: 1927–1997*, Oxford: Hart, 1998.

Willet, C., *Theorising multiculturalism: a guide to the current debate*, Oxford: Blackwell, 1998.

Wilson, R., 'Defining genocide at international criminal tribunals: towards a political understanding of genocide', available at http://www.allacademic.com/meta/p_mla_apa_research_citation/1/7/7/0/4/p177046_index.html (accessed 8 December 2009).

Witte, J., *Religion and the American constitutional experiment: essential rights and liberties*, Boulder: Westview Press, 2000.

Witte, J. and J.D. Van der Vyver, *Religious human rights in global perspective*, Vols I and II, The Hague: Martinus Nijhoff Publishers, 1996.

Wright, S., 'Economic rights, social justice and the state: a feminist reappraisal', in D. Dallmeyer (ed.), *Reconceiving reality: women and international law*, Washington, DC: American Society of International Law, 1993.

Yang, T., 'Race, religion and cultural identity', *Indiana Law Journal*, 73, 1997, 120.

Yasmin, L., 'Law and order situation and gender-based violence: Bangladeshi perspective', Regional Centre for Strategic Studies, *Policy Studies*, 16, Chapter 4, available at http://www.rscc.org/ (accessed 8 December 2009).

Index